Lives

Secret Lives

Selected by **M. R. D. Foot**

OXFORD
UNIVERSITY PRESS

OXFORD
UNIVERSITY PRESS

Great Clarendon Street, Oxford OX2 6DP

Oxford University Press is a department of the University of Oxford.
It furthers the University's objective of excellence in research, scholarship,
and education by publishing worldwide in

Oxford New York

Auckland Bangkok Buenos Aires Cape Town Chennai
Dar es Salaam Delhi Hong Kong Istanbul Karachi Kolkata
Kuala Lumpur Madrid Melbourne Mexico City Mumbai Nairobi
São Paulo Shanghai Singapore Taipei Tokyo Toronto

Oxford is a registered trade mark of Oxford University Press
in the UK and in certain other countries

Published in the United States
by Oxford University Press Inc., New York

© Oxford University Press 2002

Database right Oxford University Press (maker)

First published 2002

British Library Cataloguing in Publication Data
Data available

Library of Congress Cataloging in Publication Data
Data available

ISBN 0-19-860637-0
1006349646
10 9 8 7 6 5 4 3 2 1

Typeset in DanteMT
by Alliance Interactive Technology, Pondicherry, India
Printed in Great Britain
by T. J. International, Padstow, Cornwall

Preface

'The best record of a nation's past that any civilization has produced':
G. M. Trevelyan's view in 1944 of the *Dictionary of National Biography*
highlights the achievement of its first editor Leslie Stephen. Between
1885 and 1900 quarterly volumes rolled out from the presses in alpha-
betical order by subject. A national institution had come into existence,
making its distinctive contribution to the national aptitude for the art of
biography.

In his initial prospectus for the *DNB*, Stephen emphasized the need to
express 'the greatest possible amount of information in a thoroughly
business-like form'. Dates and facts, he said, 'should be given abundantly
and precisely', and he had no patience with the sort of 'style' that meant
'superfluous ornament'. But he knew well enough that for 'lucid and
condensed narrative', style in the best sense is essential. Nor did he content
himself, in the many longer memoirs he himself contributed to the
DNB, with mere dates and facts: a pioneer in the sociology of literature, he
was not at all prone to exaggerate the individual's impact on events, and
skilfully 'placed' people in context. Stephen's powerful machine was carried on by his work-horse of a successor Sidney Lee, who edited the first of
the ten supplements (usually decennial) which added people who died
between 1901 and 1990.

Memoirs were often written soon after the subject died and their
authors were frequently able to cite 'personal knowledge' and 'private
information'. In such cases there is always a balance to be struck between
waiting for written sources to appear and drawing upon living memory
while still abundant and fresh. Stephen had no doubts where he stood: he
published book-length biographies of his Cambridge friend Henry Fawcett
and of his brother Fitzjames within a year of their deaths, and cited
Boswell's *Johnson* and Lockhart's *Scott* as proof that the earliest biographies
are often the best. Furthermore, memoirs of the recently dead were included in the *DNB* right up to the last possible moment, the press often
being stopped for the purpose. Roundell Palmer, for example, died on 4
May 1895 and got into the 43rd volume published at the end of June.

Preface

So the memoirs published in this series are fully in line with what was *DNB* policy from the outset. Furthermore, all have the virtue of reflecting the attitudes to their subjects that were taken up during their lifetimes. They may not always reflect what is now the latest scholarship, but as G. M. Young insisted, 'the real, central theme of history is not what happened, but what people felt about it when it was happening'. So they will never be superseded, and many are classics of their kind—essential raw material for the most up-to-date of historians. They have been selected by acknowledged experts, some of them prominent in helping to produce the new *Oxford Dictionary of National Biography*, which will appear in 2004. All are rightly keen that this ambitious revision will not cause these gems of the *DNB* to be lost. So here they are, still sparkling for posterity.

Brian Harrison
Editor, *Oxford Dictionary of National Biography*

Introduction

Within living memory, it was regarded as the depth of bad form to make any public reference to secret service: it was essentially secret, and not a subject for written comment at all. (This was before the days of radio, then called wireless; let alone television.) All the same, there had been spies and spying for centuries past; in a bitterly divided nation, only too many of them round the time of the Reformation and the next century's Civil War.

None of our great warrior kings and queens, from Boudicca to Victoria, could have secured their victories without a sound intelligence system, whatever it was called; but the subject was long so secret, and the authorities that dealt with it were so senior, that there is not much from early times that has remained in writing for historians to work over. Moreover it has long been—still is—a rule in the secret world that anything really secret should not be written down at all.

DNB did what it could. The pages below give some indications of who spied, and on whom; needless to say, most of those abroad who spied on behalf of British monarchs do not appear, because they were not British citizens. Several examples are included of the Roman Catholic priests who risked coming to newly Protestant England, and suffered for it. And several examples are here also of those who set out to overturn government— Wolfe Tone and Arthur Thistlewood the most extreme of them.

British governments have sometimes set out to overturn governments abroad; hence the appearance of some agents who strove against the French Revolution, and some who worked in the special operations executive, the secret service that fostered subversion in Nazi-occupied Europe a century and a half later. Wickham, who worked closely with Windham, and Wilson provide good examples of the uses diplomats could have in the secret world.

Introduction

Spies, to secure useful results, need spymasters; a few of whom are included. One of these, William Windham, had for his cover that he was a dilettante; no one would think, reading the *DNB* article on him, that he had anything to do with spying at all, but the researches of Elizabeth Sparrow have unearthed the papers of the Aliens Office, long thought vanished, of which Windham was the head for most of the 1790s. His successor William Huskisson is only left out of these pages because the article devoted to him (which also says nothing of espionage) is so long. Similarly, Marlowe the dramatist does not appear; *DNB*'s long article on him deals with him solely as a poet. That he was a secret agent is not in doubt; though who his secret employers were, and how he died, remain more obscure.

Round the time of the French Revolution, government in London was inclined to regard every reform movement with suspicion; hence the presence below of such innocents as Thomas Hardy (the reformer, not the novelist) or the radical tailor Francis Place. From Sleeman's work in India against the thugs, in the 1820s and 1830s, many of today's police and counter-espionage methods derive.

More modern times have brought more open dealings. In 1909 the cabinet gave formal approval to the existence of two secret services, one for intelligence and one for security, and their heads—Sir Mansfield Cumming, the first 'C', and Sir Vernon Kell—can accordingly appear below, with a few of their successors and a few of their agents. That one of these agents—Edith Cavell, shot in Brussels in 1915 for having aided several score British soldiers to escape to Holland—was also a distinguished spy is a secret that the present writer has sat on for 25 years; but has just gone public, in a life of Airey Neave, himself a distinguished escaper from Colditz and a victim of Irish terror.

During the great war against the Kaiser's Germany, Cumming and Kell both secured triumphs; the best of Cumming's came in Belgium, through a group run by Walthère Dewé who went on to become head of the post-war Belgian telephone service; retired; and performed exactly the same clandestine feat during the next world war, till he was shot by the Gestapo in 1944. As a foreigner, he is of course excluded from *DNB*. Lawrence 'of Arabia' comes in: his secret services provided a wonderful propaganda relief for a nation oppressed by the casualty lists of Passchendaele.

From the Troubles in Ireland of 1916–22 two figures can stand, one from each side in the Irish civil war: Michael Collins who ran the clandestine IRA and Eamon de Valera who eventually ran the Free State. Two men who fought against them, Jo Holland and Colin Gubbins, appear also, spymasters of a kind in a greater struggle that was to follow.

Introduction

From the struggle against Bolshevik Russia, Bruce Lockhart's name stands out; every Soviet child used to be brought up on the story of the 'Lockhart plot', which Volkogonov's life of Lenin assures us was a complete fabrication—by Lenin, to save his own skin.

Some aspects of the secret world remain secret: decipher, for example. The triumphs in this field of Alan Turing, who while he was at it helped invent the electronic computer, hardly appear in his *DNB* entry, written by Helen Palmer before the ultra secret went public; at least she could record his dates of birth and death. Dilly Knox, another master of decipher, appeared at last in *DNB*'s Missing Persons volume.

One group of modern spies was too important to leave out: the 'Cambridge Five' who were the pride of the Soviet secret service, and spied against their own country, both during the war against Hitler and (in some cases) after it. Four of them—Maclean, probably the most dangerous, Burgess who bolted with him, Philby the best known of them, and Blunt whose cover was deepest—are cited; Cairncross the fifth was still alive when *DNB* went to press.

Those who search for spies in *DNB* on line deserve one word of warning: a great many of the entries are of those who were cartooned by 'Spy', Sir Leslie Ward, and were not spies at all; though a few of them, such as Balfour, Harcourt, and Rosebery, may have helped direct them.

Large gaps remain in *DNB*'s coverage of the subject; this cannot be helped. Some will be filled in the new edition, now approaching completion, such as Sir Dick White, successive head both of MI 5 and of MI 6, who wrote the appreciation, below of Kell and Hollis; more, if it too runs to supplementary volumes to include such figures as the incomparable Pearl Witherington who is still with us.

M. R. D. Foot

April 2002

Contents

Contents

Contents

Contents

Contents

Contents

Contents

O'CONNOR Brian or Bernard

(1490?–1560?)

More properly known as Brian O'Conor Faly, captain of Offaly, eldest son of Cahir O'Conor Faly, succeeded to the lordship of Offaly on the death of his father in 1511. The importance of the clan, of which he was chief, dates from the decline of the English authority in Ireland at the beginning of the fifteenth century. By the beginning of the sixteenth century the O'Conors had succeeded in extending their dominion over the Irish westward as far as the Shannon, while the extent of their power in the direction of the English Pale may be estimated from the fact that the inhabitants of Meath consented to pay them a yearly tribute or black-rent of 300*l.*, and those of Kildare 20*l.*, in order to secure immunity from their attacks. In 1520, when the Earl of Surrey was appointed lord lieutenant, Brian O'Conor was at the height of his power. Being allied to the house of Kildare he was naturally opposed to Henry's project of governing Ireland independently of that noble family, and in June 1521 he joined with O'More and O'Carrol in an attack on the Pale. Surrey at once retaliated by ravaging his territory and capturing his stronghold, Monasteroris. O'Conor for some time refused to listen to peace on any terms, but he eventually submitted, and his castle of Monasteroris was restored to him. On the departure of Surrey things reverted to their old condition. During the detention of Gerald Fitzgerald, ninth earl of Kildare, in England in 1528, the vice-deputy, Richard Nugent, seventh baron Delvin, made an unwise attempt to withhold from him his customary black-rents out of Meath. O'Conor resented the attempt, and having inveigled the vice-deputy to the borders of Offaly, on pretence of parleying with him, he took him prisoner on 12 May, and flatly refused to surrender him until his demands were conceded. The Earl of Ossory made an unsuccessful effort to procure his release by intriguing with O'Conor's brother Cahir, and Delvin remained a prisoner till early in the following year. In consequence of secret instructions from the Earl of Kildare, who repined at his detention in England, O'Conor in the autumn invaded the Pale, but shortly after the earl's restoration he was pardoned.

When Kildare's son, 'Silken Thomas', took up arms in 1534 to avenge his father's supposed death, O'Conor was one of his staunchest allies; and it was from O'Conor's castle that he addressed his fatal offer of submission to Lord Leonard Grey. Through the treachery of his brother Cahir, O'Conor was compelled to submit to Skeffington in August 1535, and he gave pledges for the payment of a fine of eight hundred head of cattle. He revenged himself by expelling Cahir from Offaly, but more than a year elapsed without any attempt on his part to redeem his pledges. Accordingly in May 1537 Grey invaded his country, and, having forced him to fly, appointed Cahir lord of Offaly in his stead. For a time O'Conor found shelter with his kinsman O'Carrol; but when O'Carrol was in turn compelled to submit, he came to Grey on a safe-conduct, and promised, if he was restored, not merely to forbear his black-rents, but also 'to yelde out of his countrie a certen sum yerely to His Grace.' Grey was unable to grant his request, but he allowed him to redeem his son, who was one of his pledges, for three hundred marks. Though 'more lyker a begger then he that ever was a captayn or ruler of a contre,' 'goyng from on to another of hys olde fryndes to have mete and drynke,' O'Conor was not subdued. With the assistance of his secret friends he invaded Offaly at the beginning of October 'with a great number of horsemen, gallowglasses, and kerns,' and forcibly expelled his brother. Grey at once marched against him, but, in consequence of recent floods, was for some time unable to enter Offaly. In November the rain subsided; but O'Conor had already escaped into O'Doyne's country, and thence into Ely O'Carrol. After destroying an immense quantity of corn and robbing the abbey of Killeigh, Grey returned to Dublin. O'Conor offered to submit, and a safe-conduct was sent him; but he had by that time come to terms with his brother Cahir, and, at his suggestion, retracted his submission. Once more Grey invaded Offaly, but he yielded to O'Conor's solicitation for a parley; and on 2 March 1538 O'Conor made full and complete submission, promising for the future to behave as a loyal subject, to pay a yearly rent of three shillings and fourpence per plowland to the crown, to renounce the pope, and to abstain from levying black-rents in the Pale. Four days later he renewed his submission before the council in Dublin, and preferred a request that he might be created baron of Offaly, that such lands as he possessed 'per partitionem, more patrie,' might be confirmed to him and his heirs, and that his brother and other landowners in Offaly might be placed on the same footing. He was pardoned, but his requests were apparently ignored.

For some time he remained quiet, but in 1540 he was implicated in a plot for the restoration by force of Gerald Fitzgerald, the young heir to the earldom of Kildare, and in April and May frequently invaded the Pale. Lord Justice Brereton retaliated by plundering Offaly, but owing to the menacing attitude of O'Donnell and O'Neill, he accepted O'Conor's offer to abide by his indentures, and concluded peace with him. O'Conor's conduct had greatly exasperated Henry, and order was sent for his extirpation, but peace had been concluded before the order arrived; and when St. Leger shortly afterwards assumed the reins of government, O'Conor renewed his submission so humbly that the deputy suggested the advisability of conceding his requests and making him baron of Offaly. Henry yielded to St. Leger's suggestion, but nothing further apparently came of the proposal; though O'Conor and his brother Cahir had meanwhile, on 16 Aug. 1541, consented to submit their differences to arbitration. So long as St. Leger remained in Ireland O'Conor kept the peace, paying his rent regularly; but during his absence some slight disturbances occurred on the borders of the Pale, which the council sarcastically ascribed to 'your lordshipes olde frende Occhonor.' St. Leger attributed the insinuation to the malice of the chancellor, Sir John Alen, and in May 1545 mooted the propriety of rewarding O'Conor's loyalty by creating him a viscount. The proposal was sanctioned by the privy council, but it was not carried into effect, though, at St. Leger's recommendation, a grant of land was made to him in the vicinity of Dublin, together with the use of a house in St. Patrick's Close whenever he visited the city. But whether it was that he was discontented at the indifference of the government, or thought that the accession of Edward VI presented a favourable opportunity to recover his old authority, he, in the summer of 1547, joined with O'More in an attack on the Pale, nominally on behalf of the exiled house of Kildare. St. Leger at once invaded Offaly, which he burnt and plundered as far as the hill of Croghan, but 'without receiving either battle or submission' from O'Conor. No sooner, however, had he retired than O'More and O'Conor's son Rory emerged from their hiding-places, burnt the town and monastery of Athy, ravaged the borders of the Pale, and slew many persons, both English and Irish. St. Leger thereupon invaded Offaly a second time, and, remaining there for fifteen days, burnt and destroyed whatever had escaped in former raids. Deserted by their followers, O'Conor and O'More fled across the Shannon into Connaught. They returned about the beginning of 1548 with a considerable body of wild kerns, but so cowed were their urraghts and tribesmen that none dared even afford them food or protection. Nevertheless, O'Conor managed to keep up a determined guerilla warfare, and it was not till winter brought him face to face with starvation that he was induced to submit, his life being promised him in order to induce O'More to follow his example. He was sent to England and incarcerated in the Tower. He managed to escape early in 1552, but was recaptured on the borders of Scotland. He was afterwards released by Queen Mary, at the intercession of his daughter Margaret. He returned to Ireland in 1554 with the Earl of Kildare, but was shortly afterwards re-arrested and imprisoned in Dublin Castle, where apparently he died about 1560.

By his wife Mary, daughter of Gerald Fitzgerald, ninth earl of Kildare, O'Conor had apparently nine sons and two daughters, several of whom played considerable parts in the history of the times, viz.: Cormac, who, after an adventurous career in Ireland, escaped to Scotland in 1550, and thence to France in 1551, where he remained till 1560, returning in that year to Scotland. He returned to Ireland in 1564, under the assumed name of Killeduff, and was for some time protected by the Earl of Desmond; but, being proclaimed a traitor, he again fled to Scotland. At the intercession of the Earl of Argyll he was pardoned in 1565. He returned to Ireland, and disappears from history in 1573. Donough, the second son, was delivered to Grey in 1538 as hostage for his father's loyalty; but, being released, he took part in the rebellion of 1547. In 1548 he was pressed for foreign service. He returned to Ireland, but being involved in an insurrection of the O'Conors in 1557, he was proclaimed a traitor and was killed in the following year, not without suspicion of treachery, by Owny MacHugh O'Dempsey. Calvach, the third son, after a long career as a rebel, was killed in action in October 1564.

Cathal or Charles O'Connor or O'Conor Faly, otherwise known as Don Carlos 1540–1596, a younger son, born about 1540, was taken when quite a child to Scotland. He accompanied D'Oysel to France in 1560, and appealed to Throckmorton to intercede for his pardon and restoration. By Throckmorton's advice he attached himself as a spy to the train of Mary Queen of Scots. In 1563 he obtained a grant of Castle Brackland and other lands in Offaly. He was implicated in the rebellion of James Fitzmaurice and the Earl of Desmond, and placed himself outside the pale of mercy by his barbarous murder of Captain Henry Mackworth in 1582. He avoided capture, and subsequently escaped in a pinnace to Scotland, and thence, disguised as a sailor, on a Scottish vessel to Spain. He joined the army of invasion under Parma in the Netherlands, and after the defeat of the Armada returned to Spain, where he was dubbed Don Carlos (a fact which has led to his being mistaken for the unfortunate prince of Spain of that name) and granted a pension of thirty crowns a month. He corresponded at intervals with Hugh O'Neill, earl of Tyrone, and endeavoured to remove the bad effects of Tyrone's conduct in surrendering Philip's letter. He embarked at Lisbon with his mother, wife, and children in November 1596, on board the Spanish armada destined for the invasion of Ireland, but the vessel—the Sonday—in which he sailed was wrecked, and he himself drowned.

[State Papers, Hen. VIII (printed); Ware's Annales Rerum Hibern.; Cal. State Papers, Eliz. (Ireland and Foreign); Cal. Carew MSS.; Annals of the Four Masters; Cal. Fiants, Hen. VIII, Ed. VI, Mary, Eliz.; Irish Genealogies in Harl. MS. 1425.]

ROBERT DUNLOP

published 1894

Diplomatist, born in 1515, was fourth of the eight sons of Sir George Throckmorton of Coughton, Warwickshire. His grandfather, Sir Robert Throckmorton (son of Thomas, and grandson of Sir John Throckmorton), was a privy councillor under Henry VII, and died in 1519 while on a pilgrimage to Palestine. His mother was Katharine, daughter of Sir Nicholas, lord Vaux of Harrowden, by his wife Elizabeth, daughter of Henry, lord Fitzhugh, and widow of Sir William Parr, K.G. She was thus aunt by marriage to Queen Catherine Parr, and Sir Nicholas claimed the queen as his first cousin. His father, Sir George, incurred, owing to some local topic of dispute, the ill-will of Cromwell, whose manor of Oversley adjoined that of Coughton. Early in 1540 Cromwell contrived to have his neighbour imprisoned on a charge of denying Henry VIII's supremacy, but Lady Throckmorton's niece, Catherine Parr, used her influence with the king to procure Sir George's release. Sir George was one of the chief witnesses against Cromwell at his trial, which took place in the same year, and was consulted by Henry VIII in the course of the proceedings. After Cromwell's fall Sir George purchased Cromwell's forfeited manor of Oversley. He was sheriff of Warwickshire and Leicestershire in 1526 and 1546, and built the great gatehouse at Coughton. He died soon after Queen Mary's accession. Sir Robert Throckmorton (d. 1570), Sir George's eldest son and successor in the Coughton estate, was succeeded by his son Thomas (d. 1614), who, as a staunch catholic, suffered much persecution and loss of property during Elizabeth's reign. Thomas Throckmorton's grandson Robert was a devoted royalist, and was created a baronet on 1 Sept. 1642. The baronetcy is still held by a descendant.

Michael Throckmorton d. 1558, a younger brother of Sir George and Nicholas's uncle, arranged in 1537 to enter the service of Cardinal Pole at Rome, with a view to acting as a spy on him in the interest of the English government; but Michael deceived Cromwell, and became the loyal and affectionate secretary of the cardinal. For a time he wrote home to the English government letters favourable to Pole without exciting suspicions of his duplicity. He is credited with the authorship of a volume entitled 'A copye of a very fyne and wytty letter sent from the ryght reuerende Lewes Lippomanus, byshop of Verona in Italy,' London, 1556, 8vo. Michael Throckmorton, who received a grant of Haseley in Warwickshire from Queen Mary in 1553, finally took up his residence at Mantua, where he died on 1 Nov. 1558 (cf. *Letters and Papers of Henry VIII; Nine Historical Letters of the Reign of Henry VIII*, by J. P. C[ollier], 1871; *Cal. State Papers*, 1547–80, pp. 67, 75–6). His son Francis was long known at Mantua by his hospitable entertainment of English visitors; he was buried at Ullenhall, Warwickshire, in 1617.

Nicholas was chiefly brought up by his mother's brother-in-law, Lord Parr. In youth he served as page to the Duke of Richmond, and probably went to Paris with his master in 1532. With two brothers he joined the household of his family connection, Catherine Parr, soon after her marriage to Henry VIII in July 1543. Unlike other members of his family, he accepted the reformed faith of his mistress, and remained a sturdy protestant till his death. He and two brothers were present as sympathising spectators at the execution of Anne Askew, the protestant martyr, in 1546 (*Narratives of the Reformation*, Camden Soc. pp. 41–2).

Throckmorton entered public life as M.P. for Malden in 1545, and sat in the House of Commons almost continuously till 1567. The accession of Edward VI was favourable to his fortunes. With the king's religious sentiment he was in thorough sympathy, and Edward liked him personally. He accompanied the army of the Protector Somerset to Scotland in August 1547, and, after engaging in the battle of Musselburgh, was sent to bear the tidings of victory to Edward. The king received him with the utmost cordiality and knighted him. He was subsequently appointed a knight of the king's privy chamber and treasurer of the mint in the Tower (*Acts of Privy Council*, iv. 76, 77, 84). He also received a grant of an annuity of 100*l.*, which he resigned in 1551 in exchange for the manor of Paulerspury in Northamptonshire and other land in adjoining counties. He was present at the unfortunate siege of Boulogne in 1549–1550, and later in 1550 attended to give evidence at Gardiner's trial. He represented Devizes in the House of Commons from 1547 to 1552, and sat for Northamptonshire in Edward's last parliament in March 1553.

Throckmorton's signature was appended to the letters patent of 7 June 1553 which limited the succession of the crown to Lady Jane Grey and her descendants (*Chronicle of Queen Jane*, p. 100). Immediately after Edward's death and Lady Jane's accession, Throckmorton's wife acted by way of deputy for Lady Jane as godmother of a son of Edward Underhill, the 'Hot-Gospeller,' at his christening in the Tower of London (19 July 1553); the boy was named Guilford after Lady Jane's husband (*Narratives of the Reformation*, p. 153). On the same day Mary was generally proclaimed queen. Throckmorton is reported to have been at the moment at Northampton, and when Sir Thomas Tresham formally declared for Mary there, he is said to have made a protest in Lady Jane's favour, which exposed him to personal risk at the townspeople's hands (*Chron. of Queen Jane*, p. 12). But

Throckmorton's devotion to Lady Jane was more specious than real, and he had no intention of forfeiting the goodwill of her rival Mary. He was credited by his friends with having taken a step of the first importance to Mary's welfare on the very day of Edward VI's death by sending her London goldsmith to her at Hoddesdon to apprise her of the loss of her brother, and to warn her of the danger that threatened her if she fell into the clutches of the Duke of Northumberland (*Legend of Throckmorton*, vv. iii et seq.; cf. Goodman's *Life and Times*, i. 117). On Mary's arrival in London she showed no resentment at Throckmorton's dalliance with Lady Jane's pretensions, and he sat as member for Old Sarum in her first parliament of October–December 1553.

But early next year Throckmorton's loyalty was seriously suspected. On 20 Feb. 1553–4 he was sent to the Tower on a charge of complicity in Wyatt's conspiracy. On 17 April 1554 he was tried at the Guildhall. Although he had not taken up arms, the evidence against him was strong. One of Wyatt's lieutenants, Cuthbert Vaughan, swore that he had discussed the plan of the insurrection with Throckmorton. Throckmorton admitted that he had talked to Sir Peter Carew and Wyatt of the probability of a rebellion, and had been in familiar relations with Edward Courtenay. Throckmorton defended himself with resolute pertinacity, and, in spite of the marked hostility of Sir Thomas Bromley and other judges, he was acquitted by the jury. The trial was memorable as affording an almost unprecedented example of the independence of a jury at the trial of one who was charged by the crown with treason. The London populace rejoiced, but the government marked its resentment by ordering the jurors to the Tower or the Fleet; they were kept in prison till the end of the year, when they were released on the payment of a fine amounting to 2,000*l.* (Holinshed, *Chronicle*, ii. 1747; *State Trials*). Nor was Throckmorton allowed to benefit immediately by the jury's courage. He was detained in the Tower till 18 Jan. 1554–5 (Machyn, *Diary*, p. 80); and next year, when a kinsman, John Throckmorton, was arrested on a charge of conspiring with Henry Dudley to rob the treasury, he was again brought under suspicion, but no action was taken against him. His kinsman was executed on 28 April 1556 (cf. *Cal. State Papers*, 1547–80, p. 78). Meanwhile he was a frequent and a welcome visitor of the Princess Elizabeth at Hatfield, though his protestant zeal exceeded that of the princess, and at times drew from her an angry rebuke.

Elizabeth's accession to the throne opened to him a career of political activity. He was at once appointed chief butler and chamberlain of the exchequer, and was elected M.P. for Lyme Regis on 2 Jan. 1558–9. In the following May the more important office of ambassador to France was bestowed on him (cf. *Cal. State Papers*, Dom., 1547–80, p. 128). On 9 Jan.

1559–60 the queen signed instructions in which he was directed to protest against the assumption of the arms of England by Francis II, who had married Mary Queen of Scots on 24 April 1558, and had ascended the French throne on 10 July 1559 (*Hatfield MSS*. i. 165–7; *State Papers*, Foreign, 1559–60, No. 557). Francis died on 5 Dec. 1560, and Throckmorton was much occupied in the weeks that followed in seeking to induce Queen Mary to forego 'the style and title of sovereign of England,' and to postpone her assumption of her sovereignty in Scotland. Throckmorton had many audiences of her, and acknowledged her fascination. They corresponded on friendly terms, and despite differences in their religious and political opinions, he thenceforth did whatever he could to serve her, consistently with his duty to his country (cf. Labanoff, *Lettres de Marie Stuart*, i. 94, 128). He now succeeded in reconciling Elizabeth to the prospect of Queen Mary's settlement in Scotland. But he endeavoured to persuade Mary to tolerate protestantism among her subjects, and did not allow his personal regard for her to diminish his zeal for his own creed. The Venetian ambassador in France described him (3 July 1561) as 'the most cruel adversary that the catholic religion has in England' (*Cal. Venetian State Papers*, 1558–80, p. 333). He showed every mark of hostility to the Guises and of sympathy with the Huguenots, and urged Elizabeth to ally herself publicly and without delay with the Huguenots in France and the reformers in Scotland. Little heed was paid to his proposals.

On 28 Oct. 1560 he wrote with disgust to Cecil of the rumour that the Earl of Leicester was contemplating marriage with the queen (Froude, vi. 439 sq.). In November he sent his secretary, one Jones, to remonstrate with the queen on the injurious effect that the reports of such a union were having on her prestige abroad (Hardwicke, *State Papers*, i. 165). Elizabeth was displeased with his frank importunity, and in September 1561 Throckmorton begged for his recall. Cecil, to whose son Thomas he was showing many kindly attentions in Paris, recommended him to remain at his post, but in September 1562 Sir Thomas Smith (1513–1577) arrived to share his responsibilities, and, as different directions were given by the home government to each envoy, Throckmorton's position was one of continual embarrassment, and his relations with his colleague were usually very strained (cf. Wright, *Queen Elizabeth*, i. 155, 174). Throckmorton never ceased to warn the queen that Europe was maturing a conspiracy to extirpate protestantism, and that it was her duty to act as the champion of the reformed faith. Largely owing to his representations, Elizabeth reluctantly agreed in October 1562 to send an English army to the assistance of the French protestants, who were at open war with their catholic rulers, and were holding Havre against the French government. Throckmorton joined the Huguenot army in Normandy, and after the battle of Dreux (19 Dec. 1562) was carried as a prisoner into the camp of the catholics and was detained. He arrived at Havre in February 1563. On 7 August 1563 he was arrested by the French government on the plea that he had no passport. Cecil expostulated with the French ambassador in London, and Throckmorton was set at liberty (*Hatfield MSS*. i. 277; cf. *Cal. Venetian State Papers*, 1557–80, p. 373; *Lettres de Catherine de Médicis*, vol. ii.). In the spring of 1564 he was engaged in negotiating at Troyes a peace with France, and found, as he conceived, his chief obstruction in the conduct of his colleague, Sir Thomas Smith. A violent quarrel took place between them while the negotiations were in progress, but the treaty of Troyes was finally signed on 1 April 1564, whereupon Throckmorton withdrew from the French embassy.

Next year another diplomatic mission was provided for Throckmorton in Scotland. On 4 May 1565 instructions were drawn up directing him to proceed to Scotland to prevent the marriage of Mary Queen of Scots with Darnley. He hurried to Mary at Stirling Castle. The queen received him reluctantly, and turned a deaf ear to his protest against her union with her cousin. He returned home leisurely, pausing at York to send Cecil the result of his observations on the temper of northern England, where he detected disquieting signs of hostility to Elizabeth's government. Later in the year he addressed a letter of advice to Mary urging her to show clemency to the banished protestant lords, and especially to the Earl of Moray (Melville, *Memoirs*, 1683, pp. 60–3).

Throckmorton was created M.A. at Oxford on 2 Sept. 1566, and next year was, on the recommendation of the Earl of Leicester, named a governor of the incorporated society which was to control the possessions and revenues of the preachers of the gospel in Warwickshire. On 30 June 1567 Throckmorton was ordered to proceed to Scotland for a second time. A dangerous crisis had just taken place in Queen Mary's affairs. Her recent marriage to Bothwell after Darnley's murder had led to the rebellion of the Scottish nobles, and they had in June imprisoned her in Lochleven Castle. As a believer in the justice of Mary's claims to the English succession and an admirer of her personal charm, Throckmorton was anxious to alleviate the perils to which she was exposed. Elizabeth's instructions gave him no certain guidance as to the side on which he was to throw English influence. He travelled slowly northwards, in the hope that Elizabeth would adopt a clearer policy. On arriving at Edinburgh in July he told Mary at a personal interview that Queen Elizabeth would come to her rescue if she would abandon Bothwell. His persuasions were in vain (*MS. Cotton*, Calig. C. 1, ff. 18–35), but on 24 July the imprisoned queen wrote thanking him for the good feeling he had shown her (Labanoff, *Lettres*, ii. 63). At the same time he opened negotiations with the Scottish lords. Elizabeth reproached him with his failure to secure Queen Mary's release (Thorpe, *Scottish State Papers*, ii. 824–46). In self-defence Throckmorton disclosed to the Scottish lords his contradictory orders, but the queen resented so irregular a procedure, and he was recalled in August (cf. Melville, *Memoirs*, 96 seq.).

Throckmorton thenceforth suffered acutely from a sense of disappointment. His health failed during 1568, but he maintained friendly relations with Cecil, to whom he wrote from Fulham on 2 Sept. 1568 that he proposed to kill a buck at Cecil's house at Mortlake. He had long favoured the proposal to wed Queen Mary to the Duke of Norfolk, and he was consequently suspected next year of sympathy with the rebellion of northern catholics in Queen Mary's behalf. In September 1569 he was imprisoned in Windsor Castle, but he was soon released and no further proceedings were taken against him. He died in London on 12 Feb. 1570–1. Shortly before he had dined or supped with the Earl of Leicester at Leicester House. According to the doubtful authority of Leicester's 'Commonwealth,' his death was due to poison administered by Leicester in a salad on that occasion (Leicester, *Commonwealth*, 1641, p. 27). Leicester, it is said, had never forgiven Throckmorton for his vehement opposition to the earl's proposed marriage with the queen. No reliance need be placed on this report. Throckmorton had continuously corresponded on friendly terms with Leicester for many years before his death, and they had acted together as patrons of puritan ministers (cf. Thorpe, *Scottish Papers*, i. 210 seq.; *Cal. State Papers*, Dom. 1547–80, p. 291); Cecil wrote to Sir Thomas Smith of their markedly amicable relations on 16 Oct. 1565, and described Throckmorton as 'carefull and devote to his lordship' (Wright, *Life and Times of Elizabeth*, i. 209). Throckmorton was buried on the south side of the chancel in St. Catherine Cree Church in the city of London.

Throckmorton married Anne, daughter of Sir Nicholas Carew, K.G., and sister and heiress of Sir Francis Carew of Beddington, Surrey. Of three daughters, Elizabeth (baptised at Beddington 16 April 1565) married Sir Walter Ralegh. Of two sons, the elder, Arthur (1557–1626), matriculated from Magdalen College, Oxford, in 1571, aged 14; he was M.P. for Colchester in 1588–9; joined in 1596 the expedition to Cadiz, where he was knighted; inherited from his father the manor of Paulerspury, Northamptonshire, of which county he was sheriff in 1605, and was buried at Paulerspury on 1 Aug. 1616. Sir Nicholas's younger son, Nicholas, who was knighted on 10 June 1603, was adopted by his uncle, Sir Francis Carew (1530–1611) of Beddington, took the name of Carew, and succeeded to the Beddington property, dying in 1643 (cf. Lysons, *Environs of London*, i. 52 et seq.; cf. art. Ralegh, Sir Walter, ad fin.).

Much of Throckmorton's correspondence as ambassador in France between 1559 and 1563 is printed in Patrick Forbes's 'Full View of Public

Transactions in the Reign of Queen Elizabeth,' 1740–1 (2 vols. fol.), in the 'Hardwicke State Papers' (1778, i. 121–62), and in the 'Calendar of Foreign State Papers.' His Scottish correspondence is calendared in Thorpe's 'Scottish State Papers.' A few of his autograph letters are at Hatfield and among the Cottonian, Harleian, Lansdowne, and additional manuscripts at the British Museum. The mass of Throckmorton's original papers came into the possession of Sir Henry Wotton. Wotton bequeathed them to Charles I, but the bequest did not take effect. After many vicissitudes the papers passed into the possession of Francis Seymour Conway, first marquis of Hertford (1719–1794), whose grandson, the third Marquis of Hertford, made them over to the public record office, on the recommendation of John Wilson Croker, before 1842 (cf. *Notes and Queries*, 3rd ser. iv. 455).

A portrait of Sir Nicholas, painted when he was forty-nine, is at Coughton. An engraving by Vertue is dated 1747.

[A poem called the Legend of Sir Nicholas Throckmorton, consisting of 229 stanzas of six lines each, gives in a vague fashion the chief facts of his life. It professes to be spoken by Throckmorton's ghost, after the manner of the poems in the Mirrour for Magistrates. The authorship is uncertain. It was first printed from a badly copied manuscript at Coughton Court by Francis Peck in an appendix to his Life of Milton in 1740, and was inaccurately assigned by Peck to Sir Nicholas's nephew, 'Sir Thomas Throckmorton of Littleton in coun. Warwick, knt.' Apparently the person intended was Thomas Throckmorton 'esquire' (son of Sir Nicholas's brother, Sir Robert Throckmorton), who died on 13 March 1614–15, aged 81, and was buried at Weston Underwood, Buckinghamshire (Lipscomb's Buckinghamshire, iv. 399). The best version of the poem is that transcribed by William Cole and now in the British Museum Addit. MS. 5841; another is in Harl. MS. 6353. John Gough Nichols prepared an improved edition from these manuscripts in 1874. Browne Willis compiled in 1730, from the family papers at Coughton, a History and Pedigree of the Ancient Family of Throckmorton; this still remains in manuscript at Coughton, but was used by Miss Strickland in her Lives of the Queens of England. There is also at Coughton a 'Gens Throckmortoniana' assigned to Sir Robert Throckmorton (cf. Hist. MSS. Comm. 3rd Rep. App. pp. 256–8). Other papers of the Throckmorton family are preserved at Buckland Court, Faringdon (see Hist. MSS. Comm. 10th Rep. No. iv. pp. 168–76). Pedigrees and accounts of the family are in Dugdale's Warwickshire, ii. 749, Lipscomb's Buckinghamshire, iv. 399, Nash's Worcestershire, i. 452, Betham's Baronetage, i. 486, and Wotton's Baronetage, ii. 359 sq. See also Froude's History; Lingard's History; Wright's Life and Times of Queen Elizabeth, passim; Fuller's Worthies, ed. Nichols, iii. 280; Strype's Annals and Memorials, passim; and the state papers and the official calendars mentioned above.]

SIDNEY LEE

published 1898

11

STUART Esmé

(1542?–1583)

Sixth Seigneur of Aubigny and first Duke of Lennox

Only son of John Stuart or Stewart, fifth seigneur of Aubigny, youngest son of John Stewart, third or eleventh earl of Lennox, by his wife, Anne de La Quelle, was born about 1542, and succeeded his father as seigneur of Aubigny in 1567. In 1576 he was engaged in an embassy in the Low Countries (*Cal. State Papers, For.* 1576–8, No. 968); on 25 Nov. he was instructed to go with all speed to the Duke of Alençon and thank him in the name of the estates for his goodwill (*ib.* No. 1030); and a little later he was instructed to proceed to England (*ib.* No. 1036).

After the partial return of Morton to power in 1579 the friends of Mary, whose hopes of triumph had been so rudely dashed by the sudden death of the Earl of Atholl, resolved on a special coup for the restoration of French influence and the final overthrow of protestantism. As early as 15 May Leslie, bishop of Ross, informed the Cardinal de Como that the king 'had written to summon his cousin, the Lord Aubigny, from France' (Forbes-Leith, *Narratives of Scottish Catholics*, p. 136). He was, however, really sent to Scotland at the instigation of the Guises and as their agent. Calderwood states that Aubigny, who arrived in Scotland on 8 Sept., 'pretended that he came only to congratulate the young king's entry to his kingdom [that is, his assumption of the government], and was to return to France within short space' (*History*, iii. 457). But he did not intend to return. As early as 24 Oct. De Castelnau, the French ambassador in London, announced to the king of France that he had practically come to stay, and would be created Earl of Lennox, and, as some think, declared successor to the throne of Scotland should the king die without children (Teulet, *Relations Politiques*, iii. 56). These surmises were speedily justified; in fact no more apt delegate for the task he had on hand could have been chosen. If he desired to stay, no one had a better right, for he was the king's cousin; and if he stayed, he was bound by virtue of his near kinship to occupy a place of dignity and authority, to which Morton could not pretend, and which would imply Morton's ruin. Moreover his personal qualifications for the rôle entrusted to him were of the first order; he was handsome, accomplished, courteous, and (what was of more importance), while he impressed every one with the conviction of his honesty, he was one of the adroitest schemers of his time, with almost unmatched powers of dissimulation. It was impossible for the young king to resist such a fascinating personality. On 14 Nov. 1579 he received from the king the rich abbacy of Arbroath *in*

commendam (*Reg. Mag. Sig. Scot.* 1546–1580, No. 2920), and on 5 March 1579–
80 he obtained the lands and barony of Torbolton (*ib.* No. 2970); the lands
of Crookston, Inchinnan, &c., in Renfrewshire (*ib.* No. 2791), and the
lordship of Lennox (*ib.* No. 2972), Robert Stewart having resigned these
lands in his favour, and receiving instead the lordship of March.

Playing for such high stakes, Lennox did not scruple to forswear himself
to the utmost extent that the circumstances demanded. According to
Calderwood, he purchased a *supersedere* from being troubled for a year for
religion (*History*, iii. 460); but the ministers of Edinburgh were so vehement in their denunciation of the 'atheists and papists' with whom the
king consorted that the king was compelled to grant their request that
Lennox should confer with them on points of religion (Moysie, *Memoirs*, p.
26). This Lennox, according to the programme arranged beforehand with
the Guises, willingly did; and undertook to give a final decision by 1 June.
As was to be expected, he on that day publicly declared himself to have
been converted to protestantism (*Reg. P. C. Scotl.* iii. 289); and on 14 July he
penned a letter beginning thus: 'It is not, I think, unknown to you how it
hath pleased God of his infinite goodness to call me by his grace and mercy
to the knowledge of my salvation, since my coming in this land'; and
ending with a 'free and humble offer of due obedience,' and the hope 'to
be participant in all time coming' of their 'godly prayers and favours'
(Calderwood, iii. 469). A little later he expressed a desire to have a minister
in his house for 'the exercise of true religion'; and the assembly resolved to
supply one from among the pastors of the French kirk in London (*ib.* p.
477). On 13 Sept. he is mentioned as keeper of Dumbarton Castle (*Reg. P. C.
Scotl.* iii. 306), and on 11 Oct. Lennox was nominated lord chancellor and
first gentleman of the royal chamber. In the excessive deference he showed
to the kirk Lennox was mainly actuated by desire for the overthrow of
Morton. Although regarded by Mary and the catholics as their arch enemy,
Morton was secretly detested by the kirk authorities. His sole recommendation was his alliance with Elizabeth and his opposition to Mary; but
the kirk having, as they thought, obtained a new champion in Lennox,
were not merely content to sacrifice Morton, but contemplated his
downfall and even his execution with almost open satisfaction. When
Morton was brought before the council on 6 Jan. 1580–1 and accused of
Darnley's murder, Lennox declined to vote one way or other, on the
ground of his near relationship to the victim; but it was perfectly well
known that the apprehension was made at his instance, and that Captain
James Stewart (afterwards Earl of Arran) was merely his instrument.
Randolph, the English ambassador, had declined to hold communication
with Lennox, on the ground that he was an agent of the pope and the
house of Guise (Randolph to Walsingham, 22 Jan. 1580–1, quoted in Tytler,

ed. 1864, iv. 32), as was proved by an intercepted letter of the archbishop of Glasgow to the pope; but Lennox had no scruple in flatly denying this, the king stating that Lennox was anxious for the fullest investigation, and would 'refuse no manner of trial to justify himself from so false a slander' (the king and council's answer to Mr. Randolph, 1 Feb. 1580–1, *ib.*). After the execution of Morton on 6 June 1581 the influence of Lennox, not merely with the king but in Scotland generally, had reached its zenith. So perfect was the harmony between him and the kirk that even Mary Stuart herself became suspicious that he might intend to betray her interests and throw in his lot with the protestants (Mary to Beaton, 10 Sept. 1581 in Labanoff, v. 258); but the assurances of the Duke of Guise dispelled her doubts (*ib.* p. 278). On 5 Aug. 1581 he was created duke (*Reg. P. C. Scotl.* iii. 413), and on the 12th he was appointed master of the wardrobe.

As early as April 1581 De Tassis had, in the name of Mary, assured Philip II of Spain of the firm resolution of the young king to embrace Roman catholicism, and had sent an earnest request for a force to assist in effecting the projected revolution. It was further proposed that James should meanwhile be sent to Spain, in order that he might be secure from attempts against his crown and liberty; that he might be educated in catholicism, and that arrangements might be completed for his marriage to a Spanish princess. To the objection that Lennox, having special relations with France, might not be favourable to such a project, De Tassis answered that he was wholly devoted to the cause of the Queen of Scots, and ready if necessary to break with France in order to promote her interests (De Tassis to Philip II in *Relations Politiques*, v. 224–8). For the furtherance of these designs, Lennox early in 1582 was secretly visited by two jesuits, Creighton and Holt, who asked him to take command of an army to be raised by Philip II for the invasion of England, in order to set Mary at liberty and restore catholicism. In a letter to De Tassis, Lennox expressed his readiness to undertake the execution of the project (*ib.* pp. 235–6); and in a letter of the same date to Mary he proposed that he should go to France to raise troops for this purpose, but stipulated that her son, the prince, should retain the title of king (*ib.* p. 237). Further, he made it a condition that the Duke of Guise should have the chief management of the plot (De Tassis to Philip, 18 May, *ib.* p. 248). The Duke of Guise therefore went to Paris, where he had a special interview with Creighton and Holt, when it was arranged that a force should be raised on behalf of catholicism under pretext of an expedition to Brittany (*ib.* p. 254). Difficulties, however, arose on account of the timidity or jealousy of Philip II, and the delay proved fatal.

The fact was that after Morton's death Lennox, deeming himself secure, ceased to maintain his submissive attitude to the kirk authorities, whose sensitiveness was not slow to take alarm. Thus, at the assembly held in October 1581 the king complained that Walter Balcanquhal was reported to have stated in a sermon that popery had entered 'not only in the court but in the king's hall, and was maintained by the tyranny of a great champion who is called Grace' (Calderwood, iii. 583). A serious quarrel between the duke and Captain James Stewart (lately created Earl of Arran) led also to dangerous revelations. As earl of Arran, the duke's henchman now deemed himself the duke's rival. He protested against the duke's right to bear the crown at the meeting of parliament in October, and matters went so far that two separate privy councils were held—the one under Arran in the abbey, and the other under the duke in Dalkeith (*ib.* iii. 592–3; Spotiswood, ii. 281). They were reconciled after two months' 'variance'; but meanwhile Arran, to 'strengthen himself with the common cause,' had given out 'that the quarrel was for religion, and for opposing the duke's courses, who craftily sought the overthrow thereof' (Spotiswood). After the reconciliation, the duke on 2 Dec. made another declaration of the sincerity of his attachment to protestantism (*Reg. P. C. Scotl.* iii. 431), but mischief had been done which no further oaths could remedy. In addition to this the duke had come into conflict with the kirk in regard to Robert Montgomerie, whom he had presented to the bishopric of Glasgow (Calderwood, iii. 577); and Arran and the duke, being now reconciled, did not hesitate to flout the commissioners of the assembly when on 9 May 1582 they had audience of the king. On 12 July a proclamation was issued in the king's name, in which the rumour that Lennox was a 'deviser' of 'the erecting of Papistrie' was denounced as a 'malicious' falsehood, inasmuch as he had 'sworn in the presence of God, approved with the holy action of the Lord's Table,' to maintain protestantism, and was 'ready to seal the same with his blood' (*ib.* p. 783). The proclamation might have been effectual but for the fact that in some way or other the kirk had obtained certain information of the plot that was in progress (*ib.* p. 634). This information had reached them on 27 July through James Colville, the minister of Easter Wemyss, who had arrived from France with the Earl of Bothwell; and the news hastened, if it did not originate, the raid of Ruthven on 22 Aug., when the king was seized near Perth by the protestant nobles.

On learning what had happened, the duke, who was at Dalkeith, came to Edinburgh; and, after purging himself 'with great protestations that he never attempted anything against religion,' proposed to the town council that they should write to the noblemen and gentlemen of Lothian to come to Edinburgh 'to take consultation upon the king's delivery and liberty' (*ib.* p. 641); but they politely excused themselves from meddling in the matter. Next day, Sunday the 26th, James Lawson depicted in a sermon 'the duke's enormities' (*ib.* p. 642); and, although certain noblemen were permitted to join him, and were sent by him to hold a conference with the king, the only answer they obtained was that Lennox 'must depart out of Scotland within fourteen days' (*ib.* p. 647). Leaving Edinburgh on 5 Sept. 1582 on the pretence that he was 'to ride to Dalkeith, the duke, after he had passed the borough muir, turned westwards, and rode towards Glasgow' (*ib.* p. 648). On 7 Sept. a proclamation was made at Glasgow forbidding any to resort to him except such as were minded to accompany him to France, and forbidding the captain of the castle of Dumbarton to receive more into the castle than he was able to master and overcome (*ib.*). At Dumbarton the duke on 20 Sept. issued a declaration 'touching the calumnies and accusations set out against him' (*ib.* p. 665). Meanwhile he resolved to wait at Dumbarton in the hope of something turning up, and on the 17th he sent a request to the king: or a 'prorogation of some few days' (*ib.* p. 673). A little later he sent to the king for liberty to go by England (*ib.* p. 689); but his intention was to organise a plot for the seizure of the king, which was accidentally discovered. The king, it is said, earnestly desired that the duke might be permitted to remain in Scotland; but was 'sharply threatened by the lords that if he did not cause him to depart he should not be the longest liver of them all' (Forbes-Leith, *Narrative of Scottish Catholics*, p. 183). Finally, after several manœuvrings, Lennox did set out on 21 Dec. from Dalkeith on his journey south (Calderwood, iii. 693). On reaching London he sent word privately to Mendoza, the Spanish ambassador, that he would send his secretary to him secretly to give him an account of affairs in Scotland (*Cal. State Papers*, Spanish, ii. 435); and the information given to Mendoza was that Lennox had been obliged to leave Scotland in the first place in consequence of a promise made by King James to Elizabeth, and in the second place in consequence of the failure of the plot arranged for the rescue of the king from the Ruthven raiders on his coming to the castle of Blackness (*ib.* p. 438). On 14 Jan. 1583 Lennox had an audience of Elizabeth, who 'charged him roundly with such matters as she thought culpable' (*Cal. State Papers*, Scottish, pp. 431–2); but of course the duke, without the least hesitation, affirmed his entire innocence, and appears to have succeeded in at least rendering Elizabeth doubtful of his catholic leanings. Walsingham endeavoured through a spy, Fowler, to discover from Mauvissière the real religious sentiments of the duke; but as the duke had prevaricated to Mauvissière—assuring him that James was so constant to the reformed faith that he would lose his life rather than forsake it, and declaring that he professed the same faith as his royal master—Walsingham succeeded only in deceiving himself (Tytler, iv. 56–7).

Early in 1583 Lennox arrived in Paris, resolved to retain the mask to the last. On the duke's secretary being asked by Mendoza whether his master would profess protestantism in France, he replied that he had been specially instructed by the duke to tell Mendoza that he would, in order that he might signify the same to the pope, the king of Spain, and Queen Mary (*Cal. State Papers*, Spanish, ii. 439). For one reason he had not given up hope of returning to Scotland; and, indeed, although in very bad health, he had 'schemed out a plan' of the success of which he was very sanguine (De Tassis to Philip II, 4 May, in Teulet, v. 265). He did not live to begin its execution; but, in order to lull the Scots to security, he at his death on 26 May 1583 continued to profess himself a convert to the faith which he was doing his utmost to subvert. He also gave directions that while his body was to be buried at Aubigny, his heart should be embalmed and sent to the king of Scots, to whose care he commended his children. An anonymous portrait of Lennox belonged in 1866 to the Earl of Home (*Cat. First Loan Exhib.* No. 459). By his wife, Catherine de Balsac d'Entragues, Lennox had two sons and three daughters: Ludovick, second duke; Esmé, third duke; Henrietta, married to George, first marquis of Huntly; Mary, married to John, earl of Mar; and Gabrielle, a nun.

[Cal. State Papers, For., Eliz., Scot., and Spanish; Teulet's Relations Politiques; Forbes-Leith's Narratives of Scottish Catholics; Reg. Mag. Sig. Scot.; Reg. Privy Council Scotl.; Labanoff's Letters of Mary Stuart; Histories by Calderwood and Spotiswood; Moysie's Memoirs and History of King James the Sext (Bannatyne Club); Bowes's Correspondence (Surtees Soc.); Lady Elizabeth Cust's Stuarts of Aubigny; Sir William Fraser's Lennox; Douglas's Scottish Peerage, ed. Wood, i. 99–100.]

THOMAS FINLAYSON HENDERSON

published 1898

PARRY William

(*d.* 1585)

Conspirator, was the son of Harry ap David, a gentleman of good family of Northop, Flintshire, and his wife Margaret, daughter of Pyrs or Peter Conway, archdeacon of St. Asaph and rector of Northop (Dwnn, *Heraldic Visitations*, ii. 326; Le Neve, *Fasti*, i. 84). Harry ap David is stated by his son to have been of the guard to Henry VIII, to have been appointed to attend on the Princess Mary, and to have died about 1566, aged 108, leaving fourteen children by his first wife and sixteen by his second, Parry's mother.

17

Parry

Parry, or William ap Harry, as he was originally called, was early apprenticed to one Fisher of Chester, who 'had some small knowledge in law.' At Chester Parry attended a grammar school, but is said to have made frequent attempts to escape from his master. At last he succeeded, and came to London to seek his fortune. A marriage with a Mrs. Powell, widow, and daughter of Sir William Thomas, brought him some means, and he became attached to the household of William Herbert, first earl of Pembroke, whom he served until the earl's death in 1570. Parry then entered the queen's service, receiving some small appointment at court, and soon afterwards made a second fortunate marriage with Catherine, widow of Richard Heywood, an officer in the king's bench. By this marriage, in addition to his own lands in Northop, worth 20l. a year, he became possessed of various manors in Lincolnshire and Woolwich, Kent, which his wife made over to him in spite of the entail devolving them upon Heywood's sons; this led to litigation in 1571 (*Proceedings of Privy Council*, 1571–5, p. 16; Hasted, *Kent*, ed. 1886, i. 151 *n.*).

Parry, however, soon squandered his own and his wife's money, and, probably with a view to avoiding his creditors, sought service as a spy abroad. His chief endeavour was to insinuate himself into the secrets of the English catholic exiles, and to report on their plans to Burghley; with this object he visited Rome, Siena, and other places. In 1577 he was again in England, and frequently appealed to Burghley for a salary, stating that he maintained two nephews at Oxford, a brother, and other relatives. In 1579 he fled precipitately without leave, probably again to avoid his creditors. He wrote to Burghley from Paris excusing his conduct, and Burghley still reposed confidence in him; for when his wife's nephew, Anthony Bacon, was going abroad, Burghley strongly recommended Parry to him. The Earl of Essex endeavoured to make capital out of the confidence which Burghley thus appeared to place in Parry, and complained to the queen; but Burghley stated his willingness to be responsible if Bacon's loyalty suffered from his intercourse with Parry (Birch, *Memoirs*, i. 12, 13). About the same time Parry secretly joined the Roman catholic church.

In 1580 Parry again returned to England, and in November, after renewed proceedings by his creditors, he made a personal assault on Hugh Hare, one of the chief of them, in the Temple; the offence was quite unlike a felony, and the indictment was drawn up in the common form for a burglary. Parry was convicted and sentenced to death, in spite of his protest that he could 'prove that the Recorder spake with the jury, and the foreman did drink' (Jardine, *Criminal Trials*, i. 246–76). He received a pardon from the queen, but was subject to further annoyance from Hugh Hare, against whom he petitioned the council on 17 Dec. 1581, stating that he had deserved better of his prince and country than to be thus tormented by a cunning and shameless usurer (*Cal. State Papers*, Dom. 1581–90, p. 33). He found sureties for his debts, one of whom was Sir John Conway, a connection of his mother's.

In July 1582 he asked leave to travel for three years, and left the country 'with doubtful mind as to his return'; he began to 'mistrust his advancement in England.' He still pretended to reveal the secrets of the catholics to Burghley, but in reality was seeking to serve their cause. He began by strenuously urging a policy of conciliation towards them in England, and recommending pardon for some of the more distinguished catholic refugees, like John and Thomas Roper, Sir Thomas Copley, and Charles Neville, sixth earl of Westmorland, who, through the Conways, seems to have been distantly connected with Parry. But by degrees he became persuaded of the necessity for more violent courses; he fell into the hands of Charles Paget and Thomas Morgan (1543–1606?), and the reading of Cardinal Allen's works seems to have suggested to him the lawfulness of assassinating Elizabeth. He sought approval of his scheme in various quarters, but it seems to have been generally discountenanced. At Milan he 'justified himself in religion before the inquisitor'; thence he proceeded to Venice, and back to Lyons and Paris. In Paris he had an interview with Thomas Morgan and Paget, who, according to the later account by Robert Parsons, sent Parry to England without Parsons's knowledge, where he revealed their plans (*Letters, &c., of Cardinal Allen*, p. 392).

Parry landed at Rye in January 1584, and proceeded at once to court, where he disclosed the existence of a plot to murder the queen and organise an invasion from Scotland to liberate Mary and place her on the throne. On the strength of this revelation he demanded the mastership of St. Catherine's Hospital, near the Tower, but was refused. Meanwhile he received a reply from Cardinal Como to a letter he had addressed to the pope from Milan. He considered it a complete approval of his plan to murder Elizabeth, and it was generally accepted as such when published in England. The letter, however, contains no reference to any definite scheme, and merely expresses general approval of Parry's intentions; its significance entirely depends upon what Parry had informed the pope his intentions were, and that is not known.

Parry still hesitated, and resolved to try the effect of a protest in parliament against the persecution of catholics before proceeding to extreme measures. With this object he was elected, on 11 Nov. 1584, member for Queenborough, Kent. Meanwhile another perusal of Cardinal Allen's book seems to have strengthened his original determination, and he had various conferences with Edmund Neville (1560?–1618), whom he terms his 'cousin'; according to their confessions they both plotted treason, but each disclaimed any intention of carrying it out.

Parliament met on 23 Nov., and one of its first acts was to pass a bill 'against jesuits, seminary priests, and other such-like disobedient persons.' It met with unanimous approval, but on the third reading, on 17 Dec., Parry rose in his place and denounced it as 'a measure savouring of treasons, full of blood, danger, and despair to English subjects, and pregnant with fines and forfeitures which would go to enrich not the queen, but private individuals.' The house was astounded, and Parry was committed to the sergeant-at-arms, placed on his knees at the bar, and required to explain his words. He was carried off in custody and examined by the council. The next day he was released by an order from the queen (D'Ewes, *Journals*, pp. 340–1).

Six weeks afterwards Neville informed against his fellow-conspirator, stating that he had plotted to murder the queen while she was driving in the park. Parry was arrested on a charge of high treason, and placed in the Tower, whence he wrote a full confession to the queen and sent letters to Burghley and Leicester. On 11 Feb. 1584–5 he was expelled from parliament, and on 18 Feb. his trial began. Probably in the hope of pardon he pleaded guilty, but he subsequently declared his innocence, said that his confession was a tissue of falsehoods, and that Como had never given any countenance to the murder. He was condemned to death, and executed on 2 March in Westminster Palace Yard. On the scaffold he again declared his innocence, and appealed to the queen for a more lenient treatment of her catholic subjects. Special prayers and thanksgivings were ordered to be used in churches for the preservation of the queen after the discovery of Parry's plot (cf. *An Order of Praier and Thanksgiving . . . with a short extract of William Parries Voluntarie Confession written with his owne hand*, 1584, 4to).

An account of Parry's execution is among the manuscripts of Lord Calthorpe, vol. xxxi. fol. 190, and on the back of fol. 191 is a poetical epitaph on him (*Hist. MSS. Comm.* 2nd Rep. App. p. 41). After his death a work, published, probably, at the instance of the government, and entitled 'A true and plaine Declaration of the Horrible Treasons practised by William Parry', charged him with various atrocious crimes quite inconsistent with Burghley's confidence in him. It made depreciatory remarks on his birth and parentage, but little reliance can be placed upon them.

There is some doubt as to Parry's guilt, and it is improbable that he would ever have summoned up sufficient resolution to carry his scheme into effect even if he had been genuine in his intention. 'Subtle, quick, and of good parts,' he was extremely weak and vacillating, and his confession and letters convey the suspicion that he was not quite sane. Parry's nephew, according to Strype, had been with him in Rome, and the younger man subsequently served the Duke of Guise and Alexander of Parma; he was executed late in Elizabeth's reign for highway robbery.

[There are numerous letters from Parry to Burghley in Lansdowne MSS., where is also an account of the proceedings relative to his trial for assault on Hugh Hare; cf. also Harl. MSS. 787 No. 49, 895 No. 3, which gives his speech on the scaffold; Cal. State Papers, Dom. Ser.; Murdin's Burghley Papers, p. 440; Hist. MSS. Comm. 5th Rep. App. p. 213, 6th Rep. App. p. 306 a; Hatfield MSS. vv. 25, 58, 59; Stubbes's Intended Treason of Doctor Parrie [1585]; A true and plaine Declaration of the Horrible Treasons practised by William Parry, &c., 1585, also reprinted with Sir W. Monson's Megalopsychy, 1681, fol.; D'Ewes's Journals, passim; Collection of State Tryals, 1719, i. 103–10; Cobbett's State Trials, i. 1097–1111; Jardine's Criminal Trials, i. 246–76; Journals of the House of Commons; Official Returns of Members of Parliament; Strype's Annals, passim; Camden's Elizabeth, ed. Hearne, ii. 426–30; Holinshed, iii. 1382–96; Somers's Tracts, i. 264; Foulis's Hist. of Romish Treasons, p. 342, &c.; Bartoli's Istoria della Compagnia di Giesù—l' Inghilterra, 1667, pp. 286–91; Hazlitt's Handbook and Collections, passim; Spedding's Bacon, viii. 37, x. 37, 55; Aikin's Memoirs of Elizabeth, ii. 143–6; Letters, &c., of Cardinal Allen, pp. 392–3; Dodd's Church History, ii. 152–3, and Tierney's Dodd, iii. 20, App. No. xiii.; Foley's Records of the English Jesuits, i. 327, 384, iv. 169; Pike's Annals of Crime; Lingard, Froude, Ranke, and Hallam's Histories; Gardiner, x. 144; Williams's Eminent Welshmen; Notes and Queries, 7th ser. vi. 468, vii. 76; cf. art. Elizabeth.]

ALBERT FREDERICK POLLARD

published 1895

CECIL alias Snowden, John

(1558–1626)

Priest and political adventurer, was born in 1558 of parents who lived at Worcester. He was educated at Trinity College, Oxford (*Douay Diaries*, p. 363), became a Roman catholic, joined the seminary at Rheims in August 1583, and in April of the following year, when he was twenty-six years of age, passed to the English college at Rome (Foley, *Records*, Diary of the College, p. 164), where he received holy orders. For eighteen months (1587–8) he acted as Latin secretary to Cardinal Allen, and afterwards spent two years in Spain, and was with Father Parsons at his newly erected seminary at Valladolid. Early in 1591 Parsons sent Cecil, with another priest, Fixer, alias Wilson, into England, via Amsterdam; but the vessel in which they sailed was captured by her Majesty's ship Hope in the Channel, and the two priests were carried to London. Here they at once came to terms with Lord Burghley. Cecil had already in 1588 corresponded, under the name of Juan de Campo, with Sir Francis Walsingham. He now declared that although he and his companion had been entrusted with treasonable commissions by Parsons, in preparation for a fresh attack upon England by the Spanish forces, they nevertheless detested all such practices, and had resolved to reveal them to the government at the first opportunity. Cecil hoped to obtain liberty of conscience for catholic priests who eschewed politics, and, with the view of helping to distinguish loyal from disloyal clergy, he willingly undertook to serve the queen as secret informer, provided that he was not compelled to betray catholic as catholic, or priest as priest. On this understanding he was sent, at his own request, into Scotland. For the next ten years this clever adventurer contrived, without serious difficulty, to combine the characters of a zealous missionary priest, a political agent of the Scottish catholic earls in rebellion against their king, and a spy in the employment of Burghley and Sir Robert Cecil. In Scotland he resided generally with Lord Seton, and acted as confessor or spiritual director of Barclay of Ladyland. When George Kerr was captured, on his starting for Spain with the 'Spanish Blanks,' 31 Dec. 1592, there were found among his papers letters from John Cecil to Cardinal Allen and to Parsons, assuring them of his constant adherence to the catholic faith and of his sufferings in consequence, also a letter from Robert Scott to Parsons, referring indeed to some false rumours in circulation to the discredit of Cecil, but recommending him to the jesuit on account of 'his probity and the good service he had done in the vineyard.' Three months later the catholic lords, when hard pressed by King James, sent Cecil on a diplomatic mission to Parsons in Spain. Here he was welcomed by his former friend and patron, who unsuspectingly introduced him to Juan d'Idiaquez as 'a good man who had suffered for the cause.' For greater secrecy Parsons sent him disguised as a soldier, and told Idiaquez that he must give him money to get back to Scotland. In the statement regarding the projects of the Scottish lords laid before Idiaquez by Cecil, he describes himself as 'a pupil of the seminary of Valladolid' (Cal. Spanish, Eliz. iv. 603, 613–617). All this time he was in constant communication with Sir Robert Cecil and Sir Francis Drake, who seemed to place some value on his services, and in 1594 he boasted to the Earl of Essex of all he had done, and how he had discovered the plots of catholics by bringing their letters to Burghley (Hatfield Papers, iv. 473, 478, 479; Cal. Dom. Eliz. 1591–4, p. 474).

In October 1594 Cecil was again sent into Spain by the Earls of Angus and Errol to represent to King Philip the condition of catholics in Scotland, and to solicit his aid. He made no secret of this mission to Sir Robert Cecil; for, writing to him, 30 (?) Dec. 1595 (Cal. Dom. Eliz.), he says: 'When last in Spain I gave such satisfaction that I was employed by the contrary party to give information of the estate of Scotland, and to see if the King of Spain would be brought to do anything to succour the nobility there and in

Ireland.' He tells that he had handed over to Drake letters of Parsons and Sir Francis Englefield, adding: 'I am again ready to serve you, always reserving my own conscience. Not a leaf shall wag in Scotland but you shall know.'

In 1596 Cecil was once more in Spain, commissioned by the catholic earls to follow up and to countermine the diplomatic intrigues of John Ogilvy of Poury, who had, or pretended to have, a secret mission from James to seek the friendship and alliance of Philip, and to assure the king and the pope of his own catholic sympathies and proclivities. Cecil met Ogilvy at Rome, where the two men endeavoured to overreach each other at the papal court and with the Duke of Sesa, with whom they had frequent interviews. They then journeyed together into Spain, and in May and June they presented to Philip at Toledo their several memorials, Cecil attacking Ogilvy, and demonstrating the hostility of James to the catholic religion and its adherents, and the falsity of all his catholic pretences. This exposure of the Scottish king enraged Father William Crichton, the aged jesuit, who, in opposition to the policy of Father Parsons, had constantly upheld James's claim to succeed to the English throne. He accordingly wrote anonymously, and disseminated in manuscript 'An Apologie and Defence of the K. of Scotlande against the infamous libell forged by John Cecill, English Priest, Intelligencer to Treasurer Cecill of England.' To this Cecil, who had received about this time the degree of doctor of divinity from the university of Paris or of Cahors, replied in the rare tract, of which the copy in the British Museum is probably unique; it is entitled 'A Discoverie of the errors committed and inivryes don his M.A. off Scotlande and Nobilitye off the same realme, and Iohn Cecyll, Pryest and D. off diuinitye by a malitious Mythologie titled an Apologie and cōpiled by William Criton, Pryest and professed Iesuite, whose habit and behauioure, whose cote and cōditions, are as sutable as Esau his hādes, and Iacob his voice.' The preface is dated 'from the monastery of Montmartre,' 10 Aug. 1599. The writer, indignant at being stigmatised as 'intelligencer' to the English government, declares that it was done to ruin him, and that, as he is about to pass into Scotland, the charge might be his death.

At the end of 1601 Cecil was in France, and apparently in company with Robert Bruce; for Cardinal d'Ossat, writing from Rome, 26 Nov., warns Villeroi against both men as spies acting on behalf of Spain. D'Ossat may have been misinformed on this point with regard to Cecil. In any case, two months later this versatile diplomatist appears in quite another company. When the four deputies of the English appellant priests, John Mush, Bluet, Anthony Champney, and Barneby, were starting on their journey to Rome to lay before the pope their grievances against the archpriest Blackwell and the jesuits, Dr. Cecil unexpectedly took the place of Barneby in the deputation; and fortified with testimonials from the French government, in spite of D'Ossat's warnings, he for the next nine months assumed a leading part in the proceedings with the pope and cardinals—proceedings in which one of the main charges brought against the jesuits was their improper meddling with the affairs of state. Parsons now in vain denounced Cecil to the pope as a swindler, a forger, a spy, the friend of heretics, and the betrayer of his brethren; for as the jesuit had made similar or more incredible accusations against all his other opponents, the charges were disbelieved or disregarded by the papal court. Cecil had several favourable audiences of the pope, and his ability and tact gained for him great credit with the clerical party, to whose cause he had attached himself. It is probably to his pen that we owe the 'Brevis Relatio,' or formal account of the proceedings in the case at Rome (printed in *Archpriest Controversy*, ii. 45–151). In 1606 he was chosen, together with Dr. Champney, to present to the pope the petition of a number of English priests for episcopal government. The indignant Parsons again denounced his adversary, and desired that he might be seized and put upon his trial (Tierney, *Dodd*, v. 10, 11, xiv–xx), but Dr. Cecil remained unharmed in fortune or character. He for some time held the appointment of chaplain and almoner to Margaret of Valois, the divorced wife of Henry IV, and settled down to a quiet life. There are even indications that he became friendly with the jesuits. He handed over, indeed, copies of certain letters touching Garnet to the English ambassador; but Carew, forwarding them to Salisbury, 2 Feb. 1607, wrote that 'he [Cecil] is of late so great with Père Cotton that I dare not warrant this for clear water' (R. O. French correspondence). He died at Paris, according to Dr. John Southcote's Note Book (MS. *penes* the Bishop of Southwark), on 21 Dec. 1626.

[Dodd's Church Hist. ii. 377; Statements and Letters of 'John Snowden,' Cal. State Papers, Dom. Eliz. 1591–4, pp. 38–71; Calderwood's Hist. v. 14–36; Documents illustrating Catholic Policy, &c., viz. (1) Summary of Memorials presented to the King of Spain by John Ogilvy of Poury and Dr. John Cecil; (2) Apology and Defence of the King of Scotland by Father William Creighton, S.J., edited, with introduction, by T. G. Law, in Miscellany of the Scot. Hist. Soc. 1893; The Archpriest Controversy (Royal Hist. Soc.), vol. ii. passim.]

THOMAS GRAVES LAW

published 1901

(1559?–1603)

Secular priest and conspirator, born on 23 April, apparently in 1559, was, like his contemporaries, Anthony Watson and Christopher Watson, a native of the diocese of Durham. His name does not occur in the 'Visitations of Durham' (ed. Foster, 1887), but his father must have been a man of some position if William's statement is to be trusted, that he was 'sent to Oxforde at 10 yeares of age with my tutor (a perfect linguist, which my father kept to teach).' He must be distinguished from the 'William Watson of Durham, pleb.,' who matriculated, aged 26, from All Souls' on 28 Nov. 1581, and graduated B.A. in the following February, for the future conspirator 'at 14 came to the inns of court,' and at 16 'passed the sea to Rheims' (Watson to the Attorney-general, printed in Law, *Archpriest Controversy*, i. 211 sqq.). Watson's family was evidently Roman catholic, and his name does not appear on the registers at Oxford or at the inns of court. According to Parsons, who is even less veracious than Watson himself, Watson came to Rheims 'a poor, little begging boy,' and obtained employment in menial offices at the English College, where he made sport for the students 'in tumbling, for which his body was fitly made, and so he passed by the name of Wil. Wat., or Wat. Tumbler' (Parsons, *Manifestation*, 1602, ff. 83–4). Watson's own account was that 'my studies until I was 18 yeares of age were in the 7 liberall sciences intermixte, with the tongues, phisicke, common lawe (and especially histories all my life time for recreacon); from 18 to 21 I studied the lawes canon and civil with positive divinitie, and perfecting of my metaphisicke and philosophie; after that, untill my return home, I plyed schoole divinitie.' His library, when he was arrested, contained, besides theological works, 'lawe bookes, Machiavels works, tragedies, cronycles, collecions of Doleman, Philopater, Leycesters Commonwealth.'

Watson was confirmed at Rheims on 25 March 1581, received minor orders on 23 Sept. 1583, was ordained subdeacon on 21 Sept. 1585, deacon at Laon on 22 March 1585–6, priest on 5 April, and on 16 June following was sent as missioner to England (*Douai Diaries*, pp. 13, 178, 198, 209, 211). He was captured almost immediately and imprisoned in the Marshalsea; he was soon released on condition of leaving England within a specified time, during which he was not to be molested. Richard Topcliffe, however, who had been commissioned to hunt out priests, seized Watson, shut him up in Bridewell, and severely tortured him (cf. *State Papers*, Dom. Eliz. ccii. 61). In 1588 Watson escaped to the continent (on 30 Aug. in that year two persons were executed for contriving his escape), and passed two years at Liège. In the autumn of 1590 he again returned to England, and officiated for some time in the west, eluding capture in spite of there being at one time sixteen warrants out against him. Eventually one of Sir William Waad's agents discovered him; but his imprisonment, apparently in the Gatehouse, was comparatively mild until Topcliffe again intervened with his tortures. Once again Watson, 'taking occasion of the dores set wyde open unto me,' effected his escape, in order, he maintained, to avoid legal proceedings on account of 200*l*. which had been 'taken up' by some one using his name; possibly this was on 18 May 1597, when he escaped from Bridewell with 'an Irish bishop' (*Cal. Hatfield MSS*. vii. 204). On 30 June 1599 it was reported 'Watson, a seminary priest, has again escaped from the Gatehouse and cannot be heard of; he is thought to have with him a servant who, with his consent, has stolen his master's best gelding and 40*l*. in money for Watson's use' (*Cal. State Papers*, Dom. 1598–1601, p. 226). He now seems to have fled to Scotland, hoping to cross thence to France, but returned to the north of England, and thence once more to London. Here apparently he was again arrested, and he was one of the thirty-three secular priests in prison at Wisbech Castle who on 17 Nov. 1600 signed the famous 'appeal' against the appointment of George Blackwell as archpriest, on the ground that he was a tool of Parsons and the jesuits. Watson's thirty articles against Blackwell's appointment are printed by Mr. T. G. Law in 'The Archpriest Controversy' (Camden Soc.), i. 90–8.

To this struggle between the secular priests and the jesuits Watson had devoted his entire energy. Like other seculars, he was bitterly opposed not only to the domination of the jesuits, but also to their anti-national intrigues, especially the project for securing the succession to the infanta of Spain; he maintained that but for these plots Elizabeth's government would grant a large measure of toleration to Roman catholics. As early as 1587, while in the Marshalsea, he had protested against Babington's plot, and the jesuits denounced him as a government spy and his sufferings in prison as fictitious; Watson himself declared that he endured more from the tongues of the jesuits than from Topcliffe's tortures. Possibly his visit to Scotland was in connection with his project of answering the 'Conference about the next Succession,' which Parsons had published under the pseudonym of Doleman in 1594, advocating the claims of the infanta. The account which Watson gives of his book is obscure and possibly untrue; at first apparently he wished to advocate the exclusion of all 'foreign' claims, the Scottish included, and he says that the queen and Essex liked what he wrote; then he maintained James's right, and when this proved unpalatable at court he suggested that he had only been entrapped into writing the book at all by jesuit intrigues.

This book does not seem to have been printed, but in 1601 appeared four works, all probably printed at Rheims and ascribed to Watson. The first, 'A Dialogue betwixt a Secular Priest and a Lay Gentleman concerning some points objected by the Jesuiticall Faction against such Secular Priests as haue shewed their dislike of M. Blackwell and the Jesuit Proceedings,' was erroneously assigned by Parsons and Anthony Rivers to John Mush, another of the appellants (Foley, *Records*, i. 42; Law, *Jesuits and Seculars*, p. cxxxvii). The second, 'A Sparing Dis-coverie of our English Iesuits and of Fa. Parsons' Proceedings under pretence of promoting the Catholike Faith in England ... newly imprinted' (Rheims? 4to), is ascribed by Rivers to Christopher Bagshaw (*ib.*). But 'the most notable of these later writings on the side of the appellants was the "Important Considerations." It forms, however, an exception to the general character of Watson's productions, both in matter and style. Indeed it has so little of Watson's manner that it is not improbable that he was the writer of no more than the prefatory epistle, which is signed with his initials. The book itself professes to be "published by sundry of us, the Secular Priests," and is a brief, and on the whole fair, historical survey of all the rebellions, plots, and "bloody designments" set on foot against England by the pope or others, mainly at the instigation of the jesuits' (*ib.* p. xci). Its title was 'Important Considerations which ought to move all true and sound Catholickes who are not wholly Jesuited to acknowledge ... that the Proceedings of Her Majesty ... have been both mild and merciful.' It was reprinted in 'A Collection of Several Treatises concerning ... the Penal Laws,' 1675 and 1688, in 'The Jesuit's Loyalty,' 1677 series, in 'A Preservative against Popery,' 1738, vol. iii., and was edited by the Rev. Joseph Mendham in 1831. It was also extensively used by Stillingfleet in his 'Answer to Cressy,' and by Joseph Berington in his 'Decline and Fall of the Roman Catholic Religion,' 1813 (*ib.*, p. cxxxv; Mendham, pref. pp. xiv–xv). In 1601 also was published Watson's longest work, 'A Decacordon of Ten Quodlibeticall Questions concerning Religion and State; wherein the author, framing himself a Quilibet to every Quodlibet, decides an Hundred Crosse Interrogatorie Doubts about the generall contentions betwixt the Seminarie Priests and Iesuits ...,' Rheims? 4to. Though dated 1602, it was described by Father Rivers in a letter to Parsons on 22 Dec. 1601. It contains a few interesting allusions to Nash, Tarlton, and Will Somers, which seem to indicate that Watson frequented the theatre (pp. 266, 329). Fuller called it a 'notable book,' and declared that no answer to it was published by the jesuits (*Church History*, 1656, bk. x. pp. 5–6). A puritan reply, however, appeared early in 1602 (Foley, i. 30) as 'Let Quilibet beware of Quodlibet,' n.d., n. pl., and 'An Antiquodlibet or an Advertisement to beware of Secular Priests' (Middelburg, 1602, 12mo) has been attributed to John Udall who, however, died ten years before.

Whatever hand other appellants had in the production of these works, their bitterness and extravagance impelled the deputation then pleading the appellants' cause at Rome to repudiate repeatedly all share in them (*Archpriest Controversy*, ii. 68, 77, 87, 89). The jesuits at the same time endeavoured to saddle them with the responsibility, and made good use of the books in their attempt to prejudice the papal court against the appellants. Parsons replied to them with equal scurrility, but more skill, in his 'Briefe Apologie' (1602) and 'Manifestation of the Great Folly...' (1602), in which he heaps on Watson all manner of personal abuse.

Meanwhile Watson had benefited by the favour shown by Elizabeth's government to the secular priests. He had probably been removed from Wisbech with the other seculars to Framlingham, but in April 1602 he was in the Clink. In a letter to Parsons, Anthony Rivers relates how the Roman catholics in that prison had made secret arrangements for celebrating mass when they were surprised by government agents, and asserts that this was prearranged by Watson, who was removed to the king's bench, but discharged the next day. He was now seen in frequent consultation with Bancroft, bishop of London, the subject of their deliberations being a form of oath of allegiance which might be taken by the more moderate catholics. This oath was taken in November following by Watson and other seculars, who were thereupon released; and to this period must probably be referred the report (dated October 1601 in *Cal. State Papers*, Dom. Addenda, 1580–1625) of Watson's 'going gallantly, in his gold chain and white satin doublet ... contrary to his priest's habit.' He had now begun to regard himself as a person of importance, and on the death of Elizabeth he hurried to Scotland to obtain from James a promise of toleration which would completely justify his own policy and cripple the influence of the jesuits. He gained access to James and boasted that his reply was favourable. When therefore no change of policy was forthcoming Watson was bitterly mortified; 'the resolution of James to exact the fines was regarded by him almost in the light of a personal insult' (Gardiner, i. 109). He began to meditate more forcible methods of effecting his aims, and communicated his grievances to Sir Griffin Markham, Anthony Copley, William Clark (*d.* 1603), and others, seculars like himself or disappointed courtiers. In May 1603 Markham suggested recourse to the Scottish precedent of seizing the king's person and compelling him to accede to their demands. Even wilder schemes were discussed; the king, not yet crowned and anointed, might, Watson thought, be set aside if he proved obdurate; the Tower could easily be seized, and Watson nominated himself future lord keeper or lord chancellor, and Copley secretary of state. Bands of catholic adherents were to be collected for 24 June, when they would press their demands on the king at Greenwich. This conspiracy became known as the 'Bye' or 'Priests' Plot,' and George Brooke, his brother, Lord Cobham, and Lord Grey de Wilton were implicated in it; but Watson also knew of Cobham's or the 'Main' plot (*Cal. State Papers*, Dom. 1603–10, pp. 34–8), and even discussed the advisability of drawing Ralegh into the 'Bye' plot (*Addit. MS.* 6177, f. 265).

Watson's plot gave the jesuits an opportunity, which they were not slow to use, of turning the tables on the seculars and revenging their defeat over the archpriest controversy. Father Gerard obtained from the pope an express prohibition of 'all unquietness,' and the whole influence of the society was exerted to frustrate Watson's scheme. Copley, who was to have brought in two hundred adherents, could not obtain one, 'for I knew never a catholic near me of many a mile that were not jesuited' (confession ap. Dodd, ed. Tierney, vol. iv. App. pp. i. sqq.). Gerard, Blackwell, and Garnett all hastened to inform the government of what was going on, and Gerard at least made a merit of this when charged with complicity in the 'gunpowder plot.' The attempt on 24 June was an utter fiasco, and on 2 July a proclamation was issued for Copley's arrest. It was by his confession on 12 July that the others conspirators were implicated, and this, coupled with the fact that Copley was pardoned, suggests that he also was playing a double part (Edwards, *Life of Ralegh*, ii. 140, 142 sqq.). It was not till 16 July that a proclamation was issued for Watson's arrest, which apparently was not effected until about 5 Aug. He 'was taken in a field by the Hay in Herefordshire (or Brecknockshire ...) by Mr. ... Vaughan. ... 'Twas observed that Mr. Vaughan did never prosper afterwards' (Aubrey, *Brief Lives*, ed. Clark, ii. 293). Watson's confession, dated 10 Aug., is printed in Tierney's 'Dodd' (vol. iv. App. pp. xix sqq.). Owing to the efforts made by the government to disentangle the obscure ramifications of the two plots, Watson was not brought to trial till 15 Nov. at Winchester Castle ('Baga de Secretis' in *Dep. Keeper of Records*, 5th Rep. App. ii. 135–9). He was condemned to death for high treason, and was executed at Winchester on 9 Dec. with William Clark. Among the manuscripts at Stonyhurst is a 'Breve relazione della morte di due sacerdoti Gul. Watsoni et Gul. Clarkei, 9 Dec. 1603.'

In the proclamation for his arrest Watson is described as 'a man of the lowest sort [= very short] ... his hair betwixt abram [= auburn] and flaxen; he looketh asquint, and is very purblind, so as if he reade anything he puttethe the paper neere to his eyes; he did weare his beard at length of the same coloured haire as is his head. But information is given that nowe his beard is cut.' Parsons says he 'was so wrong shapen and of so bad and blinking aspect as he looketh nine ways at once.'

[The most important sources for Watson's life are the documents printed from the Petyt MSS. by Mr. T. G. Law in his Archpriest Controversy (Camd. Soc. 2 pts.

1897–8), and especially Watson's autobiographical letter to the attorney-general, endorsed April 1599; a doubt whether this is the correct date, Watson's own vagueness, and a difficulty in reconciling his dates with those afforded by occasional references in the state papers, combine to render the chronology of his life somewhat tentative. See also Law's Jesuits and Seculars, 1889; Douai Diaries; Cal. State Papers, Dom.; Parsons's Brief Apologie and Manifestation, both 1602?; Foley's Records S.J. vol. i. passim; Morris's Troubles, i. 196, ii. 260, 277; Lansd. MS. 983, art. 15; Cotton. MS. Vesp. cxiv. f. 579; Hist. MSS. Comm. 3rd Rep. App. pp. 150, 152, 338, 13th Rep. App. iv. 129; Cal. State Papers, Venetian, 1592–1603, Nos. 1052, 1061, 1078, 1089; Notes and Queries, 4th ser. iv. 314, 422; and Watson's Works in Brit. Mus. Library. For his conspiracy, see Confessions and Examinations among the Domestic State Papers in the Record Office, the most important of which are printed in Tierney's Dodd, vol. iv. App. pp. i–lii; others are at Hatfield (cf. extract in Addit. MS. 6177, f. 265); further details are given in the despatches of Beaumont, the French ambassador, in the Brit. Mus. King's MS. 123, ff. 309 sqq., 329–43, and MS. 124; see also Weldon's Court of James I, pp. 340 sqq.; Birch's Court and Times of James I; Lodge's Illustrations, iii. 75–6; Edwards's Life of Raleigh, vol. ii. passim; Sharpe's London and the Kingdom, ii. 6–7; Gardiner's Hist. of England, i. 108–40; Hume's Life of Raleigh, 1897, pp. 254, 259, 263, 274; cp. also arts. Brooke, George; Brooke, Henry, eighth Lord Cobham; Clark, William, d. 1603; Copley, Anthony; Grey, Thomas, fifteenth Baron Grey of Wilton; Markham, Sir Griffin; and Ralegh, Sir Walter.]

ALBERT FREDERICK POLLARD

published 1899

BABINGTON Anthony

(1561–1586)

Leader of a catholic conspiracy against Queen Elizabeth, was descended from a family of great antiquity. John de Babington, who traced his ancestry to the Norman era, was, in the reign of Henry III, the owner of the district round Mickle and Little Babington, or Bavington, in Northumberland. By the marriage, early in the fifteenth century, of Thomas Babington, the fifth in descent from John, with the heiress of Robert Dethick, of Dethick, the main branch of the family became identified with Derbyshire, and by a series of intermarriages with neighbouring heiresses acquired additional property in adjoining counties. A northern branch of the family continued to flourish till the eighteenth century, and offshoots of the Derbyshire branch settled in Leicestershire and Oxfordshire. Lord Macaulay was named after his father's brother-in-law, Thomas Babington, of the Leicestershire branch, in whose house at Rothley Temple he was born.

Anthony was born at Dethick in October 1561. He was the third child and eldest son of Henry Babington, of Dethick, by his second wife, Mary, daughter of George, Lord Darcy, of Darcy, and granddaughter of Thomas, Lord Darcy, who was beheaded in 1538 as a principal actor in the Pilgrimage of Grace. Anthony's father is said to have been 'inclined to papistrie,' and to have 'had a brother that was a doctor of divinitie' of the same religious profession. He died in 1571, at the age of forty-one, and left Anthony his infant heir. To his three guardians—his mother, the descendant of a catholic rebel, to her second husband, Henry Foljambe, and to Philip Draycot, of Paynsley, Staffordshire—Anthony was indebted for his education. Although all the three outwardly conformed to protestantism, they were undoubtedly secret adherents of the Roman catholic faith, and in that belief Anthony was brought up. He apparently remained at Dethick till about 1577, only diversifying his life with occasional visits to Draycot's house at Paynsley, where his Roman catholic predilections were sedulously encouraged. There, too, he made the acquaintance of Margery, Draycot's daughter, whom he seems to have married about 1579, when barely eighteen. For a short time, probably before his marriage, he served as page to Queen Mary of Scotland, when she was imprisoned at Sheffield under the care of the Earl of Shrewsbury, and he then became passionately devoted to her and her cause. In 1580 Babington came to London, with the avowed intention of studying law, and he is stated to have entered as a student at Lincoln's Inn. But he soon abandoned all prospects at the bar for fashionable town life. His wealth, his cultivated intelligence, his charm of manner, his handsome features, secured for him a good reception at court, and he met there many young men of his own creed, infatuated admirers of Queen Mary, whom Jesuit conspirators from the Continent were drawing into treasonable practices. Early in 1580, on the arrival of Edmund Campion and Parsons, the Jesuits, in disguise in England, Babington joined a number of youths of good family in the formation of a secret society for the protection and maintenance of Jesuit missionaries in England. To the conversion of 'heretics' (i.e. protestants) all the members swore to devote their persons and abilities and wealth. On 14 April 1580 Pope Gregory XIII sent them a message blessing the enterprise (cf. Simpson's *Edmund Campion*, p. 157). Babington and his friends—Lady Babington, of Whitefriars, London, and Lady Foljambe, of Walton, Derbyshire—did all in their power to advance the society's cause, and frequently invited Fathers Campion and Parsons to lodge in their houses on their secret tours through England in 1580 and 1581. Early in 1582, after the capture and execution of Campion, Babington withdrew to Dethick. In the same year he came of age, and assumed the management of his vast landed property. He acknowledged the disinterested care with which his stepfather Foljambe had administered his estates during his minority by settling upon him an annuity of one hundred marks. At the same date the names of Babington and of his wife appeared in a list of Derbyshire recusants (*Cal. State Papers*, 1581–90, p. 88). Subsequently Anthony travelled in France and made the acquaintance of Charles Paget and Thomas Morgan, Mary Stuart's emissaries at Paris, who were vigorously plotting with Spain in their mistress's behalf. According to a passage in Leti's 'Vita di Sisto V' (iii. 103, ed. 1821), Babington extended his journey to Rome, and was accompanied by many fellow-members of the Roman catholic secret society. Queen Mary's friends abroad evidently marked Babington out, while on the continent, as a fitting leader of a catholic insurrection in England. After his return, in 1585, they sent him letters to be delivered to the imprisoned queen. But it was not until April 1586 that he was induced to take the leading part in the task of organising the famous conspiracy called after him, which aimed at a general rising of the catholics in England, the murder of Elizabeth and her chief advisers, and the release of Mary Stuart. John Ballard, a catholic priest of Rheims, had, in 1585, paid many secret visits to England at the instigation of the queen's supporters in France, and had secured promises of aid from the catholic gentry throughout the country towards a vigorous attack on the existing order of things. To him Babington chiefly looked for guidance. Ballard represented that the plot had already received the approval of the Spanish ambassador at Paris, and was to be supplemented by a foreign invasion. Babington eagerly consented to charge himself with the murder of Elizabeth and the release of Mary, and selected as his assistants a number of young catholic gentlemen, all members of the secret society formed in 1580. On 12 May 1586 Don Bernardino de Mendoza, the Spanish ambassador in Paris, who placed the fullest reliance in Babington, wrote to his government that news of the death of Elizabeth might be soon expected (*Papiers d'Etat*, Bannatyne Club, iii. 411). Throughout June 1586 the conspirators met in city taverns or in St. Giles's Fields almost nightly. To six of them was delegated the task of assassinating Elizabeth; for Babington, who also talked vaguely of sacking London, was reserved the duty of liberating Mary from the custody of Sir Amias Paulet at Chartley. Before the close of July all was finally determined. Babington was very sanguine of success, frequently entertained his associates at supper in London inns and at his house in Barbican, and had his portrait drawn, surrounded by his friends, and subscribed with the verse—

Hi mihi sunt comites, quos ipsa pericula ducunt,

a motto that was afterwards prudently changed to the enigmatic 'Quorsum hæc alio properantibus?' The conspirators appear to have heard mass regularly at a house in Fetter Lane, and to have been generally known among catholics at home and abroad as 'the pope's white sons for divers pieces of services, which they do to Rome against this realm' (Foley, *Records*, i. 205).

Babington's conduct was throughout marked by much 'foolish vanity.' From the first he was desirous that Mary should be informed of his plans, and was anxious to receive from her special marks of favour. As early as 29 April 1586 Morgan wrote to her from Paris that Babington was jealous of another person, whose services she had preferred to his, and that it would be expedient for her to send him an expression of gratitude by letter. On 28 June Mary sent Babington a friendly note. On 12 July the young conspirator forwarded to the Scottish queen a long reply, describing all the means to be taken for the murder of Elizabeth, and for her own deliverance. Five days later Mary wrote in answer a favourable criticism of the plot, and demanded further information. On 3 Aug. Babington informed her that a servant of Ballard had turned traitor, but, begging her not to falter, promised to carry out the enterprise or die in the attempt. Meanwhile, Mendoza was watching from Paris all the movements of Babington and his associates with the utmost anxiety, and he forwarded to Philip II on 13 Aug. a long account of their methods and of their hopes and fears. They had, he wrote, supporters throughout the country; they wanted a definite assurance that help would reach them from the Low Countries and Spain without delay; they relied on no foreign prince except Philip. The arrangements were so perfected that as soon as the queen was assassinated, the ships in the Thames were to be seized, and Cecil, Walsingham, Hunsdon, and Knollys to be captured or killed. Mendoza finally pointed out that this was the most serious of all catholic plots as yet attempted, but that all depended on the successful accomplishment of the murder of the queen. The original of this interesting letter is preserved among the Simancas archives, and its margin is scored with notes in the autograph of Philip himself. In reply the king dwelt with admiration on Babington's courage, and announced his resolve that the holy enterprise ('tan santa empresa') should not fail for lack of his assistance in money and troops (*Papiers d'Etat*, iii. 433–54).

But Babington was throughout in fear of treachery, and in this he was fully justified. Almost from the first Walsingham's spies had known of the conspiracy: by means of Godfrey Gifford, one of Ballard's adherents won over to the service of the government, every action of Babington and his associates was reported to the government during the months of June and July, and all their letters, which were always in cipher and in French, intercepted and deciphered before they were delivered. In July warrants against Ballard and Babington were prepared; but Walsingham was in no hurry to arrest the conspirators, and awaited further revelations from his spies. The letters that finally passed between Babington and Queen Mary proved to him that further delay was unnecessary, and on 4 Aug. Ballard was suddenly seized, after a meeting of the conspirators in London. No hint was given at the time that the government had information against any other member of the band, but Babington had been for some days previously thoroughly alarmed, and had already applied to Walsingham for a passport to France, where he promised to act as a spy upon Elizabeth's enemies. He had told his friends at the same time that his visit to France was necessary to supervise the final arrangements for a foreign invasion. But no passport was given him, and with unpardonable cowardice he subsequently sent word to Walsingham that he could reveal, if he chose, a dangerous conspiracy. Still Walsingham made no sign, but his servants were ordered to keep a careful watch upon Babington. One night the young man was invited to sup with them, but while in their company he caught sight of a memorandum concerning himself in Walsingham's handwriting. He hurried from the room on a trivial pretence, changed clothes with a friend who lived at Westminster, and hid himself in the thickest part of St. John's Wood. There he was joined by some of his associates. Babington disguised himself by cutting off his hair and staining his skin with walnut-juice, and travelled to Harrow, where he was sheltered by one Jerome Bellamy, a recent convert to catholicism. But before the end of August he was discovered and taken to the Tower. All the other conspirators were captured a few days later. On 13 and 14 Sept. Babington, Ballard, and five other young men (Chidiock Titchbourne, Thomas Salisbury, Robert Barnewell, John Savage, and Henry Donn) were tried before a special commission. Babington did not attempt to conceal his guilt: he declared all 'with a mild countenance, sober gesture, and a wonderful good grace'; but he laid the blame on Ballard. Ballard acknowledged the justice of the rebuke, and told Babington, before the court, that he wished the shedding of his blood could save his young companion's life. Two days later, seven more of the conspirators (Edward Abington or Habington, Charles Tilney, Edward Jones, John Charnock, John Travers, Jerome Bellamy, and Robert Gage) were tried. Sentences of hanging and quartering were passed on all the band. On 19 Sept. Babington wrote to Elizabeth, imploring her to work upon him 'a miracle of mercy,' if not for his own sake for that of his distressed family. To a friend he offered, on the same day, 1,000l. if his release could be procured. The next morning—on the day appointed for his execution—he explained the cipher which had been used in the letters to and from Mary.

Babington's prayers for pardon were not entertained, and on Tuesday 20 Sept. he and Ballard, with five of their companions, were drawn on hurdles 'from Tower Hill, through the cittie of London, unto a fielde at the upper end of Holborne, hard by the high way side to S. Giles, where was erected a scaffolde convenient for the execution' (*The Censure of a Loyall Subiect*, 1587). A great crowd collected to see the conspirators die. Babington declared from the scaffold that no private ends had influenced him, but that he honestly believed himself engaged in 'a deed lawful and meritorious.' Ballard suffered first, and Babington witnessed his barbarous death. According to an eye-witness he showed to the last 'a signe of his former pride' by standing, instead of praying on his knees, 'with his hat on his head as if he had been but a beholder of the execution' (*The Censure*). He himself followed Ballard, and underwent diabolical tortures. He was still alive when taken down from the gallows, and exclaimed, 'Parce mihi, Domine Jesu,' while the executioner was using the knife upon him (cf. Mendoza's account sent to Philip II 20 Oct. in *Papiers d'Etat*, iii. 481). When Elizabeth was informed of the revolting cruelty of his death, she directed that the other conspirators, who were to be executed on the following day, should hang till they were dead.

Babington expressed anxiety on the scaffold as to the fortunes of his property. By law the crown confiscated it all; but the entailed estates of Dethick, Derbyshire, and Kingston, Nottinghamshire, his largest manors, were allowed to pass to his brothers Francis and George. Some of his lands, and almost all his personal property, were granted by Elizabeth to Sir Walter Raleigh. Elizabeth herself took a valuable clock. At Dethick were found many books on theological controversies, and 'papers of prophecies' foretelling Elizabeth's downfall. According to the evidence of some of his tenants, examined previous to his death, Babington had been a hard landlord, and had systematically raised his rents. Shortly before his arrest he sold a large house in Derby, called Babington Hall, which was pulled down about 1822. Its site is still marked by Babington Lane. A cenotaph in Kingston Church, Nottinghamshire, among the tombs of other members of Babington's family, bears no inscription, and is locally believed on doubtful evidence to have been erected to the conspirator's memory (*Gent. Mag.* new ser. vii. 287). By his wife Margery, Babington had an only daughter, who died at the age of eight, in all probability before her father (*Harl. MS.* 1537, f. 115 b).

The discovery and death of Babington formed the subject of many contemporary ballads (cf. *Notes and Queries*, 1st ser. v. 572). One of them, full of valuable biographical details, entitled 'The Complainte of Anthonie Babington,' by Richard Williams, is among the Arundel MSS. (418, art. 3) at the British Museum. Another, entitled 'A proper new ballad, breefely declaring the Death and Execution of fourteen most wicked Traitors,' which bitterly vituperates 'proud young Babington,' has been reprinted in J. P. Collier's 'Broadside Ballads' (1868), pp. 36–41. A third poetical tract is entitled 'A short discourse; expressing the substance of all the late pretended treasons against the Queenes Maiestie;' and a fourth, by William Kempe, who is to be distinguished from the actor of the same name, bears the title 'A dutiful invective against the moste haynous treasons of Ballard and Babington,' 1587. A full description of the execution is found in 'The Censure of a Loyall Subiect,' by G[eorge] W[hetstone], 1587. Dr. George Carleton gives an account of the conspiracy in his 'Thankfull Remembrance' (1609), and reproduces there the picture of Babington and his confederates drawn in 1586. A Dutch translation of the correspondence between Babington and Queen Mary was circulated in Holland and the Low Countries in 1587.

The historical importance of the conspiracy lies in Mary Stuart's complicity. The discovery of the letter sent by her to Babington approving of the murder of Elizabeth in July 1586 brought her to the scaffold. Apologists for Mary in vain deny the genuineness of this letter, and represent it to have been a forgery of Walsingham. Babington never doubted its authenticity, and, as we have seen, on the day of his death fully explained the cipher in which it was written. And Mendoza, the Spanish ambassador at Paris, writing to Philip II on 10 Sept., states that Mary had written him a letter which left no doubt in his mind that she was fully acquainted with the whole business (*Papiers d'Etat*, iii. 458). In the presence of evidence of this kind, it is impossible to attach any weight to Mary's indignant denial at Fotheringay of all knowledge of Babington and his conspiracy (*State Trials*, i. 1182). But it is unnecessary, on the other hand, to credit the rumour circulated, as it was said, on the authority of Cecil, that Queen Mary had resolved to marry Babington.

[Collectanea Topog. and Genealog. viii. 313 et seq.; W. D. Cooper's Notices of Anthony Babington, reprinted from the Reliquary for April 1862; State Trials, i. 1127 et seq.; Thorpe's Cal. Scottish Papers; Cal. State Papers, 1581–90, and Addenda, 1580–1625, p. 202; Turnbull's Letters of Mary Stuart, pp. 344 et seq.; Froude's Hist. vol. xii.; Papiers d'Etat relatifs à l'histoire de l'Ecosse au xvie Siècle (ed. A. Teulet), pub. by Bannatyne Club, vol. iii.; Camden's Annals; Simpson's Edmund Campion.]

SIDNEY LEE

published 1885

(*d.* 1586)

Roman catholic priest, owes his fame solely to his connection with the Babington conspiracy, of which a general account is given under Anthony Babington. He was apparently educated at Rheims, and first sent upon a mission to England in 1581 (Archives of English College at Rome, in Foley's *Records*, iii. 44). He passed under various aliases, first Turner, then Thompson, but later on always under that of Foscue or Fortescue. It has been doubted whether his real name was not Thompson. The object of his coming was to 'reconcile' doubting or recalcitrant catholics to the church of Rome, and doubtless to sound their political dispositions. He was well furnished with money, was commonly called captain, and seems to have been fond of fine clothes and fine company (Tyrrell's *Confession*). Among the persons whose acquaintance he made was Anthony Tyrrell, the jesuit, whose confession, could it be accepted as trustworthy, would give us most of the facts of Ballard's career. But Tyrrell's confession was retracted, reaffirmed, and then again retracted, and is at least as much open to suspicion as the testimony of any other informer. Tyrrell made Ballard's acquaintance at the Gatehouse, Westminster, where they were both temporarily confined in 1581. In 1584 these two travelled to Rouen, and afterwards to Rheims, where they held a conference with Cardinal Allen, and from Rheims they proceeded to Rome, where they arrived on 7 Sept. 1584 (*Pilgrims' Register at Rome*, and Tyrrell). It was then that Tyrrell, in his confession, represents them as having an interview with Alfonso Agazzari, rector of the English college, in which they inquired as to the lawfulness of attempting the assassination of Elizabeth, and received assurances in the affirmative, and subsequently the blessing of Gregory XIII upon their enterprise. This account, although accepted as an undoubted fact by some historians, rests on no better authority than the confession of Tyrrell. They left Rome in October and journeyed homeward through France. In the late months of 1585 Ballard, disguised as a military officer and passing under the name of Captain Fortescue, travelled through almost every county of England and visited every catholic or semi-catholic family. In May 1586 Ballard went to Paris, where he informed Charles Paget, the adherent of Mary Queen of Scots, and the Spanish minister Mendoza, that the catholic gentry in England were willing, with the help of Spain, to rise in insurrection against Elizabeth and her counsellors. Mauvissière, the French ambassador in London, refused to countenance the scheme (Tyrrell's *Conf.*). Chateauneuf, another French envoy to England, believed

Ballard

Ballard to have been at one time a spy of Walsingham (*Mémoire de Chateauneuf* ap. Labanoff, vi. 275 seq.). But Paget and Mendoza trusted him, and on his return to England, at the end of May 1586, he instigated Anthony Babington to organise without delay his famous conspiracy. He came to England, bearing a letter of introduction from Charles Paget to Mary Queen of Scots (dated 29 May 1586, ap. Murdin, p. 531). He reported to her the condition of the country, and she sent him again to France to hasten the active co-operation of the King of Spain and of the pope (Mary to Paget, 17 July, Labanoff). Meantime Ballard imagined he had found a useful ally in his negotiations abroad and at home in Gilbert Gifford, a catholic, and to him many details of the plot were communicated; but Gifford had since 1585 been in Walsingham's secret service, and reported to the English government the progress of the conspiracy. Owing mainly to the revelations of Gifford, whom Ballard suspected too late, Ballard was suddenly arrested in London on 4 Aug., on a warrant drawn up early in July. He was committed to the Tower and severely racked, but without the government being able to extort from him more than a general confession of his guilt. Before the close of August all the leaders of the conspiracy had shared Ballard's fortune. The trial of Ballard, with Babington and five other conspirators, took place on 13 and 14 Sept., and they were all convicted. At the trial Babington charged Ballard with having brought him into his perilous situation, and Ballard acknowledged the justice of the rebuke. Ballard was executed on 20 Sept. The full penalty of the law, which involved the disembowelling of the criminal before life was extinct, was carried out with all its cruelty. Ballard, who was the first of the conspirators to be executed, is reported to have borne his sufferings with remarkable fortitude.

[MSS. Mary Queen of Scots, xix. 67, 68 (Confession of Tyrrell); cf. also Morris's Troubles of our Catholic Forefathers, second series; Teulet's Relations de la France et de l'Espagne avec l'Ecosse; Labanoff's Lettres de Marie Stuart; Murdin's State Papers; Howell's State Trials; Foley's Records of the English Province of the Society of Jesus; Froude's Hist. of England, xii. 126–36, 155, 170–4; see also under Anthony Babington.]

CHARLES FRANCIS KEARY

published 1885

GIFFORD or Giffard, Gilbert
(1561?–1590)

Roman catholic spy, belonged to the well-known Roman catholic family seated at Chillington, Staffordshire. His father, John Gifford (d. 1612), suffered imprisonment for recusancy. Gilbert is said as a schoolboy to have challenged a schoolfellow to a duel. After spending some months at Anchine he entered Douay College, then at Rheims under the direction of William Allen (1532–1594), on 31 Jan. 1576–7. In the register he was described as 'clarus adolescens.' In 1579 he removed to the English College at Rome, and in October publicly defended theses embracing all philosophy before a large assembly of prelates and noblemen (Foley, *Records*, vi. 68). He and a friend and fellow-student, Edward Gratley, made the acquaintance at Rome of Solomon Aldred, a Roman catholic spy of Sir Francis Walsingham, who lived there with his wife, and had English secret service money to dispose of. Gifford readily entertained proposals to enter the English secret service at some future date. His superiors at the English College admired his intellectual capacity and did not suspect his intentions, but they complained of his dissimulation and deceitful character, and before 1582 expelled him on grounds that are not exactly defined. He returned to Rheims to teach theology on 23 June 1582, after having apologised to Cardinal Allen for past misconduct. On 29 March 1583 Allen wrote, objecting to his remaining at either seminary, Douay or Rome. In 1583 he paid a second visit to Rome. On 16 March 1584–5 he was ordained subdeacon, and on 6 April 1585 deacon by Cardinal de Guise, in the church of St. Remigius at Rheims. He left Douay College on 8 Oct. 1585, and went to Paris.

Gifford definitely entered Walsingham's secret service in 1583 (Jebb, *De Vita et Rebus Gestis Mariæ*, 1725, ii. 281). While at Rheims he seems to have become acquainted with John Savage, afterwards an associate of Babington, a Roman catholic, who had thought of killing Elizabeth. At Paris he placed himself in communication with Thomas Morgan, a representative of Mary Queen of Scots. Morgan gave him a letter (15 Oct. 1583) recommending him to Queen Mary, then confined at Chartley. He was represented to be an enthusiastic adherent who could be trusted to convey her private correspondence from and to Chateauneuf, the French ambassador and her chief agent in London. He arrived in London about December, and was received unsuspectingly at the French embassy. Some catholic noblemen, as well as the Countess of Arundel and many catholic youths of good family, entertained him, but neither they nor members of his own family suspected his treacherous occupation. He soon presented himself to Phelippes, the chief of Walsingham's spies, and lived in his house for a short time, receiving instructions, and 'practising secretly among the catholics.' In January he went to Chartley and ingratiated himself with Queen Mary, who readily accepted his offer to direct the conveyance of her secret correspondence to London. Her gaoler, Sir Amias Paulet, knew that Gifford was an accredited government spy, and at first doubted his intentions, but quickly placed implicit trust in him.

Gifford had arranged with Phelippes and Walsingham to place all Mary's letters at their disposal. He had to adopt means to avoid rousing the slightest suspicion on the part of Mary or her London agent. Much importance attaches to his methods. He told Mary, the French ambassador, and others of Mary's friends that he secured the services of a catholic brewer of the village to take her letters in his barrels to a neighbouring catholic gentleman, who conveyed them to another catholic gentleman, and that the latter forwarded them by a servant to the French embassy in London. Letters were, he pretended, also sent from London in the same way when he himself or one of his trusted servants did not carry them direct. Mr. Froude accepted this story and, exaggerating its details, assumed that Gifford kept the letters he received from Mary only just time enough to copy them, and then at once sent them to London by means of his secret and circuitous device. As a matter of fact Gifford's account of his device was a lying tale, concocted to lull the suspicions of Mary and her friends. He himself, on receiving Mary's letters from her, usually copied them in conjunction with Paulet, but he also invariably sent the originals to Phelippes's house in London, and Phelippes at his leisure employed some agent who could be trusted to deliver them to the French ambassador. A letter written by Queen Mary on 31 Jan. was thus not delivered at the French embassy till 1 March. It lay in the interval in Phelippes's rooms. The French ambassador was nevertheless thoroughly deceived, and gave Gifford in March letters received for Queen Mary in the previous two years, which he had had no opportunity of sending her. All these Gifford took in batches to Phelippes, who deciphered them for Walsingham before forwarding them to Mary. In April Gifford was again at Chartley, and still retained the full confidence not only of Queen Mary but of her keeper Paulet. In the next few months he paid many visits to London and Paris. He was well acquainted with Anthony Babington, John Ballard, and their fellow-conspirators, and encouraged them to pursue their plot, at the same time keeping Walsingham well informed of its development. At Paris he saw Mendoza, the Spanish ambassador who had been expelled from London, and is reported to have given him the first intelligence of the Babington conspiracy. Mendoza freely promised Spanish aid. Roman catholic writers assert that it was Gifford who suggested and arranged the whole conspiracy. At present the better supported view is that the priest Ballard was its originator. Gifford continued to satisfy both his masters. He carried the fatal letters from Queen Mary to Babington, which contained her approval of the conspiracy, and duly showed them to Walsingham and his agents before they reached their destination. On 8 July 1586 he was in London, and gave Walsingham a book denouncing Parsons and the jesuits which he and Gratley had written some time before. Walsingham highly prized the manuscript, and is said to have distributed printed copies. By the end of July Gifford's work was done. All the details of Babington's plot were settled by the conspirators, and had been brought by Gifford to Walsingham's knowledge. He seems to have felt the danger of his position and hurried to Paris (29 July). After the conspirators' arrest he wrote to Phelippes and Walsingham, hoping that his departure would not be judged 'sinistrously.' On 3 Sept. he offered to do further work for Walsingham, but the offer was not accepted. That he was capable of almost any villany is clear, but that he was the concoctor of the Babington plot, and that he interpolated those passages in Queen Mary's letters which convicted her of complicity in the conspiracy and brought her to the scaffold, are charges that have some *prima facie* justification, but have not yet been proved.

Both sides soon suspected Gifford to be a traitor, although neither knew the exact extent of his treachery. His catholic associates were certainly cognisant of some portion of his action in England. Fitzherbert, writing from Paris (February 1586–7), hoped that he would 'prove honest.' In the spring of 1587 he travelled to Rheims and Rouen under the name of Jaques Colerdin. At Rheims he was ordained priest (14 March 1586–7), and expressed an intention of seeking a professorship at Rome. In 1588 he was again at Paris, dressed as disguised priests dressed in England. He quarrelled with Sir Charles Arundel, one of the chief English catholic exiles, who accused him of writing against the jesuits. In December 1588 he was found in a brothel and brought before the bishop of Paris. The bishop committed him to prison; Sir Edward Stafford, the English ambassador, made some endeavours to procure his release, but Gifford thought to serve his own ends better by bringing serious charges against Stafford. His catholic enemies proved more powerful than he anticipated, and he died in prison in November 1590. He announced to Walsingham in 1588 the arrival in Paris of Father John Gerard, and is said to have written to Cardinal Allen while in prison an account of the injuries he had done the catholic cause.

[Father Morris's Letter-book of Sir Amias Paulet, passim; Father Morris's Troubles of our Catholic Forefathers, 2nd ser. pp. 86, 361, 379, 388, 453, 492; Foley's Records of the Society of Jesus, vi. 8 et seq. (account of Gifford by Cardinal Sega written in 1596), pp. 15, 68, 135; Records of English Catholics, (1) Douay Diaries, (2) Letters, &c., of Cardinal Allen; Teulet's Papiers d'État (Bannatyne Club); Cal. State Papers (Dom.), 1581–90. Mr. Froude's account of Gifford in History of England, vol. xii., is full of errors, as Father Morris has shown in the Letter-book of Paulet.]

Sidney Lee

published 1889

Robert

(1563–1635)

Sir

Politician, born at Alderton, Suffolk, in 1563, was eldest son of Henry Naunton of Alderton, by Elizabeth Ashby, and was grandson of William Naunton, whose wife Elizabeth was daughter of Sir Anthony Wingfield, K.G. Robert was educated at Cambridge, where he matriculated as a fellow-commoner of Trinity College. On 11 Nov. 1582 he was elected a scholar, graduating B.A. in the same year; he became on 2 Oct. 1585 a minor fellow, and on 15 March 1585–6 a major fellow, and proceeded M.A. soon afterwards. In 1589 Naunton accompanied his uncle William Ashby to Scotland, where Ashby was acting as English ambassador. Naunton seems to have carried messages between his uncle and the English government, and spent much of his time at court in London in July. He returned to Scotland in August; but Ashby died in the following January, and Naunton's connection with Scotland ceased. Settling again in Cambridge, he was elected a fellow of Trinity Hall in 1592, and was appointed public orator in 1594 (Le Neve, *Fasti*, iii. 614). Soon afterwards he attracted the attention of the Earl of Essex, who determined to fit him for a diplomatic appointment by sending him abroad to study continental politics and foreign languages. Essex obtained for him the position of travelling tutor to a youth named Vernon, and Naunton undertook, while he journeyed about Europe with his charge, to regularly send to Essex all the political intelligence he could scrape together. Writing to his patron from the Hague in November 1596, he complained that his appointment combined the characteristics of a pedagogue and a spy, and he could not decide which office was 'the more odious or base, as well in their eyes with whom I live as in mine own' (*Harl. MS.* 288, f. 127). Early in 1597 Naunton was in Paris, and Essex genially endeavoured to remove his scruples. 'I read no man's writing' (Essex wrote to him) 'with more contentment, nor ever saw any man so much or so fast by any such-like improve himself. . . . The queen is every day more and more pleased with your letters.' In November, however, Naunton was still discontented, and begged a three years' release from his employment so that he might visit France and Italy, and return home through Germany. Such an experience, he argued, would the better fit him for future work in Essex's service at home (*ib.* 288, f. 128). It is probable that he obtained his request, and Essex's misfortunes doubtless prevented him from re-entering the earl's service. At any rate, he returned to Cambridge about 1600, and resumed his duties as public orator. In 1601 he served the office of proctor. A speech which he delivered on behalf of the university before James I at Hinchinbrook on 29 April 1603 so favourably impressed the king and Sir Robert Cecil that Naunton once again sought his fortunes at court (cf. *Sydney Papers*, ii. 325). A few months later he attended the Earl of Rutland on a special embassy to Denmark, and, according to James Howell, broke down while making a formal address at the Danish court (Howell, *Letters*, ed. Jacobs, i. 294). On his return he entered parliament as member for Helston, Cornwall, in May 1606. He was chosen for Camelford in 1614, and in the three parliaments of 1621, 1624, and 1625 he represented the university of Cambridge. He sat for Suffolk in Charles I's first parliament. Although he never took a prominent part in the proceedings of the House of Commons, Naunton secured, in the early days of his parliamentary career, the favour of George Villiers. He retained it till the death of the favourite, and preferments accordingly came to him in profusion. On 7 Sept. 1614 he was knighted at Windsor. In 1616, when he ceased to be fellow of Trinity Hall, he was made master of requests, in succession to Sir Lionel Cranfield (Carew, *Letters*, p. 60, Camden Soc.), and afterwards became surveyor of the court of wards. The latter post had hitherto been held 'by men learned in the law,' and Sir James Whitelocke complained that Naunton was 'a scholar and mere stranger to the law' (*Liber Famelicus*, pp. 54, 62, Camden Soc.).

On 8 Jan. 1617–18 Naunton, owing to Buckingham's influence, was promoted to be secretary of state. Sir Ralph Winwood, the last holder of this high office, had died three months earlier, and the king had in the interval undertaken, with the aid of Sir Thomas Lake, to perform the duties himself. But the arrangement soon proved irksome to the king, and Buckingham recommended Naunton as a quiet and unconspicuous person, who would act in dependence on himself. In consideration of his promotion, Naunton made Buckingham's youngest brother, Christopher Villiers, heir to lands worth 500*l.* a year. In August Naunton was appointed a member of the commission to examine Sir Walter Raleigh. Popular report credited Naunton with a large share of responsibility for Raleigh's execution on 29 Oct. 1618, and a wealthy Londoner named Wiemark publicly declared that Raleigh's head 'would do well' on Naunton's shoulders. When summoned before the council to account for his words, Wiemark explained that he was merely alluding to the proverb, 'Two heads are better than one.' Naunton jestingly revenged himself by directing Wiemark to double his subscription to the fund for restoring St. Paul's Cathedral, of which Naunton was a commissioner. Wiemark had offered 100l., but Naunton retorted that two hundred pounds were better than one (Fuller). 'Secretary Naunton forgets nothing,' wrote Francis Bacon (Spedding, *Life*, vi. 320).

Through 1619 Naunton was mainly occupied in negotiations between the king and the council respecting the support to be given by the English government to the king's son-in-law, the elector Frederick in Bohemia. Naunton was a staunch protestant, and such influence as he possessed he doubtless exercised in the elector's behalf. In May 1620 he wrote to Buckingham that he had not had a free day for two years, and that his health was suffering in consequence. In October Gondomar complained to James that Naunton was enforcing the laws against catholics with extravagant zeal. The king resented Gondomar's interference, and informed him that 'his secretary was not in the habit of acting in matters of importance without his own directions.' In the January following Naunton for once belied the king's description of his conduct by entering without instructions from James into negotiations with Cadenet, the French ambassador. He told Cadenet that the king was in desperate want of money, and, if the French government desired to marry Princess Henrietta Maria to Prince Charles, it would be prudent to offer James a large portion with the lady. The conversation reached Gondomar's ears, and he brought it to James's knowledge. Naunton was sharply reprimanded, and threatened with dismissal. His wife was frightened by his peril into a miscarriage, and, although the storm passed away, Naunton had lost interest in his work. All the negotiations for the Spanish marriage were distasteful to him. In September 1622 he begged Buckingham to protect him from immediate removal from his post, on account of his wife's condition, but in January 1623 he voluntarily retired on a pension of 1,000l. a year. Buckingham remained his friend, and, although in April he made a vain appeal for the provostship of Eton, in July 1623 he received the lucrative office of master of the court of wards. He sent the king an effusive letter of thanks for the appointment (*Harl. MS.* 1581, No. 23), but practically retired from further participation in politics. Although he was still a member of the council, he was not summoned (in July 1623) when the oath was taken to the articles of the Spanish marriage, and some indiscreet expression of opinion on the subject seems to have led to his confinement in his own house in the following October. But he sent a warm letter of congratulation to Buckingham on his return from Spain in the same month (*Fortescue Papers*, pp. 192–3, Camden Soc.). As master of the court of wards he discharged his duties with exceptional integrity; but Charles I's advisers complained that it proved under his control less profitable to them than it might be made in less scrupulous hands. In March 1635 Naunton was very ill, but Cottington vainly persuaded him to resign. At length Charles I intervened, and, after receiving vague promises of future favours, Naunton gave up his mastership to Cottington on 16 March. A day or two later he sent a petition to the king begging for the payment of the arrears of the pension granted him by James I. But his illness took an unfavourable turn, and before his petition was considered he died at his house at Letheringham, Suffolk, on 27 March.

Naunton had inherited, through his grandmother Elizabeth Naunton, daughter of Sir Anthony Wingfield, a residence at Letheringham, which had been formerly a priory of Black canons. This Sir Robert converted into an imposing mansion, and he added to it a picture-gallery. He was buried in Letheringham Church, where in 1600 he had erected a monument to his father and other members of his family. An elaborate monument was also placed there to his own memory; it is figured in Nichols's 'Leicestershire,' iii. 516; but in 1789 the church was destroyed, with all its contents. Naunton built almshouses at Letheringham, but he failed to endow them, and they soon fell into neglect. His property in the parish he bequeathed to his brother William, who died 11 July 1635. William's descendants held the property till 1758, when the Leman family became its owners. The old house was pulled down in 1770. Naunton married Penelope, daughter and heiress of Sir Thomas Perrot, by Dorothy, daughter of Walter Devereux, first earl of Essex, who survived him. Naunton's only son, James, died in infancy in 1624, and a long epitaph was inscribed by his father on his tomb in Letheringham Church. An only daughter, Penelope, married, first, Paul, viscount Bayning (*d.* 1638); and, secondly, Philip Herbert, fifth earl of Pembroke. When Lady Naunton, Naunton's widow, was invited by the parliament in 1645–6 to compound for her estate, which was assessed at 800*l.*, mention was made during the protracted negotiations of a son of hers, called Sir Robert Naunton, who was at the time imprisoned in the king's bench for debt. The person referred to seems to be a nephew of Sir Robert Naunton (*Cal. Committee for Compounding*, pp. 188, 600).

Naunton left unpublished a valuable account of the chief courtiers of Queen Elizabeth, embodying many interesting reminiscences. Although he treats Leicester with marked disdain, he made it his endeavour to avoid all scandal, and he omitted, he tells us, much information rather than 'trample upon the graves of persons at rest.' He mentions the death of Edward Somerset, earl of Worcester, in 1628, and Sir William Knollys, who was created Earl of Banbury on 18 Aug. 1626, and died in 1632, he describes as an earl and as still alive. These facts point to 1630 as the date of the composition. Many manuscript copies are in the British Museum (cf. *Harl. MSS.* 3787 and 7393; *Lansdowne MSS.* 238 and 254; *Addit. MSS.* 22591 and 28715); one belongs to the Duke of Westminster (*Hist. MSS. Comm.* 3rd Rep. p. 214, cf. 246). The work was printed for the first time with great carelessness in 1641, and bore the title, 'Fragmenta Regalia written by Sir Robert Naunton, Master of the Court of Wards.' An equally unsatisfactory reprint appeared in 1642. A revised edition was issued in 1653, as 'Fragmenta Regalia; or Observations on the late Queen Elizabeth, her Times and Favourites, written by Sir Robert Naunton, Master of the Court of Wards.' James Caulfield reprinted the 1641 edition, with biographical notes, in 1814, and Professor Arber the 1653 edition in 1870. One or other edition also reappeared in various collections of tracts, viz.: 'Arcana Aulica,' 1694, pp. 157–247; the 'Phœnix,' 1707–8, i. 181–221; 'A Collection of Tracts,' 1721; 'Paul Hentzner's Travels in England,' 1797, with portraits; 'Memoirs of Robert Cary, Earl of Monmouth,' edited by Sir Walter Scott, pp. 169–301; the 'Harleian Miscellany,' 1809, ii. 81–108, and the 'Somers Tracts.' A French translation of the work is appended to Gregorio Leti's 'La Vie d'Elisabeth, Reine d'Angleterre,' Amsterdam, 1703, 8vo, and an Italian translation made through the French appears in Leti's 'Historia o vero vita di Elisabetta,' Amsterdam, 1703. Another French version, by S. Le Pelletier, was issued in London in 1745.

Some Latin and English verses and epitaphs by Naunton on Lords Essex and Salisbury, and members of his own family, are printed in the 'Memoirs,' 1814, from manuscript notes in a copy of Holland's 'Heroologia,' once in Naunton's possession. Several of Naunton's letters to Buckingham between 1618 and 1623 are among the Fortescue Papers at Dropmore, and have been edited by Mr. S. R. Gardiner in the volume of Fortescue Papers issued by the Camden Society. Others of his letters are in the British Museum (cf. *Harl. MSS.* 1581, Nos. 22–3); at Melbourne Hall (*Cowper MSS.*), and at the Public Record Office.

A fine engraving by Robert Cooper, from a painting dated 1615 'in possession of Mr. Read,' a descendant of Naunton's brother William, appears in 'Memoirs of Sir Robert Naunton,' 1814. Another engraving is by Simon Passi.

[Memoirs of Sir Robert Naunton, knt., London, 1814, fol.; Weever's Funerall Monuments, 1631, pp. 756–7; Fuller's Worthies, 1662, pt. iv. p. 64; Birch's Memoirs of Queen Elizabeth; Lloyd's Memoirs, 1665; Nichols's Leicestershire, iii. 515 seq.; Page's Suffolk, p. 119; Spedding's Life of Bacon; Cal. State Papers, 1618–35;

Gardiner's Hist.; Strafford Papers, i. 369, 372, 389, 410–12. A paper roll, containing a 'stemma' of the Naunton family made by James Jermyn in 1806, is in Brit. Mus. Addit. MS. 17098.]

SIDNEY LEE

published 1894

GERARD John

(1564–1637)

Jesuit, second son of Sir Thomas Gerard, knight, of Bryn, Lancashire, by Elizabeth, eldest daughter and coheiress of Sir John Port, knight, of Etwall, Derbyshire, was born on 4 Oct. 1564, probably at New Bryn. He received part of his education in the English College at Douay, where he arrived 29 Aug. 1577, and apparently accompanied the students in their migration to Rheims in the following March. It seems that he subsequently returned to England, and was matriculated in the university of Oxford as a member of Exeter College about October 1579 (Boase, *Register of Exeter Coll.*, pp. 186, 218). Being unable conscientiously to comply with the religious observances of the college, he left it within twelve months and went home. In 1581 he proceeded to Paris, and studied for some time in Clermont College, which belonged to the jesuits, but ill-health compelled him again to return to England. An unsuccessful attempt which he afterwards made to leave this country without a government license resulted in his apprehension and imprisonment in the Marshalsea prison, from which he obtained his release in October 1585. In the following year he was admitted into the English College at Rome, where he was ordained priest. He joined the Society of Jesus in Rome on 15 Aug. 1588, and was at once sent on the English mission. His activity soon attracted the attention of the government, but for a long time he baffled all the attempts of spies and pursuivants to apprehend him. Eventually, while on a visit to London, he was betrayed by a servant, and was imprisoned successively in the Compter, the Clink, and the Tower, where, by order of the privy council, he underwent the horrible torture of being suspended by the wrists for hours at a time, and was nearly crippled for life. A graphic account of his extraordinary escape from the Tower in October 1597, by swinging himself along a rope suspended over the Tower ditch, is given in his autobiography. With characteristic courage he continued his missionary labours, and the government never captured him again. In 1603 Gerard, in the belief that submission to James I might bring about a removal of catholic

47

disabilities, discountenanced Watson's plot, and gave information about it to the government. Though Gerard's trust in James was soon dissipated, 'there is strong reason to believe,' writes Mr. Gardiner, 'that he was not made acquainted with the particulars' of the Gunpowder plot. The government, however, thought they could inculpate him along with Greenway and Garnett. After the discovery of the plot the search for him was therefore renewed with redoubled vigour, and it became absolutely necessary that he should leave England. Dressed in livery he embarked with the suites of the ambassadors of Spain and Flanders, and crossed the Channel on 3 May 1606, the day on which Father Henry Garnett was executed.

Proceeding to Rome, he was appointed English penitentiary at St. Peter's. In 1609 he was professed of the four vows, and was nominated 'socius' of Father Thomas Talbot, rector and novice-master in the English jesuit novitiate at Louvain. He took a leading part in the establishment of the college of his order at Liège, and became its first rector and master of novices (1614–22). After acting for some time as instructor of the tertians at Ghent, he was recalled in 1627 to Rome, and became spiritual director of the students of the English College, where he died on 27 July 1637.

His works are: 1. 'The Exhortation of Jesus Christ to the Faithful Soul,' London, 1598, 8vo; St. Omer, 1610, 8vo. A translation from the Latin of Landsberger. 2. 'The Spiritual Combat; translated from the Italian,' London, 12mo; Rouen, 1613, 12mo. 3. 'A Narrative of the Gunpowder Plot,' 1606, manuscript fol. preserved at Stonyhurst College, ff. 170. Printed under the editorship of Father John Morris in 'The Condition of Catholics under James I,' London, 1871, 8vo; 2nd edition, 1872. Portions of Gerard's valuable narrative were printed in the 'Month' in 1867–8, and these, rendered into French by Father J. Forbes, appeared in the 'Études Théologiques,' Paris, 1868, and were reprinted separately in 1872. A German translation of Father Morris's first edition was published at Cologne in 1875. 4. 'Narratio P. Johannis Gerardi de Rebus a se in Anglia gestis,' manuscript at Stonyhurst, compiled in 1609 for the information of his superiors. Considerable use was made of this autobiography by Father Morris in writing the 'Life' of Gerard, which is contained in 'The Condition of Catholics under James I.' A third edition of the 'Life,' rewritten and much enlarged, was printed at London, 1881, 8vo. The translation of the autobiography is from the pen of the Rev. G. R. Kingdon, S.J. It has been printed separately as the forty-sixth volume of the 'Quarterly Series,' under the title of 'During the Persecution,' London, 1886, 8vo, and is of very high interest.

[Life by the Rev. John Morris; Catholic Spectator, 1824, i. 257, 325, 360, 389; De Backer's Bibl. des Écrivains de la Compagnie de Jésus, 1869, i. 2089; Dodd's

Church Hist. ii. 419; Douay Diaries; Gardiner's Hist. of England, 1603–42, i. 114, 243; Gillow's Bibl. Dict.; Lives of Philip Howard, Earl of Arundel, and his Wife, p. 233; Husenbeth's Colleges and Convents on the Continent, p. 49; London and Dublin Orthodox Journal, ii. 67; More's Hist. Missionis Anglicanæ Soc. Jesu, pp. 249, 253, 256, 261, 263, 337, 339, 414; Oliver's Jesuit Collections, p. 101; Southwell's Bibl. Scriptorum Soc. Jesu, p. 452.]

THOMSON COOPER

published 1889

COPLEY Anthony

(1567–1607?)

Poet and conspirator, third son of Sir Thomas Copley, was born in 1567. He was left in England when his father went abroad, but in 1582, 'being then a student at Furnivals Inn,' he 'stole away' and joined his father and mother at Rouen. At Rouen he stayed for two years, and was then sent to Rome. There he remained for two years in the English college, having a pension of ten crowns from Pope Gregory. On leaving Rome he proceeded to the Low Countries, where he obtained a pension of twenty crowns from the Prince of Parma, and entered the service of the King of Spain, in which he remained until shortly before 1590. In that year he returned to England without permission, and was soon arrested and put in the Tower, whence we have a letter from him dated 6 Jan. 1590–1 to Wade, then lieutenant of the Tower, giving an account of his early life, and praying for pardon and employment. Other letters from him (printed by Strype) give information respecting the English exiles. Soon after we find him residing as a married man at Roughay, in the parish of Horsham, and on 22 June 1592, in a letter from Topcliffe to the queen, he is described as 'the most desperate youth that liveth. . . . Copley did shoot a gentleman the last summer, and killed an ox with a musket, and in Horsham church threw his dagger at the parish clerk. . . . There liveth not the like, I think, in England, for sudden attempts, nor one upon whom I have good grounds to have watchful eyes' (Strype, *Annals*, vol. iv.) He appears to have been an object of great suspicion to the government, and to have been imprisoned several times during the remainder of Elizabeth's reign. His writings, however, breathe fervent loyalty and devotion to the queen. In 1595 he published 'Wits, Fittes, and Fancies fronted and entermedled with Presidentes of Honour and Wisdom; also Loves Owle, an idle conceited dialogue between Love and an olde Man,' London, 1595 (Bodleian). The prose portion of this work is a collection of jests, stories, and sayings, chiefly taken from a Spanish work, 'La Floresta Spagnola,' and was reprinted in 1614 with additions, but without 'Love's Owle' (Brit. Mus.) This work was followed in 1596 by 'A Fig for Fortune' (Brit. Mus.), reprinted by the Spenser Society in 1883. It is a poem in six-line stanzas, and, like 'Love's Owle,' does not convey a very high idea of Copley's poetical powers. Extracts from it will be found in Corser's 'Collectanea,' ii. 456-9.

At the end of Elizabeth's reign Copley took an active part in the controversy between the Jesuits and the secular priests, and wrote two pamphlets on the side of the seculars, 'An Answere to a Letter of a Jesuited Gentleman, by his Cosin, Maister A. C., concerning the Appeale, State, Jesuits,' 1601, 4to (Brit. Mus.) This was followed by 'Another Letter of Mr. A. C. to his Disjesuited Kinsman concerning the Appeale, State, Jesuits. Also a third Letter of his Apologeticall for himself against the calumnies contained against him in a certain Jesuiticall libell intituled A manifestation of folly and bad spirit,' 1602, 4to (Bodleian); in this he announces 'my forthcoming Manifestation of the Jesuit's Commonwealth,' which, however, does not seem to have appeared. On the accession of James to the crown, Copley was concerned in the plot for placing Lady Arabella Stuart on the throne. (A proclamation for his apprehension in 1603 is in the Brit. Mus.) He and the other conspirators were tried and condemned to death (see *State Trials*), but Copley was afterwards pardoned (pardon dated 18 Aug. 1604), having made a confession relating the entire history of the plot, which is printed *in extenso* in the appendix to vol. iv. of Tierney's edition of Dodd's 'Church History.' We afterwards find him in 1606 (1607?) a guest, from January to April, in the English college at Rome, after which he disappears from view.

[Calendars of State Papers, Dom. Series, 1591-1594, 1603-10; Strype's Annals; Dodd's Church History (Tierney); Corser's Collectanea.]

RICHARD COPLEY CHRISTIE

published 1887

FAWKES Guy

(1570-1606)

Conspirator, only son and second child of Edward Fawkes of York, by his wife Edith, was baptised at the church of St. Michael-le-Belfrey, York, 16 April 1570. The father, a notary or proctor of the ecclesiastical courts and advocate of the consistory court of the Archbishop of York, was second son of William Fawkes, registrar of the exchequer court of York diocese from 1541 till his death about 1565. Guy's paternal grandmother was Ellen Haryngton, daughter of an eminent York merchant, who was lord mayor of that city in 1536; she died in 1575, and bequeathed to Guy her best whistle and an angel of gold. His father was buried in York Minster 17 Jan. 1578–9; he left no will, and his whole estate devolved on his son 'Guye,' at the time barely nine years old. There can be no question that his parents were protestants; it is known that they were regular communicants at the parish church of St. Michael-le-Belfrey, and it is a fair inference that Guy was brought up in their belief. He attended the free school at York, where Thomas Morton, afterwards bishop of Durham, and Sir Thomas Cheke, besides John and Christopher Wright, afterwards his fellow-conspirators, were among his schoolfellows (cf. Jardine, p. 37). In 1585 his father's brother, Thomas Fawkes, died, leaving the bulk of his estate to Guy's sisters Elizabeth and Anne, and a trifling legacy to his nephew—'my gold rynge and my bedd, and one payre of shetes with th' appurtenances.' Shortly afterwards his mother married a second time. Her husband was Dionis Baynbrigge of Scotton, Yorkshire, and Guy and his sisters removed with their mother to Scotton. Their stepfather, son of Peter Baynbrigge, by Frances Vavasour of Weston, was closely related with many great catholic families, and was doubtless of the same persuasion himself, while some near neighbours, named Pulleyn, were strong adherents of the old faith. Guy was greatly influenced by his new surroundings; the effects of his earlier training soon faded, and he became a zealous catholic. In 1591 he came of age, and succeeded to full possession of his father's property. On 14 Oct. 1591 he leased some houses and land in York to Christopher Lumley, a tailor, and soon afterwards made arrangements for disposing of the rest of his estate. In 1593 he left England for Flanders, where he enlisted as a soldier of fortune in the Spanish army. In 1595 he was present at the capture of Calais by the Spaniards under Archduke Albert, and, according to the testimony of Father Greenway, was 'sought by all the most distinguished in the archduke's camp for nobility and virtue.' Sir William Stanley, the chief English catholic who had joined the Spanish army, thought highly of Fawkes, and on the death of Elizabeth directed Fawkes and Fawkes's old schoolfellow, Christopher Wright, to visit Philip III, with a view to securing relief for their catholic fellow-countrymen.

As soon as James I had ascended the throne, and had declared himself in favour of the penal laws, the Gunpowder plot was hatched. Its originators were Robert Catesby, John Wright, and Thomas Winter. Fawkes was well known to these men, but had no share in devising the conspiracy. Early in 1604 the conspirators still hoped that Spanish diplomacy might make their desperate remedy unnecessary. Velasco, the constable of Castile, was on his way to the court of James I to discuss the terms of a treaty of peace between Spain and England. Catesby desired to communicate with him at Bergen. Winter was selected for the service about Easter, and Catesby invited Fawkes to accompany him. This was the first active part that Fawkes played in Catesby's dangerous schemes. The journey of Winter and Fawkes brought little result. Soon after their return Fawkes went by appointment to a house beyond Clement's Inn, and there, with four others (Catesby, Thomas Percy, Thomas Winter, and John Wright), took a solemn oath to keep secret all that should be proposed to him. He and Percy, a gentleman pensioner, knew nothing at the time of the proposed plot. But after the ceremony of the oath Percy and Fawkes were informed of the plan of blowing up the parliament house while the king was in the House of Lords. Both approved the proposal, and with the other conspirators withdrew to an upper room, where mass was performed and the sacrament administered by Father Gerard, the jesuit. On 24 May 1604 Percy, acting under Catesby's orders, hired a tenement adjoining the parliament house, in the cellars of which it was determined to construct a mine communicating with the neighbouring premises. Fawkes was directed to disguise himself as Percy's servant and to assume the name of Johnson. As he was quite unknown in London, the keys and the care of the house were entrusted to him. But on 7 July parliament was adjourned till the following February, and the conspirators separated to resume operations about November. In the autumn the penal laws against the catholics were enforced with renewed severity. The conspirators met at Michaelmas, and Fawkes was ordered to prepare the construction of the mine. A delay arose because the commissioners to treat of the union of England and Scotland resolved to meet in the house which Percy had hired, but about 11 Dec. 1604 the five original conspirators brought in tools and provisions by night and began operations in the cellar. The digging of the mine proved more difficult than was anticipated, and John Wright's brother Christopher and Robert Keyes, who had previously been sworn in, but had been told off to take care of a house at Lambeth, where materials for the mine were collected, were sent for to take part in the mining work. Fawkes, dressed as a porter, acted as sentinel in the house, and for a fortnight none of his companions appeared above ground. Information reached Fawkes about Christmas that the meeting of parliament originally fixed for February had been deferred till the October following. Thereupon the conspirators separated, but they resumed work in February 1604-5. In January John Grant and Thomas Winter's brother Robert were sworn of the under-taking, besides an old servant of Catesby named Bates, whose suspicions had been aroused. About March the conspirators hired in Percy's name an adjoining cellar, which ran immediately below the House of Lords, and which had just become vacant. Altering their plan, they abandoned the mine, and filled their newly acquired cellar with barrels of gunpowder and iron bars, concealing the explosives beneath lumber of all kinds.

In May 1605 the work was done, and a further adjournment took place. Fawkes was sent to Flanders to communicate the details of the plot to Sir William Stanley and the jesuit Owen. Stanley was in Spain, and Owen held out little hope that the conspiracy would meet with Stanley's approval. At the end of August Fawkes was again in London. He busied himself in replacing with dry barrels any in the cellar that were injured by damp, and learned that parliament was not to meet till 5 Nov. He took a lodging at 'one Mrs. Herbert's house, a widow that dwells on the backside of St. Clement's Church,' and when he found that his landlady suspected him of associating with Roman catholics, he hurriedly left. Mrs. Herbert stated that he was always 'in good clothes and full of money' (*Notes and Queries*, 2nd ser. ix. 277–9). About Michaelmas Sir Everard Digby, Ambrose Rookwood, and Francis Tresham, three wealthy country gentlemen, were added to the list of conspirators, and entrusted with the duty of providing armed men to second the attack on the government after the explosion had taken place. At the same time the important work of firing the gunpowder was entrusted to Fawkes, whose coolness and courage had been remarkable throughout. A slow match was to be used which would allow him a quarter of an hour to make good his escape. His orders were to embark for Flanders as soon as the train was fired, and spread the news of the explosion on the continent.

As the day approached the conspirators discussed the possibility of warning their catholic friends in the House of Lords of their impending danger. Fawkes wished to protect Lord Montague. It was decided that it was allowable for individual conspirators to do what they could without specific warning to induce their friends to absent themselves from the parliament house on the fatal date. But Tresham was especially anxious to secure the safety of Lord Monteagle, and, after the first discussion, met Catesby, Thomas Winter, and Fawkes at White Webbs in order to obtain their permission to give a distinct warning to his friend. Catesby and Winter were obdurate. On Saturday, 26 Oct., Lord Monteagle received an ambiguous letter entreating him to avoid attending the king at the opening of parliament. Monteagle showed it to Lord Salisbury the same day. The news soon reached Winter and Catesby. Fawkes, ignorant of this turn of affairs, was sent to examine the cellar on 30 Oct., and reported that it was untouched. By 31 Oct. the character of the plot was apprehended with much accuracy at court. But the ministers resolved to make no search in the parliament house till the day before the 5th, so that the conspirators might mature their plans. On Sunday, 3 Nov., a few of the leading conspirators met together and satisfied themselves that the details of the plot were unknown to the authorities. All except Fawkes prepared, however, to leave London at short notice. He undertook to watch the cellar by himself. Next day Suffolk, the lord chamberlain, accompanied by Monteagle, searched the parliament house. In the cellar they noticed abundance of coals and wood, and perceived Fawkes, whom they described as 'a very bad and desperate fellow,' standing in a corner. They were told that Thomas Percy rented the cellar with the adjoining house. The officers left, without making any remark, and reported their observations to the king. Fawkes was alarmed, but resolved to apply the match to the gunpowder on the next appearance of danger, even if he perished himself. He went forth to give Percy warning, but returned to his post before midnight, and met on the threshold Sir Thomas Knyvett, a Westminster magistrate, and his attendants. The cellar was searched; the gunpowder discovered; Fawkes was bound, and on his person were discovered a watch, slow matches, and touchwood, while a dark lantern with a light in it was found near the cellar door. Fawkes declared that had he been in the cellar when Knyvett entered it, he would have 'blown him up, house, himself, and all.'

At one o'clock in the morning the council met in the king's bedchamber at Whitehall, and Fawkes, who betrayed neither fear nor excitement, was brought in under guard. He coolly declined to give any information about himself beyond stating that his name was Johnson, and persisted in absolute silence when interrogated as to his fellow-conspirators. He asserted that he was sorry for nothing but that the explosion had not taken place. When asked by the king whether he did not regret his proposed attack on the royal family, he replied that a desperate disease required a dangerous remedy, and added that 'one of his objects was to blow the Scots back again into Scotland.' Fawkes was removed the same night to the Tower, and was subjected to further examination by the judges Popham and Coke, and Sir William Waad, lieutenant of the Tower, on each of the following days. A long series of searching questions was prepared by the king himself on 6 Nov. (cf. *Notes and Queries*, 2nd ser. viii. 369). Fawkes's name was discovered by a letter found upon him from Anne, lady Vane, but no threats of torture could extort the names of his friends, nor any expression of regret for the crime he had meditated. To overcome his obstinacy he was subjected to the rack, 'per gradus ad ima,' by royal warrant. Torture had the desired effect. On 8 Nov., although still 'stubborn and perverse,' he gave a history of the conspiracy without mentioning names. On the next day his resolution broke down, and he revealed the names of his fellow-conspirators, after learning that several had already been arrested at Holbeach. His confession is signed in a trembling hand 'Guido Fawkes.' Meanwhile parliament had met as arranged on 5 Nov., and on 9 Nov. had been adjourned till 21 Jan. On that day the 5th of November was set apart for ever as a day of thanksgiving. Guy Fawkes's name is still chiefly associated with the date. A proposal to inflict some extraordinary punishment on the offenders awaiting trial was wisely rejected. A special thanksgiving service was prepared for the churches, and many pamphlets, some in Latin verse, denounced the plotters.

On 27 Jan. 1605–6 Fawkes, with the two Winters, Grant, Rookwood, Keyes, and Bates, were tried before a special commission in Westminster Hall. All pleaded not guilty. Fawkes was asked by the lord chief justice, Popham, how he could raise such a plea after his confessions of guilt, and he replied that he would not retract his confession, but the indictment implicated 'the holy fathers' in the plot, which was unwarranted. All the prisoners were found guilty as soon as their confessions were read. Sir Everard Digby was then tried and convicted separately. Finally judgment of death was passed on all. On Friday, 31 Jan., Fawkes, with Winter, Rookwood, and Keyes, were drawn from the Tower to the old palace at Westminster, opposite the parliament house, where a scaffold was erected. Fawkes was the last to mount. He was weak and ill from torture, and had to be helped up the ladder. He spoke briefly, and asked forgiveness of the king and state.

A rare print of the plotters Fawkes, the two Wrights, the two Winters, Catesby, Percy, and Bates, was published in Holland by Simon Pass soon after their execution, and was many times reissued. There is a copy in Caulfield's 'Memoirs of Remarkable Persons,' 1795, ii. 97. A contemporary representation of the execution by N. de Visscher is also extant, besides an elaborate design by Michael Droeshout entitled 'The Powder Treason, Propounded by Sattan, Approved by Anti-Christ,' which includes a portrait of 'Guydo Fauxe.' In Carleton's 'Thankfull Remembrance' is an engraving by F. Hulsius, showing 'G. Faux' with his lighted lantern in the neighbourhood of some barrels. A somewhat similar illustration appears in Vicars's 'Quintessence of Cruelty, a Master Peice of Treachery,' 1641, a translation from the Latin verse of Dr. [Francis] Herring, issued in 1606, and translated in 1610. In most of these drawings Fawkes's christian name is printed as 'Guydo' or 'Guido,' a variant of 'Guye,' which he seems to have acquired during his association with the Spaniards. A lantern, said to be the one employed by Fawkes in the cellar, is now in the Ashmolean Museum, Oxford. A Latin inscription states that it was the gift of 'Robert Heywood, late proctor of the university, 4 April 1641.' Another lantern, to which the same tradition attaches, was sold from Rushden Hall, Northamptonshire, about 1830.

[A True and Perfect Relation of the whole Proceedings against the late most Barbarous Traitors, London, 1606, is an official version of the story of the plot. The account of the trial is very imperfect, consisting mainly of the vituperative speeches of Coke and Northampton. It was reprinted with additions as 'The Gunpowder Treason, with a Discourse of the Manner of its Discovery,' in 1679. See also the Relation of the Gunpowder under the Parliament House, printed in Archæologia, xii. 202*; Howell's State Trials; David Jardine's Narrative of the Gunpowder Plot, 1857; Winwood's Memorials; Robt. Davies's Fawkes's of York in the Sixteenth Century, 1850; Gardiner's Hist. of England, vol. i.; State Papers (Dom. James I), 1605–6; John Gerard's What was the Gunpowder Plot? 1897; S. R. Gardiner's What Gunpowder Plot was, 1897; and art. Catesby, Robert. William Hazlitt in Examiner, 12, 19, and 20 Nov. 1821, pretended to justify Fawkes; cf. Lamb's Essay on Guy Faux.]

SIDNEY LEE

published 1888

BRUCE Robert

(*d.* 1602)

Political agent and spy, was the son of Ninian Bruce, brother of the laird of Binnie. He was first heard of in February 1579, when, on account of some demonstration of catholic zeal, he was summoned, with two other gentlemen, by the privy council of Scotland to answer to the charges brought against him. For neglecting to appear he was proclaimed a rebel and put to the horn (*Reg. of Privy Council*, iii. 102, 106). He was then described as 'servant and secretary to James, sometime archbishop of Glasgow,' and from his own account it seems that he was employed at the time on some affairs of Mary Stuart. Archbishop Beaton was then in Paris, acting as Mary's ambassador at the court of France; and Bruce, retiring to the continent, entered in 1581 the newly erected Scots college at Pont-à-Mousson, sent thither probably by his patron, the archbishop, to complete his studies. Here he remained for over four years. In January 1585 Thomas Morgan (1543–1606?) wrote to Mary Stuart, specially recommending Bruce for her service in Scotland, and enclosing a letter from Bruce himself (Murdin, *State Papers*, pp. 458–63), who, referring to his former services, states that after devoting himself meanwhile to philosophy and divinity, he had now left Pont-à-Mousson for Paris, to be employed in the projects of the Duke of Guise. Bruce was accordingly sent into Scotland in the summer of that year, accompanied by two jesuits, Edmund Hay and John

Dury, disguised as his servants (Forbes-Leith, *Narratives*, p. 204), and was put into communication with the catholic earls, Huntly and Morton (Maxwell), and Lord Claude Hamilton. These noblemen sent him back to the Duke of Guise with blank letters bearing their signatures. The letters were filled up in Paris at the duke's dictation, and carried to Philip of Spain, to whom they were addressed, by Bruce, who was commended to the king as 'a nobleman of proved trust and a good catholic.' The catholic lords asked for their purpose from Philip six thousand troops and 150,000 crowns. Bruce's departure to Spain on this mission was hastened, so Mendoza reported, by orders for his arrest in France, on account of some strong declarations made by him in favour of the jesuits. In September he had an audience of the king, who seemed favourably impressed by him, and sent him back 'with fair words' to Mendoza at Paris, and thence to the Prince of Parma. With Parma Bruce remained for some time, completely gaining his confidence and that of all concerned in the Scoto-Spanish intrigues.

Meanwhile the execution of Mary Stuart in 1587 changed the aspect of Scottish affairs, and Philip decided to accede to the request of the catholic lords, so far at least as to promise to give them the 150,000 crowns three or four months after they should take up arms. Bruce was accordingly sent into Scotland, May 1587, with a message from Philip to King James, in the hope of inducing the king to throw in his lot with the catholics and to avenge his mother's death. He carried with him letters from Guise and Parma, with ten thousand crowns in gold, which he was to spend apparently at his discretion for the good of the cause. He went resolved 'to speak very plainly to the king, and to point out to him the error in which he was living'; and Mendoza, after despatching him on his mission, spoke highly to Philip of his envoy's piety and zeal, inasmuch as he had 'given his all in Scotland to the jesuits, there to aid them in their task.' Bruce had several interviews with James, but without the success he had hoped for. In August 1588 he wrote to Parma that the only course now open to him was 'to bridle the King of Scots' and to rely on the catholic lords; and even as late as 4 Nov. of that year he reports that the Spanish king has now the best opportunity ever presented of making himself 'ruler of this island'; that the principal catholics have resolved that 'it is expedient for the public weal that we submit to the crown of Spain'; and that Huntly, whose letter he encloses, had authorised him to make this statement on their behalf.

Bruce was now an important personage. John Chisholm had brought to him from Flanders another ten thousand crowns. He had from Parma five hundred crowns as a personal fee, and a pension of forty crowns a month. Almost all negotiations of the catholic nobles passed through his hands. But after the escape of Colonel William Sempill from his prison in

Bruce

Edinburgh, Pringle, the colonel's servant, indignant at not being better paid by Bruce, allowed himself to be captured in England, where he sold to the government a packet of letters from Huntly and others, including a long and important letter from Bruce himself directed to Parma (February 1589). Elizabeth sent the packet to James, and the whole conspiracy was exposed, to the consternation of the country. The king was stirred up to some feeble measures against the lords, and thereupon Bruce incited Huntly to the open insurrection which ended in the fiasco of the Brig of Dee. Bruce, whose name had already appeared in a decree of banishment pronounced against certain jesuits and others, now remained comparatively quiet for some years. In December 1589 he was at Rome.

In the summer of 1592 Bruce reappeared for a moment, under the alias of Bartill Bailzie, on the fringe of the mysterious conspiracy of the 'Spanish Blanks,' mainly directed by Father William Crichton; but in August of that year, while the plot was hatching, Sir Robert Bowes, the English agent at the Scottish court, sent to Burghley the astonishing news that Bruce, whom he still calls 'servant of the bishop of Glasgow,' had written to him from Calais, offering 'to discover the practices of Spain' (*Cal. State Papers*, Scotl. ii. 612, 618).

On 17 Nov. Bruce, still in appearance acting on behalf of his old friends, arrived once more in Scotland with money from Flanders, and on 8 Dec., to the surprise of Bowes, James passed an act of council granting 'remission' to Robert Bruce 'for high treason, negotiation with foreign princes and jesuits for the alteration of religion,' &c. It is evident that Bruce was in earnest in his new character. He wrote from Brussels, 25 May 1594: 'I have travelled of late to discredit the jesuits in all parts where they have procured to do harm heretofore ... to serve the queen, and hazard both life, means, and honesty without obligation,' and in July he sent from Antwerp information which proved to be accurate regarding the embarkation of Father James Gordon with others, with money for the insurgent earls (*Hatfield Papers*, iv. 536, 553; cf. *Cal. Scotl.* ii. 748).

Against Bruce's name in the register of the Scots college, it is noted without suspicion, in 1598, that he is still following the court. But his double dealing could not much longer escape the vigilance of his former allies. On 8 March 1599 Father Baldwin wrote to him from Antwerp, warning him that reports were in circulation that he had 'made submission to the King of Scots'; and presently Bruce was in custody at Brussels, charged with the misappropriation of funds entrusted to him, communication with English spies, the betrayal of the catholic cause, and, in particular, with preventing the fall of Dumbarton Castle into the hands of catholics for the King of Spain, by giving intelligence of its intended capture to 'the Scottish antipope' (*R. O. Scotl.* vol. lxv. Nos. 87, 88). Father

Crichton, John Hamilton, the Earls Huntly, Errol, and Westmorland, with others, gave evidence against him. He remained in prison for fourteen months, according to Hospinianus who tells a strange and incredible story of Crichton having become Bruce's accuser out of revenge, because Bruce had rejected the jesuit's proposal that he should assassinate the chancellor Maitland (*Historia Jesuitica*, p. 291). After emerging from prison Bruce appears to have visited Scotland (October 1601) under the name of Peter Nerne, with certain companions whom he was accused of attempting to murder. This Robert Bruce alias Nerne, under torture in Edinburgh, 'confessed much villainy,' and said that he was in the pay of John Cecil; and in the following month Cardinal d'Ossat, writing from Rome, warns Villeroi against certain spies then in France in the interest of Spain, mentioning Robert Bruce 'fort mauvais homme' and Dr. Cecil.

Bruce died in Paris of the plague in 1602. For some time he had been preparing a work against the jesuits, which an intelligencer from Brussels reported as being 'nearly ready to be printed' (*Cal. Dom. Eliz.* 18–28 Aug. 1599). His heir brought the unpublished book to the French nuncio, and asked 450 ducats for it, adding that the Huguenots had offered a thousand ducats (*Vatican MSS.*; *Nunziatura di Francia*. vol. ccxc. f. 146). The nuncio referred the matter to the pope, and the pope to the general of the society, who declined the offer with the remark that such writings were numerous, and that if he were to buy them all up he would be ruined.

[In addition to the sources referred to above: Spanish Papers, Eliz. iii. 580, 589–90, 595–7, iv. 144, 161, 201, 361, 478 and passim; Teulet's Papiers d'État, iii. 412–22, 469–71, 502–86; Calderwood's Church of Scotland, v. 14–36; Hamilton Papers, i. 673, 685; Thorpe's Cal. State Papers, Scotland, ii. 179, 180.]

THOMAS GRAVES LAW

published 1901

CATESBY Robert

(1573–1605)

Second and only surviving son of Sir William Catesby of Lapworth, Warwickshire, by Anne, daughter of Sir Robert Throckmorton of Coughton in the same county, was born at Lapworth in 1573. He was sixth in descent from William Catesby, of the household to Henry VI (*Rot. Parl.* v. 197) and speaker of the House of Commons in the parliament of 1484 (vi. 238), who, being on the side of Richard III, escaped from the battle of Bosworth only to be hanged at Leicester a few days afterwards (Gairdner,

Catesby

Richard III, 308). The attainder against him being reversed, his estates reverted to his family, and the Catesbys added largely to them in the century that followed. Sir William Catesby, in common with the great majority of the country gentry throughout England who were resident upon their estates and unconnected with the oligarchy who ruled in the queen's name at court, threw in his lot with the catholic party and suffered the consequences of his conscientious adherence to the old creed. He was a recusant, and for the crime of not attending at his parish church and taking part in a form of worship which he regarded as worse than a mockery, he suffered severely in person and substance during the latter half of Queen Elizabeth's reign. He had become compromised as early as 1580 by his befriending of the Roman emissaries (*Cal. State Papers*. Dom. 1580, p. 322), and he certainly was a liberal contributor to their support (*Troubles of our Catholic Forefathers*, 2nd ser. p. 156). There is some reason to believe that Robert, his son, was for a time a scholar at the college of Douay (*Diary of the English College, Douay*, ed. Dr. Knox, 1878, p. 206), but in 1586 he entered at Gloucester Hall, now Worcester College, Oxford, which was then a favourite place of resort for the sons of the recusant gentry, as Peterhouse was at Cambridge. The young men of this party rarely stayed at the university more than a year or two, the oath of supremacy being a stumbling-block to them; and Catesby never proceeded to the B.A. degree. In 1592 he married Catherine, daughter of Sir Thomas Leigh of Stoneleigh, Warwickshire, and with her had a considerable estate settled to the uses of the marriage. Next year, by the death of his grandmother, he came into possession of the estate of Chastleton, where he continued to reside for the next few years. His wife died while he was living at Chastleton, leaving him with an only son, Robert; an elder son, William, having apparently died in infancy. In 1598 his father died, and though his mother, Lady Catesby, had a life interest in a large portion of her husband's property, Catesby was by this time a man of large means and much larger expectations; but it seems that the pressure of the persecuting laws, which had been applied with relentless cruelty upon the landed gentry in the midland counties, had produced an amount of irritation and bitterness which to proud and sensitive men was becoming daily more unsupportable, and the terrible fines and exactions which were levied upon their estates, and the humiliating espionage to which they were subjected, tended to make them desperate and ready for any risks that promised even a remote chance of deliverance. As early as 1585 Sir William Catesby had compounded with the government, to the extent of a fifth of his income, for the amount of impositions to be levied upon him for his recusancy (*Hist. MSS. Comm.* 7th Rep. 640). Nevertheless we find him three years after a prisoner at Ely along with Sir Thomas Tresham and others of the recusant gentry, and indignantly protesting against the cruel treatment to which he was exposed. In 1593 he was still in durance, and with some difficulty obtained a license for fifteen days' absence to go to Bath for the recovery of his health, which presumably had suffered from his long confinement (*ib.* 5th Rep. 311). Matters did not mend for the recusants during the next few years, and the penal laws were not relaxed, though the victims were perforce kept quiet. When the mad outbreak of Robert, earl of Essex, in 1601 brought that foolish nobleman to the scaffold, Catesby was one of his most prominent adherents, and in the scuffle that took place in the streets he received a wound. He was thrown into gaol, but for once in her career the queen did not think fit to shed much blood in her anger. More money was to be made out of the conspirators by letting them live than by hanging them, and Catesby was pardoned, but a fine of 4,000 marks was imposed upon him, 1,200*l.* of which was handed over to Sir Francis Bacon for his share of the spoils (Spedding, *Bacon Letters*, iii. 11). It was an enormous impost, and equivalent to a charge of at least 30,000*l.* in our own times. Catesby was compelled to sell the Chastleton estate, and seems then to have made his home with his mother at Ashby St. Legers, Northamptonshire. Growing more and more desperate and embittered, he seems after this to have brooded fiercely on his wrongs and to have surrendered himself to thoughts of the wildest vengeance. Casting aside all caution he consorted habitually with the most reckless malcontents and brought himself so much under the notice of the government that a few days before the queen's death he was committed to prison by the lords of the council, and was probably under arrest on the accession of James I (Camden, *Ep.* p. 347; *Cal. State Papers*, Dom. James I, 1603–10, p. 1). During the first six months of his reign the new king seemed inclined to show favour to the catholic gentry, or at any rate inclined to relax the cruel harshness of the laws. The fines and forfeitures upon recusants almost disappeared from the accounts of the revenue, and a feeling of uneasiness began to spread among the protestant zealots that toleration was going too far. This forbearance lasted but a little while. Continually urged by the outcries of the puritan party to show no mercy to their popish fellow-subjects, and worried by his hungry Scotchmen to bestow upon them the rewards which their poverty needed so sorely if their services did not merit such return, James, who soon discovered that even English money and lands could not be given away without limit, began to show that he had almost as little sympathy with the romanising party as his predecessor, and the old enactments were revived and the old statutes put in force. The catholics, who had begun to hope for better days, were goaded to frenzy by this change of attitude. The more conscientious and the more sincerely desirous they were simply to enjoy the liberty of worshipping God after their own fashion, the more sullenly they brooded over their wrongs. The catholics by this time had become divided into two parties somewhat sharply antagonistic the one to the other. The one party consisted of those who had a vague idea of setting up an organised ecclesiastical establishment in England which should be placed under the discipline of its own bishops appointed by the pope, and which should occupy almost exactly the same position occupied by the Roman catholics in England at the present moment. They hoped that by submitting themselves to the government and taking the oath of allegiance they might purchase for themselves a measure of toleration of which they suspected that in process of time they might avail themselves to bring back the nation to its allegiance to the see of Rome.

The other party consisted of those who were under the paramount influence of the jesuits, and these were vehemently opposed to any submission or any temporising; they would have all or nothing, and any concession to the heretics or any weak yielding to laws which they denounced as immoral they taught was mortal sin, to be punished by exclusion for ever from the church of Christ in earth or heaven. It was with this latter party—the party who, not content with toleration, could be satisfied with nothing but supremacy—that Catesby had allied himself, and of which he was qualified to be a leading personage. At the accession of James I he was in his thirtieth year, of commanding stature (Gerard, p. 57) and great bodily strength, with a strikingly beautiful face and extremely captivating manners. He is said to have exercised a magical influence upon all who mixed with him. His purse was always at the service of his friends, and he had suffered grievously for his convictions. Moreover, he was a sincerely religious man after his light, a fanatic in fact, who subordinated all considerations of prudence to the demands which his dogmatic creed appeared to him to require. A catholic first, but anything and everything else afterwards. Such men get thrust into the front of any insane enterprise that they persuade themselves is for the advancement of a holy cause, and Catesby when he girded on his sword took care to have that sword engraved 'with the passion of our Lord,' and honestly believed he was entering upon a sacred crusade for the glory of God. In the confused tangle of testimony and contradiction, of confession under torture, hearsay reports and dexterous prevarication on which the story of the Gunpowder plot is based, it is difficult to unravel the thread of a narrative which is told in so many different ways. Thus much, however, seems to be plain, viz. that the plot was originally hatched by Thomas Winter about the summer of 1604, first communicated to Guy Faux and soon after to Catesby, who was always to be relied on to furnish money; that it was not revealed to any of the Roman priesthood except under the seal of confession, which rendered it impossible for them as priests to divulge it; that the two jesuit fathers Garnett and Gerrard, who were a great deal too astute and sagacious not to see the immeasurable imprudence of any such attempt, revolted from its wickedness, and did their best to prevent it, foreseeing the calamitous issue that was sure to result from it; finally, that it never would have gone so far as it did but for the ferocious daring of Faux, supported by the immovable obstinacy, amounting to monomania, of Catesby. The Gunpowder plot is, however, a matter of history, not of biography, and into its details it is not advisable here to enter. The full particulars are to be read in the confession of Thomas Winter, among the documents at the Record Office (*Cal. State Papers*, Dom. 1603–11, pp. 262, 279). It is sufficient to say that about midnight of 4 Nov. 1605 Faux was apprehended at the door of the cellar under the parliament house by Sir Thomas Knyvett, who found thirty-six barrels of powder in casks and hogsheads prepared in all readiness for the explosion. Catesby obtained information of his confederate's arrest almost immediately and lost no time in getting to horse. He was joined by the two Wrights, Percy, and Ambrose Rookwood, and the party reached Ashby St. Legers, a distance of eighty miles, in less than seven hours. On the evening of the 7th the whole company, about sixty strong, reached Holbeach, on the borders of Staffordshire. Next morning occurred the remarkable explosion of the gunpowder which the conspirators were getting ready for their defence of the house against assault, whereby Catesby himself was severely scorched. Some few hours after this Sir Richard Walsh arrived with his force, surrounded the house, and summoned the rebels to lay down their arms. On their refusal the attack commenced, and Catesby and Percy, standing back to back and fighting furiously, were shot through the body with two bullets from the same musket. Catesby, crawling into the house upon his hands and knees, seized an image of the Virgin, and dropped down dead with it clasped in his arms (8 Nov. 1605). Of course the property of the unhappy man was forfeited, and fell to the courtiers who scrambled for their reward; but the settlement of that portion of the estates which had been made by Sir William upon Lady Catesby preserved them from alienation, and though an attempt was made in 1618 (*Cal. State Papers*, Dom. 1611–18, p. 580) to set that settlement aside, it seems to have failed, and Robert Catesby the younger, recovering the fragments of his inheritance, is said to have married a daughter of that very Thomas Percy who perished fighting ingloriously back to back with his father when they made their last stand at Bostock. Of his subsequent history nothing is known.

The old Manor House of Ashby St. Legers is still standing, and a portrait reported by tradition to be a likeness of the conspirator is to be seen at Brockhall, Northamptonshire.

Digby

[Gairdner's Richard III; Notes and Queries, 6th series, xii. 364, 466; Genealogist, v. 61 et seq.; Cal. State Papers, Dom. 1580; Jardine's Narrative of the Gunpowder Plot, 1857; The Visitation of Warwickshire (Harl. Soc.); Morris's Condition of Catholics under James I, 2nd edit. 1872; Knox's Diary of the English College at Douay, 1878.]

AUGUSTUS JESSOPP

published 1886

DIGBY Everard

(1578–1606)

Sir

Conspirator, son of Everard Digby of Stoke Dry, Rutland, by Maria, daughter and coheiress of Francis Neale of Keythorpe, Leicestershire, was born on 16 May 1578, and was in his fourteenth year when his father died on 24 Jan. 1592. It is a common error to identify his father with Everard Digby, divine and author. His wardship was purchased from the crown by Roger Manners, esq., of the family of the Earl of Rutland, and probably re-sold at an advanced price to young Digby's mother. The heir to large estates in Rutland, Leicestershire, and Lincolnshire, and connected with many of the most considerable families in England, it was only to be expected that he should present himself at the queen's court. While still a youth he was appointed to some office in the household, which John Gerard, the jesuit father, probably erroneously, describes as 'being one of the queen's gentlemen-pensioners.' His great stature and bodily strength, however, made him an adept at all field sports, and he spent the greater part of his time in the country hunting and hawking. In 1596 he married Mary, only daughter and heiress of William Mulsho of Goathurst, Buckinghamshire, and obtained with her a large accession of fortune. About 1599 Digby fell under the influence of John Gerard, who soon acquired an extraordinary sway over him. They became close friends and companions, their friendship being strengthened by the conversion of Digby to the 'catholic doctrine and practice,' which was soon followed by the adhesion of Digby's wife and his mother. When James I came to England, Digby joined the crowd of those who welcomed the new king at Belvoir Castle, and received the honour of knighthood there on 23 April 1603. How bitterly the Romish party were disappointed by the attitude assumed by James in the following year; how their bitterness and anger made a small section of them furious and desperate; how the Gunpowder plot grew into more and more definite shape, and how the mad scheme exercised a kind of fascination over the imagination of the small band of frenzied gentlemen who were deeply implicated in it, may be read in the histories of the time, and best of all in Mr. Gardiner's first volume. Unlike Catesby, Rookwood, Tresham, and others more or less cognisant of the conspiracy, Digby had never had anything to complain of in the shape of persecution at the hands of the government. It is probable that both his parents were catholics, but they had never been disturbed for their convictions, and their son had evidently suffered no great inconvenience for conscience' sake. In the arrangements that were made by the conspirators Digby was assigned a part which kept him at a distance from London, and there are some indications that he was not trusted so implicitly as the rest. The plan agreed upon was that Faux should fire the train with a slow match, and at once make off to Flanders. Percy was to seize the person of Prince Henry or his brother Charles, with the co-operation of the others, who were all in London or the suburbs, and was to carry him off with all speed to Warwickshire. Meanwhile Digby was to co-operate by preparing for a rising in the midlands when the catastrophe should have been brought about; and it was settled that he should invite a large number of the disaffected gentry to meet him at Dunchurch in Warwickshire, and join in a hunting expedition on Dunsmoor Heath (near Rugby), where, it was whispered, strange news might be expected. This gathering was fixed for Tuesday, 5 Nov. 1605. On Monday the 4th, about midnight, Faux was apprehended by Sir Thomas Knyvett as he was closing the door of the cellar under the parliament house, where thirty-six barrels of gunpowder had been placed in readiness for the explosion intended on the morrow. The game was up; and before daybreak some of the conspirators had taken horse; and all were riding furiously to the place of meeting before the great secret had become common property. The meeting of the catholic gentry at Dunchurch had evidently not been a success, and when, late in the evening, Catesby, Rookwood, Percy, and the Wrights burst in, haggard, travel-soiled, and half dead with their astonishing ride, it became clear that there had been some desperate venture which had ended only in a crushing failure, the gentry who were not in the plot dispersed rapidly to their several homes, and the plotters were left to take their chance. The almost incredible strength and endurance of Catesby and his accomplices appears from the fact that on that very night (after a ride of eighty miles in seven or eight hours, for Rookwood had not left London till eleven o'clock in the morning) they started again before ten o'clock, and were at Huddington in Worcestershire by two o'clock the next afternoon, having broken into a cavalry stable at Warwick in the middle of the night and helped themselves to fresh horses for the distance that lay before them. On Thursday night, the 7th, they had reached Holbeach House in Staffordshire, and then it was determined to make a stand and sell their lives as dearly as they could. Next morning Digby deserted his companions; he says his object was to make a diversion elsewhere, and to attempt to bring up some assistance to prop, if possible, the falling cause. Shortly after he had gone the terrible explosion of gunpowder occurred, and the fight which ended in the death or apprehension of the whole band. Meanwhile Digby soon found that it was impossible to escape the notice of his pursuers, who were speedily upon his track, and thinking it best to dismiss his attendants, he told his servants they might keep the horses they were riding, and distributed among them the money they were carrying—let each man shift for himself. Two of them refused to leave him, one being his page, William Ellis by name, who eventually became a lay brother of the Society of Jesus. The three struck into a wood where there was a dry pit, in which they hoped to conceal themselves and their horses. They were soon discovered, and a cry was raised, 'Here he is! here he is!' Digby, altogether undaunted, answered, 'Here he is indeed, what then?' and advanced his horse in the manner of curvetting, which he was expert in, and thought to have borne them over, and so to break from them. Seeing, however, that resistance was useless, he gave himself up, and before many days found himself a prisoner in the Tower. Two miserable months passed before the prisoners were brought to trial. At last, on 27 Jan. 1606, Digby, with eight others who had been caught red-handed, was brought to Westminster Hall. He behaved with some dignity during the trial, but there could be no doubt about the verdict, and on Thursday, the 30th, he was drawn upon a hurdle, with three of his accomplices, to St. Paul's Churchyard, and there hanged and slaughtered with the usual ghastly barbarities. On the scaffold he had confessed his guilt with a manly shame for his infatuation, and a solemn protest that Father Gerard had never known of the plot, adding, 'I never durst tell him of it, for fear he would have drawn me out of it.' It is impossible for any candid reader of all the evidence that has come down to us to doubt the truth of this protest. Garnett's complicity cannot be questioned, and his subsequent equivocation was as impolitic as it was discreditable. Father Gerard was a very different man. If the plot had been revealed to him, it would never have been permitted to go as far as it did.

Digby left two sons behind him; the younger, Sir John Digby, was knighted in 1635 and became a major-general on the king's side during the civil war. He is said to have been slain 9 July 1645. The elder son was the much more famous Sir Kenelm Digby, of whom an account will be found *sub nomine.* Digby's wife survived him many years, as did his mother, and neither appears to have married again.

[Chancery Inquisitiones post mortem, 34th Eliz. pt. i. No. 64 (Rutland), in the Record Office; Books of the Court of Wards and Liveries, No. 158, u. s.; Harl. MS. 1364; Cal. State Papers, Domestic, 1603–10; Hist. MSS. Comm. 8th Rep. 434; Foley's Records of the English Province S. J., vol. ii.; John Morris's Condition of Catholics under James I., 1872, vol. ii., and the same writer's Life of Father John Gerard, 3rd edit. 1881; Bishop Robert Abbot's Antilogia, 1613; Cooper's Athenæ Cantab. ii. 146; Jardine's Narrative of the Gunpowder Plot, 1857; Gardiner's Hist. of England, vol. i. Digby's mother is called Maria in the usual pedigrees of the family, but in the Inq. post mort. she is called Mary Ann, probably by a clerical error.]

AUGUSTUS JESSOPP

published 1888

PAGET Charles

(*d.* 1612)

Catholic exile and conspirator, fourth son of William, first baron Paget, and Anne, daughter and heiress of Henry Preston, esq., was matriculated as a fellow-commoner of Gonville and Caius College, Cambridge, on 27 May 1559. He was a member of Trinity Hall when Queen Elizabeth visited the university in August 1564, but he does not appear to have taken a degree (Cooper, *Athenæ Cantabr.* iii. 53). Under his father's will he became entitled to the manor of Weston-Aston and other lands in Derbyshire. He was a zealous Roman catholic, and quitted England, in discontent with its ecclesiastical constitution, about 1572, and fixed his residence in Paris. There he became secretary to James Beaton, archbishop of Glasgow, who was Queen Mary Stuart's ambassador at the French court, and he was soon joined in the office with Thomas Morgan (1543–1606?). Morgan and Paget were in constant correspondence with Claude de la Boisseliere Nau and Gilbert Curle, the two secretaries who lived with the queen in England, and 'they four governed from thenceforth all the queen's affairs at their pleasure.' Paget and Morgan secretly opposed Archbishop Beaton, Mary's ambassador, and wrung from him the administration of the queen's dowry in France, which was about thirty million crowns a year. Joining themselves afterwards with Dr. Owen Lewis in Rome, and falling out with Dr. Allen and Father Parsons, they were the cause of much division among the catholics (Parsons, *Story of Domesticall Difficulties*,

Stonyhurst MS. No. 413, quoted in *Records of the English Catholics*, ii. 320 *n*.). Parsons states that the original cause of Paget and Morgan's division from Dr. Allen and himself was their exclusion, by desire of the Duke of Guise and the Archbishop of Glasgow, from the consultation held at Paris in 1582 relative to the deliverance of the Queen of Scots, and the restoration of England to catholic unity by means of a foreign invasion (*ib*. ii. 392). Thenceforward Paget and Morgan inspired Mary with distrust of Spain and the jesuits.

During all this time, while apparently plotting against Queen Elizabeth, Paget was acting the part of a spy, and giving political information to her ministers. As early as 8 Jan. 1581–2 he wrote from Paris to secretary Walsingham in these terms: 'God made me known to you in this town, and led me to offer you affection; nothing can so comfort me as her Majesty's and your favour.' Again he wrote, on 28 Sept. 1582: 'In my answer to her Majesty's command for my return to England, assist me that she may yield me her favour and liberty of conscience in religion. . . . If this cannot be done, then solicit her for my enjoying my small living on this side the sea, whereby I may be kept from necessity, which otherwise will force me to seek relief of some foreign prince.' On 23 Oct. 1582 he informed Walsingham of his intention to go to Rouen for his health, and to drink English beer. He professed dutiful allegiance to Elizabeth, and his readiness to be employed in any service, matter of conscience in religion only excepted.

In September 1583 Paget came privately from Rouen to England, assuming the name of Mope. It is alleged that the object of his journey was to concert measures for an invasion by the Duke of Guise and the King of Scots. For a time he lay concealed in the house of William Davies, at Patching, Sussex. On the 8th he had an interview at Petworth with the Earl of Northumberland. He was afterwards secretly conveyed to a lodge in the earl's park, called Conigar Lodge, where he lay for about eight days. His brother, Lord Paget, was sent for to Petworth, where Charles and the earl had several conferences. On the 16th Charles Paget met in a wood, called Patching Copse, William Shelley, esq., who was subsequently convicted of treason (*Baga de Secretis*, pouch 47).

Lord Paget, writing to his brother on 25 Oct. in the same year, said his stay in Rouen was more misliked than his abiding in Paris, considering that he consorted with men like the Bishop of Ross. He added that he was sorry to hear by some good friends that he carried himself not so dutifully as he ought to do, and that he would disown him as a brother if he forgot the duty he owed to England. From this letter it would seem that Lord Paget's interview with his brother at Petworth must have been of a more innocent character than has been generally supposed. However, about the end of

November Lord Paget fled to Paris, and thenceforward became suspected of complicity in all his brother's treasons. On 2 Dec. 1583 Sir Edward Stafford, the English ambassador to France, wrote from Paris to Walsingham: 'Lord Paget, with Charles Paget and Charles Arundel, suddenly entered my dining chamber before any one was aware of it, and Lord Paget says they came away for their consciences, and for fear, having enemies.' They also told him that 'for all things but their consciences they would live as dutifully as any in the world.'

From this period Charles Paget, in conjunction with Morgan and other malcontents at home and abroad, continued their machinations, which were, of course, well known to the English government; and in June 1584 Stafford, the English ambassador, made a formal demand, in the name of Queen Elizabeth, for the surrender of Lord Paget, Charles Paget, Charles Arundel, Thomas Throckmorton, and Thomas Morgan, they having conspired against the life of the English queen. The king of France, however, refused to deliver them up, although he soon afterwards imprisoned Morgan, and forwarded his papers to Queen Elizabeth.

It is clear that Paget was regarded with the utmost distrust and suspicion by Walsingham, who, in a despatch sent to Stafford on 16 Dec. 1584, says: 'Charles Paget is a most dangerous instrument, and I wish, for Northumberland's sake, he had never been born.' In May 1586 Paget, on account of illness, went to the baths of Spain. He was attainted of treason by act of parliament in 1587.

Although all his plots had signally failed, he appears still to have clung to the idea that the protestant religion in England could be subverted by a foreign force. Writing under the signature of 'Nauris,' from Paris, to one Nicholas Berden *alias* Thomas Rogers, 31 Jan. 1587–8, he observed, in reference to the anticipated triumph of the Spanish Armada: 'When the day of invasion happens, the proudest Councillor or Minister in England will be glad of the favour of a Catholic gentleman.' In the same letter he stated that all Walsingham's alphabets or ciphers had been interpreted by him.

In March 1587–8 he entered the service of the king of Spain, and went to reside at Brussels. His name appears in the list of English exiles in Flanders who refused to sign the address of the English fathers of the Society of Jesus (*Douay Diaries*, p. 408). With his habitual treachery, he continued his correspondence with Queen Elizabeth's government. To Secretary Cecil he wrote on 26 Dec. 1597: 'I am incited to boldness with you by your favour to my nephew Paget, and the good report I hear of your sweet nature, modesty, and wisdom. I desire ardently to do a service agreeable both to the queen and the king of Spain. I am under obligation to the one as an

English subject, and to the other as a catholic prince who has relieved me in my banishment.' He added that 'His Highness' was willing to treat with allies, and particularly with the queen, that the crowns of England and Spain might return to their old amity (*State Papers*, Dom. Eliz. vol. cclxv. art. 63). On 27 April 1598 he wrote from Liège to Thomas Barnes in London: 'I am unspeakably comforted that the queen inclines to listen to my humble suit. The profits of my land are worth 200*l.* a year to myself; it is a lordship called Weston-upon-Trent. ... I cannot capitulate with the Queen; but the greater my offence has been, the greater is her mercy in pardoning and restoring me to my blood and living, showing the liberality which makes her famous, and obliging me to spend my life at her feet' (*ib.* vol. cclxvi. art. 116).

The English catholic exiles eventually split into two parties—one, called the Spanish faction, supporting the claims of the infanta to the English crown; while the other, denominated the Scottish faction, advocated the right of James VI of Scotland. Paget was the acknowledged head of the Scottish faction, and in 1599 he threw up his employment under the king of Spain, and returned to Paris (*ib.* vol. cclxxi, art. 74). Among the State Papers (vol. cclxxi. art. 74) is a letter from a catholic in Brussels to his friend, a monk at Liège, giving a detailed account of Paget and his 'practices.' The writer says that 'from the first hour that his years permitted him to converse with men, he has been tampering in broils and practices, betwixt friend and friend, man and wife, and, as his credit and craft increase, betwixt prince and prince.'

Animated by intense hatred of the Spanish faction, Paget lost no time after his arrival at Paris in putting himself in communication with Sir Henry Neville, the English ambassador, who forwarded a detailed account of the circumstances to Sir Robert Cecil in a despatch dated 27 June (O.S.) 1599. Cecil seems to have been by no means anxious to encourage Paget, but Neville was more favourable to him. Paget said he felt himself slighted by the English government, but he nevertheless seems to have given from time to time important intelligence to Neville and to Ralph Winwood, the succeeding ambassador at the French court. His attainder appears to have been reversed in the first parliament of James I, probably by the act restoring in blood his nephew William, lord Paget, and it is presumed that he returned to England. His paternal estate, including the manor of Weston and other manors in Derbyshire, was restored to him on 13 July 1603; and on 18 Aug. in the same year James I granted him 200*l.* per annum, part of a fee-farm rent of 716*l.* reserved by a patent of Queen Elizabeth, bestowing the lands of Lord Paget on William Paget and his heirs. He died, probably in England, about the beginning of February 1611–12, leaving a good estate to the sons of one of his sisters.

His works are: 1. A proposition for calling the jesuits out of England, by means of the French king, during the treaty, and entitled 'A Brief Note of the Practices that divers Jesuits have had for killing Princes and changing of States,' June 1598. Manuscript in the State Papers, Dom. Eliz. vol. cclxvii. art. 67. 2. 'Answer to Dolman [Robert Parsons] on the Succession to the English Crown,' Paris, 1600. John Petit, writing from Liège to Peter Halins, 25 July (O.S.) 1600, remarks: 'A book has come out in answer to that one on the succession to the crown of England, which is all for the Scot, but I cannot get sight of it. Clitheroe was the author, and he being dead, Charles Paget has paid for its printing' (*Cal. State Papers*, Dom. Eliz. 1598–1601, pp. 456, 460). It appears that the latter part of the book was written by Paget. 3. 'An Answere made by me, Charles Paget, Esqvier, to certayne vntruthes and falsityes, tochinge my selfe, contayned in a booke [by Robert Parsons] intitled a briefe Apologie or defence of the Catholicke Hierarchie & subordination in Englande, & cet.' Printed with Dr. Humphrey Ely's 'Certaine Briefe Notes vpon a Briefe Apologie set out vnder the name of the Priestes vnited to the Archpriest,' Paris [1603], 8vo.

[Bacon's Letters (Spedding), i. 195; Birch's James I, i. 161; Collins's Peerage (Brydges), v. 185–7; Froude's Hist. of England, 1893, xi. 379, xii. 130; Hardwicke State Papers, i. 213, 214, 218, 224, 247; Harl. MS. 288, ff. 161, 165, 167; Harleian Miscellany (Malham), i. 535, ii. 81; Holinshed's Chronicles, quarto ed. iv. 608–11; Howell's State Trials; Jewett's Reliquary, ii. 185; Lansd. MS. 45, art. 75; Lingard's Hist. of England, 1851, viii. 165, 168, 169, 189, 199–211, 390; Murdin's State Papers, pp. 436–534; Nichols's Progr. Eliz. 1st ed. iii. 171; Plowden's Remarks on Panzani, pp. 104–12; Records of the English Catholics, i. 435, ii. 472; Sadler State Papers, ii. 243, 257, 260; Cal. State Papers, Dom. Eliz. and Scottish Ser.; Strype's Annals, iii. 136, 218, 308, 416, 474, App. p. 44, iv. 163, 164, fol.; Turnbull's Letters of Mary Stuart, pp. 100–4, 116, 120–6, 130, 367, 368; Tytler's Scotland, 1864, iv. 115–20, 308, 309, 337, 338; Watt's Bibl. Brit.; Winwood's Memorials; Wright's Elizabeth, ii. 486.]

THOMPSON COOPER

published 1895

LEVINZ Robert

(1615–1650)

D.C.L.

Royalist, born in 1615 (alternatively named Levens or Levinge), was a son of William Levinz of Senkworth, near Abingdon, who carried on the

Thurloe

business of a brewer at Oxford. His grandfather, William Levinz, was an alderman of Oxford, and five times mayor at the close of the sixteenth century; he was buried in All Saints Church, where there is a fine recumbent effigy to his memory. Robert was uncle of Sir Creswell Levinz, Baptist Levinz, and William Levinz. He matriculated at Lincoln College, and graduated B.A. on 4 Feb. 1634, and D.C.L. in 1642. He was commissary in 1640 to the Bishop of Norwich (*Cal. State Papers*, Dom. 1640–1, pp. 394, 397). On the outbreak of the civil war he took up arms for the king at Oxford, and obtained the rank of captain, but on the capitulation of the city to the parliament in 1646 appears to have resumed his studies. After Charles I's execution he was employed by Charles II in various negotiations, and finally received a commission to raise troops in England for the new king at the time of Charles's Scottish expedition in 1650. The plot was discovered, and he was arrested in London. His papers were seized, and many blank commissions signed by the king were discovered among them. Levinz was taken before the council of state, and was handed over as a spy to the council of war. He was tried by court-martial and sentenced to be hanged. Offers were made to spare his life if he would betray his accomplices: this he refused to do, but acknowledged the truth of the accusations against himself, while protesting the justice of his cause. He was taken to Cornhill in a coach guarded by a troop of horse, and hanged against the Exchange on 18 July 1650. Lloyd speaks of his numerous friends, his prudence, and integrity. His wife was a daughter of Sir Peregrine Bertie, and granddaughter of Robert, earl of Lindsay.

A portrait appears in Winstanley's 'Loyal Martyrology,' 1665.

[Winstanley's Loyal Martyrology, p. 28; Visitation of Oxford, 1573, private printed, by Sir T. Phillipps; Clarendon State Papers, ii. 73; Wood's Fasti (Bliss), i. 468, ii. 47; Lloyd's Memoirs, 1668, p. 560; Whitelocke's Memorials, p. 464; Topographer, 1821, vol. i.]

EMILY TENNYSON BRADLEY

published 1892

THURLOE John

(1616–1668)

Secretary of state, baptised on 12 June 1616, was the son of Thomas Thurloe, rector of Abbot's Roding, Essex ('Life' prefixed to the *Thurloe Papers*, p. xi). He was brought up to the study of the law, and 'bred from a youth' in the service of Oliver St. John (1598?–1673) (*Case of Oliver St. John*,

72

1660, pp. 4, 6). By St. John's interest Thurloe was in January 1645 appointed one of the secretaries to the commissioners of parliament at the treaty of Uxbridge (Whitelocke, *Memorials*, i. 377, ed. 1853). In 1647 he was admitted to Lincoln's Inn, and in March 1648 made receiver of the cursitor's fines under the commissioners of the great seal (*ib.* ii. 285), a post worth about 350*l.* per annum. He had nothing to do with the establishment of the republic, and, as to the king's death, he subsequently declared that 'he was altogether a stranger to that fact, and to all the counsels about it, having not had the least communication with any person whatsoever therein' (*State Papers*, vii. 914). In March 1651 he was appointed secretary to St. John and Walter Strickland on their mission to Holland, and on 29 March 1652 the council of state appointed him to be their secretary in place of Walter Frost, deceased. His salary was fixed at 600*l.* per annum, and he was given lodgings in Whitehall (*ib.* i. 205; *Cal. State Papers*, Dom. 1651–2, pp. 198, 203). In December 1652 the salary was raised to 800*l.*, and the duty of clerk to the committee for foreign affairs apparently added to his former office (*ib.* 1652–3, p. 1). In the elevation of Cromwell to the Protectorate Thurloe took a not unimportant part; the letters ordering the sheriffs to proclaim Cromwell were signed by him, and he was charged to perfect the instrument of government. At the same time (22 Dec.) he seems to have been co-opted a member of the council (*ib.* 1653–1654, pp. 297, 301, 309). He was also given charge of the intelligence department, which had been before confided to Thomas Scott (*d.* 1660) and Captain George Bishop (*ib.* p. 133). In addition to this, on 3 May 1655 the Protector entrusted him with the control of the posts both inland and foreign (*ib.* 1655, pp. 138, 286). Moreover on 10 Feb. 1654 he was made a bencher of Lincoln's Inn (*State Papers*, vol. i. p. xiii).

Thurloe fulfilled his various duties with conspicuous ability. By the intelligencers he employed in foreign parts, and by the correspondence he organised with the diplomatic agents of the government, he kept the Protector admirably informed of the acts and plans of foreign powers. When the ministers of Charles II were attacked for the ignorance which allowed the Dutch to inflict a crushing surprise upon England in 1667, Thurloe's management of intelligence was held up to them as an example. 'Thereby,' said Colonel Birch in the House of Commons, 'Cromwell carried the secrets of all the princes of Europe at his girdle.' No one denied the fact, but secretary Morrice pleaded in answer that he was allowed but 700*l.* a year for intelligence, while Cromwell had allowed 70,000*l.* (Pepys, *Diary*, 14 Feb. 1668). In reality Thurloe's expenditure for intelligence seems to have been between 1,200*l.* and 2,000*l.* per annum (*Cal. State Papers*, Dom. 1653–4, pp. 454, 458; Thurloe, vii. 483, 785). Under the head of intelligence came also the political police, and so long as Thurloe was in office no conspiracy against the government had a chance of success. His control of the post office enabled him to seize the correspondence of plotters, and his collection of papers contains hundreds of intercepted letters. The spies whom he kept at the court of the exiled king, and the plotters whom he corrupted or intimidated, supplied him with information of each new movement among the royalists (see *English Historical Review*, 1888 p. 340, 1889 p. 527). An illustration of his vigilance is supplied by the traditional story of the royalist gentleman who was told by Cromwell when he returned to England all that had passed in his secret interview with Charles II (Ludlow, ii. 42, ed. 1894). Burnet and Welwood tell many similar stories (*Own Time*, i. 121, 131, ed. 1833; Welwood, *Memoirs*, p. 105).

Thurloe's duties as secretary sometimes required him to set forth the views of the government in a declaration or explain them in a speech. Drafts of two such defences of the policy of the government towards the cavaliers are among his papers (*State Papers*, iv. 132, v. 786). To the parliament of 1656, in which, as in that of 1654, Thurloe represented Ely, he announced Blake's victory at Santa Cruz, related the discovery of Venner's and Sindercombe's plots, and spoke on behalf of the confirmation of Cromwell's ordinances (Burton, *Parliamentary Diary*, i. 353, ii. 43, 143; *State Papers*, vi. 184). On 11 April 1657 he received the thanks of the house for his care and vigilance (*Common's Journals*, vii. 522). On 13 July of the same year he was sworn in as a member of Cromwell's second council, on 2 Nov. he was elected a governor of the Charterhouse, and on 4 Feb. 1658 he was made chancellor of the university of Glasgow (*State Papers*, vol. i. p. xvii, vol. vi. p. 777). But in spite of the post which he occupied, and though his services were liberally recognised, Thurloe had very little influence in determining the Protector's policy. 'In matters of the greatest moment,' writes Welwood, 'Cromwell trusted none but his secretary Thurloe, and sometimes not even him' (*Memoirs*, p. 105). Thurloe was anxious for Cromwell to accept the crown, but was totally unable to tell Henry Cromwell what the Protector intended to do. 'Surely,' he concludes, 'whatever resolutions his highness takes, they will be his own' (*State Papers*, vi. 219). In his confidential letters to Henry Cromwell he more than once expresses his dissatisfaction with the policy of the council (*ib*. vi. 568, 579). Both agreed in their preference for parliamentary and legal ways, and their opposition to the military party among Cromwell's councillors, and the arbitrary methods they advocated (*ib*. vii. 38, 55, 56, 99). Thurloe thought that the Protector humoured them too much (*ib*. vii. 269). With Cromwell personally Thurloe's relations were very close. On one occasion Cromwell took him for a drive in Hyde Park in order to try the six horses sent the Protector by the Duke of Oldenburg; the horses ran away with the coach, and the secretary hurt his leg in jumping out (*ib.* ii. 652). He was one of the little knot of friends with whom the Protector would sometimes be cheerful and 'lay aside his greatness' (Whitelocke, *Memorials*, iv. 289) in the intervals of confidential deliberations on affairs of state. Thurloe's letters to Henry Cromwell during the Protector's illness, and his remarks on the Protector's death, show unbounded admiration for Cromwell as a ruler, and genuine attachment to him as a man (*State Papers*, vii. 355, 362, 363, 366, 372, 374).

During the brief government of Richard Cromwell, Thurloe's influence rather increased than diminished. He had played an important part in Richard's elevation; the missing letter nominating Richard as successor had been addressed to him, and the verbal nomination finally made had been made at his instance (*ib.* vii. 363, 364, 372, 374). Hyde and the royalists were convinced that Thurloe (advised in secret by Pierrepoint and St. John) was the real inspirer of Richard's government (*Clarendon State Papers*, iii. 421, 423, 425, 435). The officers of the army were jealous of his power over Richard, and complained of evil counsellors. Thurloe thought of resigning, but he could not be spared; and even Richard's reply to the complaints of the army was drawn up by him (*State Papers*, vii. 447, 490, 495). From the moment of the old Protector's death, Thurloe had feared that the government would be ruined by the dissensions of its friends rather than by the attacks of the royalists; but he endeavoured to shake off his melancholy forebodings, and set to work to secure a Cromwellian majority in the coming parliament (*ib.* vii. 364, 541, 588). He himself was elected for the university of Cambridge, for Tewkesbury, and for Huntingdon, but made his choice for Cambridge (*ib.* vii. 565, 572, 585–8).

In the parliament of January to April 1659 Thurloe was the official leader of the supporters of the government, and its recognised spokesman. On 1 Feb. he introduced a bill which he had drafted for the recognition of Richard Cromwell as lord-protector (*ib.* vii. 603, 609; Burton, *Diary*, iii. 25). On 21 Feb., and again on 24 Feb., he gave a clear exposition of the state of foreign affairs and of the policy of the government (*ib.* iii. 314, 376, 481). On 7 March he defended the authority of the second house, and on 7 April explained the state of the finances (*ib.* iv. 68, 365). During the session he was called upon to defend himself with regard to the police administration under the late Protector. From the moment the parliament met, Hyde and the royalist agents in England had regarded an attack upon Thurloe as one of the first and most necessary steps towards the overthrow of the Protectorate (*Clarendon State Papers*, iii. 426, 428, 436). He had not abused his power to extort money, as some of his colleagues were accused of doing, but he had arbitrarily committed supposed plotters to prison, and transported them without legal trial. On 25 March a certain Rowland Thomas presented a petition stating that he had been sold to Barbados by Thurloe's order, and demanded redress. Thurloe answered these and similar attacks by pleading reason of state, asserting that the persons complaining were royalist conspirators, and adding that similar conspiracies were even now on foot. But the republican opposition, backed by a number of crypto-royalists, replied by asserting that the supposed plots were pretended to justify arbitrary rule (*ib.* iii. 441, 446, 448, 453, 457, 463; Burton, iv. 254, 301). In the end Thurloe successfully weathered the storm, though some of his subordinate agents were not so fortunate (*ib.* iv. 307, 407). In spite of their pertinacity the parliamentary opposition were beaten on point after point, and the government seemed in a way to be firmly established. But the quarrel which took place between the parliament and the army proved fatal. To the last Thurloe, deserted by the rest of the council, urged Richard not to dissolve parliament, but Richard at length gave way (*Life of John Howe*, 1724, p. 9). 'I am in so much confusion that I can scarce contain myself to write about it,' said Thurloe in announcing Richard's fall to Lockhart (*Clarendon State Papers*, iii. 461). For a few days he carried on the management of foreign affairs, and received with apparent favour the offer of French aid to maintain Richard Cromwell's power; but on the restoration of the Long parliament (7 May 1659) those of his functions which were not entrusted to committees were assigned to Thomas Scott (Guizot, *Richard Cromwell*, i. 367, 376, 385, 389, 393, 401).

After the readmission of the secluded members (21 Feb. 1660) Thurloe, to the great disgust of the royalists, was reappointed secretary of state (27 Feb.) as being the only man whose knowledge of the state both of foreign and home affairs fitted him for the post (*Clarendon State Papers*, iii. 693, 701). The royalists suspected him of desiring to restore Richard, and were anxious to buy him over if possible; but, according to their information, he resisted the restoration of the Stuarts to the last, and did his best to corrupt Monck (*ib.* iii. 693, 749; Thurloe, vii. 855). In April, however, he certainly made overtures to Hyde, promising to forward a restoration, but his sincerity was suspected (Thurloe, vii. 897). Monck so far favoured Thurloe that he recommended him to the borough of Bridgnorth for election to the Convention; but even with this support his candidature was a failure (*ib.* pp. 888, 895).

After the king's return Thurloe escaped better than he could have expected. On 15 May 1660 he was accused of high treason and committed to the custody of the serjeant-at-arms. The particulars of the charge do not appear. On 29 June he was set at liberty with the proviso of attending the secretaries of state 'for the service of the state whenever they should require' (*Commons' Journals*, viii, 26, 117). He was reputed to have said that if he were hanged he had a black book which would hang many that went for cavaliers, but he seems to have made no revelations as to his secret agents (*Hist. MSS. Comm.* 5th Rep. pp. 154–84, 208). After his release he usually lived at Great Milton in Oxfordshire, residing at his chambers in Lincoln's Inn occasionally during term-time. The government desired to avail itself of his minute knowledge of the state of foreign affairs, on which subject he addressed several papers to Clarendon (Thurloe, i. 705, 759, vii. 915). An unsupported tradition asserts that Charles II often solicited him to engage again in the administration of foreign affairs, but without success (*State Papers*, vol. i. p. xix). He died at his chambers at Lincoln's Inn on 21 Feb. 1667–8, and is buried in the chapel there. An account of his last illness, written by his friend Lord Wharton, is printed in 'Notes and Queries,' 8th ser. xi. 83.

Thurloe was twice married: first, to a lady of the family of Peyton, by whom he had two sons who died in infancy; secondly, to Anne, third daughter of Sir John Lytcott of East Moulsey in Surrey, by whom he had four sons and two daughters (*State Papers*, vol. i. p. xix).

A portrait of Thurloe by Stone, belonging to Mr. Charles Polhill, was No. 812 in the National Portrait Exhibition of 1866. Another portrait, ascribed to Dobson, is in the National Portrait Gallery, London. An engraved portrait by Vertue is prefixed to the state papers.

Thurloe's vast correspondence is the chief authority for the history of the Protectorate. His papers, no doubt purposely hidden at the Restoration, were discovered in the reign of William III, 'in a false ceiling in the garrets belonging to secretary Thurloe's chambers, No. xiii near the chapel in Lincoln's Inn, by a clergyman who had borrowed those chambers, during the long vacation, of the owner of them.' The papers were sold to Lord Somers, passed from him to Sir Joseph Jekyll, master of the rolls, on whose decease they were bought by Fletcher Gyles, a bookseller (Preface to the *Thurloe Papers*, p. vi). Richard Rawlinson purchased them from Gyles in 1752, and left them to the Bodleian Library at his death in 1755 (Macray, *Annals of the Bodleian Library*, 1890, p. 236). Before this time, in 1742, Thomas Birch had printed his seven folio volumes of Thurloe state papers, adding to the original collection a certain number of papers from manuscripts in the possession of Lord Shelburne, Lord Hardwicke, and others. The manuscripts in the Bodleian Library, which include a considerable number of unpublished letters, are catalogued as Rawlinson MSS. A. vols. 1 to 73. Others which Birch obtained from Lord Hardwicke are now in the British Museum (Addit. MSS. 4157, 4158). Letters from Thurloe to English agents in Switzerland form part of Robert Vaughan's 'Protectorate of Oliver Cromwell,' 2 vols. 1836.

Talbot

[A memoir of Thurloe serves as introduction to the State Papers. Other authorities are mentioned in the article.]

CHARLES HARDING FIRTH

published 1898

TALBOT Peter
(1620–1680)

Titular archbishop of Dublin, born in 1620, was the second son of Sir William Talbot, and elder brother of Richard Talbot, earl of Tyrconnel. He went to Portugal in 1635, joined the Jesuits there, and completed his theological training at Rome. He lectured in moral theology at Antwerp, and then went again to Portugal. He was in Ireland during part of the civil war, his order being opposed to Giovanni Battista Rinuccini, and inclined to make terms with Ormonde. He seems to have left Ireland with his brother Richard, and they were at all events at Madrid together in the spring of 1653. From Spain Talbot went straight to London, where he dined with the French ambassador, and sought help from him between April and July (*Spicilegium Ossoriense*, ii. 134). He then went to Ireland, 'undergoing the same danger as others,' and arranged for the despatch of agents thence, his eldest brother Robert being among them. Later in the summer the ambassador refused even to say a word in favour of the Irish (*ib.*).

Talbot was at Cologne in November 1654, where he saw Charles II, and was entrusted by him with a message to Nickel, the general of the Jesuits, through whom it was hoped the pope would give help (*Hist. MSS. Comm.* 10th Rep. App. i. 358). He found the king 'extremely well affected, not only towards catholics, but also towards the catholic religion' (*ib.*). Nickel declined active interference, mainly on the ground that it would be too dangerous for the agents of the society in the British Isles (*Cal. of Clarendon State Papers*, ii. 437), and advised Talbot to sound the internuncio at Brussels. The internuncio said he had good reason to doubt Charles's sincerity (*ib.*). Later on Talbot attributed his small credit at Rome to the influence of Massari, dean of Fermo, who had become secretary to the propaganda, and was as violently opposed to the Irish royalists as his master Rinuccini had been (*ib.* iii. 162).

During 1655, 1656, and 1657 Talbot was in Flanders and occupied about Sexby's plot. His movements may be traced in the Clarendon papers. His Franciscan brother, Tom, frequently appears, and there is evidence to show that the friar's character was as bad as Clarendon represented it to be in his 'Life' (*ib*. iii. 116). It has often been said that Peter Talbot received Charles into the Roman catholic church during this period, but of this there is no real evidence. Talbot was in England both before and after Oliver Cromwell's death, and is said to have attended his funeral. He was in close communication with the spy, Joseph Bampfield, to whom he made proposals for setting up the Duke of York against Charles (Ormonde, *Letters*, ii. 232). Hyde tells the story very circumstantially, and vouches for its truth; but Talbot denied it (*Spicilegium Ossoriense*, ii. 178). Scott and Vane distrusted Talbot and had serious thoughts of hanging him, but he was allowed to go to France. Peter Walsh says that Talbot was formally expelled from the Society of Jesus at the instance of Charles II, whose cause he 'endeavoured to betray and utterly ruin in 1659,' and that he knew all the circumstances at the time (*Remonstrance*, p. 529). Talbot, nevertheless, remained on good terms with the society. He was in Spain in July 1659, and until after the negotiations which ended in the treaty of the Pyrenees, 7 Nov. 1659. He seems to have considered himself a kind of king-maker, but there was no visible result from his diplomacy. He was at this time on pretty friendly terms with Ormonde and with Peter Walsh, whom he so strenuously opposed later (*Spicilegium Ossoriense*, ii. 178). Bennet, much to Hyde's disgust, was inclined to trust Talbot, while the jesuits remonstrated against countenance being given him after his repudiation by the society to please Charles II. Hyde frequently warned Bennet against him, and, as the prospect of a restoration became clearer, he pointed out to Ormonde that the Talbots would certainly advance Irish claims as extreme as they had made 'when they were almost in full possession of the kingdom' (*ib*. p. 278). He thought all the brothers were 'in the pack of knaves' (*ib*. p. 64).

From Spain Talbot went to France. He was at Paris in June 1660, when the restoration had been effected, and told Ormonde that he hoped the mediation of the French and Spanish kings would not be required for Irishmen's estates. He seems to have thought it a matter of course that his elder brother and his nephew, Sir Walter Dongan, should be made viscounts (*ib*. ii. 185). He was in London in June 1660, and proposed to live there openly, 'as many more do of my condition who are winked at'; but Ormonde objected (*ib*.), and he professed at this time to be entirely guided by him. Talbot kept very quiet in England, and was in Paris again by the beginning of August. 'All the Irish nation here abroad,' he wrote thence to Ormonde, 'confess how that they owe their preservation to your excellency' (*ib*. p. 187). Talbot was at this time entirely in the Spanish interest, disliked the marriage of Princess Henrietta to the Duke of Orleans, and was strong against the match with Catherine of Braganza. He wished the king to 'send away that Portugal ambassador,' as likely only to embroil him with the house of Austria (*ib*. p. 187). Talbot, nevertheless, became one of the new queen's almoners, but did not hold the place long, for he made an enemy of Lady Castlemaine, and Clarendon had always been hostile. He wrote from Chester in December 1662, no doubt on his way to Ireland, asking for reinstatement (Russell and Prendergast, *Report on Carte Papers*, p. 123). In 1664 he was aiming at ecclesiastical promotion, and sought Peter Walsh's intercession with Ormonde, whom he believed hostile (*Remonstrance*, p. 530). He was in England in 1666, and actively engaged in thwarting Walsh's policy, and in preventing the adoption of the 'Remonstrance' by the clergy generally.

In 1668 Talbot was strongly recommended by Nicholas French, bishop of Ferns, and by the primate, Edmund O'Reilly, for the archbishopric of Dublin, especially on the ground of his opposition to Walsh. He was in London early in 1669, and jubilant at Ormonde's recall from the government of Ireland (*Spicilegium Ossoriense*, i. 470–73). On 9 May he was consecrated archbishop of Dublin at Antwerp by the bishop of Antwerp, assisted by the bishops of Ghent and Ferns. He was in London again in July, and in 1670 was in Ireland, where he was at once engaged in a contest with the new primate, Oliver Plunket, about the old question of precedency as between Armagh and Dublin (*ib*. i. 504). Books were written by both prelates, but the primacy of Armagh has long ceased to be a matter of dispute. Talbot and Plunket were never on very good terms. When Richard Talbot was chosen agent for the dispossessed Irish proprietors, his brother, the archbishop, subscribed 10*l*., but the Ulster clergy refused to raise a like sum. When Plunket established a jesuit school in Dublin, Talbot denounced the enterprise as rash and vainglorious (*Hist. MSS. Comm*. 10th Rep. App. v. 361). Talbot held provincial synods in 1670 and 1671. He used his position to persecute Peter Walsh and all who had adhered to the 'Remonstrance' (Carte, *Ormonde*, ii. 214). He was perhaps already planning the repeal of the act of settlement (King, App. p. 41).

When the bishops and regular clergy of the Roman catholic church were ordered to leave Ireland in 1673, Plunket held his ground; but Talbot went to Paris, where he was in close communication with Coleman and other conspirators. Sir W. Throckmorton thought him the 'lyingest rogue in the world,' and the 'most desperate villain' ever born (*Hist. MSS. Comm*. 13th Rep. App. vi. 58, 70). W. Leybourn called him a 'foolish impertinent busybody' (*ib*. p. 100). He was, however, on good terms with the Duke and Duchess of York, and had a pension of 200*l*. from Charles, who was favourable to his selection for the archbishopric of Dublin. He was back in England early in 1676 (*ib*. 7th Rep. p. 439 *a*), and, being protected by James, was allowed to live unmolested for two years at Poole Hall in Cheshire. Talbot returned to Ireland in May 1678, and was arrested in October for supposed complicity in the 'popish plot.' No evidence was found to implicate him. He had for a long time been afflicted with the stone, to which he succumbed in Newgate prison, Dublin, about 1 June 1680. Shortly before his death he received absolution from his old antagonist, Plunket, who was confined in the same building, and who, according to Bishop Forstall, burst through the reluctant gaolers to reach his side (*Spicilegium Ossoriense*, ii. 256). A portrait of Talbot by John Riley belongs to Lord Talbot de Malahide (*Cat. Third Loan Exhib.* No. 707).

Harris gives a long list of Talbot's writings, most of which he had not seen. None of them are in the Bodleian Library. The following are in Trinity College, Dublin, or the British Museum: 1. 'Erastus Senior, demonstrating that those called bishops in England are no bishops,' London, 1662, 16mo; reprinted London, 1844, 1850, and Sydney, 1848. 2. 'Primatus Dubliniensis,' Lille, 1674, 8vo. 3. 'The Duty and Comfort of Suffering Subjects represented in a letter to the Roman Catholics of Ireland,' Paris, May 1674, 4to (a copy in the British Museum). 4. 'Blakloanæ hæresis ... confutatio,' Ghent, 1675, 4to. 5. 'Scutum inexpugnabile fidei adversus hæresin Blakloanam,' Lyons, 1678, 4to.

The British Museum Catalogue also ascribes to him 'The Polititian's Catechisme ... written by N. N.,' Antwerp, 1658, 8vo.

[Ware's Writers of Ireland, ed. Harris; Brenan's Ecclesiastical Hist. of Ireland; Brady's Episcopal Succession; De Burgo's Hibernia Dominicana; Cardinal Moran's Spicilegium Ossoriense and Life of Oliver Plunket; Carte's Ormonde Letters, and his Life of Ormonde, esp. bk. vii.; Peter Walsh's Hist. of the Remonstrance; Clarendon's Life.]

RICHARD BAGWELL

published 1898

WILMOT John

(1647–1680)

Second Earl of Rochester

Poet and libertine, was the son of Henry Wilmot, first earl of Rochester, by his second wife. He was born at Ditchley in Oxfordshire on 10 April 1647, and on the death of his father on 9 Feb. 1657–8 succeeded to the earldom. He was left with little besides the pretensions to the king's favour bequeathed him by his father's services to Charles after the battle of Worcester. After attending the school at Burford, he was admitted a fellow commoner of Wadham College, Oxford, on 18 Jan. 1659–60. His tutor was Phineas Bury. He showed as an undergraduate a happy turn for English verse, and contributed to the university collections on Charles II's restoration (1660) and on the death of Princess Mary of Orange (1661). He was created M.A. on 9 Sept. 1661, when little more than fourteen. Next year he presented to his college four silver pint pots, which are still preserved. On leaving the university he travelled in France and Italy under the care of Dr. Balfour, who encouraged his love of literature. In 1664 he returned from his travels while in his eighteenth year, and presented himself at Whitehall. In the summer of 1665 he joined as a volunteer Sir Thomas Teddeman on board the Royal Katherine, and took part in the unsuccessful assault on Dutch ships in the Danish harbour of Bergen on 1 Aug. He is said to have behaved with credit. He again served at sea in the summer of the following year in the Channel under Sir Edward Spragge, and distinguished himself by carrying a message in an open boat under the enemy's fire.

Rochester had meanwhile identified himself with the most dissolute set of Charles II's courtiers. He became the intimate associate of George Villiers, second duke of Buckingham; Charles Sackville, earl of Dorset; Sir Charles Sedley, and Henry Savile, and, although their junior by many years, soon excelled all of them in profligacy. Burnet says that he was 'naturally modest till the court corrupted him,' but he fell an unresisting prey to every manner of vicious example. His debaucheries and his riotous frolics were often the outcome of long spells of drunkenness. Towards the end of his life he declared that he was under the influence of drink for five consecutive years. At the same time he cultivated a brilliant faculty for amorous lyrics, obscene rhymes, and mordant satires in verse, and, although he quickly ruined his physical health by his excesses, his intellect retained all its vivacity till death.

The king readily admitted him to the closest intimacy. He was Charles's companion in many of the meanest and most contemptible of the king's amorous adventures, and often acted as a spy upon those which he was not invited to share. But although his obscene conversation and scorn for propriety amused the king, there was no love lost between them, and Rochester's position at court was always precarious. His biting tongue and his practical jokes spared neither the king nor the ministers nor the royal mistresses, and, according to Gramont, he was dismissed in disgrace at least once a year. It was (Pepys wrote) 'to the king's everlasting shame to have so idle a rogue his companion' (Pepys, viii. 231–2). He clearly exerted over Charles an irresistible fascination, and he was usually no sooner dismissed the court than he was recalled. He wrote many 'libels' on the king, which reeked with gross indecency, but his verses included the familiar epigram on the 'sovereign lord' who 'never said a foolish thing and never did a wise one' ('Miscellany Poems' appended to *Miscellaneous Works of Rochester and Roscommon*, 1707, p. 135). He lacked all sense of shame, and rebuffs had no meaning for him. On 16 Feb. 1668–9 he accompanied the king and other courtiers to a dinner at the Dutch ambassador's. Offended by a remark of a fellow-guest, Thomas Killigrew, he boxed his ears in the royal presence. Charles II overlooked the breach of etiquette, and next day walked publicly up and down with Rochester at court to the dismay of seriously minded spectators. When he attempted to steal a kiss from the Duchess of Cleveland as she left her carriage, he was promptly laid on his back by a blow from her hand; but, leaping to his feet, he recited an impromptu compliment.

On one occasion, when bidden to withdraw from court, he took up his residence under an assumed name in the city of London, and, gaining admission to civic society, disclosed and mockingly denounced the degraded debaucheries of the king and the king's friends. Subsequently he set up as a quack doctor under the name of Alexander Bendo, taking lodgings in Tower Street, and having a stall on Tower Hill. He amused himself by dispensing advice and cosmetics among credulous women. A speech which he is said to have delivered in the character of a medical mountebank proves him to have acted his part with much humour and somewhat less freedom than might have been anticipated (prefixed to the 'Poetical Works of Sir Charles Sedley,' 1710; Gramont, *Memoirs*). At another time, according to Saint-Évremond, he and the Duke of Buckingham took an inn on the Newmarket road, and, while pretending to act as tavern-keepers, conspired to corrupt all the respectable women of the neighbourhood. On relinquishing the adventure they joined the king at Newmarket, and were welcomed with delight.

With the many ladies of doubtful reputation who thronged the court Rochester had numerous intrigues, but he showed their waiting women as much attention as themselves. Elizabeth Barry, 'woman to the Lady Shelton of Norfolk,' he took into his keeping. He taught her to act, and introduced her to the stage, where she pursued a highly successful career. Some of his letters to her were published after his death. A daughter by her lived to the age of thirteen.

Despite his libertine exploits, Rochester succeeded in repairing his decaying fortune by a wealthy marriage. The king encouraged him to pay addresses to Elizabeth, daughter of John Malet of Enmere, Somerset, by Elizabeth, daughter of Francis, baron Hawley of Donamore. Pepys described her as 'the great beauty and fortune of the north.' Gramont called her a 'melancholy heiress.' Not unnaturally she rejected Rochester's suit, whereupon he resorted to violence. On 26 May 1665 the lady supped with the king's mistress, Frances Teresa Stuart (or Stewart), and left with her grandfather, Lord Hawley. At Charing Cross Rochester and his agents stopped the horses and forcibly removed her to another coach, which was rapidly driven out of London. A hue and cry was raised, Rochester was followed to Uxbridge, where he was arrested, and, on being brought to London, was committed to the Tower by order of the king (Pepys, *Diary*, ed. Wheatley, iv. 419). Miss Malet was not captured, and Rochester was soon released with a pardon. In 1667 he married the lady, and remained on fairly good terms with her till his death (cf. his letters to her in *Whartoniana*, 1727, vol. ii.).

Rochester's marriage did not alter his relations with the king or the court. In 1666 he was made a gentleman of the king's bedchamber. On 5 Oct. 1667, although still under age, he was summoned to the House of Lords, and in 1674 he received a special mark of royal favour by being appointed keeper of Woodstock Park, with a lodge called 'High Lodge' for residence. On 24 Nov. 1670 Evelyn met him at dinner at the lord treasurer's, and described him as 'a profane wit' (Evelyn, *Diary*, ii. 254). In June 1676 he, (Sir) George Etherege, and three friends engaged in a drunken frolic at Epsom, ending in a skirmish with 'the watch at Epsom,' in the course of which one of the roisterers (Downes) received a fatal wound (*Hist. MSS. Comm.* 7th Rep. p. 467; *Hatton Correspondence*, i. 133).

Meanwhile Rochester played the rôle of a patron of the poets, and showed characteristic fickleness in his treatment of them. He was a shrewd and exacting critic, as his caustic and ill-natured remarks in his clever imitation of the 'Tenth Satire' of Horace, bk. i., and in the 'Session of the Poets' (printed in his works), amply prove. About 1670 he showed many attentions to Dryden, who flattered him extravagantly when dedicating to him his 'Marriage à la Mode' (1673). But Rochester fell out with Dryden's chief patron, John Sheffield, earl of Mulgrave; he is said to have engaged in a duel with Mulgrave and to have shown the white feather. By way of retaliating on Mulgrave, he soon ostentatiously disparaged Dryden and encouraged Dryden's feeble rivals, Elkanah Settle and John Crowne. He contrived to have Settle's tragedy, 'The Empress of Morocco,' acted at Whitehall in 1671, and wrote a prologue, which he spoke himself. Crowne dedicated to him his 'Charles VIII of France' next year, and at the earl's suggestion he wrote the 'Masque of Calisto,' which Rochester recommended for performance at court in 1675. The younger dramatists Nathaniel Lee and Thomas Otway also shared his favours for a time. In 1675 he commended Otway's 'Alcibiades,' and interested the Duke of York in the young author. Otway dedicated to him his 'Titus and Berenice' in 1677; but when the dramatist ventured to make advances to Rochester's mistress, Mrs. Barry the actress, Rochester showed him small mercy. Lee, who dedicated to Rochester 'Nero,' his first piece, commemorated his patronage in his description of Count Rosidore in his 'Princess of Cleves,' which was first produced in November 1681. Another protégé, whom Rochester treated with greater constancy, was John Oldham (1653–1683). Sir George Etherege is said to have drawn from Rochester the character of the libertine Dorimant in the 'Man of Mode, or Sir Fopling Flutter,' which was first acted at the Duke's Theatre in 1676 (Etherege, *Works*, ed. Verity, p. xiv; cf. Beljame, *Le Public et les Hommes de Lettres en Angleterre*, 1660–1744, Paris, 1881, pp. 92 sq.).

In 1679 Rochester's health failed, although he was able to correspond gaily with his friend Henry Savile on the congenial topics of wine and women. During his convalescence in the autumn he, to the surprise of his friends, sought recreation in reading the first part of Gilbert Burnet's 'History of the Reformation.' He invited the author to visit him, and encouraged him to talk of religion and morality. Rochester, in his feeble condition of body, seems to have found Burnet's conversation consolatory. In April 1680 he left London for the High Lodge at Woodstock Park. The journey aggravated his ailments, and he began to recognise that recovery was impossible. He showed signs of penitence for his misspent life. After listening attentively to the pious exhortations of his chaplain, Robert Parsons (1647–1714), he wrote on 25 June to Burnet begging him to come and receive his deathbed repentance. Burnet arrived on 20 July, and remained till the 24th, spending the four days in spiritual discourse. 'I do verily believe,' Burnet wrote, 'he was then so entirely changed that, if he had recovered, he would have made good all his resolutions.' Rochester died two days after Burnet left him, on 26 July. He was buried in the north aisle of Spelsbury church in Oxfordshire, but without any monument or inscribed stone to distinguish his grave (cf. Marshall, *Woodstock*, suppl. 1874, pp. 25–36). His bed is still preserved at High Lodge.

Rochester's will, with a codicil dated 22 June 1680, was proved on 23 Feb. 1680–1. His executors included, besides his wife and mother, whom he entreated to live in amity with one another, Sir Walter St. John, his mother's brother, and Sir Allen Apsley (1616–1683). Settlements had already been made on his wife and son; 4,000l. was left to each of his three daughters; an annuity of 40l. was bestowed on an infant named Elizabeth Clerke; and other sums were bequeathed to servants (*Wills from Doctors' Commons*, Camd. Soc., pp. 139–41).

Sympathetic elegies came from the pens of Mrs. Anne Wharton, Jack How [i.e. John Grubham Howe], Edmund Waller (*Examen Miscellaneum*, 1702), Thomas Flatman, and Oldham. His chaplain, Robert Parsons, preached a funeral sermon which gave a somewhat sensational account of his 'death and repentance,' and attracted general attention when it was published. A more edificatory account of Rochester's conversion, which made even greater sensation than Parsons's sermon, was published by Burnet under the title 'Some Passages of the Life and Death of John, Earl of Rochester,' 1680, 8vo. Like Parsons's volume, it was constantly reissued. A modern reprint, with a preface by Lord Ronald Gower, appeared in 1875. Of the episode of his visit to Rochester's deathbed Burnet wrote: 'Nor was the king displeased with my being sent for by Wilmot, earl of Rochester, when he died. He fancied that he had told me many things of which I might make an ill use; yet he had read the book that I writ concerning him, and spoke well of it' (Burnet, *Own Times*, 1823, ii. 288).

Rochester's widow survived him about thirteen months, dying suddenly of apoplexy, and being buried at Spelsbury on 20 Aug. 1681 (cf. *Hatton Correspondence*, ii. 6). By her he left a son and three daughters. The son, Charles, third and last earl of Rochester of the Wilmot family, baptised at Adderbury on 2 Jan. 1670–1, survived his father scarcely two years, dying on 12 Nov. and being buried on 7 Dec. 1681 by his father's side. The earldom thus became extinct, but it was recreated in favour of Lawrence Hyde on 29 Nov. 1682. Rochester's eldest daughter and heiress, Anne, married, first, Henry Bayntun of Bromham, Wiltshire; and, secondly, Francis Greville, leaving issue by both husbands, and being ancestress by her second husband of the Grevilles, earls of Warwick. Elizabeth, Rochester's second daughter, who is said to have inherited much of her father's wit, married Edward Montagu, third earl of Sandwich, and died at Paris on 2 July 1757. Rochester's third daughter, Malet, married John Vaughan, second viscount Lisburne.

The best portrait of Rochester is that by Sir Peter Lely at Hinchinbrooke, the seat of the Earl of Sandwich. In a portrait at Warwick Castle he is represented crowning a monkey with laurel. A third portrait, by Wissing, is in the National Portrait Gallery. A fourth portrait of Rochester in youth belonged in 1866 to Col. Sir E. S. Prideaux, bart. (*Cat. National Portraits at South Kensington*, 1866). Two engravings of him were made by R. White—one in large size dated 1681, and the other on a smaller scale, which was prefixed to the first edition of Burnet's 'Some Passages,' 1680. There is also an engraved miniature signed 'D[avid] L[oggan] 1671.'

Rochester had as sprightly a lyric gift as any writer of the Restoration. As a satirist he showed much insight and vigour, and, according to Aubrey, Marvell regarded him as the best satirist of his time. But he was something of a plagiarist. His 'Satire against Mankind' owes much to Boileau, and to Cowley his lyrics were often deeply indebted. His literary work was disfigured by his incorrigibly licentious temper. The sentiment in his love songs is transparently artificial whenever it is not offensively obscene. Numerous verses of gross indecency which have been put to his credit in contemporary miscellanies of verse may be from other pens. But there is enough foulness in his fully authenticated poems to give him a title to be remembered as the writer of the filthiest verse in the language. His muse has been compared to a well-favoured child which wilfully and wantonly rolls itself in the mud, and is so besmeared with dirt that the ordinary wayfarer prefers rather to rush hastily by than pause to discover its native charms (Mr. Edmund Gosse in Ward's *English Poets*, ii. 425).

It is said that on his deathbed Rochester directed all his licentious writings to be destroyed, and that after his death his mother ordered a scandalous history of contemporary court intrigues to be burnt (Cibber). Of that work nothing is known, and the order may have been carried out, but much else survives. The bibliography of Rochester's poems is difficult owing to the number of poems that are attributed to him in miscellaneous collections of verse of which he was probably not the author (cf. *Poems on Affairs of State*, passim; *Examen Miscellaneum*, 1702). No complete critical collection of his works has been attempted. His 'Satires against Mankind,' his poem on 'Nothing,' and others of 'his lewd and profane poems' and libels appeared as penny broadsides in single folio sheets at the close of his life—in 1679 and 1680—doubtless surreptitiously. According to the advertisement to Parsons's sermon, 'they were cry'd about the street.' The letter in which he summoned Burnet to his deathbed also appeared as a broadside in 1680.

Within a few months of his death a short series of 'Poems on several Occasions by the Right Honourable the E. of R——' was issued, professedly at 'Antwerpen,' but really in London (1680, 8vo). The volume was reprinted in London in 1685, with some omissions and modifications, as 'Poems on several Occasions, written by a late Person of Honour.' Some additions were made to another issue of 1691, in which are to be found all his authenticated lyrics. This was reissued in 1696.

Meanwhile there appeared an adaptation by Rochester, in poor taste, of Beaumont and Fletcher's tragedy of 'Valentinian,' under the title 'Valentinian: a Tragedy. As 'tis Alter'd by the late Earl of Rochester and Acted at the Theatre Royal. Together with a Preface concerning the Author and his Writings. By one of his Friends' (i.e. Robert Wolseley, eldest son of Sir Charles Wolseley), London, 1685. When the play was produced in 1685, Betterton played Aecius with much success, and Mrs. Barry appeared as Lucina (Downes, *Roscius*, p. 55). Three prologues were printed, one being by Mrs. Behn.

A second play (in heroic couplets) of intolerable foulness has been put to Rochester's discredit. It is entitled 'Sodom,' and was published at Antwerp in 1684 as 'by the E. of R.;' no copy of this edition is known; one is said to have been burnt by Richard Heber. Two manuscripts are extant;

one is in the British Museum (*Harl. MS.* 7312, pp. 118–45, a volume containing many of Rochester's authentic compositions), and the other is in the town library of Hamburg. The piece is improbably said to have been acted at court; it was doubtless designed as a scurrilous attack on Charles II. In a short poem purporting to be addressed to the author of the play (in Rochester's collected poems), he mockingly disclaimed all responsibility for it, and it has been attributed to a young barrister named John Fishbourne, of whom nothing is practically known (Baker, *Biogr. Dram.*). Internal evidence unhappily suggests that Rochester had the chief hand in the production. French adaptations are dated 1744, 1752, and 1767 (cf. Pisanus Fraxi, *Centuria Librorum Absconditorum*, London, privately printed, 1879).

An edition of Rochester's 'Works' which was issued by Tonson in 1714, 12mo, included his letters to Savile and Mrs. * * *, the tragedy of 'Valentinian,' a preface by Rymer, and a pastoral elegy by Oldham. There was a portrait by Van der Gucht. The fourth edition of this is dated 1732. Rochester's 'Remains,' including his 'Satyres,' followed in 1718. Probably the completest edition is the 'Poetical Works of the Earl of Rochester,' 1731–2, 2 vols.

A less perfect collection of his 'Works' included the poems of the Earl of Roscommon. The first edition appeared before 1702. An obscene appendix was called 'The Delights of Venus, now first published.' The second edition is dated 1702; others appeared in 1707 (and in 1714) with Saint-Évremond's memoir of Rochester and an additional poem of outrageous grossness called 'The Discovery.'

A volume containing not only Rochester's poems, but also those of the Earls of Roscommon and Dorset and the Dukes of Devonshire and Buckingham, first appeared in 1731, and was frequently reissued, often with an obscene appendix by various hands, entitled 'The Cabinet of Love,' London, 1739, 2 vols. 12mo; 1757, 1777. A privately printed reissue of excerpts from the 1757 edition appeared in 1884. Rochester's poems, expurgated by George Steevens, appeared in Johnson's collection, and were reprinted in the collections of Anderson, Chalmers, and Park.

Rochester's letters to Savile and to Mrs. Barry were published, with a varied correspondence collected by Tom Brown, in 'Familiar Letters,' 1685, 1697, and 1699, and seven letters—two to his son, four to his wife, and one to the Earl of Lichfield—are in 'Whartoniana,' 1727, ii. 161–8. A few more are appended to 'A New Miscellany of Original Poems,' 1720 (with preface by Anthony Hammond).

[Saint-Évremond's Memoir, prefixed to Rochester's Miscellaneous Works, 1707; Savile Correspondence (Camden Soc.); Cibber's Lives, ii. 269–300; Gramont's Memoirs; Burnet's Own Times; Aubrey's Lives, ed. Andrew Clark; Poems on

Affairs of State, passim; Marshall's Woodstock, with Supplement, 1873–4; Hunter's Chorus Vatum in Brit. Mus. Addit. MS. 24491; Johnson's Lives of the Poets, ed. Cunningham; G. E. C[okayne]'s Complete Peerage. Rochester's death is described for edificatory purposes not only in Parsons's Sermon, 1680, and Burnet's Some Passages, 1680, but also in The Libertine Overthrown, 1680, and in The Two Noble Converts, 1680. His career is depicted in an intentionally unedifying light in J. G. M. Rutherford's Adventures of the Duke of Buckingham, Charles II, and the Earl of Rochester, 1857, and in Singular Life ... of the renowned Earl of Rochester, 1864?]

SIDNEY LEE

published 1900

CUNNINGHAM Alexander

(1654–1737)

Historian, whose identity has often been confused with that of Alexander Cunningham (1655?–1730), was the son of the Rev. Alexander Cunningham, minister of Ettrick, and was, by his own assertion in his will, a relation of General Henry Cunningham, governor of Jamaica, who was a descendant of the Earls of Glencairn. He was educated at Selkirk school and in Holland, and was travelling tutor to James, afterwards Earl of Hyndford, from 1692 to 1695, and by a letter to Carstares in October 1697 appears at that date to have been established as tutor to John, marquis of Lorne, afterwards the great Duke of Argyll and Greenwich, who was then, though only nineteen years of age, colonel of a regiment in the Netherlands. He visited Rome in 1700, after giving up his tutorship to Lord Lorne, and in the following year, probably through the Campbell influence, received an important mission to Paris. He was nominally directed to prepare a trade convention, or sort of commercial treaty, between France and Scotland, but in reality he acted as a spy, and gave William III a full account of the French military preparations. The death of King William lost him his reward at the time, but he continued to be an active agent of the whig party, and visited Hanover with Addison in 1703, where he was graciously received by the Electress Sophia and the future George I of England. He was frequently consulted by the framers of the union between England and Scotland, tried to reconcile Harley and Somers, and was an acquaintance of Sir Isaac Newton; but he seems to have grown weary of political work in a subordinate capacity, and after the overthrow of the whig party in 1710, he returned to his old profession, and in 1711 accompanied Lord Lonsdale to Italy as travelling tutor. The accession of George I brought Cunningham his reward, and he was in 1715 appointed British envoy to Venice, where he remained till 1720, when he retired on a pension. He then returned to London, where he occupied himself in writing his great history in Latin, and where he died in 1737. He was buried in the church of St. Martin-in-the-Fields on 15 May 1737, and by his will, which is quoted in the 'Scots Magazine' for October 1804, left a fortune of 12,000*l*. behind him.

The controversy as to the identity of this Alexander Cunningham with Alexander Cunningham the critic was raised on the publication of his history in 1787, and has given rise to considerable literature. His manuscript history in Latin had come into the possession of the Ven. Thomas Hollingbery, archdeacon of Chichester, a relative of his, who entrusted it to Dr. William Thomson, the author of a continuation of Watson's 'Histories of Philip III and Philip IV of Spain.' Thomson published an elaborate translation of it, in two volumes 4to, in 1787 under the title of 'The History of Great Britain from the Revolution in 1688 to the accession of George I, translated from the Latin manuscript of Alexander Cunningham, Esq., Minister from George I to the Republic of Venice, to which is prefixed an Introduction containing an account of the author and his writings by William Thomson, LL.D.' The history is very valuable, and is an authority of the first order for many of the events of which it relates, but it is naturally written with a strong whig tendency and a disposition to eulogise the Duke of Argyll, and is further remarkable for the author's evident dislike to Bishop Burnet. Dr. Thomson, in a long and elaborate argument, tried to prove that his author was the same person as Alexander Cunningham the critic; he asserted that it was very unlikely there should have been two Alexander Cunninghams, both tutors to whig Scotch noblemen, both famous chess-players, and both good scholars, as the one's edition of Horace and the other's manuscript history abundantly proved. His view had many opponents and also many warm supporters, including Dr. Parr and David Irving, the author of the 'Life of Ruddiman,' and the latter's positiveness, and his declaration that every one who did not believe in the identity of the two Cunninghams was a fool, roused an anonymous critic to examine the wills preserved at Doctors' Commons, and thus in a very simple fashion to demolish Dr. Thomson's ingenious theory. The result of his investigations was published in a letter, signed 'Crito,' to the 'Scots Magazine' in October 1804, in which he gave the burial entry, and extracts from the will, of Alexander Cunningham the historian, dated 1737, and also proved the death of Alexander Cunningham the critic at the Hague in 1730. Another anonymous writer, who signs himself a 'Friend to Accuracy,' and evidently did not know of 'Crito's' letter, also demolishes the theory of identity in the 'Gentleman's Magazine' for August 1818, where he shows, from an anonymous book 'On the Present State of Holland' in 1743, that the critic died in 1730, and from his own independent inquiries he too shows that the historian died in 1737. The whole controversy is a curious one, and does not gain much additional light from Peacock's 'English-speaking Students who have graduated at Leyden University,' published by the Index Society in 1883, which contains two entries of the taking of degrees by Alexander Cunningham on 4 Sept. 1724, and by Alexander Cunningham on 25 Sept. 1709; these two Cunninghams may be the critic and historian, but if so, the degrees were probably honorary.

[Scots Mag. October 1804; Gent. Mag. August 1818; Thomson's edition of Cunningham's History; Chambers's Dict. of Eminent Scotsmen.]

HENRY MORSE STEPHENS

published 1888

SPEKE Hugh

(1656–1724?)

Political agitator, born in 1656, was the second son of George Speke of White Lackington, near Ilminster, a descendant of the ancient Yorkshire family of Le Espek or Espec, a branch of which migrated from the north to Somerset during the fifteenth century. His mother was Mary, daughter of Sir Robert Pye, knt.

The father, George Speke d. 1690, gave some pecuniary aid to Prince Rupert at Bridgwater, upon the surrender of which town to Fairfax in July 1645 he was seized as a hostage and his goods sequestrated. Before the end of 1645 he was transferred from the Tower to the Gatehouse, where he pleaded compulsion as his motive for joining the king's party, and poverty as a reason for the reduction of his fine. His income, he alleged, was but 540*l.* a year, and that was heavily encumbered. He eventually compounded for 2,390*l.*, and was released upon payment of that sum in May 1646. He lived in retirement until, in August 1679, he was chosen M.P. for the county of Somerset, at the same time that his third son John was returned for Ilchester. Parting company with his old allies—the Courtenays, the Seymours, and the Portmans—he now threw himself into the politics of the country party, joined the Green Ribbon Club with a son ('Mr. Speake junior'), and voted for the Exclusion Bill of 1680. He rendered himself still

91

further obnoxious to the court by extending a brilliant reception to Monmouth at White Lackington, during his progress in November 1681, and he was alleged to have said that he would have forty thousand men to assist the cause of Monmouth should the need arise. A heavy fine was imposed upon him for having, it was alleged, created a riot in rescuing his son-in-law, (Sir) John Trenchard, from the custody of a messenger in June 1685. In May 1689 he petitioned in vain for the remission of the fine. He died soon after the revolution. From his younger brother, William, was descended the explorer, John Hanning Speke.

Hugh Speke matriculated at Oxford from St. John's College on 1 July 1672, but took no degree: eight years later he was entered at Lincoln's Inn. Soon afterwards he and his brother Charles joined the Green Ribbon Club. Hugh first became prominent in 1683, when he inspired and partly wrote 'An Enquiry into and Detection of the Barbarous Murder of the Late Earl of Essex, or a Vindication of that noble Person from the Guile and Infamy of having destroy'd Himself'. The substance of this diffuse pamphlet, which was printed at a private press controlled, if not actually owned, by Speke, he summarised in a letter to his friend, Sir Robert Atkyns, in which it was not obscurely hinted that the Earl of Essex had been assassinated by the partisans of the Duke of York. With a view to disparaging the government and earning credit for themselves as the revealers of yet another plot, Speke and his ally, Laurence Braddon, intrigued to disperse as many copies as possible of this 'Letter,' and at the same time, if possible, to acquire fresh materials with which to discredit James and his adherents. In the autumn of 1683 Braddon was arrested at Bradford in Wiltshire, 'for spreading false news,' and a copy of Speke's 'Letter' was found on his person.

For his complicity in this affair Speke was placed in the custody of a messenger, Thomas Saywell, and detained eighteen weeks before he was admitted to bail. A few days after his release he was re-arrested in his barrister's gown at the gate of Westminster Hall, in an action of *scandalum magnatum* at the suit of the Duke of York, and imprisoned in the Gatehouse. The charge was altered to one of sedition, which was preferred by the attorney-general before Jeffreys in the king's bench on 7 Feb. 1683. Jeffreys admonished the prisoner with gentleness, in the hope that he would still be reclaimed from the 'presbyterian party.' He was sentenced to pay 1,000*l.*, and to find security for his good behaviour. Declining to pay the fine, he spent upwards of three years in the king's bench prison. His imprisonment probably saved his life. His father and brother-in-law, (Sir) John Trenchard, had to take to flight in order to escape arrest upon Monmouth's landing at Lyme Regis, and his younger brother, Charles, who had joined Monmouth, was tried before Jeffreys at Wells, and executed at Ilminster, where he was hanged from a large tree in the market-place in July 1685 (cf. *Western Martyrology*, ed. 1873, p. 228).

During his confinement, Speke acquired a printing-press which he kept working within the rules of the king's bench. He made the acquaintance of Samuel Johnson, the divine, and other disaffected persons; and from his press was issued Johnson's notable 'Address to all the English Protestants in the present Army' (1686). Ultimately, upon the payment of 5,000l. to the exchequer as a pledge of his own and his family's good behaviour, Speke was set at liberty in 1687. The sum was devoted to strengthening the fortifications of Portsmouth Harbour. Upon his release, Speke left London for Exeter, where he was chosen counsel to the municipality. When, however, towards the end of August 1688, rumours began to be circulated as to the possibility of another western invasion, Speke thought it more politic to return to London. He made his way to Whitehall, and 'diligently observed the countenances of the courtiers.' Some of the latter appear to have suggested to the king the important use that might be made of a west-countryman, like Speke, who had suffered injury from the government, in the event of the Prince of Orange's landing. The king actually saw Speke, who was profuse in his offers of service, at Chiffinch's lodgings. Eventually, James offered him 10,000l. if he would introduce himself as a spy into the camp of the prince. To win the king's confidence he declined the reward, set out on 7 Nov. 1688, with three passes signed by Lord Feversham 'for all hours, times, and seasons, without interruption or denial'; proceeded to Exeter, gave his passes to Bentinck, who made 'no little use of them,' obtained the confidence of the Prince of Orange, to whom he was devoted 'from principle,' and wrote letters at the prince's dictation to the king. These letters were adroitly calculated to work upon James's fears and excite his distrust of those around him by pretending that his chief officers only waited the opportunity to desert him. The desertion of Prince George of Denmark, and of the Duke of Ormonde at Andover, served to confirm the king in the high opinion that he formed at this juncture of Speke's discernment.

About the middle of December, when the London mob were beginning to rifle the houses of the catholics in a pretended search for arms, and when the secret presses were working day and night, a remarkable document was found one morning by a whig bookseller under his shop door. The document professed to be a supplemental declaration under the hand and seal of the Prince of Orange. In it good protestants were adjured, as they valued all that was dear to them, and commanded under pain of the prince's highest displeasure, to seize, disarm, and imprison their catholic neighbours. Injunctions so congenial to the populace were soon printed and widely circulated, and had no little effect in inflaming the rabble against the objects of their dislike. Some of the results were seen on the night of 21 Dec., when the Spanish ambassador's house and most of the Roman catholic chapels in London were looted. William of course disclaimed all responsibility for the spurious proclamation. Ferguson and others were suspected; but it was not until 1709, in his 'Memoirs of the most Remarkable Passages and Transactions of the Revolution' (Dublin, 16mo, and 8vo abbreviated), that, in answer to a libel called 'A Diary of Several Reports' (1704), Speke proudly avowed that he was responsible not only for the 'Third Declaration,' as it was called, but also for the circulation of the alarming rumours which brought about the shameful panic known as the 'Irish night.' The declaration, dated 'Sherburn Castle, 28 Nov. 1688' (O.S.), is printed in full in Speke's pamphlet, which he dedicated to Thomas, earl of Wharton. He subsequently modified his narrative, and called it 'The Secret History of the Happy Revolution in 1688 ... humbly dedicated to his most Gracious Majesty King George by the principal Transactor in it [i.e. Hugh Speke],' London, 1715, 8vo. In this pamphlet the spurious 'declaration,' the 'Irish conspiracy,' and James's flight are 'all unfolded and set in the clearest light by the only person who was the author and manager of them.' The dedication was equivalent to an appeal to the new king to reward his eminent services.

He had made a similar appeal to Anne upon her accession, claiming as a basis of a suitable recognition that the fine of 5,000*l*. which he had paid in 1687 should be refunded. Godolphin reported on his petition to the privy council in May 1703, and Speke, as 'an object of compassion,' was allowed 100*l*. He then went to Ireland, and seems to have been promised some employment by Harley. He wrote several letters to Ormonde from Dublin during 1710–11 (*Hist. MSS. Comm.* 7th Rep. App. pp. 782, 813).

Though an egregious liar (as where he states that his father had paid 10,000*l*. for his composition), there is no valid reason for disputing Speke's admission that, out of hatred for James II, he had deceived him by false reports, or that he forged the criminal 'Declaration.' The probability is that he told only half the truth, and that, with that passion for intrigue which the popish plot had engendered among men of his stamp, he was guilty of other manœuvres even more treacherous and ambiguous in character than any he revealed. It is tolerably clear that in some way he became quite discredited during the reign of William, from whom, in response to the most extravagant claims, it appears that Speke never received more than a few doles of money amounting in all to no more than 500*l*. (see his begging letter to Thomas Pelham, dated 17 Oct. 1698, in *Addit. MS.* 33084, f. 131); and it is highly significant that his pamphlets were not put forth until death had removed a number of chief actors in the revolution from the scene. George I seems to have paid no regard to his appeal, though the writer had it translated into French for the king's benefit. In March 1719 Speke was residing at High Wycombe with a Dr. Lluellyn, on whose behalf he wrote a letter to Sir Hans Sloane. He probably died between that date and 1725.

[Foster's Alumni Oxon. 1500–1714; Burke's Landed Gentry; Roberts's Life of Monmouth, passim; Burnet's Own Time; Eachard's Hist. of England, p. 1131; Mackintosh's Hist. of the Revolution; Lingard's Hist. vol. x.; Macaulay's Hist.; Luttrell's Brief Hist. Relation, vol. i. Ellis Correspondence, i. 194, ii. 356; Sir George Sitwell's The First Whig, pp. 197, 199, 200; Notes and Queries, 1st ser. xii. 403; Secret Consults, 137, 140; Speke's Works in Brit. Mus. Library, and a copy of his 'Secret History' in the London Library, containing a manuscript note in Speke's own hand.]

THOMAS SECCOMBE

published 1897

PLUNKET John

(1664–1738)

Jacobite agent, born in Dublin in 1664, was educated at the Jesuits' College at Vienna. He was a Roman catholic layman, and he was sometimes known under the alias of Rogers. He was for over twenty years in the service of the leading Jacobites, either as a spy or diplomatic agent, and his wide personal acquaintance with the statesmen of many countries illustrated the facility with which Jacobite agents approached men of the highest position. By generals and divines, by English, French, and Dutch ministers, he was received with politeness, plied with anxious inquiries about the health of James, and dismissed with promises of support, not perhaps sincere, but always fervent. The hopes of the Jacobites were naturally raised by the rout of the whigs in England in 1710. A number of the party were convinced that Harley was at heart a Jacobite, and that the negotiations which commenced with France in the autumn of 1711 were a preliminary to secret negotiations with the Pretender. Plunket therefore thought to improve the position of his employers by revealing to the tory ministry fictitious whig machinations against the success of the peace. Prince Eugène came to England in January 1712, and excited much uneasiness by his frequent conferences held at Leicester House with Marlborough, the imperial envoy (Gallas), the leading Hanoverians, and the whig opponents of the peace. Accordingly, in March 1712, Plunket sent to

95

Harley, now Earl of Oxford, two forged letters purporting to have been written by Eugène, and sent to Count Zinzendorf, the imperial ambassador at The Hague, for transmission to Vienna. According to these letters, outrages in London and the assassination of the tory chiefs were to be the means employed to upset the government and frustrate the peace. The forged letters did not for a moment deceive Oxford. They created, however, strong prejudice against Prince Eugène in influential quarters in England, and were skilfully used by St. John to convince Torcy and the French negotiators, newly assembled at Utrecht, of the danger the ministry ran in trying to conclude peace against the wishes of a powerful faction.

Meanwhile Plunket, disgusted by the incredulity of Oxford, brought his pretended revelations before Lord-keeper Harcourt and the Duke of Buckinghamshire, by whom they were submitted to the privy council. On 3 April Plunket was summoned, and, in answer to much questioning, stated that he had derived his information through a clerk in Zinzendorf's suite at The Hague. He was dismissed with a half-contemptuous direction to go over to Holland and bring back his friend. Though he must have known the facts, Swift treats the libels as substantially true in his flagrantly partisan 'Four closing Years of Queen Anne,' while Macpherson prints them, and makes similar deductions, in his 'Original Papers.' After a further period of foreign travel and intrigue, during which he made more than one visit to Rome and had several interviews with the Pretender, Plunket returned to England in 1718, and five years later was charged with complicity in Layer's plot for seizing the Tower of London. He was arrested by special warrant in January 1723, as he was about to leave his lodgings in Lambeth. He was proved to have written letters to Middleton, Dillon, and other prominent Jacobites, urging them to secure the co-operation of the regent of France at any price, and promising a wide support in England; there was also evidence that he had endeavoured to corrupt some sergeants in the British army. The bill for inflicting certain pains and penalties upon John Plunket was read in the House of Commons a second time on 28 March 1723. Plunket made no defence. Subsequently, before the House of Lords, he tried to establish that he was a person of no consideration in Jacobite counsels, a contention which derived support from his repellently ugly appearance, but was conclusively disproved by his correspondence. Eventually Plunket was confined as a state prisoner in the Tower until July 1738, when 'at the public expense he was removed into private lodgings and cut for the stone by Mr. Cheselden'. The operation failed owing to Plunket's advanced age, and he died in James Street, near Red Lion Street, in the following August. He was buried in the churchyard of St. Pancras. John is to be carefully distinguished from his cousin, Matthew Plunket, 'serjeant of invalids,' a man of the lowest character, who gave damning evidence against his old crony, Christopher Layer.

[Hist. Reg. 1723 passim, 1738 p. 32; Wyon's Hist. of the Reign of Queen Anne, ii. 368; Stanhope's Hist. of Engl. 1839, i. 75; Coxe's Life of Marlborough, 1848, iii. 289; Macpherson's Original Papers, ii. 284; Boyer's Annals, passim; Le-grelle's Succession d'Espagne, v. 600–40; Dumont's Lettres Historiques, 1710; Mémoires de Torcy, 1757, ii. 271–4; Swift's Four closing Years of Queen Anne; Bolingbroke's Works, 1798, vol. v.; Doran's Jacobite London; Howell's State Trials, vol. xvi.; Cobbett's Parl. Hist. viii. 54.]

THOMAS SECCOMBE

published 1895

PATTEN Robert

(*fl.* 1715)

Historian of the Jacobite rebellion of 1715, was at one time curate at Penrith, Cumberland, but when the rising of 1715 took place was in a similar capacity at Allendale in Northumberland. He led thence a party of keelmen to join the insurgents, and in crossing Rothbury Common met a number of Scotsmen on their way home to enlist for 'King James,' i.e. the Old Pretender. He persuaded them to accompany him. On his arrival at Wooler he was warmly welcomed by General Thomas Forster and James Ratcliffe, third earl of Derwentwater, and was forthwith appointed the general's own chaplain. Marching with the expedition to Kelso, where the main body of the Jacobites joined them, he preached to the whole army a sermon, specially intended to inspirit them for their enterprise, from Deut. xxi. 17: 'The right of the first-born is his.'

Besides officiating as chaplain to the Jacobite forces, he took an active part in military service. When the expedition reached Penrith, he was, on account of his local knowledge, engaged in an attempt to intercept William Nicolson, bishop of Carlisle, at his residence, Rose Castle. He also acted at times as a spy. At Preston in Lancashire, where on 13 Nov. 1715 the insurgents were defeated, Patten had his horse shot under him. He was there made prisoner, and carried under a close guard to London. In the leisure of his confinement he made up his mind to turn king's evidence, and his offer was accepted (cf. Doran, *Jacobite London*, i. 118). It was in gratitude for his preservation that in the interests of King George he wrote his history. It was published in two editions in the same year (1717), the second being enlarged. It is entitled 'A History of the late Rebellion, with Original Papers and the Characters of the principal Noblemen and Gentlemen concerned in it; by the Rev. Mr. Robert Patten, formerly Chaplain to Mr. Forster.' Two subsequent editions, the third and fourth, were published in 1745. Patten figures as 'Creeping Bob' in Sir Walter Besant's 'Dorothy Forster,' an historical novel of the Northumbrian share in the rising.

[Patten's History as above; Lancashire Memorials, Chetham Soc.]

HENRY PATON

published 1895

BRADSTREET Dudley

(1711–1763)

Adventurer, was born in 1711 in Tipperary, where his father had obtained considerable property under the Cromwellian grants, which, however, was much reduced by debts. Dudley, his youngest son, was left in his early years in charge of a foster father in Tipperary. While a youth he became a trooper, but soon quitted the army and traded unsuccessfully as a linen merchant, and subsequently as a brewer. For several years, in Ireland and England, Bradstreet led an erratic life, occupied mainly in pecuniary projects. During the rising of 1745, Bradstreet was employed by government officials to act as a spy among suspected persons. He was also engaged and equipped by the Dukes of Newcastle and Cumberland to furnish them with information on the movements of Prince Charles Edward and his army. Bradstreet assumed the character of a devoted adherent to the Stuart cause, and, under the name of 'Captain Oliver Williams,' obtained access to the prince and his council at Derby. There he acted successfully as a spy for the Duke of Cumberland, and, without being suspected by the Jacobites, continued on good terms with them, and took his leave as a friend when they commenced their return march to Scotland. Bradstreet's notices of Prince Charles and his associates are graphic. He describes circumstantially the executions, in August 1746, of the Earl of Kilmarnock and Lord Balmerino, at which he states he was present. Although Bradstreet's services as a secret agent were admitted by the government officials, he was unable to obtain from them either money or a commission in the army, which he considered had been promised to him. He, however, succeeded in bringing his case under the notice of the king, from whom he consequently received the sum of one hundred and twenty pounds. Bradstreet subsequently subsisted for a time on the results of schemes, his success in which he ascribed to the 'superstition' of the English people, and 'their credulity and faith in wondrous things.' The last of his devices at London appears to have been that styled the 'bottle conjurer,' which, with the assistance of several confederates, he carried out with great gains in January 1747–8. On his adventures in connection with the affair Bradstreet wrote a play, in five acts, styled 'The Magician, or the Bottle Conjurer,' which he states was revised for him by some of the best judges and actors in England, including Mrs. Woffington, who gave him 'the best advice she could about it.' This play was four times performed with great success at London, but on the fifth night, when Bradstreet was to have taken the part of 'Spy,' the principal character, it was suppressed by the magistrates of Westminster. 'The Bottle Conjurer' was printed by Bradstreet with his 'Life.' After other adventures, Bradstreet returned to Ireland, where he owned a small property in land. He attempted unsuccessfully to carry on trade as a brewer in Westmeath, and became involved in contests with officials of the excise. To raise funds, he printed an account of his life and adventures. The work is written with vivacity and descriptive power. Bradstreet died at Multifarnham, Westmeath, in 1763. His brother, Simon Bradstreet, was called to the bar in Ireland in 1758, created a baronet in 1759, and died in 1762. Sir Samuel Bradstreet, third baronet, was a younger brother of Sir Simon, the first baronet's son and heir.

[The Life and Uncommon Adventures of Captain Dudley Bradstreet, 1755; Dublin Journal, 1763; Memoirs of H. Grattan, 1839.]

JOHN THOMAS GILBERT

published 1885

MACDONALD Flora

(1722–1790)

Jacobite heroine, born in 1722, was daughter of Ranald Macdonald, tacksman, or farmer, of Milton in South Uist, an island of the Hebrides, by Marion, daughter of the Rev. Angus Macdonald, minister first of the island of Gigha, and afterwards of South Uist. She lost her father in early infancy, and when only six years old she was deprived of the care of her mother, who was abducted and married by Hugh Macdonald of Armadale, Skye. The child remained at Milton with her brother Angus till her thirteenth year, when, in order to receive some instruction from the family governess, she was taken into the mansion of the Clanranalds, of whom her own family were cadets not very distantly related. She manifested special musical tastes, becoming an accomplished player on the spinet, and delighting in singing Gaelic songs. In 1739 she was invited by Margaret, wife of Sir Alexander Macdonald of the Isles, to Monkstadt in Skye, and shortly afterwards it was arranged that she should accompany the family to Edinburgh to finish her education there. She spent some time at a boarding-school in the Old Stamp office, close to High Street, and on completing her studies she continued chiefly to reside until 1745 with Sir Alexander and Lady Macdonald in Edinburgh. In the summer of 1745 they returned to Skye.

While Flora was on a visit to the Clanranalds in Benbecula, the Hebridean island, Prince Charles Edward arrived there after the disaster at Culloden in 1746. Captain O'Niel, his companion, proposed to Flora to help in enabling the prince to escape to Skye, and she consented with some reluctance on learning that the prince would disguise himself in woman's dress (Letter of the Duke of Argyll in *Hist. MSS. Commission*, 11th Rep. pt. iv. p. 362). She afterwards informed Argyll that her sole motive was to succour one in distress, and told Frederick, prince of Wales, that she would have similarly befriended him had he been in the same plight; but it cannot be doubted that her political sympathies were with the Pretender. No one was permitted to leave the island except by especial permission. Flora, therefore, on pretence of going to visit her mother, obtained from her stepfather, Captain Hugh Macdonald, who was in charge of the militia, a passport for herself, her man-servant, 'an Irish spinning maid, Betty Burke,' and a crew of six men. Betty Burke was the Pretender, and it is clear that Captain Macdonald was aware of the fact (Alexander Macgregor, *Life of Flora Macdonald*, p. 77). At ten o'clock on the evening of 27 June the party set sail across the Minch to Skye. The presence of a large party of the Macleod militia on the beach near Waternish prevented their landing there, and amid a shower of bullets they held out to sea, disembarking early in the forenoon at Kilbride, near Monkstadt. Leaving the prince and her servant to take shelter in a small cave, she proceeded to Monkstadt. Sir Alexander Macdonald was with the Duke of Cumberland at Fort Augustus, but Lady Macdonald was at home, and among her guests was Captain John Macleod, in command of the militia. Macleod closely questioned Flora regarding the cause of her visit to Skye, and her knowledge of the prince's movements, but her self-possession completely diverted his suspicions. To Lady Macdonald, whom she knew to sympathise with the Jacobite cause, she confided her secret. Lady Macdonald agreed to aid in the prince's escape. He was sent for the night to the factor's house at Kingsburgh, Flora and her man-servant accompanying him. Next day they set out for Portree, whence a boat conveyed him to Raasay. On parting with her at Portree, the prince presented her with his portrait in a golden locket.

Unluckily the boatmen were permitted to return to Benbecula, and being arrested there, they divulged the secret of the prince's escape. As soon as she returned to her brother's house at Milton, Flora consequently received a summons to appear before Captain Macleod, and obeyed it. She declined the advice of friends to disregard the message, and take refuge in the mountain fastnesses. After being permitted to pay a parting visit to her mother in Skye, she was conveyed to London, where after a short imprisonment in the Tower she was handed over to the custody of a messenger. At the time she was thus described: 'She is a young lady about twenty, a graceful person, a good complexion, and regular features. She has a peculiar sweetness mixed with majesty in her countenance; her deportment is rather graver than is becoming her years; even under her confinement she betrays nothing of sullenness or discontent, and all her actions bespeak a mind full of conscious innocence, and incapable of being ruffled by the common accidents of life' (*Some Particulars of the Life, Family, and Character of Miss Florence McDonald, now in Custody of one of his Majesty's Messengers in London*, 1747). On receiving her liberty by the Act of Indemnity in 1747, she stayed for some time in the house of Lady Primrose, where she was visited by many persons of distinction. Before leaving London she was also presented with 1,500*l*. (printed copies of letters and receipts in a volume of pamphlets in the library of the British Museum). On her return to Scotland she was entertained at Monkstadt at a banquet, to which the principal families in Skye were invited.

On 6 Nov. 1750 Flora married Allan Macdonald the younger of Kingsburgh. At first they resided at the farm of Flodigarry; but on the death of her father-in-law they went in 1772 to Kingsburgh. Here she was visited in 1773 by Dr. Johnson, who describes her as 'a woman of soft features, gentle manners, and elegant presence.' In August of the following year she and her family emigrated to North Carolina. On the outbreak of the civil war her husband was appointed brigadier-general by the governor, and she accompanied him in his campaigns till his capture at Morres Creek. He was retained a prisoner in Halifax, Virginia, and by his advice she in 1779 returned to Scotland. The ship was unsuccessfully attacked by a French privateer. During the encounter she bravely remained on deck, and had an arm broken. For some time she resided at Milton, where her brother built her a cottage; but on the return of her husband they again settled at Kingsburgh, where she died on 5 March 1790. She was wrapped in the sheet in which the prince and Dr. Johnson had slept at Kingsburgh, and was buried in the churchyard of Kilmuir. The original marble slab erected on her grave was chipped to pieces and carried off, but subsequently an obelisk was erected by subscription to her memory. She had five sons: Charles, captain of the queen's rangers; Alexander and Ranald, naval officers, who went down with the Ville de Paris, De Grasse's flagship, which foundered on its way home to England on 12 April 1782; James of Flodigarry, and John (1759–1831). Of her daughters, Anne married Alexander Macleod of Lochbay, Skye, and Frances, Lord Donald Macleod. Two children died young.

A portrait of Flora Macdonald by Allan Ramsay is in the Bodleian Library of Oxford, and was engraved by MacArdell; another painting by W. Robertson is in the possession of Lord Donington; a third is in the townhall at Inverness.

[Particulars of Flora Macdonald's adventures with Prince Charles Edward were given to Dr. Johnson, and written down by Boswell. The account of the Wanderings of Prince Charles Edward and Flora Macdonald, from the original manuscript of one of their attendants, 1839, is grandiloquent and affected. Another account was published in the New Monthly Mag. 1840. The so-called autobiography by her granddaughter, 1870, is of little value. An Account of the Young Pretender's Escape is also printed in Appendix to Lockhart Papers, ii. 544–7. A Life by Alexander Macgregor (afterwards Mackenzie) appeared in 1882, and Flora Macdonald in Uist by W. Jolly in 1886. See also Ewald's Life and Times of Charles Edward, 1886, and Cat. Stuart Exhibition, 1889, pp. 107, 113–15.]

THOMAS FINLAYSON HENDERSON

published 1893

MACDONELL Alastair Ruadh, known as 'Pickle The Spy'

(1725?–1761)

Thirteenth chief of Glengarry, born about 1725, was eldest son of John, twelfth chief, by the only daughter of Colin Mackenzie of Hilton. While yet a mere youth he was sent in 1738 to France, where in 1743 he joined Lord Drummond's regiment of Royal Scots Guards. In March 1744 he was with the Earl Marischal, and intended starting with the futile expedition of that year. Having in the following year been sent to Scotland to give information in connection with certain jacobite disputes, he was in May despatched by the highland chiefs to France to testify to Charles their allegiance to his cause, but at the same time to warn him against an attempt to land in Scotland unless strongly backed by foreign assistance.

His mission, however, was of no avail; for Charles, before Macdonell's arrival in France, had already set sail on his rash adventure. Macdonell resolved to take part in it, but while returning to Scotland with a detachment of Drummond's guards he was captured on 25 Nov. 1745 by H.M.S. Sheerness (*London Gazette*, 26–9 Nov., quoted in Blaikie's *Itinerary of Prince Charles Edward*, Scottish Historical Society, 1897, p. 111), and sent to the Tower of London, where he was detained until July 1747. In December 1749 he helped himself to the jacobite treasure concealed at Loch Arkaig. Already or shortly afterwards he had further resolved on the betrayal of the jacobite cause, and having introduced himself to Henry Pelham, he, as Mr. Lang has elaborately and beyond cavil demonstrated, became a hired spy on Prince Charles and the jacobites, corresponding with the government under the pseudonym of 'Pickle.'

Perhaps it has been insufficiently borne in mind that Macdonell may have all along cherished resentment against the prince on account of the clan's removal to the left wing at Culloden, where it practically deserted the prince's cause by refusing to strike a blow on his behalf. True the clan gave the prince shelter during his wanderings, but Macdonell himself may on account of the treatment of the clan, or for some other reason, have cherished a personal grudge against the prince. In any case he was probably clever enough to recognise that the prince himself had become impossible; and his interest corresponding with his convictions, he may have persuaded himself that he was really saving his clan and the highlands generally from much needless suffering by frustrating the prince's madcap schemes. If, however, as is likely, his purpose was mainly selfish, it was unsuccessful, for the death of Pelham in 1754 blighted his main hopes of reward. On the death of his father in September of the same year, he became chief of the clan and succeeded to his father's impoverished fortunes. He died in 1761 in a hut adjoining his ruined castle, and having no issue was succeeded in the chieftaincy by his nephew Duncan, son of his brother Æneas, who was slain at Falkirk.

During the '45 the command of the Glengarry clan was, on account of the imprisonment of the chief, and of Alastair the chief's eldest son, entrusted to the second son, Æneas; but in the absence of Æneas in the highlands to procure reinforcements, the clan was, while on the march southwards to Derby, under the charge of Colonel Donald Macdonald of Lochgarry; and after the death of Æneas at Falkirk, Lochgarry accompanied the prince in his later wanderings and escaped with him to France, whence he wrote to his chief a 'memorial' detailing the clan's achievements during the rebellion and its loyal conduct to the prince while a fugitive in its fastnesses (printed in Blaikie's *Itinerary of Prince Charles Edward*, pp. 111–126.

[Mackenzie's History of the Macdonalds; Andrew Lang's Pickle the Spy, 1897, and Companions of Pickle, 1898, with the authorities therein mentioned; Blaikie's Itinerary of Prince Charles Edward.]

THOMAS FINLAYSON HENDERSON

published 1901

WRIGHT Patience

(1725–1786)

Mrs.

Wax modeller, was born of quaker parents named Lovell at Bordentown, New Jersey, North America, in 1725. In 1748 she married Joseph Wright, also of Bordentown, and in 1769 was left a widow with a son and two daughters. Having made a reputation in the colony by her portraits in wax, she removed to England in 1772 and settled in London, where she became celebrated as the 'Promethean modeller.' Her residence was in Cockspur Street, Haymarket, and there she arranged an exhibition of her works, comprising life-sized figures and busts of contemporary notabilities and historical groups, which was superior to anything of the kind previously seen. She modelled for Westminster Abbey the effigy of Lord Chatham, which is still preserved there. During the American war of independence Mrs. Wright, who was a woman of remarkable intelligence and conversational powers, acted successfully as a spy on behalf of Benjamin Franklin, with whom she regularly corresponded. Her house was much resorted to by artists, especially Benjamin West and John Hoppner, the latter of whom married her second daughter Phœbe. In 1781 Mrs. Wright paid a visit to Paris, and returned only shortly before her death, which took place in London on 23 March 1786. An engraving of Mrs. Wright accompanies a notice of her in the 'London Magazine' of 1775.

Joseph Wright 1756–1793, only son of Patience Wright, accompanied his mother to England, and, with the assistance of West and Hoppner, became a portrait-painter. In 1780 he exhibited a portrait of his mother at the Royal Academy, and at about the same time he painted a portrait of the Prince of Wales. In 1782 he returned to America, where he practised both painting and wax-modelling; Washington sat to him several times. He was appointed the first draughtsman and die-sinker to the mint at Philadelphia, and died in 1793.

[Dunlap's Hist. of the Arts of Design in the United States, 1834; London Mag. 1775, p. 555; Redgrave's Dict. of Artists.]

FREEMAN MARIUS O'DONOGHUE

published 1900

O'LEARY Arthur
(1729–1802)

Irish priest and politician, was born in 1729 at Acres, a townland in the parish of Fanlobbus, near Dunmanway, co. Cork, his parents being of the peasant class. Having acquired some knowledge of classical literature, he went to a monastery of Capuchin friars at St. Malo in Brittany. There he entered the Capuchin order, and was ordained priest. In the course of the war between England and France which commenced in 1756 prisoners of war made by the French were confined at St. Malo; many of them were Irishmen and catholics, and O'Leary was appointed chaplain to the prisons and hospitals. The Duc de Choiseul, minister of foreign affairs, directed O'Leary to persuade the catholic soldiers to transfer their allegiance to France, but he indignantly spurned the proposal. 'I thought it,' wrote O'Leary long afterwards in his 'Reply to Wesley,' 'a crime to engage the king of England's soldiers into the service of a catholic monarch against their protestant sovereign. I resisted the solicitation, and my conduct was approved by the divines of a monastery to which I then belonged, who unanimously declared that in conscience I could not have acted otherwise.' He continued to hold the chaplaincy until peace was declared in 1762. Among distinguished personages whose intimacy he enjoyed in France was Cardinal de Luynes, archbishop of Sens.

In 1771 he returned to Ireland, and for several years he officiated in a small edifice in the city of Cork, long known as Father O'Leary's chapel, where he preached to crowded congregations, his sermons being 'chiefly remarkable for a happy train of strong moral reasoning, bold figure, and scriptural allusion.' In 1775 a Scottish physician named Blair, residing in Cork, published a sceptical and blasphemous work under the title of 'Thoughts on Nature and Religion.' O'Leary obtained permission from Dr. Mann, protestant bishop of the diocese, to reply to this in 'A Defence of the Divinity of Christ and the Immortality of the Soul,' Cork, 1776. O'Leary's next publication appeared about 1777, under the title 'Loyalty asserted; or the new Test-oath vindicated and proved by the Principles of the Canon and Civil Laws, and the Authority of the most Eminent Writers, with an Enquiry into the Pope's deposing Power, and the groundless Claims of the Stuarts. In a letter to a Protestant Gentleman.' In 1779 the hostile French fleet rode menacing and unopposed in St. George's Channel, and much anxiety prevailed regarding the attitude of the Irish catholic body. At this critical moment O'Leary, in 'An Address to the common People of the Roman Catholic religion concerning the apprehended French Invasion,' explained to Irishmen their obligation of undivided allegiance to the British government. In 1780 he issued 'Remarks on the Rev. John Wesley's Letter on the civil Principles of Roman Catholics and his defence of the Protestant Association,' Dublin, 1760, 8vo. This witty, argumentative, and eloquent treatise elicited from Wesley a reply which was noticed by O'Leary in a few pages usually printed with the 'Remarks,' and entitled 'A rejoinder to Mr. Wesley's Reply.' Some years later the two controversialists met. Wesley noted in his 'Journal' on 12 May 1787: 'A gentleman invited me to breakfast with my old antagonist, Father O'Leary. I was not at all displeased at being disappointed. He is not the stiff, queer man that I expected, but of an easy, genteel carriage, and seems not to be wanting either in sense or learning.' About 1780 John Howard visited Cork, and was introduced to O'Leary, who was an active member of a society which had for some years been established in that city 'for the relief and discharge of persons confined for small debts.' In after times Howard frequently boasted of sharing the friendship and esteem of the friar.

O'Leary's ablest work was 'An Essay on Toleration; or Mr. O'Leary's Plea for Liberty of Conscience' [1780?]. One consequence of its publication was his election as one of the 'Monks of St. Patrick' or 'Monks of the Screw,' a political association which was started by Barry Yelverton, afterwards lord Avonmore. He was, however, only an honorary member of the association, and did not join in the orgies with which the soi-disant monks celebrated their reunions. In 1781 he collected his 'Miscellaneous Tracts,' and published them at Dublin in a single octavo volume (Lowndes, *Bibl. Manual*, ed. Bohn, iii. 1723).

In 1782 O'Leary publicly announced his support of the Irish national volunteer movement, and a body of volunteers known as the 'Irish Brigade' conferred on him the honorary dignity of chaplain. Many of the measures discussed at the national convention held in Dublin were previously submitted to him. On 11 Nov. 1783 he visited that assembly, and met with a most enthusiastic reception. He was now the idol of his catholic fellow-countrymen, who regarded him as one of the stoutest champions of the nationalist cause. But he was at the same time actually in the pay of the government. His biographer, England, gives the following account of his position: During his visit in Dublin a confidential agent of the ministry proposed to him that he should write something in defence of their measures. On his refusal, it was intimated that his silence would be acceptable to the government, and that an annual pension of 150*l*. was to be offered for his acceptance without any condition attached to it which would be repugnant to his feelings as an Irishman or a catholic. A change in the administration occurred shortly afterwards, and the promise remained unfulfilled. It is doubtful whether this story is quite accurate. Before 1784 he was obviously in receipt of a secret pension of at least 100*l*. a year, which had been conferred on him in acknowledgment of the value set by the authorities on the loyalist tone of his writings. In 1784 it was proposed to him, in consideration of an extra 100*l*. per annum, to undertake a new task, namely, to give information respecting the secret designs of the catholics. Lord Sydney, secretary of state in Pitt's ministry, wrote thus to the Duke of Portland, viceroy of Ireland, on 4 Sept. 1784: 'O'Leary has been talked to by Mr. Nepean, and he is willing to undertake what is wished for 100*l*. a year, which has been granted him;' and on 8 Sept. Orde, the chief secretary, wrote to Nepean thanking him for sending over a spy or detective named Parker, and adding: 'I am very glad also that you have settled matters with O'Leary, who can get to the bottom of all secrets in which the catholics are concerned, and they are certainly the chief promoters of our present disquietude. He must, however, be cautiously trusted, for he is a priest, and, if not too much addicted to the general vice of his brethren here, he is at least well acquainted with the art of raising alarms for the purpose of claiming a merit in doing them away.' Again Orde writes on 23 Sept.: 'We are about to make trial of O'Leary's sermons and of Parker's rhapsodies. They may be both, in their different callings, of very great use. The former, if we can depend upon him, has it in his power to discover to us the real designs of the catholics, from which quarter, after all, the real mischief is to spring.' Mr. Lecky remarks that Father O'Leary, whose brilliant pen had already been employed to vindicate both the loyalty and faith of the catholics and to induce them to remain attached to the law, appears to have consented for money to discharge an ignominious office for a government which distrusted and despised him (*History of England*, vi. 369); while Mr. Froude does not hesitate to describe him as 'a paid and secret instrument of treachery' (*The English in Ireland*, ii. 451). Francis Plowden, O'Leary's friend, ignoring the early date at which O'Leary first placed himself at the government's disposal, asserted that the pension was granted to O'Leary for life in the name of a trustee, but upon the secret condition that he should for the future withhold his pen and reside no more in Ireland (Plowden, *Ireland since the Union*, 1811, i. 6). The Rev. Mr. Buckley was informed that the pension was accepted on the understanding that Mr. Pitt would keep his word as a man of honour in promising that he would bring about the emancipation of the catholics and the repeal of the penal laws in case O'Leary consented to write nothing against the union of the Irish with the British parliament (*Life of O'Leary*, 1868, p. 356). In an endeavour to extenuate O'Leary's conduct, Mr. Fitzpatrick says: 'He had already written in denunciation of French designs on Ireland; and what more natural than that he should now be asked to track the movements of certain French emissaries who, the government heard, had arrived in Dublin, and were conspiring with the catholic leaders to throw off the British yoke? This task O'Leary, as a staunch loyalist, may have satisfied his conscience in attempting, especially as he must have known that in 1784 the catholics as a body had no treasonable designs, though doubtless some exceptions might be found' (*Secret Service under Pitt*, 2nd edit. p. 224). O'Leary's biographer represents that the pension of 200*l.* was not offered him until 1789, after he had finally left Ireland, and, although this is clearly incorrect, some doubt is justifiable as to whether the whole sum was actually paid him until he had ceased to concern himself with Irish politics.

About 1784 O'Leary was solicited to write a history of the 'No Popery' riots in London under Lord George Gordon. For a short time he entertained the idea, and began to collect materials, but eventually abandoned the design. In 1786 he wrote his 'Review of the Important Controversy between Dr. Carroll and the Rev. Messrs. Wharton and Hawkins; including a Defence of Clement XIV.' Appended to it is 'A Letter from Candor to the Right Hon. Luke Gardiner on his Bill for a Repeal of a part of the Penal Laws against the Irish Catholics.' This was written in 1779, and had appeared in the newspapers of that time. In 1785 and 1786 the peace of the county of Cork was disturbed at night by mobs under the guidance of a leader who assumed the name of 'Captain Right,' and O'Leary published 'Addresses to the Common People of Ireland, particularly such of them as are called Whiteboys,' demonstrating in a familiar, eloquent, and bold mode of reasoning the folly, wickedness, and illegality of their conduct. His personal exertions were further solicited by the magistrates of the county, and he accompanied them to different places of worship, exhorted the deluded people to obedience to the laws and respect for religion, and was successful in persuading numbers of them to quit the association. He afterwards published 'A Defence of the Conduct and Writings of the Rev. Arthur O'Leary during the late Disturbances in the Province of Munster, with a full Justification of the Irish Catholics, and an Account of the Risings of the Whiteboys; Written by Himself, in Answer to the False Accusations of Theophilus [i.e. Patrick Duigenan], and the Ill-grounded Insinuations of the Right Rev. Dr. Woodward, Lord Bishop of Cloyne.'

The controversies in which his equivocal position involved him induced him to quit Ireland in 1789, when he was appointed one of the chaplains to the Spanish embassy in London, his colleague there being Dr. Hussey, afterwards bishop of Waterford. They afterwards had a dispute, and a 'Narrative of the Misunderstanding between the Rev. A. O'Leary and the Rev. Mr. Hussey' appeared in 1791 (Fitzpatrick, p. 255 n.). On his arrival in London, O'Leary was anxiously sought after by his countrymen. Edmund Burke introduced him to the Duke of York, and always spoke with characteristic enthusiasm of the good effect of his writings. He used to attend the meetings of the English catholic committee, but he opposed its action, and took exception to the absurd appellation of 'Protesting Catholic Dissenters.' Charles Butler, the secretary of the committee, says: 'The appearance of Father O'Leary was simple. In his countenance there was a mixture of goodness, solemnity, and drollery which fixed every eye that beheld it. No one was more generally loved or revered; no one less assuming or more pleasing in his manner. Seeing his external simplicity, persons with whom he was arguing were sometimes tempted to treat him cavalierly; but then the solemnity with which he would mystify his ad-versary, and ultimately lead him into the most distressing absurdity, was one of the most delightful scenes that conversation ever exhibited' (*Hist. Memoirs of the English Catholics*, 1822, iv. 438). Successful efforts were meanwhile made by his friend Plowden to secure the full payment of the pension of 200l., with all unpaid arrears.

St. Patrick's chapel, Sutton Street, Soho Square, was, during the later years of his life, the scene of his labours. His sermons were widely admired, and his auditory included all grades of society. His collections for a pro-jected history of the Irish rebellion of 1798 he presented to Francis Plowden. He published in 1800 an 'Address to the Lords Spiritual and Temporal of the Parliament of Great Britain; to which is added an Account of Sir H. Mildmay's Bill relative to Nuns.' This was followed by 'A Me-morial in behalf of the Fathers of La Trappe and the Orphans committed to their Care,' which was probably the last of his literary labours. Towards the end of 1801 he went to France for the benefit of his health. He was again in London on 7 Jan. 1802, and died on the following morning at No. 45 Great Portland Street. His 'Funeral Oration,' pronounced by the Rev. Morgan D'Arcy, has been printed. The body was interred in Old St. Pancras churchyard, and a monument was placed over the grave by Earl Moira, afterwards marquis of Hastings (*Addit. MS.* 27488, f. 156). This monument was repaired by public subscription in 1851. Another was erected in St. Patrick's Chapel. When old St. Pancras churchyard was taken by the Midland railway for the extension of their station buildings, the remains of O'Leary were removed, and on 3 Feb. 1891 they were interred in the catholic cemetery at Kensal Green, in a grave close to that of Cardinal Wiseman (*Tablet*, 28 Feb. 1891, p. 355).

His earliest biographer, England, in portraying his character, states that 'good sense, unaffected piety, and extensive knowledge gained him the respect and admiration of the learned and grave, whilst by his unbounded wit, anecdotes, and unrivalled brilliancy of imagination he was the source of delight and entertainment to all whom he admitted to his intimacy.' A more discriminating critic, Mr. Lecky, admits that O'Leary was by far the most brilliant and popular writer on the catholic side; 'but, though his devotion to his creed was incontestable, it would be hardly possible to find a writer of his profession who exhibits its distinctive doctrines in a more subdued and attenuated form, and no one appears to have found anything strange or equivocal in the curiously characteristic sentence in which Grattan described his merits: "If I did not know him to be a Christian gentleman, I should suppose him by his writings to be a philosopher of the Augustan age"' (*Hist. of England*, vi. 446). Mr. Froude considers that O'Leary was 'the most plausible, and, perhaps, essentially the falsest, of all Irish writers' (*The English in Ireland*, ii. 37 n.). A collected edition of his works, edited by 'a clergyman of Massachusetts,' appeared at Boston in 1868, 8vo.

There is a portrait prefixed to England's biography, 'engraved by W. Bond from the scarce print, after a drawing by Murphy' (Bromley, *Cat. of Engraved Portraits*, p. 364). Another portrait, engraved by T. H. Ellis from a painting by E. Shiel, is prefixed to Buckley's 'Life.'

[England's Life of O'Leary, including Historical Anecdotes, Memoirs, and many hitherto unpublished Documents, London 1822, 8vo; Buckley's Life and Writings of O'Leary, Dublin, 1868, 8vo; Addit. MS. 5875, f. 168b; Barrington's Personal Sketches, ii. 130; Cansick's Epitaphs at St. Pancras, Middlesex, i. 80; Chalmers's Biogr. Dict.; Croly's Life of George IV, p. 129; European Mag. 1782, pt. i. pp. 192–5; Fitzpatrick's Secret Service under Pitt, 2nd edit. pp. 211–252; Froude's English in Ireland, 1881, ii. 37 n, 450, 451; Gent. Mag. February 1802; Gordon's Personal Reminiscences, i. 110, 236, 242; Kelly's Reminiscences, i. 298; Laity's Directory, 1803; Lecky's Hist. of England, iv. 330 n, 495, vi. 369, 446, vii. 211, 271; Literary Memoirs of Living Authors, 1798, ii. 92; London and Dublin Orthodox Journal, 1842, xv. 117; Lysons's Environs, Suppl. pp. 255, 262, 263; Macdonough's Irish Graves in England; McDougall's Sketches of Irish Political Characters, p. 264; Maguire's Life of Father Mathew, pp. 23–6; Lady Morgan's Memoirs, i. 2; Nichols's Illustr. of Lit. vi. 74, vii. 486, 489; Nichols's Lit. Anecd. i. 671; Notes and Queries, 25 March 1893 p. 228, 28 Oct. 1893 p. 359; O'Keeffe's Recollections, i. 244; Public Characters, 1799, i. 361; Southey's Life of Wesley, 2nd edit. 1820, ii. 546; Tablet, 22 Nov. 1890, p. 821, &c.; Cat. of Library of Trin. Coll. Dublin; Watt's Bibl. Brit. under Leary.]

THOMPSON COOPER

published 1894

French spy, born at Kildare about 1714, was son of Florence Hensey or Henchy (*d.* 1757), of Ballycumeen, co. Clare, and his wife Mary (*d.* 1748). When very young he came to England, and on 18 Oct. 1748 entered as a student of medicine at Leyden, where he graduated M.D. (*Leyden Students*, p. 48). He afterwards travelled in, and studied the languages of, Switzerland, Italy, Portugal, and Spain. He then settled at Paris, where for some years he practised as a physician, and learnt French. Finally he removed to England, and commenced practice in London. On the outbreak of the seven years' war in 1756, Hensey opened a correspondence with an old fellow-student who was then engaged in the French foreign office. As a result he entered the French service as a spy, and in return for a salary of a hundred guineas a year supplied information as to the movements and equipment of the English fleet. He warned the French of the intended expedition to Rochefort in 1757, and his warning seems to have contributed to the failure of that enterprise. Hensey conducted his correspondence through a brother who was chaplain to the Spanish ambassador at the Hague. A postman, who knew that Hensey was a Roman catholic, and had observed his frequent foreign correspondence, called the attention of his superiors to the matter, and on opening Hensey's letters evidence was obtained which led to his arrest, on 21 Aug. 1757, as he was leaving the catholic church in Soho Square. After many examinations before the secretary of state, Hensey was committed to Newgate 9 March 1758, and on 8 May was brought before the king's bench and ordered to prepare for his trial. The trial took place before Earl Mansfield on 12 June, occupying all day. The evidence of guilt was overpowering; further letters were found at Hensey's lodgings in Arundel Street, Strand, in a bureau of which he alone had the key, and were conclusively shown to be in his handwriting. There was practically no defence, and such technical objections as were raised were overruled. On the 14th Hensey was condemned to death as a traitor; but on 12 July, the very day appointed for his execution, he received a respite for a fortnight, and this period was afterwards extended, till on 7 Sept. 1759 he was admitted to bail in order to plead his pardon next term. After this Hensey disappears. There is a medallion portrait of him in the 'Genuine Account,' and a full-length one of him in fetters in the 'Genuine Memoirs.'

[A Genuine Account of the Proceedings on the Trial of Florence Hensey, M.D., London, 1758; Genuine Memoirs of the Life and Treasonable Practices of Dr.

Florence Hensey, London, 1758 (written between sentence and the day appointed for his execution); Ann. Reg. 1758, pp. 97–9; Gent. Mag. 1758 pp. 240, 287–8, 337–8, 1759 p. 438.]

CHARLES LETHBRIDGE KINGSFORD

published 1891

ARNOLD Benedict

(1741–1801)

American and afterwards English general, was born at Norwich, Connecticut, 14 Jan. 1740–1. (The date usually given of 1740 seems to have originated from a confusion between the new and old styles.) His family, of respectable station in England, had emigrated from Dorsetshire; his great grandfather had been governor of Rhode Island; his father, a cooper, owned several vessels in the West Indian trade. From his infancy he manifested a mischievous and ungovernable disposition, of which several characteristic traits are recorded. On attaining man's estate he entered into business as a bookseller and druggist at New Haven, Connecticut, married, adventured like his father in the West Indian trade, and acquired considerable property, partly, there is reason to suspect, by smuggling. Upon the outbreak of the dissensions between the colonies and the mother country he took a leading part upon the side of the patriots, and immediately on receiving the news of the battle of Lexington (19 April 1775) put himself at the head of a company of volunteers, seized the arsenal at New Haven, and marched to Cambridge, Massachusetts, where, with true military instinct, he proposed to the committee of public safety an expedition to capture Ticonderoga, on Lake George, and Crown Point, on Lake Champlain, the keys to the communications between Canada and New York. The plan was approved, and Arnold was despatched to Western Massachusetts to raise troops. While thus engaged he learned that another expedition, under the direction of Ethan Allen, was proceeding from Vermont with the same design. He hurried to join it, and claimed the command, which was refused him, and he had to be content with accompanying it as a volunteer. He took part in the successful surprise of Ticonderoga, 11 May, and a few days later, having obtained some troops of his own, anticipated Allen in surprising and capturing St. John's, also on Lake George. Differences with the Massachusetts committee occasioned him to resign his command; but shortly afterwards Washington adopted a plan proposed by him for an expedition against Quebec by way of the river

Kennebec and the mountains of Maine, to co-operate with another expedition under Schuyler proceeding by way of the northern lakes. After
enduring extreme hardships, aggravated by the desertion of one of his
officers who marched back with a part of the commissariat, Arnold
brought his troops successfully under the walls of Quebec, but was too
weak to attack the city until the arrival of Schuyler's column, now
commanded by Montgomery. On 31 Dec. 1775 the two leaders assaulted
Quebec, but were disastrously repulsed, Montgomery being killed and
Arnold severely wounded. He nevertheless maintained the blockade of
Quebec, 'with such a handful of men,' wrote his successor, 'that the story
when told hereafter will scarcely be believed.' He subsequently commanded at Montreal, and when at last want of supplies, discontent among
the troops, and inferiority of force, compelled the Americans to evacuate
Canada, he was literally the last man to leave the country. His next appointment was to the command of a flotilla on Lake Champlain, where,
after two desperate actions and one dexterous escape, he was compelled to
run his vessels ashore, but saved himself and the men under his command.
Shortly afterwards he was, as he conceived, unjustly treated by Congress,
which promoted five brigadiers to the rank of major-general over his head.
This conduct was probably occasioned by charges then pending against
him with reference to the seizure of property at Montreal; and when he
was ultimately acquitted, Congress, though consenting to his promotion,
refused to restore his seniority. The disgust thus occasioned was probably
the first motive to his subsequent treachery. He fought, however, at
Ridgefield, where he escaped death as though by miracle; relieved Fort
Stanwix, blockaded by Indians; and, placed nominally under Gates's orders, but in reality the life and soul of the American army, took the most
conspicuous part in the two battles at Saratoga which occasioned the
surrender of Burgoyne (October 1777). Congress now restored him to his
precedence; but this was the term of his good fortune. A severe wound
received at Saratoga disabled him from active service, and he was appointed governor of Philadelphia. While filling this post he exposed
himself to charges of extortion and peculation, the truth of which it is
difficult to ascertain. He resigned his command, and claimed an investigation. After vexatious delays he obtained a partial acquittal, but incurred
a reprimand which Washington, who had always protected him, administered with evident reluctance (January 1780). Arnold was now thoroughly disgusted; his fortunes were desperate. The second wife he had
recently married had strong loyalist sympathies; the sentiment of military
honour, apart from military glory, had probably never been a very strong
one with him, and he easily allowed himself to be persuaded by British
agents that he would serve his country by an act of treachery putting an

end to the war. A paper published by Barbé-Marbois, purporting to be addressed to Arnold by Colonel Beverley Robinson, is of doubtful authenticity, but probably represents the nature of the arguments to which, rather than to pecuniary temptation, his fidelity succumbed. In August 1780 he solicited and obtained the command of West Point, the key of communication between the northern and southern states, and the depository of the American stores of gunpowder, with the deliberate intention, it cannot be doubted, of betraying it to the enemy. Negotiations were immediately entered into with the British commander Clinton, being conducted on the latter's part by his adjutant, the gallant and unfortunate Major André. On Sept. 21 Arnold and André had an interview at which the surrender of West Point was arranged, and the latter departed, carrying with him particulars of the defences and other compromising documents. The circumstances of his arrest have been related under his name. The news reached Arnold on the morning of 25 Sept., only one hour before the arrival of Washington. After a hasty interview with his wife, who fell senseless at his feet, he mounted his horse, galloped down to the riverside, called a boat, and found safety on board of the British sloop Vulture, which had brought André on his fatal errand.

On joining the British, Arnold received the rank of brigadier-general. His first act was to publish a vindication of his conduct and an appeal to the American army to imitate his example; but these documents, though ably composed, failed to produce the slightest effect. He subsequently commanded expeditions against Richmond in Virginia and New London in Connecticut; both succeeded, but were mere marauding forays, without influence on the general course of operations. In 1782 he proceeded to England, where he was consulted by the king on the conduct of the war, and drew up a very able memorandum, but the suggestions it contained obviously came too late. He also obtained upwards of 6,000l. as compensation for his losses, and a pension of 500l. for his wife. Though much caressed at court, he found it impossible to procure active employment in the British army, and was even obliged to vindicate his honour by fighting a duel with Lord Lauderdale. He again entered into business, first in New Brunswick and afterwards in the West Indies. Though not in actual service, he so distinguished himself at Guadaloupe as to be rewarded by a large grant of land in Canada; he also evinced political prescience in framing a plan for the conquest of the Spanish West Indies, by exciting insurrection among the creoles. His commercial enterprises proved unfortunate, and his latter days were embittered not only by self-reproach for his treason, but by pecuniary embarrassments and the dread of want. He died in London on 14 June 1801. The threatened ruin was averted by the exertions and business ability of his devoted wife. All his four sons by her entered the British service, and one, James Robertson Arnold, an officer of engineers, rose to the rank of lieutenant-general. Descendants of his third son George still exist in England. He had three sons by his first marriage, whose posterity survive in Canada and the United States.

'It should excite but little surprise that an ambitious, extravagant man, with fiery passions and very little balance of moral principle, should betray his friends and plunge desperately into treason.' This remark of the historian of Arnold's native town leaves little further to be said on the cardinal event of his life. Under provocation and temptation he acted infamously, but his character does not deserve the exceptional infamy with which it has been not unnaturally loaded in America. A civilian soldier, he had imperfectly imbibed the traditions of military honour; and, with his loyalist connections, his desertion may have seemed to him rather a change of party than the betrayal of his country. He was eminent for courage and the strength of domestic affection, and his memoirs contain instances of generosity and humanity which better men might envy. With all these redeeming qualities he was still essentially a bad citizen, turbulent, mercenary, and unscrupulous. Washington's exclamation on hearing of his defection showed that he had no belief in his probity, though he had tolerated his vices in consideration of his military qualities. These were indeed eminent. Arnold's intrepidity, ingenuity, promptitude, sagacity, and resource are even more conspicuous in his miscarriages than in his successes. When his almost total want of military instruction is considered, he deserves to be ranked high upon the list of those who have shown an innate genius for war.

[The principal authorities for Arnold's life are the dry but clear narrative of Jared Sparks in the Library of American Biography, vol. iii., Boston, 1835; and the more copious Biography by Isaac N. Arnold (Chicago, 1880). The latter extenuates everything, the former sets down not a few things in malice, but between the two it is easy to arrive at a just estimate of Arnold's character and actions. See also Miss F. M. Caulkin's History of Norwich, Conn., pp. 409–415; Irving's and Marshall's Lives of Washington; Sargent's Life of André; and the historians of the American war of independence in general.]

RICHARD GARNETT

published 1885

WINDHAM William

(1750–1810)

Statesman, came of an old Norfolk family settled at Felbrigg, near Cromer, since the fifteenth century, whose name was the same originally as that of the town of Wymondham.

His father, Colonel William Windham 1717–1761, son of William Windham, M.P. for Sudbury 1722–7 and for Aldeburgh 1727 until his death in 1730, possessed distinguished military talent. Disputes with his father had caused him to live much on the continent. He travelled with Richard Pococke in Switzerland in 1741, and his 'Letter from an English Gentleman to Mr. Arland, giving an Account of a Journey to the Glacieres or Ice Alps of Savoy' (1744), is one of the earliest printed accounts of Chamonix and Mont Blanc (see Coxe, *Life of Stillingfleet*; C. E. Mathews, *Annals of Mont Blanc*; C. Durier, *Le Mont Blanc*, 1897, pp. 50–62; Th. Dufour, *William Windham et Pierre Martel, Genève*, 1879). He also visited Hungary, and for some time was an officer in one of Queen Maria Theresa's hussar regiments. Returning to England, he vigorously supported Pitt's scheme for a national militia in 1756, and helped the Marquis Townshend to form the Norfolk militia regiment in 1757. He published in 1760 a 'Plan of Discipline' in quarto, with plates, which came into general use, and he sat in parliament for Aldeburgh in 1754. The statesman's father married Sarah Hicks, widow of Robert Lukin of Dunmow, Essex, and died of consumption on 30 Oct. 1761 at the age of forty-four.

William, the only son, was born on 3 May (O. S.) 1750 at No. 6 Golden Square, Soho. From 1762 to 1766 he was at Eton, where he was a contemporary of Fox, and was then placed with Dr. Anderson, professor of natural philosophy in the university of Glasgow. He attended the lectures of Robert Simson, professor of mathematics, and pursued the study in later life, even composing three mathematical treatises, which, however, he never published. On 10 Sept. 1767 he entered University College, Oxford, as a gentleman commoner, and became a pupil of Robert Chambers. He was created M.A. on 7 Oct. 1782, and on 3 July 1793 he became an honorary D.C.L. Both at school and at college he was quick and industrious, but as a young man he was completely indifferent to public affairs, though distinguished both as a scholar and a man of fashion. Accordingly he refused Lord Townshend's offer of the secretaryship to the lord-lieutenant of Ireland, made while he was still at college, and left Oxford in 1771. Two years later he started with Commodore Constantine John Phipps (afterwards second baron Mulgrave) upon a voyage of polar exploration, but was compelled by sea-sickness to land in Norway and make his way home. He afterwards spent some time with the Norfolk militia, in which he attained the rank of major, and passed a couple of years abroad, chiefly in Switzerland and Italy. He also became known to Johnson and Burke. He was Johnson's favoured friend, attended him assiduously in his last days, and was a pall-bearer at his funeral. His attachment to Burke was such that he became his political pupil. He joined the Literary Club and attended its meetings almost till he died, and was also a member of the Essex Head Club.

Meantime he was gradually drawing towards a public career. He made his first public speech on 28 Jan. 1778 at a public meeting called to raise a subscription towards the cost of the American war, and opposed the project. He won some local repute by personal courage and promptitude in quelling a mutiny at Norwich, when the Norfolk militia refused to march into Suffolk, and in September 1780 he unsuccessfully contested Norwich. In 1781 he was a member of the Westminster committee, and came very near standing for Westminster in 1782. He, however, gradually drifted away from his earlier reforming opinions into a fixed antipathy to any constitutional change. In 1783 he became chief secretary to Northington, lord lieutenant of Ireland in the Portland administration, but resigned the post in August, nominally owing to ill-health, but in reality because he desired to give Irish posts to Irishmen, a policy not in favour with his superiors. After the dissolution in March 1784 he was one of the few coalition candidates who were successful, and was elected at Norwich on 5 April. For some time he acted steadily with the opposition, and Burke chose him in June to second his motion on the state of the nation. He spoke in 1785 on the shop tax and the Westminster scrutiny; he strongly supported the right of the Prince of Wales to be regent without restrictions in 1788, and in 1790 killed Flood's reform bill by the happy phrase that 'no one would select the hurricane season in which to begin repairing his house.' He was also one of the members charged with the impeachment of Warren Hastings, and undertook that part of the case which dealt with the breach of the treaty of 1774 with Faizulla Khan. He was re-elected at Norwich in 1790, and in February 1791 supported Mitford's catholic relief bill for England. Following Burke, by whom he continued to be largely guided, he took alarm at the French revolution, and in 1792 and 1793 was one of the most ardent supporters of the government's repressive legis-lation. He supported the proclamation against seditious meetings and the aliens bill, had a plan for raising a troop of cavalry in Norfolk, and on 11 July 1794, on Burke's advice, he somewhat reluctantly consented to take office under Pitt, with the Duke of Portland, Lord Fitzwilliam, and Lord Spencer (Prior, *Life of Burke*, ii. 264). A secretaryship of state was at first suggested for him, but eventually he became secretary at war, with a seat in the cabinet. This was the first time that the cabinet was opened to the holder of the secretaryship at war. His change of front was somewhat resented at Norwich, but he secured re-election, and from August to October was with the Duke of York's army in Flanders. He held that the royalists in the west of France deserved assistance, and was the person most responsible for the Quiberon expedition in July 1795. Vigorously supporting the continuance of war, and steadily opposing projects of reform, he only after a sharp fight saved his seat at Norwich, 25 May 1796. He held office till February 1801, when he resigned with Pitt. To the Irish union he had been at first opposed altogether, but consented to it in consideration of the promise that catholic disabilities should be removed. He had by no means always approved of Pitt's war policy, and had held that, as the war was fought for the restoration of the Bourbons, more efforts should have been made to assist the royalists in France. Much was done under his administration to increase the comfort of the troops. Their pay was raised, pensions were established, and the Royal Military Asylum was founded.

Windham's chance in opposition soon came. He had a rooted distrust of Napoleon, and strongly opposed the peace of 1802. He assisted Cobbett, whom he greatly admired, to found the 'Political Register,' and thoroughly agreed with its attacks on Addington. He spoke against the peace preliminaries on 4 Nov. 1801, and moved an address to the crown against the peace on 13 May 1802. As the peace was popular in the country, this attitude cost him his seat at Norwich in June 1802. He declined to contest the county, and accepted from the Grenville family the borough of St. Mawes in Cornwall, where he was elected on 7 July. This seat he held till November 1806, when he was elected for New Romney, and later in the same month for the county of Norfolk. This latter election was afterwards declared void, upon a petition alleging breaches of the Treating Act. Windham being thus ineligible for re-election for the same seat. Throughout these proceedings he retained his seat for New Romney till the dissolution of parliament 29 April 1807. At the general election in May he was returned for Higham Ferrers, and held that seat till his death.

Windham welcomed the renewal of hostilities with France. He had never supported a policy of fortifications or of large land forces, and when in office had considered the erection of martello towers a sufficient defence for the coast, his chief reliance being upon the fleet. He doubted too the value of volunteers, and made somewhat savage attacks upon them, but took part in the general movement in 1803, and raised a volunteer force at Felbrigg, and became its colonel. He now became leader of the

Grenville party in the House of Commons, and engaged in the attack on Addington, but declined to join Pitt again in May 1804, owing to the king's objection to the admission of Fox to the ministry. He then found himself once more acting with Fox and opposing Pitt, and at the time of Pitt's death he incurred some hostility in consequence. He accepted the war and colonial office in Lord Grenville's administration, and on 3 April 1806 introduced a plan for improving the condition of the military forces, and making the army an attractive profession. With this object he passed bills for reducing the term of service and for increasing the soldiers' pay. He had begun the arrangements for the South American expedition when, with the rest of the ministry, he was dismissed in March 1807. In the previous year he had refused the offer of a peerage, preferring a career in the House of Commons, and he continued to devote himself to the conduct of the war and to criticism of the policy of his successor Castlereagh. On general policy, however, he held aloof from debate, and, from growing dislike of London, lived much in the country. His only conspicuous speeches in the later years of his life on civil topics were (14 May 1805) in favour of the Roman catholic claims, to which subject he returned in 1810, and on Curwen's bill for preventing the sale of seats in May 1809. As Castlereagh's proposals with regard to the militia ran counter to his own plan of 1806, he opposed the local militia bill in 1808, and, as he was adverse to a policy of scattered and, as he thought, aimless expeditions, he spoke against the Copenhagen expedition in 1807, and the Scheldt expedition in January 1810. On the other hand, he was a very warm supporter of the Spanish cause, and even began to learn Spanish with a view to a personal visit to Spain. In his view, however, the objective of the English force should have been the passes of the Pyrenees, and not Portugal, so as to cut off the French from Spain, and he thought that Moore ought to have been sent with a much larger force to the north of Spain, and there could and should have held his ground. The Peninsular war, once begun, was to be pressed with vigour, and such an expedition as that to Antwerp did not seem to Windham consistent with the successful prosecution of the Spanish war. He continued to express these views energetically, but, by supporting a proposal made early in 1810 for the exclusion of reporters from the House of Commons, he provoked the hostility of the press, which for some time refused to report his speeches.

Windham's last speech was made on 11 May 1810. In July of the previous year he had injured his hip by his efforts in removing the books of his friend the Hon. Frederick North (afterwards fifth Earl of Guilford) out of reach of a fire. On 17 May 1810 Cline operated upon him for the removal of a tumour, but he never recovered from the shock, and died at his house in Pall Mall on 4 June, and was buried at Felbrigg. He married, on 10 July 1798,

Cecilia, third daughter of Commodore Arthur Forrest, but had no children.

Windham's personal advantages were many. He was rich, and had an income of 6,000*l.* a year. He was tall and well built, graceful and dignified in manner, a thorough sportsman, and in his youth, like his father, was very athletic and a practised pugilist. He had a good memory, and was widely and well informed; he was an ardent Greek and Latin scholar, and fluent in French and Italian. Though his voice was defective and shrill, he was, when at his best, a most eloquent orator, and was always a clear speaker and a keen debater; but his speeches were marred by occasional indiscretions of temper and want of reticence. He was pious, chivalrous, and disinterested, and his brilliant social qualities made him one of the finest gentlemen as well as one of the soundest sportsmen of his time. His diary, published in 1866, shows him to have been vacillating and hypochondriacal in private, but he seems to have relieved his feelings by this habit of private confession; and in public, though somewhat changeable, he was not irresolute. In an age of great men his character stood high, and although his conduct on two occasions in his political life led to charges of inconsistency, and earned for him the nickname of 'Weathercock Windham,' his personal integrity was unimpugned. The army undoubtedly owed much to his labours in improving its efficiency and condition. Panegyrics were pronounced upon him in the House of Lords by Lord Grey on 6 June 1810, and in the House of Commons by Lord Milton the following day, and Brougham paints him in laudatory terms in his 'Historical Sketches of British Statesmen' (i. 219). A portrait of him by Hoppner was placed in the public hall, Norwich, and there is another, by Sir Thomas Lawrence, at University College, Oxford. Hoppner's portrait was engraved by Say. Portraits by Sir Joshua Reynolds and Lawrence, and a bust by Nollekens, are in the National Portrait Gallery, London.

A valuable collection of Windham's manuscript papers, including letters to him from Pitt and Burke, was acquired by the British Museum in June 1909 (*Times*, 19 June 1909).

[Windham's Speeches, with Memoir by his secretary, Thomas Amyot (3 vols. 1806); Windham's Diary, 1784–1810, ed. Mrs. Henry Baring, 1866; Malone's Memoir of Windham, 1810, reprinted from Gent. Mag. 1810, i. 588 (cf. *ib.* 566); Mémoires du Comte Joseph de Puisaye; Lecky's Hist.; Hardy's Lord Charlemont, ii. 82, 86; Colburn's New Monthly Mag. xxxii, 555; Edinburgh Review, cxxiii. 557; Romilly's Life; Stanhope's Pitt; Boswell's Johnson, ed. Hill; Cooke's Hist. of Party, iii. 433; Harris's Radical Party.]

JOHN ANDREW HAMILTON

published 1900

ANDRÉ John

(1751–1780)

Major in the British army, was the son of a Genevese merchant settled in London. He received his education at Geneva, and upon his return to England became intimately connected with Miss Seward and her literary *coterie* at Lichfield, where he conceived an attachment for Honora Sneyd, subsequently the second wife of Richard Lovell Edgeworth. His relinquishment of mercantile for military pursuits has been attributed to the disappointment of his passion for this lady, whose marriage, however, did not take place till two years after the date of his commission, 4 March 1771. He joined the British army in America, and in 1775 was taken prisoner at St. John's. Upon his release he became successively aide-de-camp to General Grey and to Sir Henry Clinton, who entertained so high an opinion of him as to make him adjutant-general, notwithstanding his youth and the short period of his service. This position unhappily brought him into connection with Benedict Arnold, who was plotting the betrayal of West Point to the British. As Clinton's chief confidant, André was entrusted with the management of the correspondence with Arnold, which was disguised under colour of a mercantile transaction, Arnold signing himself Gustavus, and André adopting the name of John Anderson. When the negotiations were sufficiently advanced (20 Sept. 1780), André proceeded up the Hudson River in the British sloop Vulture to hold a personal interview with Arnold. To avoid treatment as a spy, he wore his uniform, and professed to be aiming at an arrangement with respect to the sequestrated property of Colonel Beverley Robinson, an American loyalist. His letter to Arnold on the subject having been shown by the latter to Washington, the American generalissimo so strongly protested against any interview that Arnold was compelled to resort to a secret meeting, which took place on the night of 21 Sept. Arnold then delivered to André full particulars respecting the defences of West Point, and concerted with him the attack which the British were to make within a few days. Meanwhile the Vulture had been compelled by the fire of the American outposts to drop further down the river, and André's boatmen refused to row him back. He spent the day at the farmhouse of Joshua Smith, a tool, but probably not an accomplice, of Arnold's, and had no alternative but to disguise himself as a civilian, which, as he was within the American lines, brought him within the reach of military law as a spy. He started the following morning with a pass in the name of Anderson signed by Arnold, and under the guidance of Smith, who only left him when he seemed past all danger. By nine on the

121

morning of the 23rd he was actually in sight of the British lines when he was seized by three American militiamen on the look-out for stragglers. Had he produced Arnold's pass, he would have been allowed to proceed, but he unfortunately asked his captors whether they were British, and, misunderstanding their reply, disclosed his character. He was immediately searched, and the compromising papers were found in his boots. Refusing the large bribes he offered for his release, the militiamen carried him before Colonel Jameson, the commander of the outposts, who had actually sent him with the papers to Arnold, when, at the instance of Captain Talmadge, André was fetched back, and the documents forwarded to Washington. Jameson, however, reported his capture to Arnold, and the news came just in time to enable the latter to escape to the British lines. André acknowledged his name and the character of his mission in a letter addressed to Washington on 24 Sept., in which he declared: 'Against my stipulation, my intention, and without my knowledge beforehand, I was conducted within one of your posts.' On 29 Sept. he was brought before a military board convoked by Washington, which included Lafayette and other distinguished officers. The board found, as it could not possibly avoid finding, that André had acted in the character of a spy. He was therefore sentenced to execution by hanging. Every possible effort was ineffectually made by the British commander to save him, short of delivering up Arnold, which of course could not be contemplated. Washington has been unreasonably censured for not having granted him a more honourable death. To have done so would have implied a doubt as to the justice of his conviction. André was executed on 2 Oct., meeting his fate with a serenity which extorted the warmest admiration of the American officers, to whom, even during the short period of his captivity, he had greatly endeared himself. A sadder tragedy was never enacted, but it was inevitable, and no reproach rests upon any person concerned except Arnold. Washington and André, indeed, deserve equal honour: André for having accepted a terrible risk for his country and borne the consequences of failure with unshrinking courage; and Washington for having performed his duty to his own country at a great sacrifice of his feelings.

André's countrymen made haste to do him honour. The British army went into mourning for him. A monument was erected to his memory in Westminster Abbey, and in 1821 his remains were transferred to the spot. His early friend Miss Seward published a monody on his fate, not devoid of poetical merit, and containing some valuable biographical particulars in the notes. To the charm of his character and manners there is a unanimous testimony, confirmed by every recorded trait and everything we have from his pen. His military promise must have been great to have justified such rapid promotion. He possessed considerable literary ability: the style of his letters is exceedingly good, and he left a satirical poem, 'The Cow Chace' (New York, 1780), in which the marauding exploits of the American general Wayne are ridiculed with much spirit. A pen-and-ink portrait by himself, sketched on the morning originally appointed for his execution, attests both his talent as an artist and his firmness of mind. It is engraved in Sparks's 'Life of Arnold' and in 'Andreana,' in which collection there are three other portraits. The original of the sketch is at Yale College.

[The fullest authority for André's life is the biography by Winthrop Sargent (Philadelphia, 1862), of which, however, only 75 copies were printed. Mr. Sargent has been somewhat more liberal with his 'Andreana,' a collection of documents relating to André's trial, of which he has printed no less than 100 copies. See also Benson's Vindication of the Captors of Major André (1817, and reprinted in 1865); and Joshua H. Smith's Narrative of the Causes which led to the Death of Major André (London, 1808); Miss Seward's Monody, with the notes; the lives of Benedict Arnold by Jared Sparks and Isaac T. Arnold; and the various biographers of Washington and historians of the American war.]

RICHARD GARNETT

published 1885

DESPARD Edward Marcus

(1751–1803)

Executed for high treason, was the youngest of six brothers, who were all in the army, except the eldest, and was born in Queen's County, Ireland, in 1751. He entered the army as an ensign in the 50th regiment in 1766, and was promoted lieutenant in 1772, when his regiment was stationed at Jamaica, where he quickly showed his talent for engineering. In 1779 he was appointed engineer in the expedition to San Juan, and so greatly distinguished himself, that Captain Polson wrote in his despatch to the governor of Jamaica: 'There was scarcely a gun fired but what was pointed by Captain Nelson of the Hinchinbrooke, or Lieutenant Despard, chief engineer, who has exerted himself on every occasion.' On his return he was promoted captain into the 78th regiment, but still employed in engineering in Jamaica. From this work he was removed by the governor, Sir John Dalling, in 1781, when he was appointed commandant of the island of Rattan on the Spanish main, whither certain English logwood-cutters had retired when driven from Honduras by the Spaniards, and soon after of the whole Mosquito shore and the bay of Honduras. Dalling recalled him in a hurry to superintend the military defences of Jamaica, when the island was threatened by the great fleet of the Comte de Grasse. All apprehension on this score was removed by Rodney's great victory, and in August 1782 Despard was permitted to take command of an expedition, consisting of the settlers of Cap Gracias à Dios, at the head of whom, with the help of a few English artillerymen, he took possession of all the Spanish possessions on the Black River. He received the special thanks of the king for these services (see Bannantine, *Memoirs of Colonel Despard*, p. 13), and was, at the special request of the House of Assembly of Jamaica, made a colonel of Provincials by Sir Archibald Campbell, who had succeeded Governor Dalling on 9 Nov. 1782. By the treaty of peace of 1783 Spain granted the peninsula of Yucatan to the English logwood-cutters, on condition that they should do nothing but cut logwood, and in March 1784 Despard was directed to take over the new territory. In this capacity he gave so much satisfaction that, at the special request of the settlers themselves, he was appointed by Campbell to be superintendent of his majesty's affairs there on 1 Dec. 1784, with the very inadequate salary of 500l. a year. He was at first most successful, and obtained leave from the Spanish authorities for the English to cultivate vegetables, and also the cession of a small island for the residence of a pilot. But his popularity did not last long; the old settlers on the peninsula, seven hundred in number, objected to the existence among them of the two thousand logwood-cutters from the Mosquito shore, whom Despard particularly favoured, and the chief of the old settlers, Robert White, sent in a number of accusations against him for cruelty and illegal actions. These accusations had no weight with the House of Assembly of Jamaica, or with Lord Sydney, the secretary of state in charge of the colonies, who dismissed them as frivolous in 1787, but Lord Grenville, Sydney's successor, suspended Despard, whom he ordered to England. He reached England in May 1790, but was kept hanging about the secretary of state's office until 1792, when he was informed that there was no real accusation against him, and that, though his old post was abolished, he would not be forgotten. Nevertheless he obtained no employment, and as he claimed compensation both violently and persistently, he was in the spring of 1798 seized and imprisoned in Coldbath Fields prison without any accusation being made against him. In a few weeks he was released, but on the suspension of the Habeas Corpus Act in the autumn of 1798 he was again seized and imprisoned in the House of Industry at Shrewsbury, and in the Tothill Fields bridewell until 1800. He was then a soured and embittered man, and began to form a plot against the government. As a man of sense and education he can never have expected his plot to succeed. According to the evidence given at his trial by spies, Despard's idea was to win over some of the soldiers of the guards, and with their help to seize the Tower and the Bank of England, assassinate the king on his way to open parliament, and stop the mails going out of London. The whole plan is so ridiculous that it cannot be regarded seriously; but the government arrested Despard and forty labouring men and soldiers, who were mostly Irish, at the Oakley Arms, Lambeth, on 16 Nov. 1802. He was tried with twelve of his poor associates before a special commission, consisting of Lord-chief-justice Ellenborough and Justices Le Blanc, Chambré, and Thompson, at the New Sessions House, Horsemonger Lane, on 7 and 9 Feb. 1803. The attorney-general prosecuted, and Serjeant Best defended Despard; but the evidence of the spies was too strong against him, and he was found guilty of high treason and condemned to death. The most interesting evidence given at the trial was that of Lord Nelson as to character, who said, referring to the days of the San Juan expedition: 'We served together in 1779 on the Spanish main; we were together in the enemies' trenches and slept in the same tent. Colonel Despard was then a loyal man and a brave officer.' After his condemnation Despard refused to attend chapel or receive the sacrament, and on 21 Feb. 1803 he was drawn on a hurdle to the county gaol at Newington with six of his associates. He delivered a long address on the scaffold in front of the gaol, which was loudly cheered, and was then hanged and his head cut off, the rest of the horrible mutilations prescribed by his sentence being re-mitted. His remains were handed to his widow, who was present at the execution, and were buried in St. Paul's churchyard, close to the north door of the cathedral.

[Memoirs of Edward Marcus Despard, by James Bannantine, his secretary when king's superintendent at Honduras, &c., 1799, on which are founded the biographies in the Georgian Biography in the Gentleman's Magazine, &c., and that prefixed to the Whole Proceedings on the Trial of Colonel Despard and the other State prisoners before a Special Commission at the New Sessions House, Horsemonger Lane, Southwark, 7 and 9 Feb. 1803, to which are prefixed original and authentic Memoirs of Colonel Despard. The best report of the trial is that taken by James and W. Brodie Gurney in shorthand, and published immediately afterwards.]

Henry Morse Stephens

published 1888

VAUGHAN Benjamin

(1751–1835)

Politician and political economist, born in Jamaica on 19 April 1751, was eldest son of Samuel Vaughan, a West India merchant and planter, who settled in London, by his wife Sarah, daughter of Benjamin Hallowell of Boston. William Vaughan (1752–1830) was his younger brother. Benjamin was educated at Newcome's school in Hackney, at the nonconformist academy at Warrington, and at Cambridge University, but was prevented by the system of religious tests from graduating, being a unitarian. He apparently became acquainted with Lord Shelburne through Benjamin Horne, the elder brother of John Horne Tooke, and soon gained the confidence of that statesman, by whom he was occasionally employed in confidential political business and as private secretary. He also studied law at the Temple and medicine in Edinburgh; it is said because William Manning, whose daughter Sarah he married on 30 June 1781, had at first refused his consent to the marriage on the ground that he had no profession (Vaughan's wife was aunt of Cardinal Manning). He subsequently returned to mercantile pursuits, and entered into a partnership with his brother-in-law, William Manning. He made acquaintance with Benjamin Franklin, with whom he afterwards contracted a warm friendship and continued to correspond after the outbreak of the war with the colonies. Like all the followers of Lord Shelburne, he sided with the colonists in their struggle with the mother country, and his political as well as his religious sympathies brought him into intimate relations with Price, Priestley, Paine, and Horne Tooke during the American war and the French revolution. In June 1782 he was sent to Paris to give private assurances to Franklin that the death of Lord Rockingham and the accession to power of Lord Shelburne had caused no change of policy in regard to the intention of recognising the independence of the United Colonies. In September of that year he took an active though unofficial part in the negotiations for peace at the secret request of Shelburne, who employed him on account of his intimate friendship with Franklin, and helped to persuade the English ministers to admit the independence of 'the United States of America' as a preliminary, and 'not as depending upon the event of any other part of the treaty.' He also urged that so great a divergence of views existed between the American and French negotiators in Paris as to give the British government an opportunity of concluding a separate peace with the colonies if this concession to their views were made. Vaughan's activity was resented by the English official negotiators, as appears by a letter of Richard Oswald to Lord Shelburne (*Life of Shelburne*, iii. 256, 321).

In 1790 Vaughan was in Paris with Lord Wycombe, the eldest son of Lord Shelburne (then Lord Lansdowne), and was in frequent communication with the leaders of the party opposed to the French court. At the 'fête de la fédération' of 14 July 1790 in the Champ de Mars he was almost the only stranger, except those belonging to the corps diplomatique, who obtained a place in the covered seats near the royal box. He describes Marie-Antoinette as looking 'well, fat, and sulky' (to Lord Lansdowne 15 July 1790). His French sympathies were not abated by the violent turn taken by subsequent events. In February 1792 he became member for Calne. He was very active at this time with his pen on commercial and economic subjects, as well as on politics. A 'Treatise on International Trade,' which was translated into French in 1789, and a series of letters to the 'Morning Chronicle' condemning the attack of the northern powers on Poland and France in 1792 and 1793, are his principal performances. There is a record of a speech by him in February 1794 on the subject of the negro population in the West Indies. But his active parliamentary career was now abruptly terminated, owing to the arrest of William Stone, brother of John Hurford Stone, a well-known supporter of the French revolution and a notorious enemy to the policy of Pitt. J. H. Stone was at the time in Paris. On William Stone a letter from Vaughan was found, apparently intended for J. H. Stone, and in consequence Vaughan was summoned before the privy council on 8 May 1794. Although the letter contained nothing that was in reality compromising, Vaughan, conscious probably that other and more dangerous documents might have fallen into the possession of the government, and aware that he had been introduced to William Jackson (1737?–1795), the Irish conspirator, left the country, and took refuge in France, where he arrived at the commencement of the reign of terror. War had been declared against England, and Vaughan was liable to be seized at any moment as a 'moderate' or as a 'foreigner.' He lived in hiding at Passy; Robespierre, at that time a member of the committee of public safety and at the height of his power, and Bishop Grégoire being among the few persons cognisant of the secret. In June his hiding-place was discovered, but he escaped with a month's imprisonment at the Carmelites, probably owing to the goodwill of Robespierre, and then left for Geneva. Thence he wrote a long letter to Robespierre, which actually arrived on 9 Thermidor (27 July) at the very moment of the fall of the dictator. It advised him to keep France within her natural limits, and to surround her with a fringe of free and allied states, a sort of anticipation of the Confederation of the Rhine (*Journal de la Montagne*, August 1794). This letter was alleged by Billaud-Varennes, in a speech on 28 July 1794, to be a proof that Vaughan was a spy of Pitt's. In 1796 he published a pamphlet at Strasburg in defence of the Directory, which he vaunted as a highly successful form of government, and one likely to be permanent. Subsequently he returned to Paris, and, though assured by Pitt, through his brother-in-law, William Manning, that he could safely return to England, he remained in France.

There are numerous allusions to Vaughan and Stone in the despatches of Barthélemy, the French minister in Switzerland, and in one of them Barthélemy describes Vaughan as a man 'dont le patriotisme, la probité, et les lumières sont infiniment recommandables' (*Papiers de Barthélemy*, iv. 593).

Vaughan preserved his good relations with Lord Lansdowne owing to the identity of their views in regard to France. About 1798 he went to America, probably despairing, like Priestley, of the political outlook in England. He joined his brothers and his relatives on the side of his mother at Hallowell, where he lived in a peaceful retirement. His political opinions are said to have adopted a very conservative hue in his later years. He died on 8 Dec. 1835, leaving three sons and four daughters. His descendants still live at Hallowell.

In 1779 Vaughan issued the first collective edition of Franklin's works in London, under the title 'Political, Philosophical, and Miscellaneous Pieces by Benjamin Franklin.' He also superintended the 'Complete Works of Benjamin Franklin,' issued in 1806 (London, 8vo), with a memoir.

[The best account of Vaughan is to be found in Alger's Englishmen in the French Revolution. See also Lord E. Fitzmaurice's Life of Lord Shelburne, vol. iii.; Papiers de Barthélemy, ed. M. Jean Kaulek, Paris, 1889; Appleton's American Biography; Sheppard's Reminiscences of the Vaughan Family; Introductory Narrative to William Vaughan's Tracts on Docks and Commerce, 1835; Diplomatic and Revolutionary Correspondence, Washington, 1887; Archives Nationales, Paris, ii. 221; Doniol's Participation de la France à l'établissement des Etats-Unis, Paris, 1886–92, v. 100, 161.]

EDMUND GEORGE FITZMAURICE

published 1899

HARDY Thomas

(1752–1832)

Radical politician, was born in the parish of Larbert, Stirlingshire, on 3 March 1752. His father, a sailor in the merchant service, died in 1760, and

Thomas, the eldest son, was taken charge of by his maternal grandfather, Thomas Walker, a shoemaker, who, after sending him to school, brought him up to his own trade. In 1774 Hardy went up to London, where he arrived with 18*d*. in his pocket. He, however, soon found employment, and in 1781 married the youngest daughter of Mr. Priest, a carpenter and builder at Chesham, Buckinghamshire. In 1791 he set up a bootmaker's shop at No. 9 Piccadilly, and soon afterwards began to take an active interest in politics. In January 1792 Hardy with a few friends founded 'The London Corresponding Society,' with the object of promoting parliamentary reform. The first meeting was held at the Bell, Exeter Street, Strand, when only nine persons were present, and Hardy was appointed secretary and treasurer. The first address of the society, signed by Hardy as secretary, and dated 2 April 1792, was distributed throughout the country in the form of handbills. On 27 Sept. a congratulatory address to the National Convention of France was agreed to by the society, and before the end of the year it was in correspondence with 'every Society in Great Britain which had been instituted for the purpose of obtaining by legal and constitutional means a Reform in the Commons' House of Parliament' (Hardy, *Memoir*, p. 24). In December 1793 the Edinburgh convention was dispersed, and Margarot and Gerrald, the delegates from the London Corresponding Society, were arrested. It was accordingly settled that another convention should be held in England, to which the Scottish societies should send delegates. This the government determined to prevent, and on 12 May 1794 Hardy was arrested on a charge of high treason, and his papers seized. After being examined several times before the privy council he was committed to the Tower on 29 May 1794. While he was a prisoner his wife died in child-bed on 27 Aug. On 2 Oct. a special commission of six common law judges, presided over by Sir James Eyre, the lord chief justice of the common pleas, was opened at the Clerkenwell session-house. On the 6th the grand jury returned a true bill against Hardy, John Horne Tooke, John Augustus Bonney, Stewart Kyd, Jeremiah Joyce, Thomas Holcroft, John Thelwall, and five others. On the 28th Hardy's trial for high treason commenced. It lasted eight days. Sir John Scott, the attorney-general (afterwards Lord Eldon), was the leading counsel for the prosecution, while Erskine, Gibbs assisted by Dampier, and two other barristers defended the prisoners. The evidence for the prosecution broke down, and the attorney-general's attempt to establish 'constructive treason' failed. Sheridan was called as a witness for the defence, and deposed that Hardy had offered him permission to peruse the whole of the books and papers in his possession. Philip Francis bore witness to the 'quietness, moderation, and simplicity of the man as well as his good sense,' while one Florimond Goddard, a member of the same division of the London Corresponding Society as Hardy, testified to Hardy's peaceable disposition, and asserted that when the society was dispersed from the public-houses, Hardy 'desired particularly, when we got to a private house, that no member would even bring a stick with him.' On 5 Nov. the jury returned a verdict of 'not guilty,' and Hardy was drawn in his coach by the crowd in triumph through the principal streets of London. A dinner was held at the Crown and Anchor on 4 Feb. 1795 'to celebrate the happy event of the late trials for supposed high treason,' at which Charles, third earl Stanhope, presided, and Hardy's health was drunk. Owing to his imprisonment Hardy had lost his trade, and had spent all his money in his defence at the trial. In November 1794 he was, however, enabled by the assistance of some friends to recommence business at 36 Tavistock Street, Covent Garden. At first he was overwhelmed with orders, and his shop crowded with people anxious to get a sight of him. The business eventually fell off, and in September 1797 he removed to Fleet Street, where he kept a shop until his retirement from business in the summer of 1815. While in the city he became a freeman of the Cordwainers' Company, and a liveryman of the Needlemakers' Company. During the last nine years of his life he was supported by an annuity contributed by Sir Francis Burdett and a few other friends. He died in Pimlico on 11 Oct. 1832 in the eighty-first year of his age, and was buried at Bunhill Fields, where Thelwall, after the funeral service, delivered an address. A number of his letters are preserved at the British Museum (Addit. MS. 27818). The Place Collection of Papers of the London Corresponding Society will also be found among the Additional MSS. (27811–17). One of these volumes (27814) contains a sketch of the history of the London Corresponding Society by Thomas Hardy. His own 'Memoir ... written by himself' (London, 1832, 8vo) was published shortly after his death, with a preface signed 'D. Macpherson, October 16, 1832.' A portrait of Hardy will be found in the third volume of Kay's 'Original Portraits' (No. 360).

[Memoir of Thomas Hardy, 1832; Edward Smith's Story of the English Jacobins, 1881; Howell's State Trials, 1818, xxiv. 199–1408; Annnal Register, 1832, pp. 220–1; Gent. Mag. 1832, vol. cii. pt. ii. pp. 480–1; Kay's Original Portraits, 1877, ii. 482–3.]

GEORGE FISHER RUSSELL BARKER

published 1890

WICKHAM William

(1761–1840)

Politician, eldest son of Henry Wickham of Cottingley in Yorkshire, a colonel in the 1st foot guards, by his wife Elizabeth, daughter of William Lamplugh, vicar of Cottingley, was born at Cottingley in October 1761. He was educated at Harrow and at Christ Church, Oxford, where he matriculated on 27 Jan. 1779, obtained a studentship, and became intimate with Charles Abbot (afterwards Lord Colchester) and William Wyndham Grenville (afterwards Lord Grenville). He took his B.A. degree in 1782, and then proceeded to Geneva, where he studied civil law under Amadie Perdriau, a professor in the Genevese university. He then graduated M.A. in February 1786. He was called to the bar at Lincoln's Inn in the ensuing Michaelmas term, and obtained a commissionership in bankruptcy in 1790. In Geneva he became acquainted with Eleonora Madeleine Bertrand, whose father was professor of mathematics in the university, and on 10 Aug. 1788 they were married. She lived until 1836.

Wickham's early intimacy with Lord Grenville and his Swiss residence and connections first brought him into public employment. Grenville, then foreign secretary, made use of his services in a secret foreign correspondence in August 1793, and in 1794 he was appointed superintendent of aliens in order to enable him to extend his foreign communications. His letters were carefully kept from the knowledge of the diplomatic service generally, and only reached Grenville's hands through Lord Rosslyn. In October 1794 he was sent to Switzerland on an exceedingly confidential mission, and the fact that he was thus engaged was assiduously concealed from the foreign office. When the fact became known about the end of 1794 it excited great jealousy, and secrecy being no longer attainable, Lord Robert Fitzgerald (then minister plenipotentiary to Switzerland) was recalled, and Wickham was appointed chargé d'affaires during his absence. In the summer of 1795 Fitzgerald was appointed to Copenhagen, and Wickham became minister to the Swiss cantons. His correspondence in this post was most extensive, and the information which he thus gathered for his government proved very accurate and valuable, particularly in connection with the condition of Provence and the royalist movements in La Vendée. He was in fact the government's principal spy on the continent, and his activity and success were so great that in 1797 the directory formally demanded his expulsion on the ground that he acted not as a diplomatic agent but as a fomenter of insurrection (Mallet du Pan, *Correspondance avec la Cour de Vienne*, ii. 355). He was privately pressed to relieve the Swiss government from its embarrassment by voluntarily retiring, and in November he thought it wise to comply, and withdrew to Frankfort.

In January 1798 Wickham returned to England and was appointed under-secretary of state for the home department, which office had been promised him some years before and kept temporarily occupied during his service in Switzerland. It was a busy and important post. His correspondence with Castlereagh during the Irish rebellion fills a considerable part of the first two volumes of the 'Memoirs and Correspondence of Viscount Castlereagh,' and portions of it are also to be found in Ross's 'Correspondence of Lord Cornwallis.' Wickham was also private secretary to the Duke of Portland. He returned as envoy to the Swiss cantons and the Russian and Austrian armies in June 1799, while still retaining his post at home, and was entrusted with very extensive powers of negotiating treaties and arranging supplies for the anti-revolutionary forces. He travelled via Cuxhaven, Hanover, and Ulm, and reached Switzerland on 27 June. His wife narrowly escaped capture at the battle of Zürich, and was announced in the Paris papers to have fallen into the hands of the French. He was engaged abroad until, early in 1802, he was appointed on Abbot's advice chief secretary for Ireland. He was then sworn of the privy council, and came into parliament for Heytesbury. Emmett's rising was the chief event of his term of office in Ireland, but the position was distasteful to him, and he resigned early in 1804. He would have been sent in 1802 and 1803 as minister either to Berlin or Vienna, but for the objection made by those courts to his nomination on the ground of his being personally obnoxious to the French government. He accordingly retired from active service on a pension of about 1,800l. per annum. This was the conclusion of Wickham's public career, except that for a short time (February 1806 to March 1807) he was a member of the treasury board under Lord Grenville, and went on one or two missions to Germany in connection with subsidies. In 1807 he retired into the country. He was made honorary D.C.L. at Oxford in 1810, and died at Brighton on 22 Oct. 1840. His portrait by Füger belongs to the family (*Cat. Third Loan Exhib.* No. 35).

He had one son, Henry Lewis Wickham 1789–1864, who was born on 19 May 1789, was educated at Westminster and Christ Church; having been called to the bar from Lincoln's Inn (13 May 1817), he was appointed receiver-general of Gibraltar. He was principal private secretary to Althorp when chancellor of the exchequer, and from 1838 to 1848 was chairman of the boards of stamps and taxes. He published with his cousin, John Antony Cramer, a 'Dissertation on the Passage of Hannibal over the Alps' (2nd edit. London, 1828), and died in Chesterfield Street, Mayfair, on 27 Oct. 1864 (*Gent. Mag.* 1864, ii. 794; Foster, *Alumni Oxon.* 1715–1886). His son,

William Wickham (1831–1897), was M.P. for the Petersfield division of Hampshire from 1892 to 1897.

[Correspondence of the Right Hon. W. Wickham, 1870; Berville et Barrière, Collection de Mémoires relatifs à la Révolution Française, vol. lviii. ch. xxxiv. p. 99; Lecky's History of England in the Eighteenth Century; Lord Malmesbury's Correspondence, iii. 454, 531; Lord Colchester's Diary; Ann. Reg. 1841; Mémoires et Correspondance de Mallet du Pan, ii. 336.]

JOHN ANDREW HAMILTON

published 1900

TONE Theobald Wolfe

(1763–1798)

United Irishman, eldest son of Peter Tone (*d.* 1805) and Margaret (*d.* 1818), daughter of Captain Lamport of the West India merchant service, was born in Stafford Street, Dublin, on 20 June 1763. His grandfather, a small farmer near Naas, was formerly in the service of the family of Wolfe of Castle Warden, co. Kildare (afterwards ennobled by the title of Kilwarden in the person of Arthur Wolfe, viscount Kilwarden). Hence Theobald derived his additional christian name of Wolfe. Upon the grandfather's death in 1766, his property, consisting of freehold leases, descended to his eldest son, Peter, at that time engaged in successful business as a coachmaker in Dublin; he subsequently was involved in litigation, and became insolvent, but towards the end of his life held a situation under the Dublin corporation.

The intelligence manifested by Tone as a boy led to his removal in 1775 from a 'commercial' to a 'Latin' school, but soon after this his father met with a serious accident and had to abandon business and retire to his farm at Bodenstown. Left to his own devices, Tone shirked his lessons, and announced his desire to become a soldier. Very much against his will he entered Trinity College, Dublin, as a pensioner in February 1781. At college he was incorrigibly idle, and, becoming mixed up as second to one of his companions in a duel, in which the opposing party was killed, came near to being expelled the university.

Meanwhile he fell in love with Matilda Witherington, who at the time was living with her grandfather, a rich old clergyman of the name of Fanning, in Grafton Street. He persuaded her to elope, married her, and went for the honeymoon to Maynooth. The girl was barely sixteen, he barely twenty-two. But, though much sorrow and privation awaited them, the union proved a happy one. The marriage being irreparable, Tone was forgiven, took lodgings near his wife's grandfather, and in February 1786 graduated B.A. But a fresh disagreement with his wife's family followed, and, having no resources of his own, he went for a time to live with his father. Here a daughter was born to him. With a view to providing for his family, he repaired alone to London in January 1787, entered himself a student-at-law in the Middle Temple, and took chambers on the first floor of No. 4 Hare Court. But this, he confesses, was about all the progress he made in his profession; for after the first month he never opened a law book, nor was he more than three times in his life in Westminster Hall. In 1788 he was joined by his younger brother, William Henry, who, having run away from home at sixteen and entered the East India service, found himself without employment, after he had spent six years in garrison duty at St. Helena. With him Tone generously shared his lodgings and ill-filled purse. They spent some of their evenings in devising a scheme for the establishment of a military colony on one of the South Sea islands, the object of which was 'to put a bridle on Spain in time of peace and to annoy her grievously in that quarter in time of war.' The scheme, drawn up in the form of a regular memorial, was delivered by Tone at Pitt's official residence, but failed to elicit any notice. Tone's indignation was not mollified by a mild rebuke from his father on the misuse of his time, and in a transport of rage he offered to enlist in the East India service. His offer was declined by the company. His brother, William Henry Tone, however, re-entered the company's service in 1792. Subsequently, in 1796, William went to Poona and entered the Mahratta service. He wrote a pamphlet upon 'Some Institutions of the Mahratta People,' which has been praised by Grant Duff and other historians. He was killed in 1802 in an action near Choli Mahéswur, while serving with Holkar (see Compton, *Military Adventurers of Hindustan*, 1892, p. 417).

Meanwhile a reconciliation was effected between Wolfe Tone and his wife's family on condition of his immediate return to Ireland. He reached Dublin on Christmas day 1788, and, taking lodgings in Clarendon Street, purchased about 100l. worth of law books. In February 1789 he took his degree of LL.B., and, being called to the Irish bar in Trinity term following, joined the Leinster circuit. Despite his ignorance of law, he managed nearly to clear his expenses; but the distaste he had for his profession was insurmountable, and, following the example of some of his friends, he turned his attention to politics. Taking advantage of the general election, he early in 1790 published 'A Review of the Conduct of Administration, addressed to the Electors and Free People of Ireland.' The pamphlet, a defence of the opposition in arraigning the administration of the Marquis of Buckingham, attracted the attention of the leaders of the Whig Club.

Tone, though holding even at this time views much in advance of theirs, listened to their overtures and was immediately retained in the petition for the borough of Dungarvan, on the part of James Carigee Ponsonby, with a fee of a hundred guineas. But, perceiving that his expectations of obtaining a seat in parliament through the whigs were not likely to be realised, he soon severed his connection with them.

Coming to the conclusion 'that the influence of England was the radical vice of' the Irish government, he seized the opportunity of a prospect of war between England and Spain in the matter of Nootka Sound to enunciate his views in a pamphlet signed 'Hibernicus,' arguing that Ireland was not bound by any declaration of war on the part of England, but might and ought as an independent nation to stipulate for a neutrality. The pamphlet attracted no notice.

About this time, while listening to the debates in the Irish House of Commons, Tone made the acquaintance of Thomas Russell (1767–1803), who perhaps more than himself deserves to be regarded as the founder of the United Irish Society. The acquaintance speedily ripened into friendship, and the influence of Russell, who held a commission in the army, led to a revival of Tone's plan for establishing a military colony in the South Seas. The memorial, when revised, was forwarded to the Duke of Richmond, master of the ordnance, who returned a polite acknowledgment and suggested that it should be sent to the foreign secretary, Lord Grenville. A civil intimation from the latter to the effect that the scheme would not be forgotten convinced Tone that he had nothing to hope for in that direction, and satisfied him that it only remained for him to make Pitt regret the day he ignored his merits. During the winter of 1790–91 Tone started at Dublin a political club consisting of himself, Whitley Stokes, William Drennan, Peter Burrowes, Joseph Pollock, Thomas Addis Emmet, and several others. But the club, after three or four months' sickly existence, collapsed, leaving behind it a puny offspring of about a dozen essays on different subjects—a convincing proof, in Tone's opinion, 'that men of genius to be of use must not be collected together in numbers.'

Meanwhile the principles of the French revolution were making great progress, especially among the Scottish presbyterians in the north of Ireland. On 14 July 1791 the anniversary of the capture of the Bastile was celebrated with great enthusiasm at Belfast, and Tone, who was becoming an ardent republican, watched the progress of events with intense interest. He had recently convinced himself that, if Ireland was ever to become free and independent, the first step must be the laying aside of religious dissensions between the protestants and Roman catholics. 'To subvert the tyranny of our execrable government, to break the connection with England, the never-failing source of all our political evils, and to assert the independence of my country—these were my objects. To unite the whole people of Ireland, to abolish the memory of all past dissensions, and to substitute the common name of Irishman in place of the denominations of protestants, catholics, and dissenters—these were my means.' He had little hope that the protestants of the established church could be induced to surrender their privileges in the interest of the nation at large; but that the protestant dissenters could be persuaded to unite with the Roman catholics seemed to him not only feasible, but, in the light of the Belfast resolutions, not very difficult to effect. To promote this object he in September published a well-written pamphlet, under the signature of a 'Northern Whig,' entitled 'An Argument on behalf of the Catholics of Ireland.' It was addressed to the dissenters, and its main object was to prove that no serious danger would attend the enfranchisement of the catholics. It is said that ten thousand copies were sold. Besides bringing him into personal contact with the leaders of the catholic party, it obtained for him the honour—an honour he shared with Henry Flood alone—of being elected an honorary member of the first or green company of Belfast volunteers.

Tone, at the suggestion of Russell, paid a visit to Belfast early in October to assist at the formation of 'a union of Irishmen of every religious persuasion in order to obtain a complete reform of the legislature, founded on the principles of civil, political, and religious liberty.' This was accomplished during a stay of three weeks, 'perhaps the pleasantest in my life,' in Belfast. He returned to Dublin 'with instructions to cultivate the leaders in the popular interest, being protestants, and, if possible, to form in the capital a club of United Irishmen.' He met with an ardent ally in James Napper Tandy, who, like himself, had strong leanings towards republicanism, but was content for the present to limit his object to a reform of parliament. With Tandy's assistance a club was started in Dublin; but Tone was surprised, and not a little mortified, to find that he speedily lost all influence in its proceedings. After a little time he drifted out of contact with it. Nevertheless, the rapid growth of the society gratified him, and his firmness, in conjunction with Archibald Hamilton Rowan, in supporting Tandy in his quarrel with the House of Commons, during which time he acted as pro-secretary of the society, strengthened its position.

But an intimacy with John Keogh, the actual leader at the time of the catholic party and himself a prominent United Irishman, had given a new turn to his thoughts, and, in consequence of the mismanagement of the catholic affairs by Richard Burke, he was early in 1792 offered the post of assistant secretary to the general committee at an annual salary of 200*l*. The offer was accepted, and his discreet behaviour won him the general respect of the whole body. After the concession of Langrishe's relief bill

(February 1792), and the rejection of their petition praying for 'some share of the elective franchise,' the catholics set about reorganising their committee with a view to making it more thoroughly representative. A circular letter was prepared inviting the catholics in every county to choose delegates to the general committee sitting in Dublin, who were, however, only to be summoned on extraordinary occasions, leaving the common routine of business to the original members. The publication of this plan alarmed the government, and at the ensuing assizes the grand juries were prompted to pass strong resolutions condemning it as illegal. Tone, at the request of the committee, drew up a statement of the case for the catholics, and submitted it to two eminent lawyers, who pronounced in its favour. Defeated on this point, the government, as Grattan said, 'took the lead in fomenting a religious war ... in the mongrel capacity of country gentlemen and ministers.' The catholics themselves were not united on the propriety of the step they were taking. In itself, indeed, the secession of the aristocracy, headed by Lord Kenmare, had strengthened rather than weakened the body. But the seceders had found sympathisers among the higher clergy, and of the episcopate there were several exercising considerable influence in the west of Ireland who regarded the present plan with disapproval. Tone paid several visits to the west of Ireland and to Ulster with a view to restoring harmony to the divergent parties that were concerned in the agitation. During the autumn of 1792 he was busily preparing for the great catholic convention which assembled in Tailors' Hall in Back Lane on 3 Dec. Of the proceedings of this convention he left a very valuable account, and as secretary he accompanied the delegation appointed to present the catholic petition to the king in London. Hitherto he had managed to work in harmony with Keogh. But in 1793 Keogh (who had 'a sneaking kindness for catholic bishops') allowed himself to be outmanœuvred by secretary Hobart, and, instead of insisting on 'complete restitution,' acquiesced in a bill giving the catholics merely the elective franchise, and consented to a suspension of the agitation. Before terminating its existence, the catholic convention voted Tone 1,500l. and a gold medal in recognition of his services. But he was bitterly disappointed, and more than ever inclined to look for the accomplishment of his plans to the co-operation of France.

Hitherto, notwithstanding his position as founder of the United Irish Society, he had avoided compromising himself in any openly unconstitutional proceedings. It was an accident that drew him within the meshes spread for him by government. Early in 1794 William Jackson (1737?–1795) visited Dublin with the object of procuring information for the French government relative to the position of affairs in Ireland. Hearing of Jackson's arrival from Leonard MacNally, with whom (unsuspecting his real character) he was on intimate terms, Tone obtained an interview with Jackson and consented to draw up the memorial he wanted, tending to show that circumstances in Ireland were favourable to a French invasion. This document he handed over to Jackson, but, fearing that he had committed an indiscretion in confiding it to one who, for all he knew, might be a spy, he transferred it to MacNally, by whom it was betrayed to government. The arrest of Jackson (24 April 1794), followed by the flight of Hamilton Rowan, alarmed him so effectually that he revealed his position to a gentleman, probably Marcus Beresford, 'high in confidence with the then administration.' He admitted that it was in the power of government to ruin him, and offered, if he were allowed and could possibly effect it, to go to America. The only stipulation he made was that he should not be required to give evidence against either Rowan or Jackson. The government acceded to his terms. But the prospect which just then presented itself of a radical change in the system of administration, in consequence of the appointment of Earl Fitzwilliam, induced him to delay his departure, and it was only after the collapse of Fitzwilliam's government in March 1795 that he began seriously to prepare to leave the country. That he might not be charged with slinking away, he exhibited himself publicly in Dublin on the day of Jackson's trial, and, having deliberately completed his arrangements, he sailed, with his wife, children, and sister, on board the Cincinnatus from Belfast on 13 June, just a month after the United Irish Society had been reorganised on a professedly rebellious basis. Prior to his departure he had an interview with Emmet and Russell at Rathfarnham, in which he unfolded his projects for the future. His compact with government he regarded as extending no further than to the banks of the Delaware. Arrived in America, he was, in his opinion, perfectly free 'to begin again on a fresh score.' His intention was immediately on reaching Philadelphia to set off for Paris, 'and apply in the name of my country for the assistance of France to enable us to assert our independence.' His plan was warmly approved by Emmet and Russell, and the assent of Simms, Neilson, and Teeling having been obtained, he regarded himself as competent to speak for the catholics, the dissenters, and the defenders.

After a wearisome voyage, during which he narrowly escaped being pressed on board an English man-of-war, he and his family landed safely at Wilmington on the Delaware on 1 Aug. Proceeding at once to Philadelphia, he waited on the French minister, Adet, and at his request drew up a memorial on the state of Ireland for transmission to France. Having little expectation that the French government would pay any attention to it, but satisfied with having discharged his duty, he began to think of settling down as a farmer, and was actually in negotiation for the purchase of a small property near Princeton in New Jersey when letters reached him from Keogh, Russell, and Simms, the last with a draft for 200*l*., advising him of the progress Ireland was making towards republicanism, and imploring him 'to move heaven and earth to force his way to the French government in order to supplicate their assistance.' Repairing to Philadelphia, and meeting with every encouragement from Adet, who had received instructions to send him over, Tone sailed from New York on 1 Jan. 1796 on board the Jersey, and, after a rough winter passage, landed at Havre a month later. With no other credentials than a letter in cipher from Adet to the Committee of Public Safety, with only a small sum of money necessary for his own personal expenses, without a single acquaintance in France, and with hardly any knowledge of the language, Tone, *alias* citizen James Smith, arrived at Paris on 12 Feb. and took up his residence at the Hôtel des Étrangers in the Rue Vivienne. Within a fortnight after his arrival he had discussed the question of an invasion of Ireland with the minister of foreign affairs, De la Croix, and been admitted to an interview with Carnot. He was soon at work preparing fresh memorials on the subject. His statements as to the strength of the revolutionary party in Ireland were doubtless exaggerated, but in the main he tried to delude neither himself nor the French government.

Every encouragement was given him to believe that an expedition on a considerable scale would be undertaken; but weeks lengthened out into months, and, seeing nothing done, he found it at times hard to believe in the sincerity of the government. Although his loneliness and his scanty resources depressed him, he liked Paris and the French people, and looked forward, if nothing came of the expedition, to settling down there with his wife. Money, for which he reluctantly applied, was not forthcoming, but a commission in the army, which he trusted would save him in the event of being captured from a traitor's death, was readily granted, and on 19 June he was breveted chef de brigade. With the appointment about the same time of Hoche to the command of the projected expedition matters assumed a brighter aspect. For Hoche, whom he inspired with a genuine interest in Ireland, Tone conceived an intense admiration, and on his side Hoche felt a kindly regard for Tone, whom he created adjutant-general. But even Hoche's enthusiasm was unable to bring order into the French marine department, and it was not until 15 Dec. that the expedition, consisting of seventeen ships of the line, thirteen frigates, and a number of corvettes and transports, making in all forty-three sail, and carrying about fifteen thousand soldiers, together with a large supply of arms and ammunition for distribution, weighed anchor from Brest harbour. Disaster, for which bad seamanship and bad weather were responsible, attended the fleet from the beginning. Four times it parted company, and when the Indomptable, with Tone on board, arrived off the coast of Kerry, the

Fraternité, carrying Hoche, was nowhere to be seen. Grouchy, upon whom the command devolved, had still between six and seven thousand men, and in spite of the absence of money and supplies (for the troops had nothing but the arms in their hands), he would have risked an invasion. But before a landing could be effected a storm sprang up, and, after a vain attempt to weather it out at anchor, the ships were compelled to seek the open sea.

On New Year's day 1797 Tone, after a perilous voyage, found himself back again at Brest, whence he bore Grouchy's despatches to the directory and the minister of war. Reaching Paris on the 12th, he heard of his wife's arrival at Hamburg, but being ordered to join the army of the Sambre and Meuse under Hoche, it was not till 7 May that he obtained a short leave of absence, and joined his family at Groningen.

Meanwhile another expedition against Ireland was planning, in which the Dutch fleet was to play an important part. Tone was allowed by Hoche to accompany the expedition. He received a friendly reception from General Daendels, and on 8 July embarked on board the admiral's ship, the Vryheid, of 74 guns. But the wind, which up to the point of embarkation had stood favourable to them, veered round and kept them pent up in the Texel till the expedition, owing to shortness of provisions and the overwhelming strength of the British fleet under Admiral Duncan, had to be abandoned. Other plans were formed, and at the beginning of September Tone was despatched to Wetzlar to consult Hoche. Here a fresh disappointment awaited him. Five days after his arrival Hoche died.

Hoche's death broke Tone's connection with the army of the Sambre and Meuse, and he proceeded to Paris. He had lost much of his old enthusiasm, while the intrigues of Tandy and Thomas Muir against him and Edward John Lewins gave him a disgust for the agitation which it required a strong sense of duty to overcome. On 25 March 1798 he received letters of service as adjutant-general in the Armée d'Angleterre, and, having settled his family in Paris, he set out for headquarters at Rouen on 4 April. But as the spring wore on his scepticism as to Bonaparte's interest in Ireland increased. His doubts were justified, for when the news of the rebellion in Ireland reached France, Bonaparte was on his way to Egypt. He himself, when he heard of the rising in Wexford, hastened to Paris to urge the directory to equip an expedition before it was too late. His efforts were warmly supported by Lewins, but, owing to the disorganised state of the French navy, an expedition on a large scale was out of the question, and all that could be done was to arrange that a number of small expeditions should be directed simultaneously to different points on the Irish coast. Inadequate as this might seem to accomplish the object in hand, Tone had no doubt as to his own course of conduct. He had all along protested that

140

if only a corporal's guard was sent he would accompany it. The first French officer to sail, on 6 Aug., was General Humbert, with a thousand men and several Irishmen, including Tone's brother Matthew. On 16 Sept. Napper Tandy, with the bulk of the Irish refugees, effected a landing on Rutland Island. Tone joined General Hardy's division, consisting of the Hoche and eight small frigates and a fast sailing schooner, La Biche. Three thousand men were on board, and they set sail from Brest on 20 Sept. Making a large sweep to the west with the intention of bearing down on Ireland from the north, but encountering contrary winds, Admiral Bompard arrived off the entrance to Lough Swilly on 10 Oct. Before he could land the troops a powerful English squadron, under Sir John Borlase, hove in sight. The brunt of the action was borne by the Hoche, and Tone, who had refused to escape in La Biche, commanded one of the batteries. After a determined resistance of four hours the Hoche struck, and two days later Tone and the rest of the prisoners were landed and marched to Letterkenny. On landing he was recognised by Sir George Hill, and, being placed in irons, was sent to Dublin, where he was confined in the provost's prison. On 10 Nov. he was brought before a court-martial, presided over by General Loftus. He made no attempt to deny the charge of treason preferred against him, but he pleaded his rights as a French officer. He had prepared a statement setting forth his object in trying to subvert the government of Ireland; but the court, deeming it calculated to inflame the public mind, allowed him to read only portions of it. He requested that he might be awarded a soldier's death and spared the ignominy of the gallows. To this end he put in his brevet of chef de brigade in the French army. His bearing during the trial was modest and manly. He was condemned to be executed within forty-eight hours, and, being taken back to prison, he wrote to the directory, commending his wife and family to the care of the republic; to his wife, bidding her a tender farewell; and to his father, declining a visit from him. His request to be shot was refused by Lord Cornwallis. Strenuous efforts were made by Curran to remove his cause to the civil courts. On the morning of the day appointed for the execution application was made in his behalf for an immediate writ of habeas corpus, and his application was granted by Lord Kilwarden. But the military officials, pleading the orders of Lord Cornwallis, refused to obey the writ, and the chief justice at once ordered them into custody. It was then that it was discovered that Tone had taken his fate in his own hands, having on the previous evening cut his throat with a penknife he had secreted about him. All that it remained for the chief justice to do was to issue an order for the suspension of the execution. The wound, though dangerous, had not proved immediately fatal. It had been dressed, but only, it is asserted, to prolong life till the hour appointed for the execution. After lingering for more than a week in great agony, Tone expired on 19 Nov. His remains, together with his sword and uniform, were given up to his relatives, and two days afterwards he was quietly buried in Bodenstown churchyard. A monument, erected by Thomas Osborne Davis in 1843, was chipped away by his admirers, and had to be replaced by a more substantial one, surrounded by ironwork.

His brother Matthew was taken prisoner at Ballinamuck and hanged at Arbour Hill, Dublin, 29 Sept. 1798.

Tone's widow survived him many years. On the motion of Lucien Bonaparte, the conseil des cinq-cents made her a small grant, and she continued to live at Chaillot, near Paris, till the downfall of the first empire. In September 1816 she married a Mr. Wilson, an old and highly esteemed friend of Tone, and, after a visit to Scotland, emigrated to America. She survived her second husband twenty-two years, dying at Georgetown on 18 March 1849, aged 81.

Wolfe Tone's 'Journals' (which begin properly in October 1791, but are of most interest during the period of his residence in France) supply us with a vivid picture of the man. At the same time it must not be forgotten that these journals were written expressly for the amusement of his wife and his friend Thomas Russell, neither of whom was likely to be misled into treating them too seriously. For Tone was a humourist as well as a rebel. Otherwise one might easily be induced, like the Duke of Argyll (see a very able but extremely hostile criticism in the *Nineteenth Century*, May and June 1890), into regarding him as an unprincipled adventurer of a very common type, whose only redeeming quality was that he was devoid of cant. That he had a weakness for good liquor and bad language is patent; but at bottom he was a sober, modest, brave man, whose proper sphere of action was the army, and whom circumstances rather than predilection turned into a rebel. He has no claim to rank as a statesman. His object was the complete separation of Ireland from England with the assistance of France, and the establishment of Ireland as an independent kingdom or republic. 'I, for one,' he wrote in the thick of the preparations for the invasion, 'will never be accessory to subjugating my country to the control of France merely to get rid of that of England.' After the suppression of the rebellion and the rise of O'Connell and constitutional agitation, his schemes as well as himself fell into disrepute; but when later on the ideas of the Young Ireland party gained the upper hand, he was elevated into the position of a national hero and his methods applauded as the only ones likely to succeed.

There are two portraits of Tone. One, drawn on stone by C. Hullmandel from a portrait by Catherine Sampson Tone, represents him in French uniform (published in 1827, reproduced in 'Autobiography,' 1893, vol. ii.). The other, some years earlier in date, 'from an original portrait representing him in volunteer uniform,' forms the frontispiece to the 'Autobiography' and to the second series of Madden's 'United Irishmen,' which also has a portrait of Tone's son, William Theobald Wolfe Tone, from a drawing by his wife.

Of Tone's three children, only one attained a mature age, William Theobald Wolfe Tone 1791–1828, born in Dublin on 29 April 1791. After his father's death he was declared an adopted child of the French republic, and educated at the national expense in the Prytaneum and Lyceum. He was appointed a cadet in the imperial school of cavalry on 3 Nov. 1810, and in January 1813 promoted sub-lieutenant in the 8th regiment of chasseurs. He took an active part in the campaigns of that year—at Gross Görschen, Bautzen, and Leipzig, where he was severely wounded. Being made lieutenant on the staff, aide-de-camp to General Bagnères, and a member of the legion of honour, he retired from military service on the abdication of Napoleon, but returned to his standard after his escape from Elba, and was entrusted with the organisation of a defensive force on the Rhine and the Spanish frontiers. He quitted France after the battle of Waterloo, and in 1816 settled down in New York, where for some time he studied law. On 12 July 1820 he was appointed second lieutenant of light artillery, and was transferred to the 1st artillery on 1 June 1821, but resigned on 31 Dec. 1826. He married Catherine, daughter of his father's friend, William Sampson, in 1825, but died of consumption on 10 Oct. 1828, and was buried on Long Island. Besides a juvenile work, entitled 'L'État civil et politique de l'Italie sous la domination des Goths' (Paris, 1813), he was the author of 'School of Cavalry, or a System for Instruction . . ., proposed for the Cavalry of the United States' (Georgetown, 1824). Shortly before his death he published his father's journals and political writings, to which he appended an account of Tone's last days under the title 'Life of Theobald Wolfe Tone' (2 vols. Washington, 1826).

[Life of Theobald Wolfe Tone, Washington, 1826; the only complete edition containing both the 'Journals' and Tone's political writings. An edition re-arranged with useful notes by Mr. Barry O'Brien, under the title 'The Auto-biography of Wolfe Tone' (with two mezzotint portraits), was published in 1893; Madden's United Irishmen; Gent. Mag. 1798, ii. 1084; Cat. of Graduates Trinity Coll. Dublin; Howell's State Trials, xxvii. 613–26; Cornwallis Corresp. ii. 341, 362, 415, 434–5; Biographical Anecdotes of the Founders of the late Irish Rebellion; Webb's Compendium of Irish Biography; Biographie Nouvelle des Contemporains; Appleton's Cyclopædia of American Biography.]

ROBERT DUNLOP

published 1898

THELWALL John

(1764–1834)

Reformer and lecturer on elocution, son of Joseph Thelwall (1731–1772), a silk mercer, and grandson of Walter Thelwall, a naval surgeon, was born at Chandos Street, Covent Garden, on 27 July 1764. On his father's death in 1772 his mother decided to continue the business, but it was not until 1777 that John was removed from school at Highgate and put behind the counter. His duties were distasteful to him, and he devoted most of his time to indiscriminate reading, which he varied by making copies of engravings. Discord prevailed in the family, his eldest brother being addicted to heavy drinking, while the mother was constantly reproaching and castigating John for his fondness for books. To end this state of things he consented to be apprenticed to a tailor, but here again exception was taken to his studious habits. Having parted from his master by mutual consent, he began studying divinity until his brother-in-law, who held a position at the chancery bar, caused him to be articled in 1782 to John Impey, attorney, of Inner Temple Lane. Here, again, his independent views precluded the pursuit of professional success. He studied the poets and philosophers in preference to his law-books, avowed his distaste for copying 'the trash of an office,' and refused to certify documents he had not read. His moral exaltation was such that he conceived not only a dislike for oaths, but a rooted objection to commit himself even to a promise. Impey formed an attachment for him in spite of his eccentricities, but he insisted on having his indentures cancelled on the score of the scruples which he entertained about practising the profession. He was now for a time to become dependent wholly upon his pen. He had already written for the periodicals, and in 1787 he published 'Poems upon various Subjects' (London, 2 vols. 8vo) which was favourably noticed in the 'Critical Review.' About the same time he became editor of the 'Biographical and Imperial Magazine,' for which he received a salary of 50l. He made perhaps as much by contributions to other periodicals, and devoted half his income to the support of his mother, who had failed in her business.

Thelwall commenced his political career by speaking at the meetings of the society for free debate at the Coachmakers' Hall. In the course of the discussions in which he took part a number of radical views became grafted upon his original high tory doctrines, and when the States-General met at Versailles in 1789, he rapidly became 'intoxicated with the French doctrines of the day.' Though he suffered originally from a marked

144

hesitation of speech and even a slight lisp, he gradually developed with the voice of a demagogue a genuine declamatory power. He made an impression at Coachmakers' Hall by an eloquent speech in which he opposed the compact formed by the rival parties to neutralise the voice of the Westminster electors in 1790. When it was determined to nominate an independent candidate, he was asked to act as a poll clerk, and he soon won the friendship of the veteran Horne Tooke when the latter resolved to contest the seat. Tooke so appreciated his talents that he offered to send him to the university and to use his influence to obtain his subsequent advancement in the church. But Thelwall had formed other plans for his future. His income was steadily increasing, and during the summer of 1791 he married and settled down near the Borough hospitals in order that he might attend the anatomical and medical lectures of Henry Cline, William Babington, and others. He was also a frequent attendant at the lecture-room of John Hunter. He joined the Physical Society at Guy's Hospital, and read before it 'An Essay on Animal Vitality,' which was much applauded (London, 1793, 8vo).

In the meantime the advanced opinions which Thelwall shared were rapidly spreading in London, and 1791 saw the formation of a number of Jacobin societies. Thelwall joined the Society of the Friends of the People, and he became a prominent member of the Corresponding Society founded by Thomas Hardy (1752–1832) in January 1792. One of 'Citizen Thelwall's' sallies at the Capel Court Society, in which he likened a crowned despot to a bantam cock on a dunghill, caught the radical taste of the day. When this rodomontade was reproduced with some embellishments in 'Politics for the People, or Hogswash' (No. 8; the second title was in reference to a contemptuous remark of Burke's upon the 'swinish multitude'), the government precipitately caused the publisher, Daniel Isaac Eaton, to be indicted at the Old Bailey for a seditious libel; but, in spite of an adverse summing-up, the jury found the prisoner not guilty (24 Feb. 1794), and the prosecution was covered with ridicule owing to the grotesque manner in which the indictment was framed—the phrase 'meaning our lord the king' being interpolated at each of the most ludicrous passages in Thelwall's description. The affair gave him a certain notoriety, and he was marked down by the government spies. One of these, named Gostling, declared that Thelwall upon a public occasion cut the froth from a pot of porter and invoked a similar fate upon all kings. He was not finally arrested, however, until 13 May 1794, when he was charged upon the deposition of another spy, named Ward, with having moved a seditious resolution at a meeting at Chalk Farm. Six days later he was sent to the Tower along with Thomas Hardy and Horne Tooke, who had been arrested upon similar charges. On 6 Oct. true bills were found against them, and on 24 Oct. they were removed to Newgate. His trial was the last of the political trials of the year, being held on 1–5 Dec. at the Old Bailey before Chief-baron Macdonald. The testimony as to Thelwall's moral character was exceptionally strong, and his acquittal was the signal for a great outburst of applause. At the beginning of the trial he handed a pencilled note to counsel, saying he wished to plead his own cause. 'If you do, you will be hanged,' was Erskine's comment, to which he at once rejoined, 'Then I'll be hanged if I do' (Britton). Soon after his release he published 'Poems written in Close Confinement in the Tower and Newgate' (London, 1795, 4to). He was now living at Beaufort Buildings, Strand, and during 1795 his activity as a lecturer and political speaker was redoubled. When in December Pitt's act for more effectually preventing seditious meetings and assemblies received the royal assent, he thought it wisest to leave London; and Mathias, in the 'Pursuits of Literature,' mentions how

> Thelwall for the season quits the Strand,
> To organise revolt by sea and land

(Dial. iv. l. 413). But he continued for nearly two years denouncing the government to the provinces, and commenting freely upon contemporary politics through the medium of 'Lectures upon Roman History.' He was warmly received in some of the large centres; in the eastern counties, especially at Yarmouth (where he narrowly escaped capture by a pressgang), King's Lynn, and Wisbech, mobs were hired which effectually prevented his being heard.

About 1798 he withdrew altogether from his connection with politics and took a small farm near Brecon. There he spent two years, gaining in health, but suffering a great deal from the enforced silence; and about 1800 he resumed his career as a lecturer, discarding politics in favour of elocution. His illustrations were so good and his manner so animated that his lectures soon became highly popular. At Edinburgh during 1804 he had a fierce paper war with Francis Jeffrey, whom he suspected of inspiring some uncharitable remarks about him in the 'Edinburgh Review.' Soon after this he settled down as a teacher of oratory in Upper Bedford Place, and had many bar students among his pupils. He made the acquaintance of Southey, Hazlitt, and Coleridge (who spoke of him as an honest man, with the additional rare distinction of having nearly been hanged), and also of Talfourd, Crabb Robinson, and Charles Lamb. From the ordinary groove of elocutionary teaching, Thelwall gradually concentrated his attention upon the cure of stammering, and more generally upon the correction of defects arising from malformation of the organs of speech. In 1809 he took a large house in Lincoln's Inn Fields (No. 57) so that he might take the complete charge of patients, holding that the science of correcting impediments involved the correcting and regulating of the whole mental and moral habit of the pupil. His system had a remarkable success, some of his greatest triumphs being recorded in his 'Treatment of Cases of Defective Utterance' (1814) in the form of a letter to his old friend Cline. Crabb Robinson visited his institution on 27 Dec. 1815, and was tickled by Thelwall's idea of having Milton's 'Comus' recited by a troupe of stutterers, but was astonished at the results attained. Much as Charles Lamb disliked lectures and recitations, his esteem for Thelwall made him an occasional visitor at these entertainments in Lincoln's Inn Fields. Reports of some cases of special interest were contributed by him to the 'Medical and Physical Journal.'

Thelwall prospered in his new vocation until 1818, when his constitutional restlessness impelled him to throw himself once more prematurely into the struggle for parliamentary reform. He purchased a journal, 'The Champion,' to advocate this cause; but his Dantonesque style of political oratory was entirely out of place in a periodical addressed to the reflective classes, and he soon lost a great portion of his earnings. He subsequently resumed his elocution school at Brixton, and latterly spent much time as an itinerant lecturer, retaining his cheerfulness and sanguine outlook to the last. He died at Bath on 17 Feb. 1834.

He married, first, on 27 July 1791, Susan Vellum, a native of Rutland, who died in 1816, leaving him four children. She supported him greatly during his early trials, and was, in the words of Crabb Robinson, his 'good angel.' He married secondly, about 1819, Cecil Boyle, a lady many years younger than himself. A woman of great social charm and some literary ability, she wrote, in addition to a 'Life' of her husband, several little works for children. She died in 1863, leaving one son, Weymouth Birkbeck Thelwall, a watercolour artist, who was accidentally killed in South Africa in 1873.

Talfourd and Crabb Robinson testify strongly to Thelwall's integrity and domestic virtues. His judgment was not perhaps equal to his understanding; but, apart from a slight warp of vanity and self-complacency, due in part to his self-acquired knowledge, few men were truer to their convictions. In person he was small, compact, and muscular, with a head denoting indomitable resolution. A portrait engraved by J. C. Timbrell, from a bust by E. Davis, forms the frontispiece to the 'Life of John Thelwall by his Widow,' London, 1837, 8vo. A portrait ascribed to William Hazlitt has also been reproduced. The British Museum possesses two stipple engravings—one by Richter.

Apart from the works already mentioned and a large number of minor pamphlets and leaflets, Thelwall published: 1. 'The Peripatetic, or Sketches of the Heart of Nature and Society,' London, 1793, 3 vols. 12mo. 2. 'Political Lectures: On the Moral Tendency of a System of Spies and Informers, and the Conduct to be observed by the Friends of Liberty during the Continuance of such a System,' London, 1794, 8vo. 3. 'The Natural and Constitutional Rights of Britons to Annual Parliaments, Universal Suffrage, and Freedom of Popular Association,' London, 1795, 8vo. 4. 'Peaceful Discussion and not Tumultuary Violence the Means of redressing National Grievance,' London, 1795, 8vo. 5. 'The Rights of Nature against the Usurpation of Establishments: a Series of Letters on the recent Effusions of the Right Hon. Edmund Burke,' London, 8vo, 1796. 6. 'Sober Reflections on the Seditious and Inflammatory Letter of the Right Hon. Edmund Burke to a Noble Lord,' London, 1796, 8vo. 7. 'Poems chiefly written in Retirement (including an epic, "Edwin of Northumbria"),' Hereford, 1801, 8vo; 2nd ed. 1805. 8. 'Selections from Thelwall's Lectures on the Science and Practice of Elocution,' York, 1802, 8vo; various editions. 9. 'A Letter to Francis Jeffrey on certain Calumnies in the "Edinburgh Review,"' Edinburgh, 1804, 8vo. 10. 'Monody on the Right Hon. Charles James Fox,' London, 1806, 8vo; two editions. 11. 'The Vestibule of Eloquence ... Original Articles, Oratorical and Poetical, intended as Exercises in Recitation,' London, 1810, 8vo. 12. 'Selections for the Illustration of a Course of Instructions on the Rhythmus and Utterance of the English Language,' London, 1812, 8vo. 13. 'Poetical Recreations of the Champion and his Literary Correspondents; with a Selection of Essays,' London, 1822, 8vo.

Thelwall's eldest son, Algernon Sydney Thelwall 1795–1863, born at Cowes in 1795, entered Trinity College, Cambridge, and graduated B.A. as eighteenth wrangler in 1818, and M.A. in 1826. Having taken orders, he served as English chaplain and missionary to the Jews at Amsterdam 1819–26, became curate of Blackford, Somerset, in 1828, and then successively minister of Bedford Chapel, Bloomsbury (1842–3), and curate of St. Matthew's, Pell Street (1848–50). He was one of the founders of the Trinitarian Bible Society. From 1850 he was well known as lecturer on public reading and elocution at King's College, London. He died at his house in Torrington Square on 30 Nov. 1863 (*Gent. Mag.* 1864, i. 128).

Among his voluminous writings, the most important are: 1. 'A Scriptural Refutation of Mr. Irving's Heresy,' London, 1834, 12mo. 2. 'The Iniquities of the Opium Trade with China,' London, 1839, 12mo. 3. 'Old Testament Gospel, or Tracts for the Jews,' London, 1847, 12mo. 4. 'The Importance of Elocution in connexion with Ministerial Usefulness,' London, 1850, 8vo. 5. 'The Reading Desk and the Pulpit,' London, 1861, 8vo. He also compiled the 'Proceedings of the Anti-Maynooth Conference of 1845' (London, 8vo).

[Life of John Thelwall, 1837, vol. i. (no more published); Gent. Mag. 1834, ii. 549; Talfourd's Memoirs of Charles Lamb, ed. Fitzgerald; Crabb Robinson's Diary, passim; Smith's Story of the English Jacobins, 1881; Britton's Autobiography, 1850, i. 180–6 (a warm eulogy from one who knew him well); Coleridge's Table Talk; Life of William Wilberforce, 1838, iii. 499; Edmonds's Poetry of the Anti-Jacobin; Wallas's Life of Francis Place, 1898; Trial of Tooke, Thelwall, and Hardy, 1795, 8vo; Howell's State Trials, xxiii. 1013; Watt's Bibl. Britannica; Penny Encyclopædia; Brit. Mus. Cat.]

THOMAS SECCOMBE

published 1898

THISTLEWOOD Arthur
(1770–1820)

Cato Street conspirator, born at Tupholme, about twelve miles from Lincoln, in 1770, was the son of William Thistlewood of Bardney, Lincolnshire, and is said to have been illegitimate. His father was a well-known breeder of stock and respectable farmer under the Vyners of Gautby. Thistlewood appears to have been brought up as a land surveyor, but never followed that business; his brother, with whom he has been confused, was apprenticed to a doctor. He is said to have become unsettled in mind through reading the works of Paine, and to have proceeded to America and from America to France shortly before the downfall of Robespierre. In Paris he probably developed the opinions which marked him through life, and, according to Alison (*Hist. Eur.* ii. 424), returned to England in 1794 'firmly persuaded that the first duty of a patriot was to massacre the government and overturn all existing institutions.' He was appointed ensign in the first regiment of West Riding militia on 1 July 1798 (*Militia List*, 1799), and on the raising of the supplementary militia he obtained a lieutenant's commission in the 3rd Lincolnshire regiment, commanded by Lord Buckinghamshire.

He married, 24 Jan. 1804, Jane Worsley, a lady older than himself, living in Lincoln and possessed of a considerable fortune. After his marriage he resided first in Bawtry and then in Lincoln. On the early death of his wife her fortune reverted to her own family, by whom he was granted a small annuity. Being obliged to leave Lincoln owing to some gambling transaction which left him unable to meet his creditors, he drifted to London, and there, being thoroughly discontented with his own condition, he became an active member of the Spencean Society, which aimed at revolutionising all social institutions in the interest of the poorer classes. At the society's meetings he came in contact with the elder James Watson

149

Thistlewood

(1766–1838) and his son, the younger James, who were in hearty sympathy with his views. In 1814 he resided for some time in Paris. Soon after his return to England, about the end of 1814, he came under the observation of the government as a dangerous character. Under the auspices of the Spencean and other revolutionary societies, the younger Watson and Thistlewood organised a great public meeting for 2 Dec. 1816 at Spa Fields, at which it was determined to inaugurate a revolution. At the outset the Tower and Bank were to be seized. For several months before the meeting Thistlewood constantly visited the various guardrooms and barracks, and he was so confident that his endeavours to increase the existing dissatisfaction among the soldiery had proved successful, that he fully believed that the Tower guard would throw open the gates to the mob. The military arrangements under the new régime were to be committed to his charge. The government was, however, by means of informers, kept in touch with the crude plans of the conspirators, and was well prepared; consequently the meeting was easily dispersed after the sacking of a few gunsmiths' shops. The cabinet was, however, so impressed by the dangers of the situation that the suspension of the habeas corpus bill was moved in the lords on 24 Feb. 1817, and the same day a bill for the prevention of seditious meetings was brought forward in the commons. Warrants had already been taken out against Thistlewood and the younger James Watson on the charge of high treason on 10 Feb. 1817, and a substantial reward offered for their apprehension. Both went into hiding, and, although the government appears soon to have been informed of their movements, it was not thought fit to effect Thistlewood's capture until May, when he was apprehended with his (second) wife, Susan, daughter of J. Wilkinson, a well-to-do butcher of Horncastle, and an illegitimate son Julian, on board a ship on the Thames on which he had taken his passage for America. The younger Watson succeeded in sailing for America at an earlier date. Thistlewood and the elder Watson were imprisoned in the Tower. It was arranged that the prisoners charged with high treason should be tried separately. Watson was acquitted, and in the case against Thistlewood and others, on 17 June 1817, a verdict of not guilty was found by the direction of the judge on the determination of the attorney-general to call no evidence. This narrow escape had little effect on Thistlewood; the weekly meetings of the Spenceans were immediately renewed, and the violence of his language increased. A rising in Smithfield was projected for 6 Sept., the night of St. Bartholomew's fair; the bank was to be blown open, the post-office attacked, and artillery seized. This and a similar design for 12 Oct. were abandoned owing to the careful preparation of the authorities, in whose possession were minute accounts of every action of Thistlewood and his fellow-committeemen.

The want of success attending these revolutionary attempts seems to have driven Thistlewood towards the end of October 1817 to active opposition to Henry Hunt and the constitutional reformers, and to considerable differences with the Watsons and other old associates, who, though ready to benefit by violent action, were not prepared to undertake the responsibility of assassination. About this period he appears for the first time to have considered plans for the murder of the Prince of Wales and privy council at a cabinet or public dinner, if sufficient numbers for 'a more noble and general enterprise' could not be raised (*Home Office Papers*, R. O.). Though naturally opposed to all ministers in authority, Thistlewood entertained a particular dislike to the home secretary, Lord Sidmouth, to whom he wrote about this period a number of letters demanding in violent language the return of property taken from him on his arrest on board ship. Failing to secure either his property or the compensation in money (180*l*.) which he demanded, he published the correspondence between Lord Sidmouth and himself (London, 1817, 8vo), and sent a challenge to the minister. The result was his arrest on a charge of threatened breach of the peace. At his trial on this charge on 14 May 1818 he at first pleaded guilty but withdrew his plea, and was found guilty and sentenced to twelve months' imprisonment, and at the expiration of the term to find two sureties for 150*l*. and himself for 300*l*., failing which to remain in custody. A new trial was moved for on 28 May, but refused. Thistlewood was confined in Horsham gaol. His sentence and treatment appear to have been exceptionally severe. On 29 June he applied to the home secretary for improved sleeping accommodation, and described his cell as only 9 feet by 7 feet, while two and sometimes three men slept in the one bed. During his period of imprisonment his animosity towards Hunt appears to have increased, though Hunt wrote to him in friendly fashion of his attempts 'to overturn the horrid power of the Rump.'

The full term of Thistlewood's imprisonment expired on 28 May 1819, and after a little difficulty the sureties requisite for his liberation were secured. Directly after his release he commenced attending the weekly meetings of his old society at his friend Preston's lodgings; a secret directory of thirteen were sworn, and more violent counsels immediately prevailed. In July 1819 the state of the country, especially in the north, was critical; the lord lieutenants were ordered back to their counties, and the authorities in London were in a constant state of preparation against meetings which it was feared would develop into riots. For a short time Thistlewood worked once again in apparent harmony with the parliamentary reformers, spoke on the same platform with Hunt, 21 July, and as late as 5 Sept. organised the public reception of the same orator on his entry into London; but the new union society was formed, 1 Aug., with the intention of taking the country correspondence out of the hands of Thistlewood and Preston, whose violence caused alarm to their friends. Thistlewood and Watson organised public meetings at Kennington on 21 Aug. and Smithfield on 30 Oct. which passed off without disturbance, although attended by men in arms. Thistlewood designed simultaneous public meetings in the disaffected parts of the country for 1 Nov., but this course was not approved by either Hunt or Thomas Jonathan Wooller, from whom he appears now to have finally separated. The reformers were at this period so nervous about traitors in their midst that even Thistlewood was denounced as a spy (Nottingham meeting, 29 Oct.). Despite, however, increased caution and endeavours to secure secrecy, the government was in receipt of almost daily accounts of the doings of the secret directory of thirteen. In November Thistlewood and his friends grew hopeless as to their chances of successfully setting the revolution on foot in London. They now looked to the north for a commencement. Thistlewood was invited to Manchester at the beginning of December, but lack of funds prevented him from going. No effective support seemed coming from Lancashire; Thistlewood regarded a 'straightforward revolution' as hopeless, and concentrated his efforts on his old plan of assassination. One informer not in the secret wrote on 1 Dec.: 'There is great mystery in Thistlewood's conduct; he seems anxious to disguise his real intentions, and declaims against the more violent members of the party, but is continually with them in private.' His exact intentions were being reported to the home office by George Edwards, who was one of the secret committee of thirteen, and especially in Thistlewood's confidence. At first an attack on the Houses of Parliament was meditated, but, the number of conspirators being considered insufficient for the purpose, assassination at a cabinet dinner was preferred. A special executive committee of five, of whom Edwards was one, was appointed on 13 Dec.; and the government permitted the plot to mature. From 20 Dec. 1819 to 22 Feb. 1820 Thistlewood appears to have been waiting anxiously for an opportunity; his aim was to assassinate the ministers at dinner, attack Coutts's or Child's bank, set fire to public buildings, and seize the Tower and Mansion House, where a provisional government was to be set up with the cobbler Ings as secretary. About the end of January 1820, wearied with waiting, he took the management of the plot entirely into his own hands, Edwards alone being in his confidence. A proclamation was prepared and drawn up with the assistance of Dr. Watson, who at this time was, fortunately for himself, in prison. In it the appointment of a provisional government and the calling together of a convention of representatives were announced. The death of the king, George III, on 29 Jan. was regarded as especially favourable to the plot, and the announcement of a cabinet dinner at Lord

Harrowby's house in Grosvenor Square in the new 'Times' of 22 Feb., to which Thistlewood's attention was called by Edwards, found Thistlewood ready to put his scheme into execution. The meeting-place which the conspirators had hitherto attended about twice a day had been at 4 Fox's Court, Gray's Inn Lane, but as a final rendezvous and centre to which arms, bombs, and hand grenades should be brought, a loft over a stable in Cato Street was taken on 21 Feb. Hither they repaired (about twenty-five in number) on the evening of 23 Feb., and, warrants having been issued the same day, the greater number of them were apprehended about 8.30 p.m. They were found in the act of arming preparatory to their start for Lord Harrowby's house. Shots were fired. Thistlewood killed police-officer Smithers with a sword, and escaped immediate capture in the darkness and general confusion. Anonymous information was, however, given as to his whereabouts, and he was taken the next day at 8 White Street, Moorfields. He was again imprisoned in the Tower, and was the first of the gang to be tried before Charles Abbott (afterwards first lord Tenterden) and Sir Robert Dallas and two other judges on the charge of high treason. After three days' trial, 17, 18, and 19 April, during which Edwards was not called as evidence, Thistlewood was found guilty and sentenced to a traitor's death. He was hanged, with four other conspirators, in front of the debtor's door, Newgate, on 1 May 1820. The criminals were publicly decapitated after death, but the quartering of their bodies was not proceeded with. Thistlewood died defiantly, showing the same spirit that he exhibited at the end of his trial when he declaimed 'Albion is still in the chains of slavery. I quit it without regret. My only sorrow is that the soil should be a theatre for slaves, for cowards, for despots.'

In appearance Thistlewood was about 5 ft. 10 in. high, of sallow complexion and long visage, dark hair and dark hazel eyes with arched eyebrows; he was of slender build, with the appearance of a military man. A lithographed portrait of him is prefixed to the report of the 'Cato Street Conspiracy,' published by J. Fairburn, Ludgate Hill, 1820.

[State Trials; Times, 2 May 1820; Annual Reg.; European Rev.; Gent. Mag.; Pellew's Life of Lord Sidmouth; Hansard's Parl. Debates, May 1820; Home Office Papers, 1816–1820, at the Record Office.]

WILLIAM CARR

published 1898

(1771–1798)

Irish informer, of Scottish parentage, was born on 29 June 1771, at Downpatrick. He tells us that he ran away from home when he was seventeen and became a sailor, making a short voyage to Cadiz. In a year he returned home, and after serving as apprentice to a painter and glazier, followed the trade of a glass-stainer for two years, but failed in attempts to start business in Dublin and Limerick. Early in 1796 he went to Belfast, and practised the profession of portrait-painting in miniature. There he joined the United Irishmen, and worked for the cause for thirteen months, neglecting his business in his enthusiasm. He was, however, distrusted by some of the leaders, and in revenge, as he admits, became an informer. Early in 1797 he was taken to Edward Cooke, under-secretary of state for Ireland, and gave him a great deal of information, most of which he avowedly invented, although he charges the under-secretary with adding names to the list of innocent people which he himself supplied. Cooke sent him to Newry, where General Gerard Lake was then stationed, directing the latter to treat him well and follow Newell's advice. He was lavishly supplied with money, all of which he confesses to have spent in debauchery. When examined before a secret committee of the Irish House of Commons, on 3 May 1797, he was 'with great ceremony placed in a high chair, for the benefit of being better heard,' and coolly admits that he deliberately exaggerated, 'and fabricated stories which helped to terrify them' (*Life and Confessions*, 1846? pp. 42–43). While in Dublin Newell lodged in Dublin Castle. Early in 1798 he pretended to feel remorse for his treachery, and announced to Cooke his intention of giving up his employment as a spy. It was arranged that he should go to England, with a pension, on 16 Feb. 1798, and settle in Worcester, under the name of Johnston, ostensibly to carry on his profession as a painter. Shortly after the final interview with Cooke he brought out 'The Life and Confessions of Newell, the Informer,' which purports to be written and printed in England. But it was privately printed at Belfast, by a printer named Storey, and Newell was then in that city. He confessed to receiving 2,000*l.* as a reward 'for having been the cause of confining 227 innocent men to languish in either the cell of a bastile or the hold of a tender, and, as I have heard, has been the cause of many of their deaths' (*Life and Confessions*). The work, which is unquestionably genuine, was dedicated to John Fitzgibbon, earl of Clare, and contains a portrait of the author by himself. It aroused much attention, and had a large sale.

Newell finally prepared to leave for America, taking with him the wife of an acquaintance whom he had persuaded to elope, but he was assassinated in June 1798 by those whom he had betrayed. He was induced, it is said, to go out in a boat to meet the ship which was to convey him to America, and is supposed to have been thrown into the sea. Another account says he was shot on the road near Roughford, and a third that he was drowned at Garnogle. Madden gives some particulars of the finding of bones thought to be Newell's on the beach at Ballyholme, ten miles from Belfast (*United Irishmen*, 2nd ser. i. 352).

[Froude's English in Ireland, iii. 245, where the name is wrongly given as 'Nevile;' Life and Confessions of Newell the Informer, 1798; Fitzpatrick's Secret Service under Pitt, 1892, pp. 12, 104, 173; Madden's Lives of United Irishmen, 2nd ser. i. 347 et seq.]

DAVID JAMES O'DONOGHUE

published 1894

PLACE Francis

(1771–1854)

Radical reformer, was born on 3 Nov. 1771. His father, Simon Place, was an energetic but dissipated man who had begun life as a working baker, and was in 1771 a bailiff to the Marshalsea court and keeper of a 'sponging house' in Vinegar Yard, Drury Lane. Place was sent to various schools near Fleet Street and Drury Lane from his fifth till his fourteenth year. His father (who had meanwhile taken a public-house) desired to apprentice him to a conveyancer, but the boy preferred to learn a trade, and was accordingly bound, before he was fourteen years old, to a leather-breeches maker. In 1789 he became an independent journeyman, and in 1791 married Elizabeth Chadd (he being nineteen years old and she not quite seventeen), and set up house in one room in a court off the Strand. Hitherto Place had lived rather an irregular life, but now he became rigidly economical and industrious. Leather-breeches making, however, was a decaying trade, and he had great difficulty in obtaining work. In 1793 the London leather-breeches makers struck, and Place was chosen as organiser. The strike having failed, Place was refused work by the masters, and for eight months suffered extreme privation. It is a singular proof of his resolute character that during those months he studied laboriously such books on mathematics, law, history, and economics, as he could get access to. He became secretary to his trade club, and in 1794, during another period of slack work, was secretary for several other trade clubs of carpenters, plumbers, and other workmen.

In 1794 he also joined the London Corresponding Society, whose secretary, Thomas Hardy (1752–1832), had just been arrested. After Hardy's acquittal on a charge of high treason, the society rapidly increased, and in May 1795 it had seventy London branches, with an average weekly attendance of over two thousand. Place was at that time the usual chairman at the weekly meetings of the general committee of the society (see the original minute-book, Brit. Mus. Add. MS. 27813). But after the passing of the 'Pitt and Grenville Acts' in November and December 1795, the corresponding society quickly declined. Place, who had always belonged to the moderate party on the committee, resigned in 1797, in consequence of the tactics of the more violent members. In 1798 all the remaining members of the committee, including Place's friend, Colonel Edward Marcus Despard, were arrested and kept in prison without trial for three years. During that period Place managed the collection and distribution of subscriptions for their families.

Meanwhile Place was not only improving his education, but was building up a connection with customers of his own, and gaining credit with the wholesale dealers. In 1799 he and a partner opened a tailor's shop at 29 Charing Cross, but after about a year the partnership was broken up, and Place moved to a new shop of his own at 16 Charing Cross.

He now gave up politics and devoted himself entirely to his business, reading, however, for two or three hours every evening after work was over. The shop was from the first extremely successful, and in 1816 he cleared, he says, over 3,000*l.* He had a large family, fifteen children being born to him between 1792 and 1817; five of them died in infancy.

In 1807 Place returned to political life, and took a leading part during the general election of that year in bringing forward Sir Francis Burdett as an independent candidate for Westminster. Burdett was put at the head of the poll without cost to himself, and after an unprecedentedly small expenditure by the committee.

For the next three years Place seems to have kept pretty closely to his business, but from 1810 onwards his time was more and more taken up by public affairs. When Burdett (April 1810) barricaded his house in order to resist the warrant committing him to the Tower, Place attempted to bring the sheriff and a body of constables to his help. When Burdett was released (21 June 1810), Place organised a great procession, which, however, was stultified by Burdett's absence. Burdett and Place quarrelled over this incident, and did not speak to each other for the next nine years.

Meanwhile Place was becoming known to the political thinkers as well as to the politicians of the time. In 1810 William Godwin the elder sought his acquaintance, and borrowed money of him at intervals till Place threw him off in 1814. About the same time Place began a long friendship with James Mill (1773–1836), who used to call at Charing Cross on his journeys between Stoke Newington and Bentham's house in Queen's Square Place. In 1813 Robert Owen came to London, and Place helped him to put his essays on the 'Formation of Character' into shape. In 1812 Place met Bentham, and from 1814 used to write long weekly letters of London news to Mill and Bentham during their visits to Ford Abbey. Since 1804 Place had regularly subscribed to the educational schemes of Joseph Lancaster, and in 1813 he helped to organise the West London Lancasterian Association. When the Royal Lancasterian Society became the British and Foreign School Society, Place was put upon the committee. But Burdett's ill-will and Place's notoriously 'infidel' opinions made his position in both societies difficult, and he left the West London committee in 1814 and the British and Foreign committee in 1815.

In 1817 Place prepared to give over his business to his eldest son, and went to stay some months with Bentham and Mill at Ford Abbey. Here he occupied himself in learning Latin grammar, and in putting together 'Not Paul, but Jesus,' from Bentham's notes. Sir Samuel Romilly, who met him at Ford Abbey, wrote to Dumont: 'Place is a very extraordinary person. . . . He is self-educated, has learned a great deal, has a very strong natural understanding, and possesses great influence in Westminster—such influence as almost to determine the elections for members of parliament. I need hardly say that he is a great admirer and disciple of Bentham's' (Bain, *Life of James Mill*, p. 78).

Romilly was elected for Westminster in 1818, but Place, who was always a bitter opponent of the official whig party, did not support him. After Romilly's death, Place helped John Cam Hobhouse, afterwards baron Broughton, as an independent reformer against George Lamb, Lord Melbourne's brother, the whig candidate. Lamb beat Hobhouse in February 1819, but was beaten by him in the general election of 1820.

Joseph Hume was introduced to Place by Mill about 1812, and Place used afterwards to collect much of the materials on which Hume founded his laborious parliamentary activity. The library behind the shop at 16 Charing Cross (where Place had gathered a splendid collection of books, pamphlets, and parliamentary papers) was a regular resort of the reformers in and out of parliament. An informal publishing business was carried on there by means of occasional subscriptions. Mill's essays from the supplement to the 'Encyclopædia Britannica' and many tracts by Place and others were thus issued. Place sometimes wrote forcibly and well, but the greater part of the tracts, newspaper articles, and unpublished letters and manuscripts which he left behind him are diffuse, and often almost unreadably dull. His only published book is 'The Principles of Population' (1822), a reply to Godwin's 'Enquiry,' which contains some of his best work. He wrote two articles in the 'Westminster Review,' which are both in his dullest manner.

Place was more successful as a practical politician. He was no speaker, and disliked publicity; but he was untiring in providing members of parliament and newspaper editors with materials, in drafting petitions, collecting subscriptions, organising agitations, and managing parliamentary committees.

From 1820 to 1830 he was continually gathering facts and arguments on such questions as the libel laws, the Newspaper Stamp Acts, the laws against the freedom of political meetings and associations, the laws of creditor and debtor, the wool laws, the duties on printed cotton, the cutting and flaying acts, &c. From 1816 to 1823 he carried on a campaign against the sinking fund. His greatest triumphs were seen in 1824, when after ten years of almost unaided work, he succeeded in getting the laws against combinations of workmen repealed, and in 1825, when he prevented an intended re-enactment of them (see Webb, *History of Trade Unionism*, chap. ii.). By this time Place was beginning to be talked about, and an article in the 'European Magazine' of March 1826 states: 'No one needs to be told that the whole popular liberties of this country, and, by connection and consequence, of the world, depend upon the electors of Westminster; and just as necessarily as the sinking of lead depends upon its weight, do these electors depend on Mr. Place, not only in the choice of the men whom they intrust as their representatives, but in the very subjects in which those men deal. When it is said that Sir Francis Burdett or John Cam Hobhouse made a proposition or a speech, thus or thus, there is a misnomer in the assertion; for the proposition or the speech belongs in justice to Mr. Place, and in all that demonstration of frantic freedom—that tumultuary tide of popularity which they propel—he is the influential luminary—the moon which stirs up the waters. ... Look over the notices of motions, and see when Joseph [Hume] is to storm sixpence laid out in the decoration of a public work, or sack the salary of a clerk in a public office; and when you find that in a day or two it is to astonish St. Stephen's and delight the land, then go, if you can find admission, to the library of this indefatigable statesman, and you will discover him schooling the Nabob like a baby.'

In 1827 Place's first wife died, and he seems, at least for a time, to have estranged many of his friends by his second marriage in 1830. But after the introduction of the Reform Bill in 1831 his library again became the meeting-place of the more extreme reformers, and he and his friend, Joseph Parkes, made active preparations during the crisis of May 1832 for the expected civil war. A placard drawn up by Place with the words 'Go for Gold and stop the Duke,' produced a partial run upon the Bank of England, and is said to have been one of the causes which prevented the Duke of Wellington from forming a government (see 'The Story of Eleven Days,' *Contemporary Review*, 1892).

After the passing of the Reform Bill Place's political influence rapidly declined. Westminster had been partially disfranchised by the 10l. clause, and no longer held the peculiar position which as a huge popular constituency it had occupied in the 'borough-mongering' days. Place himself lost the greater part of his fortune through the blunders of his solicitor in 1833, and was compelled to leave Charing Cross and take a house in Brompton Square. He helped, however, Joseph Parkes with the preparation of the municipal corporations report in 1835, and worked furiously, though vainly, to secure the complete abolition of the newspaper stamp at the time of its reduction to one penny in 1836. He and Roebuck published 'Pamphlets for the People' on these and other points in 1835. William Lovett and several other working-class leaders of the early chartist movement in London (1837–8) were his personal friends and disciples, and Place drafted at Lovett's request the 'People's Charter' itself (1838). But when once the chartist movement had begun, his influence over it was small. His individualist political opinions and the neo-malthusian propaganda which he had carried on by correspondence and conversation for nearly twenty years made Feargus O'Connor, James [Bronterre] O'Brien, and the other leaders of the chartists in the northern and midland counties hate him nearly as much as he hated them. At the same time being thoroughly disgusted with the weakness of Lord Melbourne's government after 1835, and with the refusal of the reformers in parliament (with the exception of Roebuck) to take up an independent attitude, he withdrew almost entirely from his parliamentary connection. The years between 1836 and 1839 were mostly spent on a long history of the Reform Bill, which remains (in manuscript) in the British Museum. In 1840 Place joined the Metropolitan Anti-Corn Law Association, and acted for some years as chairman of the weekly business committee. In 1844 he was attacked with what seems to have been a tumour on the brain, and, though he lived for ten more years, his health was always feeble. In 1851 he was separated from his second wife, and died in his eighty-third year, 1 Jan. 1854, at a house belonging to his daughters in Hammersmith.

From about 1814 till the time of his death Place carefully kept and indexed his political correspondence. In 1823, on the advice of Bentham, he commenced an autobiography which branched out into a series of long accounts of the corresponding society, the Westminster elections, the repeal of the anti-combination laws, and other political events in which he was concerned. All the accounts were illustrated by 'guard books' of documents. Seventy-one volumes of his manuscripts and materials are in the British Museum. The autobiography and letters are in the possession of his family.

It is difficult to convey the impression of almost incredible industry which one derives from a study of Place's manuscripts and correspondence. Through nearly the whole of his long life he began work at six in the morning, and sat often at his desk till late at night. That his political writings are not of greater value may be due partly to the fact that he did not get free from a very laborious and engrossing business till he was nearly fifty years old, partly to the fact that he habitually overworked, and was forced into a tired and mechanical style. His remains form an unequalled mine of information for the social history of this century, but he deserves to be remembered not so much for what he wrote as for what he did, and for the passionate sympathy and indomitable hope which was always the driving force of his activity.

[Place MSS. Brit. Museum, Add. MSS. 27789–27859; Principles of Population, 1822, and numerous pamphlets; Place Family papers; Bain's James Mill, pp. 77–9; Robert Owen's Autobiography, vol. i. *a*, p. 122; Webb's Hist. of Trade Unionism, chap. ii. For contemporary accounts of Place, besides that in the European Magazine (supra), see Chambers's Journal, 26 March 1836; Fraser's Mag. 1 April 1836 (with a portrait by Maclise); Monthly Mag., May 1836 (by 'A. P.' i.e. Richard Carlile); Northern Liberator, 30 Dec. 1837. A good appreciation of his life appeared in the Spectator of 7 Jan. 1854, and another in the Reasoner of 26 March 1854. A Life of Francis Place by Graham Wallas was published in 1898.]

GRAHAM WALLAS

published 1895

MORIER John Philip

(1776–1853)

Diplomatist, was the eldest of the four sons of Isaac Morier, and was born at Smyrna 9 Nov. 1776. He was attached to the embassy at Constantinople 5 April 1799, where he acted as private secretary to the ambassador, the seventh Earl of Elgin, best known for his acquisition of the 'Elgin marbles.' Morier was despatched on 22 Dec. 1799 on special service of observation to Egypt, to accompany the grand vezîr in the Turkish expedition against General Kléber, whom Napoleon had left to hold the country. Morier joined the Turkish army at El-'Arîsh, on the Egyptian frontier, 31 Jan. 1800, and remained with it until July. He published an admirable account of the campaign, under the title of 'Memoir of a Campaign with the Ottoman Army in Egypt from February to July 1800' (London, 8vo, 1801). According to the 'Nouvelle Biographie' he was taken prisoner by the French, but in spite of his character as the representative of a hostile power, entrusted, moreover, with a secret mission to co-operate diplomatically with the Turks with a view to the expulsion of the French from Egypt, he was set at liberty, with a warning that should he again be found in Egypt he would meet the fate of a spy. No authority, however, is adduced for this story, which is unsupported by any public or private evidence. In December 1803 Morier was appointed consul-general in Albania, where the policy of 'Alî Pasha of Jannina, the most powerful of the semi-independent vassals of the Porte, was for many years a subject of solicitude both to English and French diplomacy (Lane-Poole, *Life of Stratford Canning*, i. 104). In April 1810 he was promoted to be secretary of legation at Washington, and in October 1811 was gazetted a commissioner in Spanish America. On his return to England he became for a while acting under-secretary of state for foreign affairs in August 1815. In the following year, 5 Feb., he was appointed envoy extraordinary to the court of Saxony at Dresden, which post he held till his retirement, on pension, 5 Jan. 1825. He died in London 20 Aug. 1853. He had married, 3 Dec. 1814, Horatia Maria Frances (who survived him only six days), eldest daughter of Lord Hugh Seymour, youngest son of the first Marquis of Hertford, by whom he had seven daughters, one of whom married the last Duke of Somerset.

[Foreign Office List, 1854; London Gazette, 1 Oct. 1811; Ann. Reg. 1853; information from Sir E. Hertslet; private information.]

STANLEY LANE-POOLE

published 1894

WILSON Robert Thomas

(1777–1849)

Sir

General and governor of Gibraltar, fourth child and third son of the portrait painter Benjamin Wilson, was born in Great Russell Street, Bloomsbury, London, on 17 Aug. 1777. He was educated at Westminster school, and also under Dr. Joseph Warton at Winchester. After the death of his father and mother, his elder sister, Frances, married early in 1793

Colonel Bosville of the Coldstream guards, who was killed on 15 Aug. 1793 at the battle of Lincelles; with her assistance Wilson joined the Duke of York in the following year at Courtray, furnished with a letter of recommendation from the king. He was at once enrolled as a cornet of the 15th light dragoons.

He took part in the storm and capture of Prémont on 17 April 1794 and the action of the 18th. On the 24th he was one of eight officers with the two squadrons of the 15th light dragoons who, with two squadrons of Leopold's hussars, mustering altogether under three hundred sabres, attacked and routed a very superior French force at Villiers-en-Couché. This action prevented the capture of the emperor Francis II, whom the French were endeavouring to intercept on his journey from Valenciennes to Catillon, and had already cut off by their patrols. The results of this magnificent charge, undertaken with the full knowledge of the danger incurred and of the object to be attained, were twelve hundred of the enemy killed and wounded, three pieces of cannon captured, and the withdrawal of all French posts from the Selle, with the consequent safety of the emperor. Wilson's horse was wounded under him. Four years later the emperor caused nine commemorative gold medals to be struck—the only impressions—one to be deposited in the imperial cabinet, and the others to be bestowed upon the eight British officers of the 15th light dragoons. George III gave permission for them to be worn 'as an honorary badge of their bravery in the field' (*London Gazette*, 9 June 1798). In 1800 the emperor conferred upon the same officers the cross of the order of Maria Theresa, which George III on 2 June 1801 permitted them to accept, with the rank of baron of the holy Roman empire and of knighthood attached.

Two days after the affair of Villiers-en-Couché, Wilson was engaged with his regiment in the action at Cateau (26 April). He also took part in the battle of Tournay, or the Marque, on 10 May; in the capture of Lannoy, Roubaix, and Mouveaux on the 17th; in the disastrous retreat on the 18th to Templeuve, when he commanded the rearguard, and when the light cavalry, according to an eye-witness, 'performed wonders of valour' (Brown, *Journal*); at the battle of Pont à Chin on 22 May; and at the action of Duffel on 16 July. He greatly distinguished himself in September at Boxtel-on-the-Dommel, when, with Captain Calcraft and the patrol, he penetrated to the French headquarters, captured an aide-de-camp of General Vandamme and two gendarmes, mounted them on the general's horses, and, notwithstanding that a regiment of red hussars and a regiment of dragoons pursued for six miles by separate roads to cut him off, made good his retreat with the captives; and on the same evening falling in with a party of French infantry cut it to pieces. The British army having retreated into Germany, Wilson returned to England at the end of 1795, and joined the depôt at Croydon in February 1796.

He was promoted to be lieutenant, by purchase, on 31 Oct. 1794, and on 21 Sept. 1796 he purchased his troop. He married in 1797, and in May 1798 accompanied Major-general St. John to Ireland, and served as brigade-major on his staff, and afterwards as aide-de-camp during the rebellion of 1798. He rejoined his regiment in 1799, and accompanied it to the Helder; in this campaign the 15th light dragoons were greatly distinguished at Egmont-op-Zee on 2 Oct. Wilson also took part in the actions of 6 and 10 Oct., and returned with the regiment to England in November.

On 28 June 1800 he purchased a majority in Hompesch's mounted riflemen, then serving under Sir Ralph Abercromby in the Mediterranean, and in the autumn travelled across the continent to Vienna on a mission to Lord Minto, by whom he was sent to the Austrian army in Italy. Having communicated with General Bellegarde and Lord William Bentinck, he proceeded to join Abercromby. He landed at Aboukir Bay on 7 March 1801, and took part in the action of the 13th and in the battle of Alexandria on the 21st, when Abercromby fell and was succeeded by Major-general (afterwards Lord) Hutchinson; the latter employed Wilson on several missions. In July he entered Cairo with Hutchinson, was at the siege of Alexandria in August, and its capitulation on the 25th. Wilson left Egypt on 11 Sept. and returned to England by Malta and Toulon, arriving at the end of December. He was made a knight of the order of the Crescent of Turkey for his services in Egypt.

In 1802 Wilson published 'The History of the British Expedition to Egypt' (l.p. 4to), which went through several editions, was translated into French in 1803 from an octavo edition in two volumes published that year, and also appeared in an abridged form. The fourth edition in 1803 contained 'A Sketch of the Present State of the Country and its Means of Defence,' with a portrait of Sir Ralph Abercromby. Lord Nelson wrote a characteristic letter to Wilson, on receipt of a presentation copy, which is printed in Randolph's 'Life of Nelson.' The work derived especial popularity from the charges of cruelty which it brought against Buonaparte, both towards his prisoners at Jaffa and his own soldiers at Cairo. Of these charges the emperor complained to the British government, but, receiving no satisfaction, caused a counter report to be issued by Colonel Sebastiani. Wilson was appointed inspecting field-officer in Somerset and Devonshire under General Simcoe.

In 1804 Wilson published an 'Inquiry into the Present State of the Military Force of the British Empire with a View to its Reorganization,' 8vo, in which he made his first public protest against corporal punishment in the army, and was complimented by Sir Francis Burdett in a letter dated 13 Aug. 1804 for the service thus rendered to humanity.

Wilson purchased a lieutenant-colonelcy in the 19th light dragoons in this month, and on 7 March 1805 exchanged into the 20th light dragoons. He sailed with 230 of them in the expedition under Sir David Baird and Sir Home Popham on 27 Aug. from Cork harbour for the Cape of Good Hope, and after a voyage to Brazil, where he purchased horses for the cavalry, and a narrow escape from shipwreck, disembarked with General Beresford on 7 Jan. 1806 in Saldanha Bay, Cape of Good Hope, as an advanced guard. After the battle of Blaauwberg, which took place just before his arrival, Wilson was employed in command of the cavalry on outpost duty until the terms of the capitulation were settled, and in receiving arms, colours, guns, and horses at Simon's Bay until General Janssen and the Dutch troops were deported in February. In June he obtained leave of absence and returned to England in the Adamant, but was nearly lost at sea in passing from one ship to another of the fleet.

On 3 Nov. 1806 Wilson having been attached to the staff of Lord Hutchinson, then going on a special mission to the Prussian court, embarked with him at Yarmouth in the frigate Astræa, and was nearly wrecked in the Cattegat on the Anhalt shore, the guns having to be thrown overboard. He accompanied Lord Hutchinson and the king of Prussia to Memel in January 1807, and in February joined General Beningsen at the Russian headquarters of the army at Jarnova. He was present at the battle of Eylau on the 7th and 8th, and accompanied the headquarters to Heilsberg in March, and in April to Bartenstein, where on the 26th the emperor of Russia bestowed upon him the cross of St. George for his services at Eylau. Wilson took part in the campaign of June, was present at the action of the Passarge on the 5th, at the battle of Heilsberg on the 10th, and the battle of Friedland on the 14th, after which he retreated with the army to Tilsit.

On the conclusion of the peace of Tilsit he went to St. Petersburg, and thence to England with despatches, arriving on 19 Sept. On 2 Oct. he left England with a confidential communication from Canning to the emperor of Russia, arriving at St. Petersburg on the 20th. He left again on 8 Nov. with despatches from Lord Granville to Canning, containing intelligence which Wilson had himself been the first to procure, that the emperor of Russia was about to invade Swedish-Finland and declare war against England. Notwithstanding the fact that a Russian courier had preceded him by thirty-six hours (Wilson's passport having been expressly withheld to give the courier the advantage), Wilson pushed from Abo across the Gulf of Bothnia, in very bad weather, reached Stockholm before the courier, arranged that the courier should be delayed, sailed for England, landed in the Tees on the evening of the 29th, posted to London, and saw Canning in bed at four o'clock in the morning of 2 Dec. He was directed to keep quiet until Canning's orders to the naval authorities at Portsmouth had been executed; and on his return to breakfast with Canning the following morning he was complimented upon his activity, which had resulted in the seizure of the Russian frigate Sperknoi, with money to pay the Russian fleet, while a fast vessel had been despatched to Sir Sidney Smith to intercept the Russian fleet.

In 1808 Wilson was given the command of the loyal Lusitanian legion, a body raised out of Portuguese refugees in England under British officers, and in August went to Portugal as a brigadier-general in the Portuguese army. He was engaged in various encounters with the enemy in Castille and Estramadura during the retreat of the British to Coruña in 1808–9; and after the battle of Coruña on 16 Jan. 1809, acting in conjunction with the Spaniards beyond the Agueda, by a series of spirited and judicious movements, he kept open the communications with Ciudad Rodrigo and Almeida, and held the enemy in check. He had a good deal of desultory fighting, took part in the pursuit of Soult, and with the Lusitanian legion and three thousand Spaniards advanced to within nine miles of Madrid. After the battle of Talavera on 27 and 28 July Wilson found himself at Escalona, cut off by the enemy from Arzobispo; crossing the Tietar, he scrambled over the mountains, and with difficulty gained the pass of Baños on 8 Aug., as Ney's corps was approaching on its march from Placentia to the north. Wilson endeavoured to stay its advance, and defended the pass with spirit for some hours, but was eventually dislodged, and retreated to Castello Branco.

When the British army went into winter quarters, Wilson returned home, and, as the Lusitanian legion was absorbed in the new organisation of the Portuguese army, offered himself to Lord Wellesley for special service on 6 May 1810. For his services in the Peninsula he was promoted on 25 July to be colonel in the army, and appointed aide-de-camp to the king, and in 1811 received the Portuguese medal, and was made a knight-commander of the Portuguese order of the Tower and Sword. In this year Wilson published, in quarto form, 'Brief Remarks on the Character and Composition of the Russian Army; and a Sketch of the Campaign in Poland in 1806 and 1807.' In the autumn of 1811 his offer of service was accepted, and on 26 March 1812 he was given the local rank of brigadier-general in the British army, and accompanied Sir Robert Liston, the newly appointed ambassador to the Porte, to Constantinople, with instructions to assist in the conduct of negotiations for peace between Turkey and Russia (see Wilson's diary of the journey in *Addit. MS.* 30160). He arrived at Constantinople on 1 July, and on 27 July went on a mission from Liston to the grand vizier at Shumla, to the Russian admiral Tchichagoff, commanding the Danube army corps at Bucharest, and finally to the emperor of Russia at St. Petersburg. He reached the headquarters of the Russian army under Barclay de Tolly in time to take part in the battle of Smolensk on 16 Aug., arrived in St. Petersburg on the 27th, and had an audience with the emperor on 4 Sept. Having satisfactorily completed all the affairs entrusted to him, and received the thanks of Liston and of Lord Cathcart, British ambassador at St. Petersburg, he proceeded on the 15th, accompanied by his aide-de-camp, Baron Brinken, and by Lord Tyrconnel, to join the Russian army at Krasnoi Pakra, near Moscow, as British commissioner, with instructions to keep both Lord Cathcart and Liston informed of the progress of events.

Wilson took part in the successful attack on Murat at Winkowo on 18 Oct., in the battles of Malo-Jaroslawitz on the 24th, of Wiasma on 3 Nov., of Krasnoi on 17 Nov., and in all the affairs to the cessation of the pursuit of the French. He exchanged into the 22nd light dragoons on 10 Dec. 1812. Early in 1813 he marched across Poland to Kalish, and thence to Berlin, where he arrived on 31 March. On 8 April he proceeded by Dessau and Leipzig to Dresden. On 2 May he took a prominent part in the battle of Lützen, where, aided by Colonel Campbell, he rallied the Prussians, carried the village of Gros Gorschen, which he held until night, and subsequently drove the enemy back on Lützen. He further distinguished himself at the battle of Bautzen on 20 and 21 May, and at the action of Reichenbach on the 22nd. During a review of the troops near Jauer on the 27th the emperor of Russia decorated Wilson in front of the imperial guard with the cross of the third class or knight commander of the order of St. George, taking it from his own neck and making a most complimentary speech, in which he stated his desire to mark his esteem for Wilson's courage, zeal, talent, and fidelity throughout the war.

Wilson was promoted to be major-general on 4 June 1813. During the armistice he travelled about the country inspecting the fortresses. When Austria joined the alliance against Buonaparte and hostilities were resumed, Wilson was conspicuous in the attack upon Dresden on 26 Aug., when he took part in storming the grand redoubt, and was the first to mount the parapet, followed by Captain Charles. On this occasion he lost his cross of the order of Maria Theresa in the mélée, and the emperor of Austria presented him with another, which was sent to him with a complimentary letter from Count Metternich (dated Töplitz, 24 Sept. 1813). In the battle of 27 Aug. Wilson was with the emperor of Russia and General Moreau when the latter was mortally wounded. He was also present at the battles of Kulm and Kraupen on the 29th and 30th, and charged repeatedly with the Austrian cavalry on the 30th.

On 7 Sept. Wilson joined the Austrian army at Leitmeritz as British commissioner, having been transferred from the Russian army. On the 27th he received from the king of Prussia the grand cross of the order of the Red Eagle, of which order he had received the fourth class in the last war. He was with the staff of Marshal Prince Schwartzenberg, commanding the allied armies, at the battles of Leipzig on 16 and 18 Oct., and at the capture of the city on the 19th. Schwartzenberg wrote to Lord Aberdeen, the British ambassador, attributing the success at Leipzig on the 16th chiefly to Wilson's intelligence and able dispositions.

Shortly after the battles of Leipzig Lord Castlereagh appointed Lord Burghersh to be British commissioner with Schwartzenberg, and transferred Wilson to the Austrian army in Italy. Both the emperors and also the king of Prussia desired to retain Wilson with them. Metternich wrote to Aberdeen that he was commanded by the emperor to express his sense of Wilson's great services, and his wish that he should remain with the army, and Schwartzenberg told him that conspicuous as were Wilson's services in the field, they fell short of those he had rendered out of the field. Aberdeen wrote to Castlereagh (Despatch, 11 Nov. 1813): 'From his intimate knowledge of the Russian and Prussian armies, and the great respect invariably shown him by the emperor of Russia and the king of Prussia, he is able to do a thousand things which no one else could do. He was the means of making up a difference between the king and Schwartzenberg which was of the utmost importance.' Castlereagh was, however, firm; he deemed the applications of the foreign sovereigns an unwarrantable interference, and observed that if Wilson had the confidence of all other governments he lacked that of his own. Party politics alone account for the fact that, although loaded with distinctions by allied foreign sovereigns, he received none from his own. In November the emperor of Russia bestowed upon him the Moscow medal for the campaign of 1812.

On 22 Dec. 1813 Wilson went to Basle by Aberdeen's direction to join the allied commission, but on the 25th his instructions arrived from Castlereagh to join the Austrian army in Italy, and to report direct to him, keeping the British ambassador to Austria informed. Before leaving, the emperor of Russia presented him with the first class or grand cross of the order of St. Anne at Freiburg on 24 Dec., and the emperor of Austria promoted him to be knight commander of the order of Maria Theresa on 4 Jan. 1814. He joined Marshal Bellegarde at Vincenza on 12 Jan., accompanied him in the occupation of Verona early in February, and was present on the 8th at the battle of Valeggio, where he greatly distinguished himself and was nearly captured by the French. On the 10th he was present at the action on the right bank of the Mincio. On 28 March he went to Bologna, where he met Lord William Bentinck and Murat, with whom he commenced negotiations. The abdication of Buonaparte put an end to his mission, and in June he left Italy for Paris.

On 10 Jan. 1816 Wilson was instrumental, in conjunction with Michael Bruce and Captain John Hely-Hutchinson (afterwards third Earl of Donoughmore), in the escape from Paris of Count Lavalette, who, having been condemned to death, had escaped from prison by changing dress with his wife. Wilson passed the barriers in a cabriolet with Lavalette disguised as a British Officer, and conveyed him safely to Mons. He sent a narrative of the adventure to Earl Grey (reprinted in *Gent. Mag.* 1816), which was intercepted. He was arrested in Paris on 13 Jan. The three Englishmen were tried in Paris on 2 April and sentenced on the 24th to three months' imprisonment (see *Annual Register*, 1816). On 10 May a general order was issued by the Duke of York, commander-in-chief, expressing the prince regent's high displeasure at the conduct of Wilson and Hutchinson.

In 1817 Wilson published 'A Sketch of the Military and Political Power of Russia,' which went through several editions, and was severely attacked by the 'Quarterly Review' (vol. xix., September 1818). In 1818 Wilson was returned as member of parliament for Southwark, defeating Charles Barclay, the brewer, and on this occasion he replied to the attack of the 'Quarterly Review' in 'A Letter to his Constituents in Refutation of a Charge for despatching a False Report of a Victory to the Commander-in-chief of the British Army in the Peninsula in 1809.' In 1820 he was again returned for Southwark, defeating Sir Thomas Turton.

Queen Caroline (1768–1821), who had been friendly to Wilson and to whom his eldest son was equerry, died on 7 Aug. 1821. Wilson attended the funeral on the 14th, when an encounter took place between the household cavalry and the mob at Cumberland Gate, Hyde Park. Shots were fired, and Wilson interposed to prevent bloodshed. He was peremptorily dismissed from the army on 15 Sept. without any reason being assigned, or any opportunity of explanation afforded. Having purchased all but his first commission, he lost a large sum of money, and a subscription was raised to compensate him for the loss. On 13 Feb. 1822 in his place in parliament Wilson moved for papers, and in a long and able speech (see *Hansard*) vindicated his action, and called in question the prerogative of the crown to dismiss any officer without cause. The government, confining themselves to the questions of prerogative, easily defeated the motion. In 1823 Wilson went to Spain to take part in the war first in Galicia and then at Cadiz. He was again returned to parliament for Southwark in 1826, when the poll lasted six days, and he defeated Edward Polhill. He made a speech in the House of Commons on 12 Dec. on the policy of aiding Portugal when invaded by Spain, which was published separately. He was an active politician, and took a prominent part in the formation of the Canning ministry (see Wilson, *Canning's Administration: Narrative of Formation, with Correspondence, &c., 1827*, ed. Herbert Randolph, 1872, 8vo). He was again returned to parliament for Southwark in 1830. On the accession of William IV Wilson was reinstated in the army with the rank of lieutenant-general, to date from 27 May 1825. The Reform Bill was introduced in the House of Commons on 1 March 1831. Wilson voted for the second reading, but spoke without voting in favour of Gascoigne's amendment opposing the reduction of the number of members for England and Wales which was carried against the government. He did not seek re-election after the consequent dissolution of April 1831. He finally regarded the measure as 'the initiatory measure of a republican form of government.' By his attitude he lost for a time the colonelcy of a regiment.

On 29 Dec. 1835 Wilson was appointed colonel of his old regiment, the 15th hussars. On 23 Nov. 1841 he was promoted to be general, and in 1842 he was appointed governor and commander-in-chief at Gibraltar. He had only recently returned home when he died suddenly on 9 May 1849 at Marshall Thompson's hotel, Oxford Street, London. He was buried on 15 May beside his wife in the north aisle near the western entrance of Westminster Abbey, and a fine memorial brass, next to the grave of John Hunter, marks the vault (for will cf. Chester, *Westminster Abbey Register*, 513).

Wilson married Jemima (1777–1823), daughter of Colonel William Belford of Harbledown, Kent, eldest son of General William Belford of the royal artillery. She was coheiress with her sister, Mrs. Christopher Carleton, of their uncle, Sir Adam Williamson. Both Wilson and Miss Belford were wards of chancery and under age, and the marriage ceremony, with the consent of both families, took place on 8 July 1797 at Gretna Green and again on 10 March 1798 at St. George's, Hanover Square, London. They had a family of seven sons and six daughters. Of the latter, Jemima married, as his second wife, Admiral Sir Provo William Parry Wallis.

There are several engraved portraits of Wilson; one by Ward, from a painting by Pickersgill, represents him in uniform with all his orders; another is by Cooper after Wivell. A miniature was painted by Cosway and engraved by William Holl, and is reproduced for the frontispiece of Randolph's 'Life.' He also figures in the well-known painting of the death of Abercromby.

The following are works by Wilson not mentioned above: 1. 'An Account of the Campaign in 1801 between the French Army of the East and the English and Turkish Forces in Egypt,' translated by Wilson from the French of General Regnier, with observations, London, 1802, 8vo. 2.

'Narrative of Events during the Invasion of Russia by Napoleon Bonaparte and the Retreat of the French Army,' 1812, edited by Wilson's nephew and son-in-law the Rev. Herbert Randolph, London, 1860, 8vo. The introduction gives a brief memoir of Wilson up to 1814; 2nd edit. the same year. 3. 'Private Diary of Travels, Personal Services, and Public Events during Missions and Employment with the European Armies in the Campaigns of 1812, 1813, and 1814, from the Invasion of Russia to the Capture of Paris,' edited by the same, London, 1861, 2 vols. 8vo. 4. 'Life from Autobiographical Memoirs, Journals, Narratives, Correspondence,' &c., edited by the same, London, 1863, 2 vols. 8vo. This work was never completed, and stops at the end of 1807.

[Besides the materials for a biography supplied by Wilson himself in his works, and in election and other pamphlets, see especially A Letter in reply to Wilson's Enquiry, 1804; Forgues's Guerre de Russie en 1812, 1861; Dupin's Procès des trois Anglais, 1816; Nightingale's Trial of Sir R. Wilson, &c., 1816; see also War Office Records; Despatches; Alison's History of Europe (frequent allusions); Alison's Lives of Lord Castlereagh and Sir Charles Stewart (frequent allusions); Quarterly Review, vols. v. xiii. xvi. xvii. and xix.; Gent. Mag. 1816, 1822, and 1849; Ann. Reg. 1816, 1822, 1830, 1849; Blackwood's Mag. vols. viii. xiv. xvi. xxi. xxii. and xxviii.; Hall's Atlantic Monthly, April 1865; Mayne's Narrative of the Campaigns of the Loyal Lusitanian Legion under Sir R. Wilson, &c., 1812, 8vo; Public Characters, 1806–7, vol. ix.; Burke's Celebrated Naval and Military Trials; Royal Military Calendar, 1820; Royal Military Chronicle, vols. iii. and v.; Notes and Queries, 4th ser. vols. viii. and ix. 5th ser. vols. i. ii. iii. and v.; Tait's Edinburgh Mag. 1849 (obituary notice); Lavalette's Memoires et Souvenirs; London Times, 10 May 1849; Cathcart's Commentaries on the War in Russia and Germany, 1812–13; Londonderry's Narrative of the War in Germany and France, 1813–14; Odleben's Campaign in Saxony, 1813, translated by Kempe; Phillippart's Northern Campaign, 1812–13; Porter's Campaign in Russia in 1812; Walsh's Campaign in Egypt, 1801; Anderson's Journal of the Expedition to Egypt, 1801; Gleig's Leipsic Campaign.]

ROBERT HAMILTON VETCH

published 1900

EMMET Robert

(1778–1803)

United Irishman, third and youngest son of Dr. Robert Emmet, physician to the viceroy in Ireland, was born in Dublin in 1778. After being educated at several private schools in Dublin, he entered Trinity College on 7 Oct.

1793, and greatly distinguished himself there by winning prizes and by his eloquence in the Historical Society. A fellow student, Thomas Moore, the poet, describes his oratory as of the loftiest and most stirring character. His politics were, as might have been expected from the brother of Thomas Addis Emmet, violently nationalist, but his youth prevented him from having any weight in the councils of the society of United Irishmen. He was, however, one of the leaders of that party among the students of Trinity College, and he was one of the nineteen ringleaders pointed out to Lord Clare and Dr. Duigenan during their famous visitation held in February 1798, for the purpose of testing the extent of the sympathy exhibited by the students for the United Irishmen. When summoned before the visitors, Emmet took his name off the college books. This turn of events put an end to his thoughts of a professional career, but he continued to take the keenest interest in politics, and in 1800 visited his brother, a prisoner at Fort St. George, and discussed with him the expediency of a rising in Ireland. He then travelled on the continent, visiting Belgium, France, Switzerland, and Spain; he met his brother after his release at Brussels and studied books on military science. In 1802 he had interviews with Napoleon and Talleyrand. The former promised to secure Irish independence, but Emmet doubted his sincerity. Emmet returned to Dublin in October 1802 with his mind made up on the subject. He had no combined plan like that of the United Irishmen of 1798; he had little hope of military help from France, although Napoleon had promised to invade England in August 1803; he seems indeed to have laid his plans without expecting them to be successful. He had 3,000*l.* of his own, and 1,400*l.* was advanced him by a Mr. Long, and with this money he purchased a few stand of arms, forged pikes, and collected a few desperate or ignorant conspirators. His father's death in December 1802 gave increased opportunities for pursuing his plans. In the spring he formed depôts of arms at Irishtown, in Patrick Street, and at Marshalsea Lane, where forty men were employed in manufacturing weapons of war. He printed proclamations and a scheme of national government which should guarantee life and property and religious equality. An explosion in the Patrick Street depôt on 16 July hastened his plans. He took up his residence in Marshalsea Lane and prepared for an immediate outbreak. The details of the plot were precisely similar to those of Despard's in London, with which it had probably some connection. Emmet resolved to seize Dublin Castle, Pigeon House Fort, and the person of the viceroy, who was to be held as a hostage. What to do next Emmet does not seem to have determined, and he certainly made no attempt to get the feeling of the country on his side. On Saturday, 23 July 1803, the projected rising took place. A few men came in from Kildare and Wexford, others were at Broadstone, but all were without orders. At nine o'clock in the evening Emmet, dressed in a green coat, white breeches, and a cocked hat with feathers, together with a hundred wild followers, marched from Marshalsea Lane in utter disarray; they came across the carriage of Lord Kilwarden on its way to the castle, and murdered the old man with their pikes. Emmet was disheartened by this violence, and hastened to Rathfarnham. His followers assassinated Colonel Brown of the 4th regiment, whom they met on the Coombe. At the castle all was consternation; the Irish military authorities seemed in despair, and ordered the general assembly of all the troops in garrison; but before they had collected, and while the officials were in despair, news arrived that the ordinary guard had turned out and had easily dispersed the rioters. Emmet fled from Rathfarnham to the Wicklow mountains with a few friends. Anne Devlin, a daughter of his servant, brought him letters, and he returned with her in order to take leave of Sarah Curran, to whom he was engaged to be married, before escaping to France. His hiding-place was transferred to Harold's Cross, and there he was arrested by Major Sirr, the capturer of Lord Edward Fitzgerald, on 25 Aug. 1803. He was tried on 19 Sept. before a special court, consisting of Lord Norbury and Barons George and Daly, and though defended by Ball, Burrowes, and McNally, he was condemned to death, and hanged upon the following day. He made a thrilling speech before receiving sentence, and also spoke from the scaffold. The youth and ability of Emmet have cast a glamour of romance over his career, and that glamour has been enhanced by his affection for Sarah Curran, the daughter of the great lawyer, to whom Moore addressed his famous poem, 'She is far from the land where her young hero sleeps'; the lady afterwards (24 Nov. 1805) married a very distinguished officer, Major Sturgeon of the royal staff corps. Emmet was first interred in Bully's Acre near Kilmainham Hospital, and his remains are said to have been afterwards removed either to St. Michan's churchyard or to Glasnevin cemetery. An uninscribed tombstone in each burial-place is now pointed out as marking his grave.

[There are many biographies of Emmet, but far the best is that contained in Madden's Lives of the United Irishmen, 3rd ser. vol. iii.; see also W. H. Curran's Life of John Philpot Curran, and Moore's Diaries.]

HENRY MORSE STEPHENS

published 1888

(1780–1829)

[handwritten: X BUT CONTEMPORARY OF WELLINGTON]

Lieutenant-colonel, was son of Duncan Grant of Lingieston, Morayshire, and brother of Colonel Alexander Grant, C.B., in the East India Company's service, a distinguished Madras officer. Through General James Grant of Ballindalloch, Colquhoun Grant's widowed mother obtained for him an ensigncy in the 11th foot, to which he was appointed on 9 Sept. 1795, before he was fifteen, with leave to remain at a military school near London until promoted. He became lieutenant the year after, and in 1798 was taken prisoner, with the greater part of his regiment, in the unsuccessful descent on Ostend, and detained for a year at Douai. He obtained his company on 19 Nov. 1801, and served some years in the West Indies, at the capture of the Danish and Swedish West India islands, and afterwards on the personal staff of Sir George Prevost. He subsequently was with the 1st battalion of his regiment at Madeira and in the Peninsula. Napier, who was an intimate friend of Grant, wrote of him in after years, and describes his position as one of the 'exploring officers,' of whom Wellington said that 'no army in the world ever produced the like.' He conducted the secret intelligence, but never acted as a spy like his namesake John Grant (1782–1842). He often passed days in the enemy's lines, but always in uniform, trusting to his personal resources of sagacity, courage, and quickness (memorandum in *Autobiog. of Sir James MacGrigor*, App.). Grant, who had a talent for picking up languages and dialects, was a special favourite with the Spaniards, among whom he was known far and near as 'Granto bueno.' His position on the British staff was that of a deputy assistant adjutant-general. He became brevet-major on 30 May 1811.

As an example of the valuable character of Grant's services, Napier tells us that when Marmont came down on Beira in 1812, and was supposed to contemplate a *coup de main* against Ciudad Rodrigo, Grant entered the enemy's cantonments, and succeeded in obtaining information as to Marmont's numbers and supplies, which proved that he had no such intention. While watching the French movements on the bank of the Coa immediately afterwards, Grant was surprised by some French dragoons, his guide was killed, and himself carried prisoner to Salamanca. His popularity among the French officers, and his intimacy with Patrick Curtis and other members of the Irish College at Salamanca, caused uneasiness to Marmont, who appears to have confused the major with Grant the spy. After accepting Grant's parole, Marmont ultimately sent him off under an escort of three hundred men to Bayonne, with secret orders to put him in irons on reaching French soil. Holding himself thus absolved from his parole, Grant made his escape at Bayonne, introduced himself as an American officer to the French general Souham, with whom he travelled unsuspected to Paris, where he found out an English secret agent, and with his aid remained in the city openly for several weeks, sending intelligence thence to Wellington, as he had done from Salamanca. Finding Paris getting too perilous for him, he shipped in the Loire for the United States, escaped in disguise as a sailor to England, where he put himself right by arranging for the exchange of a French officer of equal rank, and then returned to Spain, arriving at Wellington's headquarters within four months after his capture. He was employed on intelligence duties during the rest of the Peninsular war, became a brevet lieutenant-colonel on 19 May 1814, and major in his regiment on 13 Oct. following.

On the return of Napoleon from Elba, Wellington recalled Grant, who had just joined the senior department of the Royal Military College, and placed him in charge of the intelligence department of the army, with the rank of assistant adjutant-general. In some of the staff returns he is wrongly described as 'Sir' Colquhoun Grant, 11th foot (compare *Army Lists*, 1815). On 15 June Grant, who was at Condé, received information from his spies that a great battle would be fought within three days. The tidings were accidentally delayed, and did not reach the duke until delivered to him by Grant on the field of Waterloo. Grant was afterwards useful in Paris, where he was on the watch to prevent the allies from appropriating spoils of war without regard to the rights of the British troops.

Grant was put on half-pay as major 11th foot in 1816, and so remained until October 1821, when he was brought in as lieutenant-colonel to the 54th foot, then proceeding from the Cape to India. He commanded a brigade of the forces under General Morrison (H.M. 44th and 54th and native troops) employed in Arracan during the first Burmese war, for which he was made C.B. A fever there contracted completely broke down his health, and the effects appear to have been aggravated by a sense of the official neglect with which he had been treated. He sold out of the service on 1 Oct. 1829, and died on the 20th of the same month at Aix-la-Chapelle (*Gent. Mag.* xcix. pt. i. p. 477), where a monument was erected to him in the protestant burying-ground. Sir James MacGrigor, army medical department, who married Grant's youngest sister, describes him as a kindly, amiable man, possessing in a higher degree than any other officer he had met all the better and brighter attributes of a Christian soldier.

[Army Lists; Napier's Hist. Peninsular War, vol. iv. bk. xvi. chap. vii.; Autobiog. of Sir James MacGrigor (London, 1861), pp. 289–95, also App. pp. 413–17, where is a memorandum of the services of Brigadier-general Colquhoun Grant, addressed by General Sir William Napier to the Duke of Cambridge in September

1857. A biography, chiefly compiled from these sources, is given in Chambers's Eminent Scotsmen, vol. ii. A good account of the operations in Arracan appears in Thomas Carter's Hist. Rec. 44th foot. Colquhoun Grant has been repeatedly confused with more than one other officer of the name of Grant, and particularly with Colonel Colquhoun Grant, 15th Hussars, who at no time was connected with the intelligence department of the Duke of Wellington's troops.]

HENRY MANNERS CHICHESTER

published 1890

GRANT John
(1782–1842)

[handwritten: X BUT CONTEMPORARY OF WELLINGTON.]

Lieutenant 2nd royal veteran battalion, and lieutenant-colonel Portuguese service, a famous spy in the Peninsular war, began his military career as a subaltern in the Glamorganshire militia, with which he served in Ireland in 1799. In the same year he volunteered to the line from the embodied militia, and was appointed a lieutenant in the 4th foot, but was placed on half-pay at the peace of Amiens. On the renewal of the war he was brought on full pay as a lieutenant of foot, which rank he held throughout the war. He served under Sir Robert Thomas Wilson on the Portuguese frontier in 1808–9, with the irregular force known as the Lusitanian legion, and was wounded. When Wilson was defeated and left Portugal, Grant joined the Portuguese army under Marshal William Carr Beresford, in which he became major, and afterwards lieutenant-colonel. Grant was much employed as a partisan leader and spy, in which capacity he assumed a variety of disguises, and underwent most extraordinary adventures. There is much confusion of his exploits with those of Major Colquhoun Grant (1780–1829), 11th foot, a scouting officer. Wellington wrote to Beresford, on 19 Feb. 1811, apparently in reference to John Grant: 'I wish he had sent us the examination of some of his prisoners. He appears to be going on capitally, and likely to save much valuable property in the Estrada. I shall be much obliged if you will tell him how much gratified I have been at reading the accounts of his operations' (*Naval and Military Gazette*, 1 July 1848, p. 429). At the end of the war Grant was appointed lieutenant in the late 2nd royal veteran battalion, and was retired on full pay when the veteran battalions were abolished. Grant acted as secretary to the committee formed in London by the Earl of Durham, Lord William Bentinck, and others in 1820, when Marshal Beresford was dismissed from his Portuguese command by the constitutional government. In 1823, at the time of the invasion of Spain by the French troops under the Duc d'Angoulême, Grant's committee despatched Sir Robert Thomas Wilson on a fruitless mission to the Peninsula. The promised volume of Wilson's memoirs dealing with the Lusitanian legion episode of 1808–9 and the Spanish mission of 1823 have not been published (see introduction to *Life of Sir R. T. Wilson*, 1793–1807, London, 1862), and Grant's share in these transactions has never been treated in detail.

Grant died, after a long and painful illness, broken in health and circumstances, at the age of sixty, at Kensington on 14 July 1842. His appeals and those of his widow for assistance were left unanswered (*Naval and Military Gazette*, 4 March 1843, p. 137). Sir Robert Peel, when prime minister, conferred a gift of 100l. and a lieutenant's widow's pension of 40l. a year on Grant's widow, Sophia Grant, who died at Chelsea on 26 May 1848 (*ib.* 3 Jan. 1848, and 1 July 1848, p. 429).

[Army and Militia Lists; Naval and Military Gazettes, 1842–3, 1848.]

HENRY MANNERS CHICHESTER

published 1890

SLEEMAN **William Henry**

(1788–1856)

Sir

Major-general and Indian administrator, born at Stratton, Cornwall, on 18 Aug. 1788, was the son of Philip Sleeman (*d.* 1798) of Pool Park, St. Judy, Cornwall, yeoman and supervisor of excise, and his wife, Mary Spry (*d.* 1818). In 1809 he was nominated to an infantry cadetship in the Bengal army, and, going to India in the same year, was gazetted ensign 24 Sept. 1810, and lieutenant 16 Dec. 1814. He served in the Nepal war (1814–1816), when his regiment, the 12th Bengal infantry, lost five British officers by jungle fever, and he himself suffered severely from this ailment. In 1802 he was appointed junior assistant to the governor-general's agent in the Ságar and Nerbudda territories; nor did he again revert to military duties, being henceforth employed in civil and political posts, retaining, however, in accordance with the regulations, his right to military promotion. He was gazetted captain 23 Sept. 1825, major 1 Feb. 1837, lieutenant-colonel 26 May 1843, colonel 5 Dec. 1853, and major-general 28 Nov. 1854.

Between 1825 and 1835 he served as magistrate and district officer in various parts of what are now the Central Provinces. On being posted to the Jabalpur district in 1828, he issued a proclamation forbidding any one to aid or abet in a suttee, but hardly twelve months later a Brahmin widow was burnt alive in his presence, and with his reluctant assent, given when it became evident that the woman would otherwise starve herself to death. In 1831 he was transferred to Ságar, where, two years later, he displayed commendable firmness during a time of scarcity, refusing, though urged to do so by the military authorities, to put any limit on the market price of grain. In 1827 he had introduced the cultivation of the Otaheite sugar-cane in India. But his most memorable achievement was an exposure of the practices of the thugs, an organised fraternity of professional murderers. In 1829, in addition to his district work he acted as assistant to the official charged with the special task of dealing with this crime; and in January 1835 he was appointed general superintendent of the operations for the suppression of thuggi. In February 1839, additional duties being assigned to his office, he became commissioner for the suppression of Thuggi and dacoity. During the next two years he was actively engaged in investigating and repressing criminal organisations in Upper India. During 1826 and 1835 over fourteen hundred thugs were hanged or transported for life. One man confessed to having committed over seven hundred murders, and his revelations were the basis of Meadows Taylor's 'Confessions of a Thug,' 1839 (Introd. p. vi). Detection was only possible by means of 'approvers,' for whose protection from the vengeance of their associates a special gaol was established at Jabalpur. In 1841 Sleeman was offered the post of resident at Lucknow, but he refused to accept this lucrative appointment in order that it might be retained by an officer who, as he heard, had been impoverished through the failure of a bank.

In 1842 he was sent into Bundelkhand to inquire into the disturbances that had taken place there, and from 1843 to 1849 he was political resident in Gwalior. Three years after the defeat of the Gwalior troops by a British force at Maharajpur he was able to report that the measures initiated by Lord Ellenborough for the maintenance of British influence in Sindhia's territory had proved signally successful. The turbulent aristocracy had been brought under subjection, and the people, delivered from lawless violence, were able to pursue their avocations without fear of robbery or murder (*General Letter*, 6 March 1847). On the residency at Lucknow again becoming vacant, Lord Dalhousie offered it to Sleeman (16 Sept. 1848), who now accepted it. The reports he submitted during a three months' tour in 1849–50 largely influenced Lord Dalhousie in his resolve to annex the kingdom, though this measure was opposed to the advice of the resident, who believed that reforms were possible under native rule. In December 1851 an attempt was made to assassinate him. In 1854 he was compelled by ill-health to leave for the hills, but the change failed to restore him, and he was ordered home. He died on 10 Feb. 1856 on board the Monarch, off Ceylon, on his way to England. On the recommendation of Lord Dalhousie the civil cross of the Bath was conferred on him four days before his death.

He married, on 21 June 1829, Amélie Josephine, daughter of Count Blondin de Fontenne, a French nobleman, by whom he had a son, Henry Arthur, born 6 Jan. 1833, cornet 16th dragoons January 1851.

A portrait in oils of Sleeman, by Beechey, is in the possession of Mrs. L. Brooke. It hung on the walls of the residency, Lucknow, throughout the siege.

Sleeman wrote: 1. 'Ramaseeana, or a Vocabulary of the Peculiar Language used by the Thugs,' &c., Calcutta, 1836 (cf. *Edinburgh Review*, January 1837, pp. 357–95). 2. 'History of the Gurka Mandala Rajas' (Journal Asiatic Society of Bengal, vi. 621, 1837). 3. 'Rambles and Recollections of an Indian Official,' London, 1844; reprinted London, 1893 (Constable's 'Oriental Series'). 4. 'An Account of Wolves nurturing Children in their Dens,' Plymouth, 1852. 5. 'A Journey through the Kingdom of Oudh in 1849–50,' London, 1858.

[Memoir prefixed to A Journey through Oudh, 1858; Memoir by Vincent A. Smith, prefixed to Rambles and Recollections, 1893; Calcutta Review, vol. xxxv.; Meadows Taylor's Confessions of a Thug, 1839, Introd. passim; Gent. Mag. 1856, ii. 243; Boase and Courtney's Bibl. Cornub.; Britten and Boulger's English Botanists.]

Stephen Wheeler

published 1897

BEACH Thomas Miller

(1841–1894)

Known as 'Major Le Caron,' government spy, second son of J. B. Beach, was born at Colchester on 26 Sept. 1841, where his father was a rate-collector. He himself passed by his own account a restless youth. While serving as apprentice to a Colchester draper he paid many illicit visits to London, and finally went to Paris. Learning of the outbreak of the American civil war in 1861 he sailed in the Great Eastern for New York. On 7 Aug. 1861 he enlisted with the federalists in the 8th Pennsylvanian reserves under the name of Henri Le Caron. He afterwards exchanged into the Andersen cavalry, in which corps he served for two years with McClellan's army of the Potomac. In April 1864 he married. In July 1864 he received a commission as second lieutenant. In December he was wounded near Woodbury, and was present at the battle of Nashville. In 1865 he acted as assistant adjutant-general, and at the end of the war attained the rank of major. Le Caron then settled at Nashville and began studying medicine. Before leaving the federal army he joined the Fenian organisation, and in 1866 he furnished the English government with information about the intended Fenian invasion of Canada, which led to the easy defeat of John O'Neill's movement on 1 June 1866.

During 1867 Le Caron visited England, and, being introduced by John Gurdon Rebow, M.P. for Colchester, to the authorities, agreed to return to the United States as a paid spy, under cover of an active membership of the Fenian body. Le Caron continued in direct and frequent communication with the British or Canadian government from this time till February 1889.

Immediately after his return he resumed relations with the Fenian leader O'Neill, now United States claim-agent at Nashville. On 31 Dec. 1867 O'Neill became president of the Fenian organisation (Irish Republican Brotherhood), and soon afterwards Le Caron began to organise a Fenian circle in Lockport, Illinois. As 'centre' of this he received O'Neill's reports and sent them and other documents to the English government. At this time Le Caron was at Chicago as resident medical officer of the state penitentiary (prison), but resigned the position in the course of the year, when he was summoned by O'Neill to New York, and accompanied him to an interview at Washington with President Andrew Johnson, the object of which was to obtain the return of the arms taken from the Fenians in 1866. He was now appointed military organiser of the 'Irish Republican Army,' and sent on a mission to the eastern states. At the Philadelphia convention of December 1868 a second invasion of Canada was resolved on by the Fenians. Le Caron, who was entrusted with the chief direction of the preparations along the frontier, paid a visit to Ottawa and arranged with the Canadian chief commissioner of police (Judge McMicken) a system of daily communications. He dissipated some suspicions that were entertained of him by the Fenians, and early in 1869 he was appointed their assistant adjutant-general, and forwarded to the authorities copies of the Fenian plans of campaign. He had already obtained a dominant influence over Alexander Sullivan, an important member of the brotherhood, and in the winter of 1869 he further strengthened his position by providing O'Neill with a loan wherewith to cover his embezzlement of Fenian funds.

Early in 1870 Le Caron, who now held the rank of brigadier and adjutant-general, had distributed fifteen thousand stand of arms and three million rounds of cartridge along the Canadian frontier. Owing to information furnished by Le Caron to the Canadian authorities, the invading force at once (26 April) fell into an ambush, and were obliged to retreat.

O'Neill was arrested by order of President Grant for a breach of the neutrality laws. Le Caron fled with his followers to Malone, but on the 27th made his way to Montreal. Next day he set out for Ottawa, but was arrested at Cornwall as a recognised Fenian, and was only allowed to proceed under a military escort. After a midnight interview with McMicken he left Canada early next day by a different route.

After the repulse of the second invasion Le Caron resumed his medical studies, but was soon invited by O'Neill, who suspected nothing, to help in the movement being prepared in conjunction with Louis Riel. Le Caron betrayed the plans to the Canadian government. In consequence of his action O'Neill was arrested with his party at Fort Pembina, on 5 Oct. 1871, just as they had crossed the frontier, and Riel surrendered at Fort Garry without firing a shot. O'Neill was given up to the American authorities, but was acquitted by them on the ground that the offence was committed on Canadian soil. Le Caron incurred some blame in Fenian circles in consequence of the failure of the last movement, and for the next few years was chiefly occupied in the practice of medicine, first at Detroit (where he graduated M.D.) and then at Braidwood, a suburb of Wilmington. But at Detroit he watched on behalf of the Canadian government the movements of Mackay Lomasney, who was afterwards concerned in the attempt to blow up London Bridge with dynamite; and he was still in the confidence of former Fenian friends.

Le Caron was not an original member of the Clan-na-Gael (the re-organised Fenian body). But by circulating the report that his mother was an Irish woman, he gradually regained his influence and obtained the 'senior-guardianship' of the newly formed 'camp' at Braidwood. He was now able to send copies of important documents to Mr. Robert Anderson, chief of the criminal detective department in London. In order to do this, however, he was obliged to evade by sleight of hand the rule of the or-ganisation that documents not returned to headquarters were to be burned in sight of the camp.

The years 1879–81 witnessed what was called 'the new departure' in the Irish-American campaign against England, whereby an 'open' or consti-tutional agitation (represented in Ireland by the Land League and its successor) was carried on side by side with the old revolutionary Fenian movement. The relations between the two were very intricate, and Le Caron was closely connected with both. He entertained at Braidwood and professionally attended Mr. Michael Davitt when he came to America to organise the American branch of the Land League, and early in 1881 he saw much of John Devoy, who represented the revolutionary side of the movement. Devoy's confidences were exhaustive, and Le Caron imparted them fully to Mr. Anderson. In the spring of 1881 he was entrusted by

Devoy with sealed packets to be delivered in Paris to John O'Leary (the intermediary of the Irish and American branches), and Patrick Egan, treasurer of the Land League. On his arrival in England in April Le Caron showed these to Anderson, and, proceeding to Paris, obtained important information from well-known Fenians.

Egan came back with Le Caron from Paris to London, and introduced him to Irish members of parliament. He had an important interview with Charles Stewart Parnell in the corridor outside the library of the House of Commons, and Parnell commissioned him to 'bring about a thorough understanding and complete harmony of working' between the constitutionalists and the partisans of the secret movement. Le Caron had another interview with the Irish leader at the tea room of the house, when Parnell gave him his signed photograph. After pursuing his inquiries in Dublin, maintaining throughout the fullest touch with the London authorities, he returned to New York in June 1881, attended the convention of the Clan-na-Gael at Chicago, and laid Parnell's views before the foreign relations committee. He also saw much of Dr. Gallagher and Lomasney, who were preparing the 'active' or dynamite policy.

Le Caron was also present at the so-called Land League Convention at Chicago in November 1881, which was packed in the interests of the Clan-na-Gael; he followed the movements of the clan with the closest attention, and all details of the 'secret warfare' (dynamite campaign) were at his command. When a schism arose in the clan Le Caron found it politic to join the majority, headed by Alexander Sullivan and his colleagues, who were termed the 'Triangle.' In August 1884 he attended, both as league delegate and revolutionary officer, the Boston Convention of the Irish National League of America. In 1885 he stood for the House of Representatives, but lost the election on account of the cry of 'Fenian general' raised against him. As a delegate to the National League Convention of August 1886 Le Caron attended the secret caucuses presided over by Egan. In April 1887 he paid another visit to Europe, and was sent by the English police to Paris to watch General Millen, who was then negotiating a reconciliation between the English and American branches of the clan. Le Caron went back to the United States in October, but in December 1888 he finally left America.

Subpœnaed as a witness for 'The Times' in the special commission appointed to inquire into the charges made by that paper against the Irish members and others, Le Caron began his evidence on 5 Feb. 1889, and was under examination and cross-examination for six days. The efforts of Sir Charles Russell, the counsel for the Irish members, failed to impair the damaging effect of the bulk of his testimony. At the close of the commission (14 Nov. 1889) Sir Henry (now Lord) James, counsel for 'The

Times' newspaper, defended Le Caron from attacks made upon his character. After the trial he lived quietly in England. He died in London of a painful disease on 1 April 1894, and was buried in Norwood cemetery. His wife returned to America some time after his death.

Le Caron himself, in his 'Twenty-five Years in the Secret Service,' maintained that he acted from purely patriotic motives. Between 1868 and 1870 he received about 2,000l. from the English and Canadian governments, but since that time (he told the commission) his salary had not covered his expenses. His identity was known to no one but Mr. Anderson, who always corresponded with him under his real name, Beach. He was a dapper, neatly made little man, with cadaverous cheeks and piercing eyes. He was a teetotaller but a great smoker. His coolness and presence of mind were unequalled. An excellent sketch of him as he appeared before the Parnell Commission appears in a portfolio of sketches drawn by Louis Gache and published as a 'Report of the Parnell Commission by a Stuff Gownsman' (1890).

[Twenty-five Years in the Secret Service, with Portraits and Facsimiles, by Major Henri Le Caron, 6th ed. 1892 (some excisions had to be made under government influence, and the portrait of the author was for obvious reasons suppressed); Essex County Standard, 7 April 1894, with portrait; Times, 2, 29 April 1894, Report of the Parnell Commission, reprinted from Times, ii. 180–233; J. Macdonald's Diary of the Parnell Commission (from Daily News), pp. 120–37, &c.]

GERALD LE GRYS NORGATE

published 1901

DAVITT Michael

(1846–1906)

Irish revolutionary and labour agitator, born on 25 March 1846, at Straide, co. Mayo, came of a Roman catholic peasant stock, originally from Donegal. His father, who subsisted with his family on a small holding, was head of an agrarian secret society in his youth, and was evicted in 1852 during the clearances that followed the great Irish famine. He emigrated with his wife and children to Lancashire, and settled at Haslingden. Here the boy Michael, as soon as he was able to work, was sent to a cotton mill. Forced in 1857 to mind a machine ordinarily attended by a youth of eighteen, he was caught in the machinery, and his mangled right arm had to be amputated. Thus disabled before he was twelve, he was removed from the factory and sent to a Wesleyan school. While still a lad, he organised a band of youths to defend catholic churches at Rochdale, Bacup, and Haslingden, which were threatened with destruction in anti-catholic riots. On leaving school, at about fifteen, he became in 1861 printer's devil and newsboy with a printer, who was also postmaster at Haslingden; afterwards he worked as book-keeper and assistant letter-carrier in the same employment. In 1865 he joined the Fenian organisation, and soon became 'centre' of the local (Rossendale) 'circle.' In February 1867 he was one of those told off to attack Chester Castle and seize the arms there. He first showed his abilities in extricating himself and his comrades from this fiasco. In 1868 he was appointed organising secretary of the Irish Republican Brotherhood for England and Scotland, and left his employment at Haslingden to assume the rôle of a commercial traveller in firearms, as a cloak for his revolutionary work—buying firearms and shipping them to Ireland. On 14 May 1870 he was arrested at Paddington while awaiting a consignment of arms from Birmingham. Tried at the Old Bailey by Lord Chief Justice Cockburn, he was sentenced to fifteen years' penal servitude for treason-felony. The principal evidence against him was a letter which he had written to prevent a young Fenian (whose name Davitt never would reveal) from assassinating a supposed spy, but which bore on the face of it (as Davitt's aim in writing was to gain time for the interference of the heads of the organisation) an apparent approval of the deed. He spent over seven years in prison—ten months in Millbank, and the remainder (except one month at Portsmouth in 1872) in Dartmoor. A pamphlet prepared by him in 1878, as the basis of his evidence (20 June 1878) before the royal commission on the working of the Penal Servitude Acts, gives a full account of what he endured, and how every prison rule was strained against him. On 19 Dec. 1877 he was released on ticket-of-leave, as a result of the exertions of Isaac Butt and the Amnesty Association. In prison he had thought out his plans for an Irish movement of a new kind, to blend revolutionary and constitutional methods, while abandoning secret conspiracy. He at once rejoined the Fenian movement, with the view of converting its heads to this plan. After lecturing for some months in Great Britain on behalf of the amnesty movement, he went in August 1878 to America, whither his family had emigrated. Here he met not only all the leaders of the constitutional and extreme Nationalists but also Henry George. The latter's land programme harmonised with and developed the views which Davitt had already formed independently in prison. Before leaving America, he made a speech at Boston, on 8 Dec. 1878, in which he outlined the new departure in Irish agitation. The essence of his suggestion was to bring the movement for Irish independence into close touch with the realities of life in Ireland by linking it up with the agrarian agitation, and to give the latter a wider scope by demanding the complete abolition of landlordism. On his return to Ireland he laid his plan before the supreme council of the Irish Republican Brotherhood, which rejected it. Davitt proceeded with the work on his own responsibility, enlisting the sympathy of most of the rank and file Fenians. He organised a meeting at Irishtown, Mayo, on 20 April 1879, when the new land programme was put forward. A second meeting, at Westport on 8 June, was attended by Charles Stewart Parnell, whom Davitt had convinced of the possibilities of the new movement. The agitation rapidly spread through the west; in August Davitt grouped the various local committees into the 'Land League of Mayo.' The 'Land League of Ireland,' in which Parnell's influence was soon to clash with Davitt's, came into being in October. In November Davitt and others were arrested and tried at Sligo for their share in the movement; but the prosecutions were dropped early in 1880. After the general election of 1880, in which Davitt assisted to procure the successes of Parnell's party, he was expelled from the supreme council of the Irish Republican Brotherhood; he remained an ordinary member of the body till 1882. In May 1880 Davitt went to America to organise the American Land League, and to raise funds. On his return he founded the Ladies' Land League, and devoted himself to the task of preventing outrages in connection with the policy of 'boycotting.' He also penetrated into Ulster, and addressed an enthusiastic meeting of Orangemen at Armagh on the land question. He urged the issue of the 'No Rent' manifesto in Feb. 1881 instead of later, but the Parliamentary section of the movement postponed its publication till Oct., when the liberal government retorted by suppressing the Land League. Meanwhile Davitt had been arrested as a ticket-of-leave man on 3 Feb. 1881, and endured a second but milder term of penal servitude in Portland. While in prison he was elected to parliament for co. Meath (24 Feb. 1882), but was disqualified as a treason-felony prisoner. He was released on 6 May 1882, and forthwith learned from Parnell that he had concluded the 'Kilmainham Treaty' with the government, that the agitation was to be mitigated, and that the Ladies' Land League had been suppressed by Parnell for declining to accept the compromise. Davitt at once prepared to fight Parnell in favour of a resumption of the agitation; but the assassination of Lord Frederick Cavendish, which took place on the day of Davitt's release, threw him back into alliance with Parnell, whose proposed co-operation with liberalism was necessarily for the time at an end.

After another visit to America, in June 1882, Davitt induced Parnell to found the National League, successor of the suppressed Land League; the programme of the new organisation, however, marked the triumph of parliamentarianism over the more revolutionary ideas of Davitt. He declined office in the National League, but spoke regularly on its platforms.

In 1883 (Jan. to May) he was imprisoned on a charge of sedition for a further period of four months in Richmond Bridewell, Dublin. Between 1882 and 1885 he devoted much of his time to advocating land national-isation, lecturing throughout Great Britain, either alone or in company with Henry George, who was touring in the United Kingdom. He brought George to Ireland, and spoke with him at a meeting in Dublin, on 9 April 1884. This brought on him a categorical repudiation of land nationalisation by Parnell. In 1885, his health having broken down, Davitt visited Italy, Palestine, and Egypt. He opposed the policy adopted by Parnell at the general election of that year, of throwing the Irish vote in England for the conservatives. In 1886 he again visited America, and married Miss Mary Yore, of Michigan. As a token of national regard, his wife was presented with a house, known as Land League Cottage, at Ballybrack, co. Dublin. This was the only occasion on which Davitt accepted any material gift from the Irish people; he always refused to assent to any public testi-monial, supporting himself, often with great difficulty, by his labours as a journalist. It was not till near the close of his life (1901) that a legacy from a relative of his wife relieved him of financial anxiety.

In 1887–8–9 Davitt was engrossed in the work involved by 'The Times' commission, which was appointed to investigate the charges brought by 'The Times' against Parnell and others, namely, that their real aim was to bring about the total independence of Ireland, that they had instigated assassination and other outrages, and that they had accepted money and other assistance from open advocates of crime and dynamite. Davitt was not originally included in these charges, but on his presenting himself before the tribunal, 'The Times' repeated the same charges against him, with two additional ones, namely, that he had been a convicted Fenian, and that he had brought about the alliance between the Parnellite home rule party in Ireland and the party of violence in America—both of which were undenied facts. The chief labour of the defence fell on him, as the link between the constitutional and extreme nationalists, between the Irish and American branches of the movement. It was Davitt who first suspected Richard Pigott, and he, by the aid of a volunteer secret service, countered every move of 'The Times' in the collection of evidence (*Fall of Feudalism*, ch. 44–49). When Parnell and the other Nationalists withdrew from the proceedings of the commission, as a protest against the refusal of the judges to order the production of the books of the 'Loyal and Patriotic Union,' Davitt dissented from this course, and continued to appear. Conducting his own case, he made a five-days' speech before the tribunal (Oct. 24–31, 1889), afterwards published as 'The Defence of the Land League,' a book which contains the best record of Davitt's life and work up to that time. In the report of the commission, the chief findings relating to

Davitt were that he had entered the agrarian movement with the intention of bringing about the absolute independence of Ireland, and that he had in a special manner denounced crime and outrage. Immediately after the commission's attack had failed, came the proceedings in the divorce court against Parnell. Davitt had been led by Parnell to believe that the suit brought by William Henry O'Shea was another conspiracy, destined to the same collapse as the Pigott forgeries. He resented Parnell's misrepresentation, and immediately flung himself into the campaign against Parnell's leadership. He had just started 'The Labour World' (first number, 21 Sept. 1890) to be the organ of the labour movement in Great Britain, which was on a fair way to success, but was ruined by Davitt's attitude towards Parnell, and by his personal absorption in the political struggle. The paper lived only till May 1891. Davitt had many times declined a seat in parliament, but he now yielded to the urgencies and needs of the anti-Parnellite party, and in the end of 1891 contested Waterford City against Mr. John Redmond, the leader of the Parnellites after Parnell's death. Defeated here, he was elected for North Meath at the general election of 1892, and was unseated on petition, owing to the use in his favour of clerical influences which he had done his best to stop. He was returned unopposed for North-East Cork at the bye-election of Feb. 1893, but having been declared bankrupt was unseated next June. In 1895 he went lecturing in Australia, and returned home to find himself M.P. for two constituencies, East Kerry and South Mayo; he chose to sit for South Mayo. He was not a parliamentary success, but was always listened to with respect, especially on prison reform, a subject he had long made his own. In 1897 he visited the United States to stop the projected Anglo-American Alliance; his active work was mainly responsible for the rejection of that year's Anglo-American Arbitration Treaty by the United States Senate. In 1898 he helped Mr. William O'Brien to found the United Irish League, an organisation which brought about the reunion of the Parnellite and anti-Parnellite sections. On 25 Oct. 1899 he dramatically withdrew from parliament as a protest against the Boer War. Early in 1900 he went to South Africa in a capacity partly journalistic and partly diplomatic; he held the threads of a plot to bring about European intervention on behalf of the Boers—a plot which broke down because of the hesitancy at a critical moment, and the subsequent death, of Colonel de Villebois Mareuil, who was to have led the French contingent. Davitt fiercely attacked the Dunraven conference report on the land question (1903) and the Wyndham Land Purchase Act of the same year, the purchase terms of which he regarded as a surrender of much that had been gained by the twenty-five years' agitation that he had started. Temporarily overborne by Mr. William O'Brien, he had the satisfaction of seeing, in little over a year, a complete revulsion of feeling in the Nationalist party with regard to Mr. O'Brien's policy. In 1903–4–5 he paid, mainly as the representative of American journals, three visits to Russia, where his sympathies were with the revolutionary party. At the general election of 1906 he devoted himself to supporting the labour party in England, and helped to secure many of their notable victories. The last months of his life were occupied with a struggle over the English education bill, on which he fell foul of the catholic clergy. The Irish Press having been closed to his letters advocating secular education, he was contemplating the establishment of a weekly paper, to express strongly democratic as well as nationalist views, when he caught cold after a dental operation. Blood poisoning set in, and he died in Dublin on 31 May 1906. He was buried in Straide, co. Mayo, where the 'Davitt Memorial Church' has been erected. His wife survived him with five sons and one daughter. A portrait by William Orpen is in the Dublin Gallery of Modern Art. Another was painted by Mr. H. J. Thaddeus.

Davitt stood for the reconciliation of extreme and constitutional nationalism; although he never wavered, as his latest writings show, from the ultimate idea of an independent Ireland he abandoned at an early stage all belief in those methods of secret conspiracy and armed rebellion which are generally associated with the separatist ideal. His notions of constitutional agitation were, however, always permeated by the vigour of his early revolutionary plans. He also stood for the harmonising of democracy and nationality. With his whole-hearted nationalism he combined from early life a growing conviction that any thoroughgoing regeneration of government and society in Ireland, and indeed throughout the world, must rest on a socialistic basis. In his collectivist, as in his anti-clerical, views he differed from most of the Irishmen with whom he was politically associated. His political affinities inclined to industrial and secularist democracy. His strength of character, disinterestedness, and steadiness of purpose won him the personal respect even of those who held his doctrines to be erroneous or pernicious.

Davitt's principal published works are: 1. 'Leaves from a Prison Diary,' 1884 (to be distinguished from the pamphlet on his experiences in Dartmoor, mentioned above). 2. 'The Defence of the Land League,' 1891. 3. 'Life and Progress in Australasia,' 1898. 4. 'The Boer Fight for Freedom,' 1902. 5. 'Within the Pale' (a study of anti-semitism in Russia), 1903. 6. 'The Fall of Feudalism in Ireland' (a history of the land agitation), 1904. He also wrote many pamphlets and a mass of uncollected journalistic work.

[Davitt's own books, especially The Defence of the Land League and The Fall of Feudalism; Michael Davitt: Revolutionary, Agitator, and Labour Leader, by

F. Sheehy Skeffington, 1908; see also Cashman's Life, 1882; R. Barry O'Brien's Life of Parnell, 1898; Life of Henry George, 1900; D'Alton, History of Ireland, vol. iii. 1910.]

FRANCIS SHEEHY SKEFFINGTON

published 1912

BADEN-POWELL Robert Stephenson Smyth

(1857–1941)

First Baron Baden-Powell

Lieutenant-general, and founder of the Boy Scouts and Girl Guides, was born in London 22 February 1857, the sixth son among the ten children of the Rev. Baden Powell, Savilian professor of geometry at Oxford, by his third wife, Henrietta Grace, eldest daughter of Admiral William Henry Smyth, who claimed collateral descent from John Smith of Virginia and was a great-niece of Nelson. Robert was named after his godfather, Robert Stephenson, the engineer. His father died in 1860, and Mrs. Baden-Powell had to bring up a large family on moderate means. She encouraged the children to study natural history, and, when they were old enough, allowed the boys to go camping and boating in their holidays.

In 1870 Baden-Powell went as a gown-boy foundationer to Charterhouse. He owed much to the influence of the headmaster, William Haig Brown. Although pre-eminent neither as scholar nor as athlete, Baden-Powell took his share in all activities. His triumphs were gained in theatricals and as a cartoonist. His love of outdoor life led him to break bounds and spend hours in the woods increasing his knowledge of woodcraft. In 1876 he entered for an army examination before going to Oxford where his brothers, George (Sir George Smyth Baden-Powell) and Frank, had been at Balliol College; but Benjamin Jowett did not think Robert 'up to Balliol form'. The search for another college ended when the results of the army examination were announced; Robert was placed second on the cavalry list and was thus excused Sandhurst. He was gazetted sub-lieutenant, and sailed for India to join his regiment, the 13th Hussars.

After his general training he specialized in reconnaissance and scouting. His technical knowledge was set down in two books, *Reconnaissance and Scouting* (1884) and *Cavalry Instruction* (1885). He was promoted captain in

1883, and served as adjutant from 1882 to 1886. He was a keen polo player, and in 1883 won the Kadir Cup for pigsticking, a sport on which he wrote a standard book, *Pigsticking or Hoghunting* (1889). Lighter diversions were theatricals and sketching.

In 1884 the 13th Hussars left India, but disembarked in Natal to be in reserve should Sir Charles Warren need support in Bechuanaland. Baden-Powell surveyed the lesser-known passes of the Drakensberg; disguised as a reporter, he gained important information and corrected the maps. When the crisis passed the regiment sailed for England, but he remained for a hunting expedition in East Africa. In 1888 he was appointed aide-de-camp to his uncle, (Sir) H. A. Smyth, who had been made G.O.C. in South Africa. Baden-Powell took part in the Zululand campaign of 1888; in 1889 he was secretary to the mixed British and Boer commission on Swaziland, and in 1890 he joined Smyth as his assistant military secretary and aide-de-camp at Malta, where Smyth had been appointed governor. The formal official life was little to Baden-Powell's liking and he welcomed his appointment in 1891 as intelligence officer for the Mediterranean. In the course of his investigations he had some of the experiences afterwards recorded in *My Adventures as a Spy* (1915). He was promoted major in 1892 and in the following year rejoined his regiment in Ireland.

Baden-Powell's next task was to organize and train a native levy for the Ashanti expedition of 1895–6; pioneering the route and scouting for the enemy were his responsibility. For his services he received the brevet of lieutenant-colonel, and he wrote an account of the expedition in *The Downfall of Prempeh* (1896). It was during this bloodless war that he first wore the cowboy hat associated with him; by the natives he was known as 'Kantankye'—'he of the big hat'. Within a few months, in May 1896, he was called again for special duties, this time as chief staff officer in Matabeleland where a native rising necessitated the use of imperial troops. It was mainly through his night scouting that the positions of the natives in the fastnesses of the Matopos were discovered; they called him 'Impeesa'—'the wolf that never sleeps'. After the war Baden-Powell received the brevet of colonel, and during his leave he wrote *The Matabele Campaign* (1897).

In 1897 at the age of forty Baden-Powell was appointed to the command of the 5th Dragoon Guards, then stationed in India. He now had full opportunity to develop training in scouting as part of a soldier's work; for this he instituted a special badge (the first of its kind) for efficiency. He described the course of instruction in *Aids to Scouting* (1899). Great stress was put on developing the powers of observation and of deduction, and by organizing the men in small units he emphasized the need for initiative.

While home on leave in 1899, Baden-Powell was again gazetted for extra-regimental employ. The tense situation in South Africa made war likely; he was therefore sent out to raise two regiments for the defence of Bechuanaland and Matabeleland. When war broke out he was at Mafeking. General Piet Cronje at once invested the town. The total defence force was 1,251 men; equipment was inadequate and much of it antiquated.

The romance of the siege gave Mafeking an exaggerated value in popular opinion; nevertheless, this small town was of strategic importance, for the defence held 9,000 Boers inactive at a critical period. It was Baden-Powell's own genius for organization and improvisation which sustained the siege for 217 days. The deterioration in food supplies, the constant bombardment, and the series of British defeats might well have disheartened the people in Mafeking, but Baden-Powell was resourceful in schemes to puzzle the besiegers and in devising ways of keeping the besieged busy and cheerful. One improvisation gave some offence at home. Postage stamps were needed; the first design, printed without Baden-Powell's knowledge, bore his head; he had these withdrawn at once and there was substituted a new design showing a boy on a bicycle, recording thus the work of the cadets whose efficiency made a lasting impression on him. Mafeking was relieved 17 May 1900; the news was received in London with such wild rejoicing that a new verb was added to the language ('to maffick'). Baden-Powell was rewarded by promotion to the rank of major-general at the age of forty-three.

After the relief he was in command of a force attempting to capture General Christiaan De Wet until in August 1900 Sir Alfred (later Viscount) Milner, having decided to establish a constabulary to police the country after the war, chose Baden-Powell for the task of raising and training the force. This was a congenial duty, for it was without precedent and gave full scope for his special method of training men in small units. The prolongation of war meant that the South African Constabulary took service in the field. After the war their work to which Joseph Chamberlain referred as a 'great civilizing and uniting influence' showed how well they had been trained for a delicate task.

Sick leave at home in 1901 gave this country an opportunity of hero-worshipping Baden-Powell. He took such demonstrations as they came but did not seek them. When, for instance, he was summoned to Balmoral to be invested as C.B. by King Edward VII, he took a circuitous route to avoid the crowds. Early in 1903 he was appointed inspector-general of cavalry. After studying cavalry training in other countries, he established the Cavalry School at Netheravon in 1904, and in the following year founded the *Cavalry Journal*. During 1906 he accompanied the Duke of Connaught to South Africa and afterwards travelled north to Egypt, a tour which gave birth to his book *Sketches in Mafeking and East Africa* (1907); an exhibition in 1907 of the original water-colours and sketches for this book, and the acceptance in the same year of a bust of John Smith by the Royal Academy displayed his considerable talent as an artist. His term of inspector-general ended in 1907, but he was persuaded by R. B. (later Viscount) Haldane to take command in 1908 of the Northumbrian division of the newly formed Territorials. Haldane and he had frequently discussed the Territorial scheme together. Baden-Powell ceased to hold this command in March 1910, and on 7 May he retired from the army, at the age of fifty-three. He had been promoted lieutenant-general in 1907.

Baden-Powell gave up the prospect of higher rank in order that he might devote himself to the interest which came to fill his life—the Boy Scouts. On his return from South Africa in 1903 he had been surprised to learn that his *Aids to Scouting* was being used by teachers. His interest in boys had been roused by the success of the cadets in Mafeking, and by the many letters he received from young hero-worshippers. At an inspection of the Boys' Brigade in 1904 he was greatly impressed by their bearing and efficiency, and he wondered how more boys could be attracted. He discussed the question with (Sir) William Alexander Smith, founder of the Brigade, who suggested that *Aids to Scouting* should be rewritten for boys. Baden-Powell's thoughts turned to his camping days with his band of brothers and his own delight in woodcraft. With these in mind he drew up a preliminary scheme which he discussed with friends and experts. Amongst his sympathizers was (Sir) C. Arthur Pearson who encouraged and initially financed the separate organization of Boy Scouts. A trial camp was held on Brownsea Island in Poole Harbour in July and August 1907, for which Baden-Powell tried the experiment of selecting boys from varied social classes; he found that they mixed happily together and thoroughly enjoyed the outdoor activities of 'backwoodsmen, explorers, and frontiersmen'. The key to success lay in the patrol organization by which the boys were divided into small units of five, each unit having its own leader with responsibility for maintaining keenness and a high standard of behaviour. As an aid to the latter, he framed a scout law setting out in positive terms the code of conduct a scout promises to observe.

Scouting for Boys was published in parts in 1908. Boys bought them eagerly and within a few weeks Boy Scout troops sprang up all over the country. The same result came when copies of the book reached the Dominions and Colonies and some foreign countries. A rally at the Crystal Palace in 1909 brought together 11,000 Boy Scouts. Girls demanded that they too should have the same fun, so the parallel scheme of Girl Guides was framed with Baden-Powell's sister, Agnes (died 1945), as first president of their council. It soon became clear that this rapidly spreading movement would need careful guidance, so the founder decided, with the approval of King Edward VII, to leave the army and give all his time to the Boy Scouts and Girl Guides. In 1910 he made the first of many extensive tours of the Empire and other countries to ensure that the main principles of his scheme were observed.

Opposition came from those who saw in the Boy Scouts a subtle attempt to give military training under another name; Baden-Powell replied that the aim of the movement was to develop those qualities of character which serve the country best in peace or in war. On the outbreak of war in 1914 he wrote a small manual, *Quick Training for War*, which had enormous sales. The Boy Scouts were soon familiar figures in public offices, in hospitals, during air raids, and in the harvest fields. Their most sustained effort was undertaken at Kitchener's request: Sea Scouts (started in 1909) replaced coast-guardsmen and during the war over 20,000 scouts were so employed. Baden-Powell made many visits to the western front, and took an active part in organizing recreation huts provided by the Young Men's Christian Association and by Boy Scouts. There is no foundation for the popular belief that he was engaged in secret-service work.

In spite of the loss of scoutmasters, the movement expanded; patrol leaders carried on until they too were called up. There was a demand for training for boys below Boy Scout age. After a period of experiment, the Wolf Cubs were started in 1916. Baden-Powell made use of the stories of Mowgli from the *Jungle Books* to give these young boys an imaginative world of their own. The scheme was explained in *The Wolf Cub's Handbook* (1916). To meet the needs of those above Boy Scout age a scheme of Rover Scouts was developed after the war, and for the guidance of these youths Baden-Powell wrote *Rovering to Success* (1922).

A rally of scouts was arranged for 1920. To this Baden-Powell gave the name of 'Jamboree', a word of uncertain origin but now with a new meaning. What at first was planned as a British gathering was expanded to include scouts from many countries. At the final rally, Baden-Powell was acclaimed as Chief Scout of the world. There were four other Jamborees during his lifetime: 1924 in Denmark, 1929 in England, 1933 in Hungary, and 1937 in Holland. On the occasion of the Jamboree of 1929 he was raised to the peerage as Baron Baden-Powell, of Gilwell, in the county of Essex, taking his territorial title from the training camp for scoutmasters which he had established in 1919; this soon became an international centre from which trained men carried Baden-Powell's interpretation of scouting to many lands. He left the detailed conduct of the movement to his headquarters commissioners; he was opposed to too great a centralization of direction, and wished those training the boys to have wide liberty within the scheme. As the years passed, so his interest became more concentrated on the international development of the scouts and guides; in this he saw a means of furthering friendliness amongst nations. His work for peace was recognized by the award of the Carnegie Wateler peace prize in 1937.

Baden-Powell spent his eightieth birthday in India in a farewell parade with his old regiment of which he had become honorary colonel in 1911. In the same year (1937) he was appointed to the Order of Merit; this was the last of a long series of honours from many countries. Honorary degrees were conferred on him by the universities of Edinburgh (1910), Toronto, McGill, and Oxford (1923), Liverpool (1929), and Cambridge (1931). He had been appointed K.C.V.O. and K.C.B. in 1909, created a baronet in 1922, G.C.V.O. in 1923, and G.C.M.G. in 1927. In 1913 he was master of the Mercers' Company.

In the autumn of 1938 Baden-Powell went to Kenya in the hope of regaining health. To the last he was fertile in ideas and suggestions for the development of scouting. He found his pleasure in sketching and painting. His doctors forbade his return to England when war broke out in 1939 and he died at Nyeri, Kenya, 8 January 1941. A stone to his memory was unveiled in Westminster Abbey in 1947. He was succeeded as second baron by his son (Arthur Robert) Peter (born 1913).

Baden-Powell was of medium height and slender build; he was sandy-haired and freckled. He was a man of simple habits and of the friendliest disposition. He was little affected by the hero-worship to which he had to submit during the greater part of his life. His chief recreation after leaving India was fishing; this gave him the solitude he needed and the joys of river and mountain scenery. His sketch-book was seldom out of reach.

He wrote some thirty books; nearly all were illustrated by himself. In addition to those mentioned above, two should be noted: *Indian Memories* (1915) and *Lessons from the 'varsity of Life* (1933); both are autobiographical. His plain style was lightened by many touches of the humour which characterized his talk and his speeches.

During one of his world tours Baden-Powell met Olave St. Clair, younger daughter of Harold Soames, a retired business man, of Lilliput, Dorsetshire. They were married in 1912, and had one son and two daughters. Lady Baden-Powell showed that she had gifts of her own to bring to the Girl Guide movement, and she was elected Chief Guide in 1918. She was appointed G.B.E. in 1932.

There are painted portraits of Baden-Powell by G. F. Watts (1901) at Charterhouse School; by (Sir) Hubert von Herkomer (1901) at the Cavalry Club; by Harold Speed (1905) in the possession of the family; by David Jagger (1929), two versions, one at the Mercers' Hall, the other at Boy Scout headquarters; by Simon Elwes (1930) at Girl Guide headquarters.

Cumming

The first three show him in the uniform of the South African Constabulary and the last three as Chief Scout.

[E. E. Reynolds, *Baden-Powell*, 1942; records at Boy Scout headquarters; private information; personal knowledge.]

E. E. REYNOLDS

published 1959

CUMMING Mansfield George Smith

(1859–1923)

Sir

The first chief of the modern secret service (CSS or C), was born Mansfield George Smith 1 April 1859 in India, the youngest in the family of five sons and eight daughters of Colonel John Thomas Smith, of the Royal Engineers, of Föellalt House, Kent, and his wife Maria Sarah Tyser. After entering the Royal Naval College, Dartmouth, at the age of thirteen, he began his career afloat as acting sub-lieutenant on HMS *Bellerophon*. He served in operations against Malay pirates 1875–6 and in Egypt in 1883. He suffered, however, from severe seasickness and in 1885 he was placed on the retired list.

Cumming (he changed his name in 1889 after marriage) spent the early 1890s largely as a country gentleman on his second wife's Morayshire estate. In 1898, while still on the Royal Navy retired list, Cumming was posted to Nelson's old flagship *Victory* 'for special service at Southampton'. The 'special service' included occasional intelligence work abroad, but his main work for the next decade was the construction and command of the Southampton boom defences.

In 1909 Cumming was appointed head of what became the foreign section of the Secret Service Bureau (the forerunner of the Secret Intelligence Service, better known as SIS or MI6). He described pre-1914 espionage as 'capital sport', but was given few resources with which to pursue it. His early operations were directed almost entirely against Germany. Between 1909 and 1914 he recruited part-time 'casual agents' in the shipping and arms business to keep track of naval construction in German shipyards and acquire other technical intelligence. He also had agents collecting German intelligence in Brussels, Rotterdam, and St Petersburg.

With the outbreak of World War I, Cumming's control of strategic intelligence gathering as head of the wartime MI 1c was challenged by two rival networks run by GHQ. Cumming eventually out-performed his rivals. His most important wartime network, 'La Dame Blanche', had by January 1918 over 400 agents reporting on German troop movements from occupied Belgium and northern France. Cumming was less successful in post-revolutionary Russia. Despite a series of colourful exploits, his agents obtained little Russian intelligence of value.

Like the rest of the British intelligence community, the postwar SIS was drastically cut back. Cumming succeeded, however, in gaining a monopoly of espionage and counter-intelligence outside Britain and the empire. He also established a network of SIS station commanders operating overseas under diplomatic cover. To the end of his life Cumming retained an infectious, if sometimes eccentric, enthusiasm for the tradecraft and mystification of espionage, experimenting personally with disguises, mechanical gadgets, and secret inks in his own laboratory. His practice of writing exclusively in a distinctive green ink was continued by his successors. He was appointed CB in 1914 and KCMG in 1919.

Cumming had a fascination with most forms of transport, driving his Rolls at high speed around the streets of London. In his early fifties he took up flying, gaining both French Aviators' and Royal Aero Club certificates. But his main passion was boating in Southampton Water and other waters calmer than those which had ended his active service career. In addition to owning 'any number' of yachts, Cumming acquired six motor boats. In 1905 he became one of the founders and first rear-commodore of the Royal Motor Yacht Club.

In 1885 Cumming married Dora, daughter of Henry Cloete, esquire, of Great Constantia, Cape of Good Hope, South Africa. After her death he married, in 1889, a Scottish heiress, Leslie Marian ('May'), daughter of Captain Lockhart Muir Valiant (afterwards Cumming), of the 1st Bombay Lancers and Logie, Morayshire. As part of the marriage settlement he changed his surname to Smith-Cumming, later becoming known as Cumming. Their only son, Alastair, a dangerous driver like his father, was killed in October 1914, driving Cumming's Rolls in France. Cumming himself lost the lower part of his right leg in the same accident. He died suddenly at his London headquarters 14 June 1923, shortly before he was due to retire.

[Christopher Andrew, *Secret Service: the Making of the British Intelligence Community*, 1985; Nicholas Hiley, 'The Failure of British Espionage Against Germany, 1907–1914', *Historical Journal*, vol. xxvi, 1983, pp. 867–89; family information.]

CHRISTOPHER ANDREW

published 1993

WINGATE Sir (Francis) Reginald

(1861–1953)

First baronet

Soldier and governor-general of the Sudan, was born at Port Glasgow in Renfrewshire 25 June 1861, the seventh son and youngest of the eleven children of Andrew Wingate, textile merchant, and his wife, Elizabeth, daughter of Richard Turner, of Hammersmith, county Dublin. He was a cousin of the father of Orde Wingate. In 1862 his father died and the family moved to Jersey where living was cheap.

Wingate went to St. James' Collegiate School where he showed 'determination and initiative', and in December 1878 entered the Royal Military Academy, Woolwich. He passed out tenth in 1880 and was gazetted as second lieutenant in the Royal Artillery. He was posted to India but soon after his arrival his battery was sent to Aden. There he studied Arabic, later becoming an expert. In June 1883 he joined the reorganized Egyptian Army.

Before General Gordon left Cairo for the last time in 1884 Wingate had been appointed aide-de-camp to Sir Evelyn Wood, sirdar of the Egyptian Army. He assisted in the preparations for the Gordon relief expedition and took part in it with distinction; he was mentioned in dispatches and received three decorations. But Gordon's death and the consequent withdrawal of the troops put an end to Wingate's active service. He was appointed assistant military secretary to the sirdar; shortly afterwards assistant adjutant-general; then in 1889 director of military intelligence with responsibility for gathering information of every kind from the Sudan. His book *Mahdiism and the Egyptian Sudan* (1891) and the accounts of Father Ohrwalder's and R. C. Slatin Pasha's experiences as prisoners of the Mahdi, which he translated and edited, bear witness to his profound knowledge of the Sudan.

His intelligence system was to prove its value when in 1895 the reoccupation of the Sudan was begun under Sir H. H. (later Earl) Kitchener. Dongola Province was occupied without difficulty in 1896 and the successful battles of the Atbara and Omdurman followed in 1898. The Khalifa's power was broken and a year later a force under Wingate brought him to battle and he was killed at Debeikerat.

In late 1899 Wingate succeeded Kitchener as governor-general of the Sudan and as sirdar and during the next seventeen years Wingate brought the country from anarchy to stable and progressive government. Slave raiding and trading were abolished; courts of justice and the rule of law were established; communications (railways, steamer services on the Nile, posts and telegraphs) were opened up and the various departments of a modern state were founded. An administrative machine was created, whereby a chain of authority ran from the governor-general to the district officers in the most remote parts of the country. Economic progress was encouraged and experiments in cotton growing led ultimately to the vast Gezira irrigation scheme. This project Wingate sponsored wholeheartedly and in 1913 he gained the support of Lloyd George, then chancellor of the Exchequer. Wingate presided over all this creative work and chose good subordinates in Slatin, (Sir) Edgar Bonham-Carter, (Sir) James Currie, and (Sir) Edgar Bernard. By constant touring and inspection he encouraged his officials, winning their sincere respect and the affectionate nickname of 'Master'. He laid the foundations of an administration which in later years won much praise for its efficiency, humanity, and progressive ideals.

When war came in 1914 it was doubtful whether the Sudan peoples would remain loyal to the British or side with Turkey as a Moslem power, but headed by their civil and religious leaders they remained unaffected, except for the Sultanate of Darfur, which Wingate occupied in 1916 after a short and well-planned operation. Lord Cromer wrote to Wingate to say, 'It is to my mind the most remarkable compliment that could possibly be paid to British rule that the Sudan should have remained quiet: and this is mainly due to your wise government.'

The Arab revolt in the Hejaz gave Wingate other problems and he carefully fostered the strength of Sharif Hussain with money, food, and men in conditions of much difficulty and uncertainty; work he was able to continue when in January 1917 he became high commissioner in Egypt.

This was the most difficult and unhappy part of Wingate's career. As a British base, Egypt was full of British troops to whom the delicacy of the constitutional position was unknown; for the civil population supplies were short, and the requisitioning of animals and foodstuffs upset the peasant population; conscription was imposed to provide labour for the army and in spite of Wingate's efforts to ensure honest dealing, there was much discontent.

The Sultan and his ministers, like all Egyptians, wanted self-government, and were under some pressure from the extremists. Wingate foresaw and continually warned the British Government that when peace came relations between Britain and Egypt would deteriorate. The Anglo-French declaration, promising self-determination to the Arabs, who had been freed from Turkish rule, brought things to a head in November 1918.

The British Government were too occupied with Europe and the start of the peace conference to heed Wingate's warnings, and in January 1919 Wingate went to Paris and London to persuade the British ministers to receive an Egyptian delegation. Lord Curzon, however, was adamant in refusing and his telegram to Cairo was followed by the immediate resignation of the Egyptian Government: agitation, disorder, and the death of Europeans and British officers resulted, and for a time law and order were completely overthrown. Although Wingate had given correct advice and this had been ignored, he clearly could no longer represent the British Government in Egypt, and he did not return. Lord Allenby was appointed in his place with instructions to carry out a conciliatory policy on the lines of Wingate's previous recommendations, and Wingate was allowed to bear the blame for the Government's failure to take his advice until forced to do so by bloodshed and disaster.

Wingate, who had reached the rank of general, was never again employed and henceforth occupied himself in other ways. A director of various companies, colonel commandant of the Royal Artillery, a governor of the Gordon College in Khartoum, and president of several local organizations at his home at Dunbar, he led a long and useful life. He married in 1888 Catherine Leslie Rundle, sister of a brother officer (Sir) (H. M.) Leslie Rundle. She was his devoted partner and helper and Wingate never recovered from her death in 1946. He died in his ninety-second year at Dunbar 28 January 1953. He had three sons and a daughter; the eldest son, Ronald Evelyn Leslie (born 1889), succeeded his father, but the second died an infant and the third was killed in action in 1918.

Wingate was appointed K.C.M.G. (1898), K.C.B. (1900), G.C.V.O. (1912), G.C.B. (1914), G.B.E. (1918), and created a baronet in 1920. He was appointed to the D.S.O. in 1889.

A cartoon by 'Spy' was published in *Vanity Fair* in 1897; and a portrait by W. W. Ouless was presented to the borough council of Dunbar.

[Sir Ronald Wingate, *Wingate of the Sudan*, 1955; personal knowledge.]

J. W. ROBERTSON

published 1971

CASEMENT Roger David

(1864–1916)

British consular official and Irish rebel, the younger son of Captain Roger Casement, third Light Dragoons, of Ballymena, co. Antrim, by his wife, Anne Jephson, of Dublin, was born at Kingstown, co. Dublin, 1 September 1864, and educated at the Academy, Ballymena. He belonged to an Ulster protestant family, whose ancestors had come from the Isle of Man early in the eighteenth century. He travelled widely in Africa as a young man. In 1892 he was appointed travelling commissioner to the Niger Coast Protectorate. Shortly afterwards he entered the British consular service, and in 1895 was appointed British consul at Lourenço Marques; in 1898 he was transferred to the west coast as consul successively at Loanda for Angola and at Boma for the Congo Free State. In 1903 the agitation against the administration of the Congo Free State had reached its height, and public opinion in England made it necessary for the British government to take the lead in investigating the charges made. Casement was therefore ordered to report on the conditions prevailing in connexion with the rubber trade in the interior, and visited the Upper Congo. He had seen this region in 1887, and he admitted that much advance had been made in transport and European building since that time. But his report, dated 11 December 1903, disclosed that the whole system of collecting rubber was based virtually on unpaid labour enforced by penalties of which mutilation was among the commonest. The report was all the more damning because of its moderation in tone; its testimony was never shaken; it was, in fact, confirmed by the report of the official Belgian commission of inquiry two years later, and it was the solid foundation for the movement which ended in the extinction of the Congo Free State (1908).

Casement's report had brought his name into prominence, and his personal distinction of manner and dark beauty added to the impression created wherever he appeared. He received the C.M.G. in 1905. Having been transferred to Brazil he became consul at Santos in 1906 and at Para in 1908; he was promoted to be consul-general at Rio de Janeiro in 1909. In 1910 he was directed by the Foreign Office to accompany a commission of inquiry sent out by the Peruvian Amazon Company to investigate charges of ill-treatment of the natives in the rubber-bearing regions by agents of the company. He accordingly went with the commission to the company's stations on the Putumayo river, and returned after eight weeks spent there. His report had the concurrence of the company's commission, and it charged the agents with 'crimes of the most atrocious kind, including murder, violation, and constant flogging'. A list was appended of those agents against whom the charges were worst and the evidence strongest, and their punishment was demanded. This report was submitted in December 1910, but was withheld from the public by Sir Edward Grey until it was seen that the Peruvian government was taking no steps to punish adequately the atrocities disclosed. Its publication as a Blue Book in 1912 created an immense sensation, enhanced by the authority which its writer had already acquired. But the advent of the European War prevented effective action from being taken and the whole matter was allowed to drop.

Casement

Casement was knighted for his services in 1911. In acknowledging the honour done him, he wrote to the foreign secretary a letter beginning, 'I find it very hard to choose the words with which to make acknowledgement of the honour done to me by the King'. He begged that his 'humble duty' might be presented, and that his 'deep appreciation' of the honour might be conveyed. He retired on pension shortly after, having completed nineteen years of valuable and conspicuous public work. He returned to Ireland in 1913.

The European War showed Casement in a new light. From boyhood an extreme nationalist, in spite of his Ulster protestant stock, he identified himself in 1904 with the Gaelic League. This was then a non-political organization; but while still employed by the British government he contributed articles to separatist papers signed 'Sean Bhean Bhocht'. When the Irish National Volunteers were formed in 1913, to counter the Ulster force, he formed one of the governing committee; and, when the European War broke out in 1914, he sided with the minority of volunteers who separated themselves from Mr. Redmond. His first thought was to gain German aid to win complete Irish independence. He made his way to America, and thence, by way of Sweden, to Berlin in November 1914. Here he saw important political and military personages, and wrote a letter, which was published in the Irish separatist papers, indicating Germany's intentions to recognize Ireland's independence and to send her friendly assistance. He made an attempt also to induce Irish soldiers who had been captured by the Germans to join an Irish brigade in the German service. His appeal was solely to their nationalist ideals: but even when the Germans reinforced his efforts by bribes and threats, only a handful were persuaded to join.

Before long Casement found that he neither trusted the Germans nor was trusted by them: he felt that he was spied on both by German and by British agents; and he became convinced that Germany had no intention of risking an expedition to Ireland, without which he considered rebellion hopeless. By means of submarines he conveyed to the Irish volunteer headquarters verbal messages designed to deter action. But a rising was in preparation for Easter 1916, and a German vessel, the *Aud*, was being laden with arms and ammunition for dispatch, under the Norwegian flag, to Ireland. Casement persuaded the Germans to send him also in a submarine, his purpose being to reinforce in person his advice against the projected rebellion. They set out on 12 April; but the adventure miscarried. The British government had been warned. The *Aud* was captured by a patrol boat on 21 April off the Kerry coast, and sunk by her crew while being taken to Queenstown. Casement, with two companions, was successfully landed from the submarine at Banna, near Tralee, but was arrested by the police and taken to London (24 April). He had succeeded, however, in sending a message to Dublin, announcing the capture of the *Aud* and urging postponement of the rebellion. He was brought up at Bow Street police court on 15 May and charged with high treason. After three days' trial at the Old Bailey (26–9 June) he was convicted and sentenced to death. Strong efforts for a reprieve were made on the ground of Casement's public services in the past. The Court of Criminal Appeal dismissed his appeal (18 July), and he was hanged at Pentonville prison 3 August 1916. He had been previously received into the Church of Rome. His knighthood had been annulled on 30 June, and his name taken off the companionage. His acceptance of these honours is difficult to reconcile with the limitations to his allegiance; but, when they were bestowed, all the world thought them richly earned. And those who knew Roger Casement knew him to be honourable and chivalrous as well as able far beyond the ordinary measure of men.

[Parliamentary Papers, vol. lxii, 357 (Congo), 1904, and vol. lxviii, 819 (Putumayo), 1912–1913; P. S. O'Hegarty, *The Victory of Sinn Fein*, 1924; Evelyn, Princess Blücher, *An English Wife in Berlin*, 1920; L. G. Redmond Howard, *Sir Roger Casement*, 1916; private information; personal knowledge.]

STEPHEN LUCIUS GWYNN

published 1927

CAVELL Edith

(1865–1915)

Nurse, was born at Swardeston, Norfolk, 4 December 1865, the eldest daughter of the Rev. Frederick Cavell, vicar of Swardeston, by his wife, Louisa Sophia Walming. She was educated at home, at a school in Somerset, and in Brussels. In 1888, having inherited a small competency, she travelled on the Continent. When visiting Bavaria, she took much interest in a free hospital maintained by a Dr. Wolfenberg, and endowed it with a fund for the purchase of instruments. In 1895 she entered the London Hospital as a probationer. In 1897 she took charge of an emergency typhoid hospital at Maidstone. Having attained the position of staff nurse at the London Hospital, she engaged in poor law nursing, serving in the Highgate and Shoreditch infirmaries. Subsequently she took temporary charge of a Queen's district nursery in Manchester. In 1906 she went to Brussels to co-operate with Dr. Depage in establishing a modern training school for nurses on the English system, the best nurses hitherto obtainable in Belgium having been sisters belonging to Catholic religious orders. Edith Cavell was appointed in 1907 the first matron of Depage's clinic—the Berkendael medical institute—the success of which soon made it of national importance. Shortly before the European War it obtained official recognition, a new and larger building being added to it from state funds. She also organized and managed the hospital of St. Gilles. In August 1914 Dr. Depage went away to organize military hospitals, and Miss Cavell remained in charge. The German authorities gave her permission to continue her work in Brussels, the institute became a Red Cross Hospital, and she and her assistants devoted themselves to the care of the wounded, Germans as well as Allies.

When, in the latter part of 1914, the French and British forces were compelled to retire from Belgium, many soldiers from both these armies were cut off from their units. They hid themselves as best they could, for some, at least, of those who fell into German hands were summarily executed. But many escaped with the aid of the Belgian farmers and peasants. A regular system grew up under which these men were enabled to escape from the country. Miss Cavell was naturally one to whom those who needed aid applied; and she readily responded. Her conduct, careful as it was, aroused suspicion. Suspicion led to espionage. On 5 August 1915 she was arrested and placed in solitary confinement in the prison of St. Gilles. Nine weeks later (7 October) she was brought to trial together with some thirty-five other prisoners. The charges against all were of a similar kind; the tribunal before which these persons, many of them women, were arraigned was a court martial; the proceedings were conducted in German, though a French interpreter was provided.

During the weeks when Miss Cavell lay in prison Mr. Brand Whitlock, the United States minister in Brussels, was active on her behalf. He wrote to Baron von Lancken, the civil governor of Belgium, stating that he had been instructed to take charge of her defence, and he asked that a representative of his legation might see her. This letter elicited no reply. When Mr. Whitlock wrote again he was told that the prisoner had already confessed her guilt, and that a M. Braun had been engaged by her friends to conduct the defence. In fact the defence was handed over to a member of the Brussels bar, M. Sadi Kirschen, who did everything possible under the circumstances. But, as the event showed, the conviction of Miss Cavell was a foregone conclusion. In accordance with the usual procedure of such courts in Germany, the prisoner was not allowed to see her advocate before the trial, nor was he granted access to the documents in the case. The allegation was that she had enabled no less than 130 persons to escape from Belgium. Merely assisting these men to escape to Holland would have constituted no more than an *attempt* to 'conduct soldiers to the enemy'. Under German military law this is not a capital offence. But the confession which Miss Cavell is alleged to have signed on the day previous to the trial stated that she had actually assisted Belgians of military age to go to the front, and that she had also concealed French and English soldiers, providing them with funds and with guides whereby they had been enabled to cross the Dutch frontier.

That such a confession was made by Miss Cavell is probable enough. Nine weeks of solitary confinement, the absence of any adviser who might have insisted that she should put her accusers to the proof of their charges, the conviction that what she had done was morally right, though legally wrong—all these considerations might well have induced her to tell the full story. But for her confessions, however, the capital charge would seem not to have been sustainable. The prosecution appears to have had no evidence that she had succeeded in enabling military refugees to reach England. She stated at the trial, however, that she had received letters of thanks from those whom she had helped to repatriate. In the absence of this admission she could only have been found guilty of an attempt to conduct soldiers to the enemy. Her statement showed that her attempt had been successful. So the penalty was death. The trial ended on Friday, 8 October. At eight o'clock on the evening of the following Monday (11 October) an official of the United States Legation was told unofficially that three hours previously sentence of death had been pronounced on Miss Cavell and that she would be shot at 2 a.m. on the following morning (12 October). Strenuous, but unavailing, efforts were made both by Mr. Whitlock and the Spanish minister to obtain at least a respite. All that they were granted was permission for the chaplain of Christ Church, Brussels, the Rev. H. S. T. Gahan, to visit her before the end, and he brought away her last messages.

Memorials of Miss Cavell have been set up in England and elsewhere. On 15 May 1919 her body was brought to Norwich Cathedral after a memorial service in Westminster Abbey. A statue of her, the work of Sir George Frampton, R.A., stands in St. Martin's Place, London, to record the price which she paid for doing what she conceived to be her duty.

To many English minds the execution of Miss Cavell was a judicial murder. British tribunals throughout the War avoided passing sentence of death upon women, even when found guilty of the most dangerous espionage. There is no evidence that Miss Cavell was in any sense a spy. She did nothing for pecuniary reward. Charity and the desire to aid the distressed were the mainsprings of her life. But the German military code prescribed the penalty of death for the offence of which she was found guilty. The procedure in this case was the same as that in other courts martial. Deference to her sex and some allowance for honourable motives might have been expected from humane judges. Presumably the judges were afraid to be humane and thought that the obedience of the Belgian population must be assured by severe sentences. The execution then was justified according to German standards. But, if legally justifiable, it was assuredly a blunder. Popular opinion in the allied countries considered Nurse Cavell to be a martyr.

[*The Times*, 16 and 22 October 1915; *Correspondence with the United States Ambassador respecting the Execution of Miss Cavell at Brussels*, Cd. 8013, 1915; *La Vie et la Mort de Miss Edith Cavell*, 1915; private information. Portraits, *Royal Academy Pictures*, 1916 and 1917.]

BENEDICT WILLIAM GINSBURG

published 1927

KELL Vernon George Waldegrave

(1873–1942)

Sir

Intelligence officer, was born in Great Yarmouth 21 November 1873, the only son of Major Waldegrave Charles Vernon Kell of the South Staffordshire Regiment, who served in a number of Imperial outposts and with distinction in the Zulu wars, and his wife, the daughter of a Polish count named Konarpki, with exiled relatives in other parts of Europe by whom her son was helped to become an accomplished linguist. Before entering Sandhurst, he was privately educated and in 1894 joined his father's old regiment, in which his languages immediately proved useful. He became an interpreter in French and German and in 1899 was posted to Moscow for further language studies and in 1900 to Shanghai, where he served in the Boxer campaign and was mentioned in dispatches. Later he became chairman of the Japan Society.

In time for her to accompany him to China, he married Constance Rawdon, daughter of James W. Scott of Westlands, Queenstown, county Cork. They had two sons and one daughter. On returning to England he served as a staff captain in the War Office and then as an assistant secretary to the Committee of Imperial Defence, an appointment which was to alter completely the course of his career.

During the span of his appointment, the CID was considering how best to fill a serious gap in the country's defence arrangements. There existed no organization to cope with the rising dangers of German espionage nor one to obtain secret intelligence on German military expansion. The Committee finally proposed and the cabinet approved the creation of a Secret Service Bureau to cover both these functions. At thirty-six years of age Kell was chosen as one of its first two directors and shortly afterwards took over full responsibility for the defensive side. He was to hold this position for the next thirty-one years and must therefore be regarded as a founding father of the organization which later became known as MI5.

Kell started work in October 1909 and was characteristically slow and methodical in his approach to his utterly new functions. By 1914 he still employed only three officers, one barrister, and seven clerks. Nevertheless, on the first night of the war he was able to round up a ring of twenty-one German spies in an effectively timed and executed coup which probably deprived the Germans of any information on Britain's initial military dispositions. By the end of the war he accounted for thirty-five more spies to complete a wartime record which impressed the general staff and ensured the continuance of his organization into the peace, though on a much reduced basis from his final wartime strength of 800.

The period between the wars coincided with the remainder of his working life and was highly formative for Britain's later intelligence system. In 1919 a Secret Service committee of senior ministers was established to monitor its development and decide the delicate issues involved in fitting it into its democratic framework. This took time, and it was not until 1931 that Kell was chosen as the director around whom something like a national security service could be built. This meant adding a civil commitment to his existing military one and augmenting his staff from selected members of the civilian staff at Scotland Yard. It was a considerable tribute to his growing reputation in high official circles, and the fact that he was proposed for it by Sir John Anderson (later Viscount Waverley), then permanent under-secretary at the Home Office, indicates that he already enjoyed the trust of the home departments he would henceforth be serving.

Kell was appointed CB in 1917 and KBE in 1919. He was an officer of the Legion of Honour and had many other foreign decorations. He reached the rank of major-general and received the Jubilee medal in 1935. He was a calm, modest, and patient man, which made it seem obvious that fly-fishing was his chosen hobby. From first to last he kept himself out of the public limelight. He selected his staff by personal recommendation and from men nearing the end of their careers in other public services, the army and navy, the home and overseas police. It was a safe and economical procedure which also initially guaranteed the loyalty and discretion needed for the maintenance of security. He ruled his staff with a light touch and a delightful sense of humour, thereby setting standards of unity and comradeship which were gratefully inherited by his successors. But the end of the 1930s was a time of trial for him. His health began to fail as a result of severe attacks of asthma. He worried over the pace of his build-up, which he knew should be quickened though resources for this were severely limited. In the early summer of 1940 he was quietly retired and he died at Emberton, Olney, Buckinghamshire, 27 March 1942.

[F. H. Hinsley and C. A. G. Simkins, *British Intelligence in the Second World War*, vol. iv, 1990; Constance Kell (wife), 'A Secret Well Kept', unpublished MS in Imperial War Museum, London; personal knowledge.]

DICK WHITE

published 1993

MAUGHAM William Somerset

(1874–1965)

Writer, was born in Paris, at the British Embassy, 25 January 1874, youngest of the four sons of Robert Ormond Maugham, solicitor and legal adviser to the embassy, by his wife, Edith Mary, daughter of Major Charles Snell, of the Indian Army. His grandfather, Robert Maugham, and his brother, Frederic (later Viscount) Maugham, were both eminent lawyers.

Maugham lived in France until he was ten, when his father died (his beloved mother having died two years earlier), and he was transported to the guardianship of his uncle, the Revd Henry Macdonald Maugham, vicar of Whitstable, Kent; he was educated at the King's School, Canterbury, and then at Heidelberg University, where he attended lectures for a year but did not take a degree. French was his first language, and during his later childhood he was a foreigner in his own country; he stammered, and he was unhappy both at school and in the vicarage. His escape was travel, which was to become a lifelong habit. At sixteen, on the suspicion that he had tuberculosis, he was sent for a time to Hyères on the Riviera. He read de Maupassant and became familiar with French authors. His uncle wanted him to go into the Church, but he had £150 from his father's estate, and in 1892 he enrolled as a medical student at St. Thomas's Hospital, London. He completed the course, but at the same time he continued to read omnivorously and to keep a writer's notebook. When he began to work in the wards he was 'exhilarated' by his contact with 'life in the raw', and in 1895 he was for three weeks an obstetric clerk in the slums of Lambeth, which he found 'absorbing'.

His first novel, *Liza of Lambeth*, was published in 1897; its vivid portrayal of low life gave it a mild *succès de scandale*, and Maugham, who later that year qualified MRCS, LRCP, was encouraged to abandon medicine for literature. He went to Spain, which was to become, after France, the country of his heart, and lodged in Seville. He read; he travelled; he wrote. After his return to England, he published further books without making any mark, although he attained a certain entrée into literary and social circles, where a lack of money humiliated him. In 1903 his first play, *A Man of Honour*, was performed by the Stage Society, but not until 1907, at the age of thirty-three, did he wake one morning to find himself, at last, famous. *Lady Frederick* had been mounted as a stopgap at the Court theatre, but its success was so sweeping that within a short time Maugham had four plays running simultaneously in the West End, and a sketch by (Sir) Bernard Partridge in *Punch* (24 June 1908) showed the shade of Shakespeare turning enviously from the playbills. From then onwards Maugham never looked back. His wit was sharp but rarely distressing; his plots abounded in amusing situations, his characters were usually drawn from the same class as his audiences and managed at once to satirize and delight their originals.

The theatre was never entirely to satisfy him. Although he attempted to use it as a platform for less amiable subjects, he was constrained by the exigencies of the managers and by his audiences' expectations. Yet by the mid twenties he was an acknowledged master of light, sometimes mordant comedy. He attempted serious themes with courage and assurance, but the public wanted to be amused. In 1933 he ceased writing plays altogether, but already as early as 1911 he had retired temporarily from the theatre to work on his long novel, *Of Human Bondage*. He was to correct the proofs under the admiring eyes of (Sir) Desmond MacCarthy in a small hotel at Malo, near Dunkirk; the two men were drivers in an ambulance unit for which they had volunteered at the outbreak of war in 1914. MacCarthy became one of the most vociferous of Maugham's literary advocates, but his voice was never wholly to prevail against those who regarded public success as evidence of vulgarity.

In 1915 Maugham was recruited into the Intelligence Department; his facility with languages made him a 'natural' for the work, and he was sent to Geneva where he posed with no great difficulty as a literary man. Willie Ashenden, his *alter ego* in many spy stories and novels, was born of this experience. In 1917 he was selected by Sir William Wiseman to go to Russia, where the overthrow of the Tsar threatened to lead to a Russian withdrawal from the war. He was to say later that he believed that, had he gone six months earlier, he might have averted the Bolshevik revolution and held Kerensky to the Allied cause. By the time Lenin came to power, Maugham's health had temporarily failed, and after spending three months in a sanatorium he remained an invalid for the next two years.

The war years were also eventful in his literary and private life. In 1916 he married Gwendoline Maude Syrie Wellcome, daughter of the philanthropist Thomas John Barnardo, after being cited co-respondent in her divorce from (Sir) Henry Wellcome. Their liaison had existed for some years, but the marriage was not happy. By the time Maugham and his wife were again together for long enough to set up house, he had discovered a new interest: the East, which he first visited in the year of his marriage. Travelling in the company of a young American, Gerald Haxton, who became the companion of his middle years, he 'stepped off his pedestal', as he put it. So far as the British were concerned, Haxton was an undesirable alien; Maugham could not both live in England and retain his friendship. He went frequently on his travels, and in 1928 decided to live permanently in the south of France. His marriage had been dissolved the previous year; he and Syrie, who became a fashionable interior decorator, had one daughter, Elizabeth Mary ('Liza'), whose second husband was Lord John Hope (later Lord Glendevon).

Of Human Bondage was published in 1915. It was less noticed in wartime London than in New York, where Theodore Dreiser reviewed it with enthusiasm. It remains Maugham's most impressive literary work, and by the time of his death was said to have sold ten million copies. *The Moon and Sixpence* (1919), *The Painted Veil* (1925), and *Cakes and Ale* (an elegant piece of literary malice, 1930), followed and found a prompt public. Having quit the theatre, he discovered a fertile new field in the short story and was widely regarded as the supreme English exponent of both the magazine squib and the more elaborate *conte*.

At his home, the Villa Mauresque at St. Jean, Cap Ferrat, he entertained smart company with stylish generosity, although he himself ate sparsely of the lotus he offered others: he worked steadily. His prose style changed little; he prided himself on his plain speaking and lack of literary frills. He was never a modern: he neither favoured experiment nor disdained public success. His books sold hugely; one short story, *Rain* (1921), was filmed several times. No one denied his intelligence, but the more severe critics never conceded his importance. He affected indifference.

In 1940 he had to leave France in a coal boat: he was on the Nazis' wanted list. He went to America, where he lived quite modestly: although rich, he refused to be too much at his ease while England was in sore straits. In 1944 he published his last substantial novel, *The Razor's Edge*, in which he paid tribute to the ascetic mysticism he had encountered in

India and of which he was more an admirer than a practitioner. He returned to France after the liberation and resumed life at the Villa Mauresque. Gerald Haxton had died in America in 1944 and Alan Searle, a man of more reliable stamp, took his place as Maugham's private secretary.

During the twenty years which remained to him, Maugham established himself in many eyes as a cosmopolitan oracle. He had a talent for worldly moralizing, already displayed with concise elegance in *The Summing Up* (1938), and he now turned to the essay, although he continued to write short stories and historical novels. Some of the stories were filmed, with his usual success, and he himself appeared on the screen to provide introductions. He had become perhaps the most famous living English author, and claimed casually that sales of his books exceeded 64,000,000 copies; yet he was not a happy man. He was rather short, about five feet seven, and prognathous in appearance, with olive complexion and penetrating eyes. He was tortured by his stammer, and by the conviction that he was unloved. He was drawn to religion, although he affected sturdy agnosticism. He was very widely read, but claimed to be uneducated. His tongue was sharp and he could make enemies easily, yet he was capable of great courtesy, and his uncensorious scepticism brought comfort as well as diversion both to millions of readers and to private acquaintances. His conversation was urbane and he was a good listener no less than an amusing commentator. His old age was soured by public wrangles with his daughter and, in the regrettable memoir *Looking Back* (1962), with the ghost of his wife, who had died in 1955. However, he could be kind as well as caustic. He was a thoughtful correspondent and a generous private critic of unsolicited manuscripts. In 1947 he founded the Somerset Maugham Award, which gives young writers an opportunity to travel. He died in hospital in Nice 15 December 1965, and left a substantial legacy, including his books, to the King's School, Canterbury, where his ashes were interred, next to the library he had endowed.

He was appointed CH in 1954, and C.Lit. in 1961. He was a fellow of the Royal Society of Literature, a commander of the Legion of Honour, and an honorary D.Litt. of the universities of Oxford and Toulouse. On his eightieth birthday the Garrick Club gave a dinner in his honour; only Dickens, Thackeray, and Trollope had been similarly honoured.

There are many portraits of Maugham: Sir Gerald Kelly painted him about thirty times—for example, 1911, in the National Portrait Gallery; 1935, privately owned; and 1948, at the King's School, Canterbury; a bronze by (Sir) Jacob Epstein (1951, lent by the Tate Gallery) is in the National Portrait Gallery, where there is also a portrait by P. Steegman (1931). A drawing by Sir William Rothenstein is reproduced in *Contemporaries* (1937),

Dansey

while the best-known portrait, by Graham Sutherland (1949), is in the Tate Gallery. Others, by Marie Laurencin (1936), H. A. Freeth (1946), and Vasco Lazzolo (1953), are in private hands.

[W. Somerset Maugham, *The Summing Up*, 1938; *The Times*, 17 December 1965; Robin Maugham, *Somerset and All the Maughams*, 1966; Frederic Raphael, *Somerset Maugham and his World*, 1976; Richard B. Fisher, *Syrie Maugham*, 1979; personal knowledge.]

FREDERIC RAPHAEL

[Ted Morgan, *Maugham, a Biography*, 1980.]
published 1981

DANSEY Claude Edward Marjoribanks

(1876–1947)

Sir

Intelligence officer, was born at Cromwell Place, South Kensington, 10 September 1876, the second child and eldest son in the family of four sons and five daughters of Edward Mashiter Dansey, captain and later lieutenant-colonel in the 1st Life Guards, and his wife Eleanore, daughter of Robert Francis Gifford, second Baron Gifford. His parents removed him from Wellington College in 1891, following a diphtheria epidemic, to a school in Bruges, whence too he was removed after a homosexual scandal. In childhood he acquired fluent French, a language he often pretended hardly to speak.

In 1895 he went to the new colony of Rhodesia and became a trooper in the Matabeleland regiment of the British South Africa Police. He helped suppress the Matabele rising in 1896, and learned the elements of scouting and intelligence gathering. In 1898 he returned to England and secured a militia commission in the Lancashire Fusiliers.

He spent ten weeks in the winter of 1899–1900 with the British North Borneo Company police force as a sub-commandant, in operations against Mohammed Salleh, before rejoining his regiment in South Africa in 1900. He took part in the relief of Mafeking, was briefly a fellow-subaltern with (Sir) Winston Churchill in the South African Light Horse, and spent the rest of the war in the field intelligence department. In 1900 he received a regular commission as lieutenant in the 6th battalion of the Lancashire Fusiliers. He stayed in South Africa, on intelligence duties, till 1904, and

210

then spent five years in British Somaliland as a political officer, trying to counter the 'Mad Mullah'.

While in England on sick leave he was recruited into the security branch of the secret service. He spent three years in New York State as resident secretary of the Sleepy Hollow Country Club, a rich men's recreation park on the Hudson River, whence he could keep an eye on wealthy Irish-Americans.

In August 1914 he was recalled to England, and placed in charge of port security. He revisited the USA in 1917 to play a decisive part in helping to set up the first official American military intelligence service. He was promoted lieutenant-colonel and transferred to the Secret Intelligence Service to unravel a disastrous muddle in the Netherlands. He next took over SIS's organization in Switzerland.

In 1919 the service's staff was cut back; he spent most of the 1920s in private business ventures on both sides of the Atlantic. From 1929 to 1936 he was re-employed, under the cover of passport control officer, in Rome. His chief, C (Sir Hugh Sinclair), then realized that German secret police had penetrated several SIS stations. Dansey left Rome in 1936; word seeped out that he had been caught with his hand in the till and sacked. He settled into an export-import office in Bush House in the Strand, and set up parallel networks of secret intelligence agents to cover the penetrated areas, using the codename Z and avoiding the use of wireless.

In September 1939 Z's networks amalgamated with C's, and Dansey went back to Berne. In November C died; Dansey returned to London, and became assistant chief to his friend (Sir) Stewart Menzies, the new C. He was in charge of all active espionage till 1945. All the arrangements for stay-behind agents in north-west Europe collapsed, but Dansey was able to charm most of the governments in exile in London into recruiting spies.

Dansey was closely involved with the Special Operations Executive in its early stages—(Sir) Frank Nelson, its first executive head, had been a Z agent. Dansey did not seek to influence its policy, so long as it kept out of his agents' way. He often used to display there his sharp tongue, as notorious as his charm. He also kept a keen eye on MI9, the secret escape service. At the end of the war he was persuaded to retire, to Bathampton Manor, near Bath.

He was appointed CMG in 1918 and KCMG in 1943. In 1915 he married Mrs Pauline Monroe Cory Ulman, daughter of David Cory, doctor of medicine, of New York. She separated from him in 1929 and later divorced him. His second wife, whom he married in 1945, was Mrs Frances Gurney Rylander, daughter of Dr D. F. K. Wilson. There were no children of either marriage but he had a stepdaughter from each. He died in a Bath nursing home 11 June 1947.

[Anthony Read and David Fisher, *Colonel Z*, 1984; private information.]

M. R. D. FOOT

published 1993

MEINERTZHAGEN Richard

(1878–1967)

Naturalist and intelligence officer, was born 3 March 1878 in Rutland Gate, Knightsbridge, the second son and third child in the family of four sons and five daughters of Daniel Meinertzhagen, London merchant banker, whose German family had long settled in Bremen, and his wife Georgina, an elder sister of Beatrice Webb, the daughter of Richard Potter, railway and industrial magnate. Though registered as Oliver, he was christened Richard, and called Dick by his intimates. He was at two preparatory schools, Aysgarth, where he learnt self-reliance, and Fonthill, where he was sadistically beaten by a master—till he hit back.

Much of his childhood he spent at Mottisfont Abbey, on the Test above Romsey; there he began his lifelong study of birds. He was educated at Harrow, from where he went for a few months into his father's City office, which he hated; and he spent a term in Göttingen, learning German. A subaltern's commission in the Hampshire Yeomanry in 1897–8 gave him a liking for army life, and in January 1899 he was commissioned into the Royal Fusiliers. He missed the South African war, as he was serving in south Asia. In 1902–6 he had four adventurous years' attachment to the King's African Rifles, serving up-country in Kenya, where he discovered a new species (*Hylochoeros meinertzhageni*, the giant forest hog). He was wounded, mentioned in dispatches, and promoted captain; he saved most of his pay.

His regiment released him again to pass the Staff College in Quetta, and at the start of World War I in 1914 he was made intelligence officer to the Tanga expeditionary force. In 1916 he was appointed to the DSO for exceptionally valuable work with this force. He then became chief intelligence officer to the Egyptian expeditionary force that advanced into Palestine. In October 1917 the Turks held an entrenched front from Gaza to Beersheba. Sir E. H. H. Allenby (later first Viscount Allenby of Megiddo) misled them as to which flank he was about to attack, in part through a bloodstained haversack full of papers dropped by Meinertzhagen on reconnaissance: a classic of practical deception.

After a brief spell at the War Office, Meinertzhagen was next posted to the intelligence branch of the GHQ in France, commanded by Sir Douglas (later first Earl) Haig. Never one to sit behind a desk if he could help it, he tried to see the battle front for himself, and was severely wounded. He recovered in time to join, as a colonel, the staff of 400 that A. J. Balfour (later first Earl of Balfour) took to the Paris peace conference, where he watched politicians disputing over Levantine problems. After a short spell as chief political officer in Palestine and Syria, he spent 1921–4 as military adviser to the colonial office, sharing a room there with his friend T. E. Lawrence.

By now he had become a convinced Zionist. This conviction did not sit well either with regimental soldiering or with Whitehall. In 1925 he re-signed from the army, and spent most of the rest of his long life travelling—mainly in western and central Asia—and studying birds, partly as cover for observing international politics. He returned to the War Office in the winter of 1939–40, and was wounded again off Dunkirk in June 1940, when he took a small boat across to join the rescue. For the rest of the war he was in the Home Guard. After it, he rejoiced in the creation of the state of Israel in 1948; he was an active eyewitness. While on his way to watch birds, he slipped ashore during a skirmish at Haifa, disguised as a Coldstream private, and shot several men.

He was a lifelong diarist, and published some of the results: *Kenya Diary 1902–1906* (1957), *Middle East Diary 1917–1956* (1959), *Army Diary 1899–1926* (1960), and *Diary of a Black Sheep* (1964). Apart from many articles in *Ibis*, he wrote *Nicholl's Birds of Egypt* (2 vols., 1930), *Birds of Arabia* (1954), and *Pirates and Predators* (1959). In 1951 he received the Godman Salvin medal of the British Ornithologists' Union, and in 1957 was appointed CBE for services to ornithology.

He was twice married: in 1911 to Armorel, daughter of Colonel Herman le Roy-Lewis of Westbury House, Petersfield; and in 1921 to Anne Constance (died 1928), daughter of Major Randle Jackson of Swordale, Easter Ross. By his second wife he had a daughter and two sons; his elder son was killed aged nineteen in the Guards Armoured division on the Dutch-German border in 1944. Of him he wrote a memoir, *The Life of a Boy* (1947). He died in Kensington, London, 17 June 1967.

[John Lord, *Duty, Honour, Empire: the Life and Times of Colonel R. Meinertzhagen*, 1971; *The Times*, 19 June 1967; works cited above.]

M. R. D. Foot

published 1993

(1879–1961)

Sir

Public servant, was born at Inveravon 9 September 1879, the second son of Thomas Petrie, master millwright, of Inveravon, Banffshire, and his wife, Jane Allan.

After graduating MA at Aberdeen University (1900), Petrie entered the Indian Police in December 1900 and was posted to the Punjab. His early service included a five-year secondment to the Samana Rifles in the North-West Frontier Province. In 1909 he became assistant to the deputy inspector-general, Punjab CID and, in 1911, assistant director with the Central Criminal Intelligence Department of the Government of India. In the same year he won the gold medal of the United Service Institution of India for an essay on 'The maintenance of law and order in India considered in relation to the mutual co-operation of the civil and military power in the country'.

In December 1912 a bomb was thrown at the viceroy and Petrie played a leading part in the ensuing investigation. He remained on special duty investigating subversion and terrorism throughout the war of 1914–18. In January 1915 this took him to the Far East where he met his wife.

During 1921–2 Petrie was on the staff first of the Duke of Connaught, and later of the Prince of Wales, during their Indian tours. As a member of the Public Services Commission, India, 1931–2, and its chairman, 1932–6, he helped to secure concessions which persuaded some subsequently distinguished police officers to pursue careers which they might otherwise have terminated prematurely.

In 1924 Petrie became director of the Intelligence Bureau of the Home Department of the Government of India (as the Central Criminal Intelligence Department came to be called), the first Indian police officer to hold this post. He filled it with great distinction in very troubled times, when law and order were threatened not only by extreme nationalist terrorism but also by Communist subversion. On leaving the Bureau in 1931 he was appointed first a member, and then, in 1932, chairman, of the Indian Public Services Commission. He also became chairman of the Indian Red Cross Society and St. John Ambulance Association and was appointed a Knight of Grace of the Order of St. John of Jerusalem in 1933. Honours had accumulated steadily—the King's Police medal (1914), CIE (1915), OBE (1918), CBE (1919), CVO (1922), and a knighthood (1929).

Petrie retired in 1936. In 1937–8 he visited Palestine with another distinguished retired police officer, Sir Charles Tegart, to advise on police organization and counter-terrorism. In 1939, with war threatening, he hoped to find employment with one of the professional intelligence services, but it was not until May 1940 that he was commissioned in the Intelligence Corps and posted to Cairo. He was recalled at the end of November to report to the lord president of the Council, Sir John Anderson (later Viscount Waverley), on the organization of MI5 (the Security Service, concerned with the defence of the realm against espionage, sabotage, and subversion), then at the nadir of its fortunes. Precisely how the fortunate choice of Petrie for this task came to be made is uncertain. It is believed that he was first suggested by a former Indian Police officer. He would have been known at least by reputation to Sir John Anderson, who had been governor of Bengal from 1932 to 1937, and he was personally known to Sir S. Findlater Stewart, formerly permanent under-secretary at the India Office, who held a key position on the Home Front. In March 1941 Petrie was appointed head of MI5 to carry out his own recommendations and held the newly created post of director-general for the next five years.

The main problems confronting him on taking office were organization and morale. He introduced major changes designed to create a machine capable of bearing the manifold strains of war. These changes were immediately successful. Morale was at a low ebb. Now the atmosphere changed dramatically, and it rose rapidly to the very high level which it maintained for the rest of the war. There was a wealth of talent in MI5 (much, but by no means all of it, recruited during the war), and with sound organization and strong leadership MI5 played a distinguished part in the defeat of Germany's intelligence services which was as complete as that suffered by her armed forces.

Petrie brought to MI5 what it most needed—leadership and administrative ability. But he also had a thorough grasp of the techniques of the work. He was very industrious and did nearly all his own drafting. He always made himself perfectly clear, but was occasionally pompous and inclined to overlook the virtues of brevity and tact in his external correspondence. Thanks to his Indian experience, he understood bureaucracy. He briefed himself with great care for meetings, where he generally spoke little but to the point. Aided by his impressive bearing and distinguished record, he left his comparatively few Whitehall contacts in no doubt that he was vastly experienced and totally reliable, and could safely be trusted with the conduct of a highly secret organization which was still very much on the periphery of government. His relations with Lord Swinton and Alfred Duff Cooper (later Viscount Norwich), who were successively *in loco parentis* to MI5, were good, but he made no attempt to cultivate influential people and described himself as a bad publicity merchant for the service.

Petrie was always authoritative and occasionally irascible, but he was also sensitive to the feelings of others. The loyal support which he invariably gave his subordinates won him much respect. With very few exceptions his relations with them were rather formal; as was the custom of his generation, he called even those closest to him by their surnames. Nevertheless, he enjoyed convivial occasions at which he more than held his own. He was a man of perfect integrity and somewhat puritanical morality, a proud Scotsman, a lover of the countryside, and a skilful fisherman.

Petrie finally retired in 1946. He had been appointed KCMG in 1945 and after the war became a commander of the US Legion of Merit and of the Order of Orange Nassau with swords, and was awarded class iii of the Czechoslovak Order of the White Lion.

He married in 1920 Edris Naida (died 1945), daughter of W. Henry Elliston Warrall, a captain in mercantile marine; they had no children. Petrie died at Sidmouth 7 August 1961.

[*The Times*, 8 August 1961; private information; personal knowledge.]

ANTHONY SIMKINS

published 1981

VANSITTART Robert Gilbert

(1881–1957)

Baron Vansittart

Diplomatist, from a long line of distinguished forebears. He was born at Wilton House, Farnham, 25 June 1881, the eldest of three sons among the six children of Robert Arnold Vansittart, of Foots Cray Place, Kent, a captain in the 7th Dragoon Guards, and his wife, Susan (Alice), daughter of Gilbert James Blane, of Foliejon Park, Berkshire.

'Van' to his many friends, 'Bob Vansittart' to the fringe, and just Vansittart to the rest, he spent a full seven years at Eton, unusual at any time. He confesses in his autobiography to a devotion to, and a hope of success in, ball games which was not wholly fulfilled; but he won two school races and was in the cricket Twenty-two. His forte was modern languages and he won the rare, if not unique, distinction of both the French and German Prince Consort prizes in the same year. He finished his career as captain of the Oppidans and was, of course, in Pop. He left regretfully and, as others before and since, lingered on at the last day, after the rest had gone home. This was perhaps symbolic of his loyal attachment to all he held dear—places, family, friends, and last but not least his country.

He next turned to serious work for the diplomatic examination. A second visit to Germany, less unpleasant than an earlier one which was perhaps the foundation for his subsequent attitude to the Germans, was followed by a sojourn in Paris. He entered the service as an attaché and was posted to Paris (1903) becoming a third secretary in 1905. In 1907 he was transferred to Tehran and in 1909 to Cairo where, as in Tehran, he qualified for an allowance for knowledge of the local language. Two years later he established himself in the Foreign Office which was thenceforward his headquarters.

During the war of 1914–18 he was joint head of the contraband department; then head of the prisoners of war department under Lord Newton. He attended the peace conference in Paris and emerged in 1920 as an assistant secretary in the Foreign Office and in 1920–24 was private secretary to the secretary of state. In 1928 he became private secretary to the prime minister, Stanley Baldwin, and continued in the same post with Ramsay MacDonald until on 1 January 1930 he was appointed permanent under-secretary in the Foreign Office. Eight years later, after serving through some of the most critical years in modern times, he was removed to the specially created post of diplomatic adviser.

The story of this 'kick upstairs' is long and tortuous. It has been put in a nutshell by (Sir) Winston Churchill in *The Gathering Storm* (1948). It begins in 1935 with what Churchill rightly calls Vansittart's 'fortuitous connection with the Hoare–Laval pact' which at the time was regarded as a scuttle. His connection may only be judged, if at all, as that of a wise adviser; the ultimate decision lay with the Government, with whom must lie also responsibility for the country's weakened situation. As the policy of appeasement grew in strength the direction of foreign affairs passed from the Foreign Office to 10 Downing Street and Vansittart was blamed for his warnings against imminent German aggression and for hostility to Germany. He was removed from his direction of the Foreign Office to the unique post, created *ad hoc*, of 'chief diplomatic adviser to His Majesty's Government' which he held from 1938 until he retired in 1941. Whether his advice was ever taken is doubtful, but in any case it was by then too late for it to be effective. He continued his theme both publicly and in the House of Lords which he entered on his retirement; the vigour of his campaign against the Nazis was such that it was seriously asked whether he was not perhaps at heart a pro-German whose campaign was deliberately planned to produce the reaction of 'Don't let's be beastly to the Germans'. Nothing could have been farther from the truth.

The epilogue to Vansittart's autobiography, *The Mist Procession* (1958), one of the outstanding contemporary accounts of the time, begins with the words 'Mine is a story of failure'. But failure is an expression of various facets, and though he may have 'failed' to convince the Government at the climax of his career that he was right and they were wrong, no life can be called a failure which was enriched by so noble, affectionate, and loyal a character, by such wide experience, and such remarkable ability. Vansittart's literary style, like his speech, was rapid, incisive, and idiomatic. It often needed an effort to keep up with his thoughts, but if you could 'take' the speed, you could 'take' the meaning. His writings were numerous and varied and included poems and plays. Perhaps his most original feat was to have a play in French run for four months in Paris when he was a secretary at the embassy.

Vansittart's first marriage (1921) to Gladys, daughter of William C. Heppenheimer, of the United States Army, happy in other respects, was clouded by the tragic death in an accident of her son by a former marriage; and she herself died in 1928. They had one daughter. In 1931 Vansittart married Sarita Enriqueta, daughter of Herbert Ward, of Paris, and widow of his late colleague, Sir Colville Barclay. She sustained him through the years of frustration and enabled him to surmount with cheerfulness disappointments which he was perhaps too much inclined to take to heart, and the inevitable concomitants of advancing age which he bore without complaint. He died at their beautiful home at Denham 14 February 1957. The peerage became extinct. A portrait by A. R. Thomson remained in the possession of the artist.

Vansittart was appointed M.V.O. (1906); C.B. (1927), K.C.B. (1929), G.C.B. (1938); C.M.G. (1920), G.C.M.G. (1931); he was sworn of the Privy Council in 1940 and created a baron in 1941.

[*The Times*, 15 February 1957; Lord Vansittart, *The Mist Procession*, 1958; Ian Colvin, *Vansittart in Office*, 1965; personal knowledge.]

NEVILE BLAND

published 1971

DE VALERA Eamon

(1882–1975)

Prime minister and later president of the Republic of Ireland, was born in New York 14 October 1882, the only child of a Spanish father, Vivion Juan de Valera, artist, and an Irish mother, Catherine (Kate), daughter of Patrick Coll, a farm labourer of county Limerick. His father died when he was two. His mother took him home to Ireland in 1885 before returning to America. He was brought up on the small farm of his mother's brother Patrick Coll.

He obtained his education the hard way. He went to the village school at Bruree, a more advanced school in Charleville, to which he frequently had to walk seven miles a day, and thence as a lay boarder at the age of sixteen to Blackrock College in Dublin. Two years later he secured a place at University College, Blackrock. By the age of twenty he had acquired the passion for mathematics which remained with him to the end of his days. At twenty-one he obtained a teaching appointment at Rockwell College near Cashel. In 1904 he gained a pass degree in mathematical science in the Royal University of Ireland. Later he became a professor of mathematics in the training college of Our Lady of Mercy, Carysfort, Blackrock.

He came to acquire a lifelong interest in the Irish language of which he knew little as a boy. Among his teachers was a young woman about four years older than himself, Sinéad Flanagan, who had already won a gold medal in a major competition. She was the daughter of Laurence Flanagan, of Carbery, county Kildare. Their marriage on 8 January 1910 in St. Paul's Church, Arran Quay, Dublin, was to prove the happiest of partnerships. Mrs de Valera was a woman of strong personality and literary gifts, but she dedicated herself to her husband and their seven children (five sons, one of whom was killed in a riding accident in 1936 at the age of twenty, and two daughters).

In 1913 a Home Rule Bill had been passed through the British House of Commons, but overwhelmingly rejected by the Lords. It could not become law until summer 1914. The Ulster Protestants set up a provisional government and organized full-scale military resistance. De Valera was crucially affected by these developments. In November 1913 a public meeting was held in Dublin to found a volunteer force in the South in reply to the Ulstermen. De Valera attended, joined the Volunteers, and committed himself irrevocably to a share in the armed conflict which he thought was inevitable.

de Valera

He became a wholehearted and efficient Volunteer. He was in no way concerned with the decisions which led to the 1916 rising, but in that traumatic week his military performance was impressive. He expected the death sentence but he was not among the first to be court-martialled, and his sentence was commuted to life imprisonment. He was saved by the delay and a change in government policy, not, as is sometimes said, because of his American birth. After the executions it was natural that he should be looked on as the senior commander. In various British prisons he exhibited a marked gift for leadership. Along with other prisoners he was released by a general amnesty in June 1917. Soon after his release he won a memorable by-election in East Clare on a policy of complete and absolute independence for an Irish Republic. At a convention on 25 October 1917, in the Mansion House, Dublin, he was elected as president of Sinn Fein. By now he was becoming a thorn in the British side.

In May 1918 he was rearrested and imprisoned in Lincoln Gaol, from which he made a sensational escape in February 1919. By this time a republic had been declared in Ireland and an alternative and 'illegal' system of government established. De Valera, the newly elected president, remained in hiding till he set off for the United States in June 1919. He did not return to Ireland until December 1920, by which time the guerrilla war of independence was reaching a climax. One purpose of his visit, that of raising funds, was achieved most successfully; the wider propagandist purpose, less obviously. But at least the Irish case was placed fairly and squarely before the American people, and identified henceforward with that of other struggling nations, India and Egypt among them.

Back in Ireland at the end of 1920, de Valera was once again in hiding. During the first half of 1921 the British government fluctuated between a policy of stepping up coercion and putting out fresh feelers. On 23 June King George V, opening the new Stormont parliament, set up under the 'Partition Act' of 1920, made a historic plea for reconciliation. The next step was to hand de Valera a letter which invited him to a conference in London with Lloyd George and Sir James Craig (later Viscount Craigavon), prime minister of Northern Ireland. De Valera could on no account accept a parity between his position and that of Craig. But the latter in any case refused. A truce was negotiated. De Valera went to London and had several meetings with Lloyd George. There was no meeting of minds personally or politically. De Valera reaffirmed the Irish demand for a republic. Lloyd George offered dominion status, an immense advance compared with the Act of 1920, or the Home Rule Bill of 1912, but hedged round with significant qualifications.

The Irish Cabinet found the Lloyd George terms quite unacceptable. De Valera now worked out the notion of external association, of which much would be heard later and which to the end of his life probably expressed his own conception of the best Anglo-Irish relationship. Ireland would not be a dominion or a member of the Commonwealth, but a friendly country externally associated with the latter. After prolonged correspondence five Irish delegates came to London in October 1921. Two months of intense negotiations followed. A treaty was signed in the small hours of 6 December 1921. The Irish Free State would be established as a dominion, and thus after 750 years the British occupation of twenty-six counties would be ended.

De Valera had not gone to London for these negotiations—a decision which was to have fateful consequences. To the end of his life he was anxious to defend his decision at considerable length. But in essence he had believed at the time that he would be able to exercise a stronger influence if he stayed in reserve. In the event he misjudged his control over the delegates, especially Arthur Griffith and Michael Collins. At the crunch, under threats of 'immediate and terrible war' they signed the treaty without referring back to him. A nominally republican delegation agreed to an arrangement in which a republic could have no place. In the light of his declared convictions, de Valera had little option but to repudiate the document. The Dáil however supported the treaty by 64 votes to 57. He was supplanted as president and became an unofficial leader of the opposition. Many republicans prepared to resist the treaty in arms. A civil war followed inexorably. De Valera was bitterly attacked by the treaty party in Ireland and by almost everyone of influence in England for causing the civil war. It is fairest to conclude that once he had repudiated the treaty there was nothing which he could do to avert the tragedy. The republicans were totally defeated. De Valera who had been on the run made a spectacular reappearance at Clare in the general election of 1923. He was not released until nearly a year later (July 1924). His fortunes seemed to be at a nadir, his career quite possibly at an end.

But he had never ceased to plan a political resurrection for the republican cause. In 1926 he launched a new party, Fianna Fáil. Initially their elected deputies declined to take their seats in the Dáil because of the required oath of allegiance to the British Crown. But in 1927 de Valera made a much derided volte-face, doing the right thing it must seem now, but showing far less consistency than usual. On 12 August 1927 the Fianna Fáil deputies took their seats in the Dáil. In the general election of 1932 they increased their seats from 57 to 72. This did not give them an overall majority but an arrangement with the Labour Party enabled de Valera to form a government. At the age of fifty, after an interval of ten years, he was once again the official leader of the Irish people.

The pre-war years, 1932–9, were disfigured by the economic dispute with Britain which ended in a kind of draw with the agreement of 1938. De Valera and his eventual successor, Sean Lemass, made a virtue of necessity and introduced measures of self-sufficiency which were in any case in line with Fianna Fáil and Sinn Fein thinking. On the constitutional front de Valera's largest personal achievement was the new constitution of 1937. In social policy it gave expression to Catholic social teaching. The special position of the Catholic Church in Ireland was emphasized, but Protestant and Jewish Churches were explicitly mentioned. Protestants at the time were pleased, but many years later the special position accorded to the Catholic Church came to seem sectarian and the clause in question was repealed.

The name of the state was changed from Irish Free State to Eire. The Anglo-Irish side of the constitutional revolution has been well summed up by Professor P. N. S. Mansergh—'Taken together, the External Relations Act and the new Constitution destroyed the dominion settlement of 1921. Relations with Britain and the Commonwealth had been taken out of the Constitution, where Mr de Valera felt that they had no place, and had become matters of external policy for the Government of the day. This was the most significant development in the whole period' (1926–39). (N. Mansergh, 'The Implications of Eire's Relationship with the British Commonwealth of Nations', *International Affairs*, January 1948.) After the agreement of 1938, and six years of neutrality in the war, it was manifest to all that total independence for the twenty-six counties had been secured. Under the agreement of 1938, de Valera secured what he had hardly hoped for, the return of 'the ports'—that is to say the renunciation by Britain of the naval and air facilities in certain Irish ports enjoyed under the treaty. De Valera and Neville Chamberlain, the British prime minister, struck up a remarkably cordial relationship. If war had not come so soon, an effective defence arrangement might have led to a united Ireland. In retrospect, de Valera dwelt occasionally on this 'might have been'.

In the event, war came all too rapidly. De Valera instantly proclaimed neutrality. The British representative in Dublin, Sir John Maffey (later Lord Rugby) privately advised the British Cabinet that no government could exist in Ireland that 'departed from the principle of neutrality'. In various secondary ways de Valera made his neutrality highly benevolent to the Allies; it will always remain a matter of dispute as to how far the Allied cause was damaged by the non-availability of the ports. At the beginning of the war Churchill showed an interest in recovering the facilities by force. Sir John Maffey, who maintained throughout the war an excellent relationship with de Valera, played a notable part in defeating any such initiative. At different times during the war the Germans, the British, and the French brought extreme pressure to bear, but de Valera maintained his iron nerve throughout six desperately anxious years. Perhaps the most successful address he ever delivered was a radio reply to Churchill at the end of the war. Churchill had boasted of the restraint and poise which the British government had shown in not laying violent hands on Ireland. De Valera's speech was moderate and conciliatory, but contained the telling question 'could he [Mr Churchill] not find in his heart the generosity to acknowledge that there is a small nation ... that could never be got to accept defeat and has never surrendered her soul?' Never had he spoken so clearly for the nation and never had the nation been so proud of him. Churchill privately conceded that de Valera had the better of the exchanges.

After the war, the independence of the twenty-six counties was not in dispute. But, although large numbers of southern Irishmen had served often with distinction in the British forces, this could not weigh against Britain's conviction that her foothold in the North had been essential to survival and victory. Partition was thus more firmly entrenched than ever. In the general election of 1948 de Valera was not surprised to be defeated by a rather strange combination of Fine Gael, traditionally more pro-British than Fianna Fáil and Clann na Poblachta, a new radical republican party, under the charismatic Sean MacBride. The new government proceeded to sever the last link with the Commonwealth by repealing the External Relations Act which de Valera had sedulously preserved. De Valera acquiesced but he did not pretend that he would have proceeded along these lines. The change was announced in the clumsiest way possible. The British responded by strengthening their guarantee to Northern Ireland.

De Valera was returned to power in 1951, but was out of office from 1954 to 1957. In the latter year, aged seventy-five, he came back with the first overall majority since the wartime election of 1944, but by 1959 he recognized that the time had come to hand over to a younger generation and to repair as president to 'The Park' where he served for fourteen years, a model of mellow dignity. One great regret in old age was his failure to make any headway with the ending of partition. From 1920 onwards he had insisted that 'Ulster must not be coerced', that force, in other words, must be renounced, in seeking to achieve Irish unity. It sometimes seemed that the distinctiveness of the Northern Unionist culture never fully came home to him. They were all Irishmen and equally dear accordingly. He persisted in the belief that the Gaelic Ireland which he had tried so hard, though with limited success, to establish in the twenty-six counties, would itself be instrumental in promoting Irish unity. Not many today would share that opinion. On the other hand, the modern notion that a united Ireland should be of a federal rather than a unitary character was completely in line with his later thinking.

In international affairs, one speculates wistfully about what he could have achieved if he had been at the head of a great state instead of a small nation. He was by chance president of the council of the League of Nations in 1932, the same year that he became head of the Irish government. He made a profound impression on that occasion. His opportunities of exercising widespread international influence were afterwards limited, but in his dealings, usually at a disadvantage with world leaders, he proved himself fully their equal. Churchill who at one time had no good word to say of him came to recognize at the end his pre-eminent quality.

Eamon de Valera was six feet one inch in height and looked even taller by reason of his upright carriage. His athletic frame was that of a man who had once played in a Munster trial at rugby football. His features were strongly developed, his eyes were dark and deep set behind the spectacles he had worn since he was a youth. He never lost his passion for mathematics. For many years before his death he was virtually blind. For most of his life he was involved in bitter controversy, but no one ever denied the dignity and courtesy of his bearing. His religious devoutness would be hard to parallel among statesmen. Once installed in the president's residence he visited the oratory five times a day. He had long been a daily communicant. But he was no Catholic bigot. It was Daniel O'Connell who said 'I take my religion from Rome, but my politics from Ireland'. It was a phrase de Valera himself might have coined. In the civil war of 1922-3 the Irish bishops condemned the side that he was nominally leading. At the end of his life he was at pains to point out to more than one visitor that he had *not* been excommunicated. He had taken the matter up with the pope of the day a few years after the civil war and found that the pope agreed with him. He was asked 'what would you have thought if the pope had disagreed with you?' He replied with his familiar dead-pan humour 'I should have considered that His Holiness was misinformed.' One of his chaplains, later a bishop, is on record as saying of him: 'He would have made a good Protestant.'

Though he was a man of subtle mind and complex personality, he stood through life for simple conceptions: religion, the family, democracy, law and order, fair dealing between nations, justice for the oppressed. In all these respects, he left an indelible mark on the state which he did so much to create and foster.

He died in Dublin 29 August 1975 at the age of ninety-two. His personality had dominated the Irish scene for nearly sixty years. No Irishman in this century, or indeed any other, has achieved so prolonged an eminence in his lifetime.

[The Earl of Longford and Thomas P. O'Neill, *Eamon de Valera*, 1970; private information; personal knowledge.]

FRANK LONGFORD

published 1986

NELSON Frank

(1883–1966)

Sir

Organizer of Special Operations Executive, was born at Bentham, Gloucestershire, 5 August 1883, the son of Henry Ellis Hay Nelson, general manager of the Army and Navy Auxiliary Co-operative Supply, and his wife, Catherine Haviland. After education at Bedford Grammar School and Heidelberg, he went to India to work in a mercantile firm in Bombay in which he rose to become senior partner. In the war of 1914–18 he served in the Bombay Light Horse. Subsequently he was chairman of the Bombay Chamber of Commerce and its representative on the Bombay Legislative Council (1922–4) and president of the Associated Indian Chamber of Commerce (1923). In 1924 he was knighted and returned to England. He was Conservative member of Parliament for Stroud from 1924 to 1931 when the depression forced him to resign to go into business.

On the outbreak of war in 1939 Nelson was employed on intelligence work in Basle, but this came to an end with the fall of France when he returned to England. Even before 1939 it had been recognized that the Government would have to weaken any potential enemy by political subversion, sabotage, and other clandestine operations. When war broke out the work suffered from lack of co-ordination, for it was split up between several bodies, responsible to different authorities. By 1940, when the British were left to fight the Axis powers alone, co-ordination was more than ever essential. The War Cabinet consequently decided on 16 July 1940 that all these functions were to be put in the charge of a new body, the Special Operations Executive (SOE), with Hugh (later Lord) Dalton, who continued to be minister of economic warfare, at its head. Dalton records that the prime minister then said to him, 'And now set Europe ablaze'. He at once divided SOE into three bodies—SO1 for underground propaganda, SO2 for unacknowledgeable action, sabotage, and the support of resistance in enemy-occupied territory, and SO3 for planning. In August 1940 Dalton appointed Nelson to be head of SO2. The functions of SO3 were assumed by SO2 in January 1941, and in the following August those of SO1 by a separate body called the Political Warfare Executive. From that point Nelson was responsible for all the remaining activities of SOE.

Nelson had a formidable task. Not only was there not a single agent in enemy-occupied France, but SOE was a new body for which no precedent existed. As such it incurred the suspicion and jealousy of the established secret organizations, the Foreign Office, and the Service ministries, all of which were professional bodies which had existed for many years and which were concerned by the inevitable amateurishness at first displayed by SOE. Another difficulty was recruitment, for by the autumn of 1940 most men of ability were employed elsewhere. Above all Nelson found he had to obtain for SOE facilities, such as secret wireless sets, aircraft for parachute training and getting agents into Europe, and special devices for sabotage. But it was no easy task to get these scarce resources unless SOE could show results, and without the resources there could be no results. Finally, Nelson had somehow to get the confidence of Whitehall and the Services.

He set to work at once with tireless energy, and surrounded himself with a group of able people, notably (Sir) Colin Gubbins, who at first took charge of the important job of training and operations and was to finish the war as head of SOE. Gradually Nelson overcame the difficulties by his unshakeable integrity of purpose. It was a disappointment to him when in early 1941 the chiefs of staff ruled against supplying secret armies in Europe by air in favour of the bombing offensive. But he persisted, and by the winter of 1941 SOE was in touch with agents and supporters in most of the countries of occupied Europe. Above all, Nelson made people believe that, given facilities, results could be achieved. In less than two years SOE had become an established force with the confidence of the chiefs of staff, and was recognized in every theatre of war. It is no disparagement of his successors to say that he created the groundwork without which SOE's later successes in Europe and the Far East would have been impossible.

But Nelson was never physically strong, and in 1942 his health began to fail. He resigned in May, was appointed KCMG, and subsequently held appointments as an air commodore in Washington and Germany. He married in 1911 Jean, daughter of Colonel Patrick Montgomerie; they had one son. She died in 1952 and he then married Dorothy Moira Carling. He died in Oxford 11 August 1966.

[Hugh Dalton, *The Fateful Years*, 1957; M. R. D. Foot, *SOE in France*, 2nd impression, with amendments, 1968, and *Resistance*, 1976; Bickham Sweet-Escott, *Baker Street Irregular*, 1965; personal knowledge.]

B. SWEET-ESCOTT

published 1981

KNOX (Alfred) Dillwyn

(1884–1943)

Classical scholar and cryptographer, was born 23 July 1884 in Oxford, the fourth of six children (four sons and two daughters) of the Revd Edmund Arbuthnott Knox, a tutor at Merton College (later bishop of Manchester) and his first wife, Ellen Penelope, daughter of Thomas Valpy French, bishop of Lahore. By any standards his family was remarkable, with the evangelical father and Dillwyn's three brothers: 'Evoe', for seventeen years editor of *Punch*, Wilfred, an Anglo-Catholic priest, and Ronald, Roman Catholic priest and translator of the Bible. Ellen Knox died in 1892 but three years later Edmund Knox remarried.

'Dilly', as he was called, went to Summer Fields, Oxford, at the age of eleven and after a year was first in his election to Eton. He went to King's College, Cambridge, in 1903 as a scholar. He obtained a first class in part i (1906) and a second (division I) in part ii (1907) of the classical tripos. A friend of G. Lytton Strachey and J. Maynard (later Baron) Keynes, he was not an 'Apostle' himself, although his name was put forward for election to the society. He was greatly influenced by Walter Headlam and inspired by his great love and knowledge of Greek literature. When Knox became a fellow of King's in 1909 he inherited the then deceased Headlam's work on Herodas and applied himself to the fragmentary texts of the Herodas papyri in the British Museum. The inconsequential and bawdy mimes proved difficult to unravel but Knox was determined to succeed, exercising on them the scholarship combined with inspired guesswork which was to be his forte in his future career. Like his brothers, he was addicted to puzzles and a devotee of Lewis Carroll (Charles L. Dodgson). The sort of question he was apt to ask, 'Which way does a clock go round?', was pure Carroll.

Soon after war broke out in 1914 he was asked to join ID 25, the department of naval intelligence known as Room 40, as a cryptographer. By 1917 he had succeeded in breaking much of the German admirals' flag code, detecting, with his ear for metre, lines of poetry in the repeated bigrams of a message, which provided a crib. Instead of returning to Cambridge, he decided to continue working in Room 40, renamed the Government Code and Cipher School. He did, however, finally manage to get the Headlam–Knox Herodas published in 1922. Following German intervention in Spain he solved the Spanish military code and collaborated with the French on Italian naval codes used in Abyssinia.

Immediately before Hitler's invasion of Poland Knox went with A. G. Denniston, the head of GC and CS, to a secret base at Pyry, where he was shown a reconstruction of the Enigma cipher machine, which was used by the Germans. The Polish replica moved the breaking of Enigma on from a theoretical exercise to a practical one and Knox always gave the Poles credit for the part they played. His own section, Intelligence Services Knox (ISK), which worked in 'the Cottage' at Bletchley Park, achieved some notable cryptographic successes, including breaking the Italian naval code which enabled the Matapan signals to be read in March 1941. Although absorbed to the point of stuffing his pipe with sandwiches when obsessed with puzzle-solving, it would be wrong to see Knox's code-breaking as a detached intellectual exercise. It was he who insisted that in order not to compromise Ultra (the breaking of the German high command codes), there should be an immediate press release that aerial reconnaissance had made possible the important naval victory off Cape Matapan in southern Greece (1941). Although ill with cancer, he worked tirelessly on breaking the Abwehr (a German secret service) traffic. A typical short cut was the successful assumption that some indicators set up by the operators in the four machine windows were not random but girls' names or four-letter dirty German words.

Knox worked from his bed to the last, only getting up and dressing in order to receive the CMG (1943) from the Palace emissary appropriately. He died 27 February 1943 at his home, Courn's Wood, near High Wycombe, Buckinghamshire. There is a drawing of him by Gilbert Spencer in the possession of the family.

In 1920 he married his former secretary, Olive, daughter of Lieutenant-Colonel Roddam. They had two sons.

[Penelope Fitzgerald, *The Knox Brothers*, 1977; personal knowledge.]

MAVIS BATEY

published 1993

KNATCHBULL-HUGESSEN Hughe Montgomery (1886–1971)

Sir

Diplomat, was born in London 26 March 1886, the fourth son of the Revd Reginald Bridges Knatchbull-Hugessen, rector of Mersham, Kent, and his second wife, Rachel Mary, daughter of Admiral Sir Alexander Leslie Montgomery; his grandfather, Edward Knatchbull had been paymaster-general in 1834–5 and 1841–5. The history of the Knatchbull family is recounted in Sir Hughe's *Kentish Family* (1960).

After education at Eton and Balliol College, Oxford, where he obtained a third class in modern history in 1907, Knatchbull-Hugessen entered the Foreign Office in 1908. In 1912 he married Mary (died 1978) daughter of Colonel (later Brigadier-General Sir) Robert Gordon-Gilmour; they had one son and two daughters. During the war of 1914–18 he worked in the Contraband Department, and, in 1919, was a member of the British delegation to the peace conference. After the war it became possible for Foreign Office staff to serve abroad, and in November 1919, Knatchbull-Hugessen went to The Hague as secretary to the legation. He served for four years in this post under Sir Ronald Graham, and then, for a year, worked under Lord Crewe as head of chancery in Paris. In 1926 he became counsellor of embassy in Brussels, and stayed there until 1930 when he was appointed minister to the three Baltic States, Estonia, Latvia, and Lithuania. He expected to remain in Europe, but, in 1934, was surprised to be asked to go to Tehran as minister; he embarked upon his new work with some anxiety, but, when he was again transferred in 1936, he looked back on his time in Persia (Iran) as one of the most interesting and pleasant periods of his life. He was on leave in London when he was offered the post of ambassador in China, in succession to Sir Alexander Cadogan who was returning to London to become permanent under-secretary of the Foreign Office. In 1920 he had been gazetted CMG, and now, in 1936, he was promoted KCMG.

It is clear from Knatchbull-Hugessen's autobiography, *Diplomat in Peace and War* (1949), that, by the time he set out for China, he was thoroughly enjoying diplomatic life; he liked the protocol and ceremony, and the variation of scene that attended each new move; through his skill at sketching, he was able to capture some of the more interesting sights in the course of his travels. He also found pleasure in the companionship and loyalty of his staff.

Knatchbull-Hugessen

During the two years Knatchbull-Hugessen spent in China, that country was in turmoil. Chiang Kai-shek and the Kuomintang government had succeeded in driving the Communists into the north-west, but the efforts of the generalissimo to assert his authority throughout China were threatened by unco-operative warlords and by the Japanese. At the ambassador's first meeting with Chiang Kai-shek in Nanking it appeared that some accommodation could be reached with the Japanese. However, in August 1937, the shooting of two Japanese officers in Shanghai led to open war. Knatchbull-Hugessen regarded it as his duty to visit the British community in Shanghai, and set out by car from Nanking with his financial adviser and military attaché. The Union Jacks on the windscreen were insufficient protection, however; a Japanese aeroplane fired on the party and the ambassador was severely wounded.

Although disappointing to Knatchbull-Hugessen, it was essential to his recovery that he should have long leave in England, and because of the situation in China, his post there had to be filled without delay. After a year recuperating from his wound, he was posted as ambassador to Turkey. The war of 1939–45 had already broken out when he arrived in Ankara. In the autumn of 1939 Turkey signed a tripartite treaty with Britain and France, and throughout the next five years Knatchbull-Hugessen's task was to counter the efforts of Franz von Papen, the German ambassador, to thwart any closer understanding between Turkey and the Allies. During 1941 and 1942, when the war seemed to be going in Hitler's favour, the Turks concentrated on keeping the peace with both sides. As the war progressed, they seemed to be as suspicious of Russian ambitions as of those of the Germans. Although early in 1943 (Sir) Winston Churchill visited Turkey and conferred with President Inönü about Turkey taking an active part in the war, the Turks maintained their cautious neutrality until February 1945 when they declared war on Germany. It seems unlikely that Knatchbull-Hugessen, in spite of his cordial relations with the Turkish leaders, was able to make any marked impression upon their policy. He himself expressed the view that Turkey was so unprepared for war in the years between 1939 and 1944 that it was better that she should remain a friendly neutral.

After a period of some ten years in the Middle East and China, in his final posting abroad he returned to Europe. Brussels had been relieved by British and American troops when he arrived there in September 1944 as ambassador in Belgium and minister in Luxemburg, but V1s were still falling nearby. During the next three years he witnessed the gradual recovery of Belgium from the effects of the German occupation; he thoroughly enjoyed the enthusiasm aroused by Churchill's visit to Brussels in 1945. In 1947 he retired.

Knatchbull-Hugessen's years of retirement were clouded by his anxiety to clear his name of the imputation that, while he was ambassador in Ankara, his failure to observe strict security measures had provided Franz von Papen with information regarding the plans for the Allied invasion of Europe. In consequence of a brief lapse of essential precautions to ensure the secrecy of important documents, the ambassador's Albanian valet was able to obtain a duplicate key to a box in which highly confidential papers were kept. The man had been vetted by the normal security procedure, but he seized his opportunity to make easy money, and was able from November 1943 to February 1944 to sell to the German embassy in Ankara films of documents to which he should not have been able to gain access. After the war sensational accounts appeared of the activities of this spy, to whom the Germans had given the code name 'Cicero', and, for years, Knatchbull-Hugessen was preoccupied with his concern to put the record straight. The information passed to the Germans included accounts of the Moscow, Cairo, and Tehran conferences, and may have included a reference to 'Overlord'. Von Papen may have deduced that this related to the D-Day landings, but it is certain that the British ambassador had no information regarding the details of the Allied plans and that no knowledge of those plans could have been revealed to the Germans through 'Cicero'. Nevertheless, a successful diplomatic career was marred by this unfortunate misadventure.

Towards the end of his life Knatchbull-Hugessen was crippled as a result of the injury he had suffered in China. He died at his home near Canterbury 21 March 1971.

[Sir Hughe Knatchbull-Hugessen, *Diplomat in Peace and War*, 1949; family papers; private information.]

H. F. OXBURY

published 1986

LOCKHART Robert Hamilton Bruce

(1887–1970)

Sir

Diplomatist and writer, was born 2 September 1887 in Anstruther, Fife, the eldest of the five sons of Robert Bruce Lockhart, headmaster of the Waid Academy, and his wife, Florence Stuart, daughter of John McGregor. A younger brother was J. H. Bruce Lockhart, headmaster of Sedbergh

School (1937–54), and another, Sir Rob Lockhart, became a general in the Indian Army. His only sister, Freda, made a reputation as film critic and journalist.

Bruce Lockhart took pride in having 'no drop of English blood' in his veins, his mother being Highland, the Lockharts Lowlanders. He won a foundation scholarship to Fettes College at the age of twelve but failed to fulfil his scholastic promise and, as he recorded in *My Scottish Youth* (1937), spent five years 'in the worship of athleticism'. To rid him of this fetish, his father sent him to work under an austere professor in Berlin, then to Paris. This paternal move was an important influence on his subsequent career for it opened up the horizon of foreign countries; and learning fluent German and French developed his talent for mastering languages which later stood him in good stead. His wide reading in the literatures of the languages he learned shaped his own style.

For three years (1908–10) Lockhart was a rubber planter in Malaya where his mother's family had interests. Acute malaria brought him home and he then entered the consular service, passing first in his examinations. In January 1912 he went to Moscow as vice-consul. Owing to the illness of his chief, he was acting consul-general during the war years and very much in the centre of the efforts to keep Russia in the war. But in 1917, some six weeks before the Bolsheviks took over, he was quietly recalled to London 'on sick leave', in reality because of an affair with a Russian Jewess which was 'being talked about'. Early in 1918, when the British Government wished to establish unofficial relations with the Soviets, Lockhart returned to Russia as head of a special mission, bearing a letter of introduction to Trotsky from Litvinov then still in England. When Anglo-Soviet relations deteriorated, Lockhart was arrested in September for 'espionage' and imprisoned in the Kremlin for a month before he and Litvinov were exchanged. For what is known in the Soviet Encyclopaedia as 'the Lockhart conspiracy' he was condemned to death *in absentia*. It was clear, however, that he had never believed in the wisdom of anti-Bolshevik intervention and had only unwillingly acquiesced in Allied policy. Later he wrote of coping with 'an impossible situation' and how the interventionists would 'never forgive' him for his advocacy of understanding with the Bolsheviks.

Lockhart's health had suffered, probably as much from hard living as the strain of his work, and it was not until November 1919 that he was appointed commercial secretary at the British legation in Prague. In a politically insignificant career there he formed a deep affection for the Czechoslovak people, and Dr Benes and Jan Masaryk became his close friends for the rest of their lives. He had a weakness for living beyond his means and to reinstate his finances he left the Foreign Service for international banking in October 1922 and continued to spend most of his time in Central Europe which had become his natural habitat. Although banking was certainly not his *métier*, his conviviality smoothed negotiations. In 1924 he was received into the Roman Catholic Church.

Lockhart had already been summoned to see Lord Beaverbrook after the Moscow débâcle and in 1928 he joined the *Evening Standard* as editor of the Londoner's Diary, a job which he performed until 1937 with superb urbanity. An early scoop was the first English interview, in 1929, with the exiled Kaiser Wilhelm II. It was during this period that he wrote his first book, *Memoirs of a British Agent* (1932), in which his Russian years are brilliantly recorded. It had an immediate success and was reprinted eighteen times between 1932 and 1946. It was followed by *Retreat from Glory* (1934) and *Return to Malaya* (1936). After 1937 authorship became his career, for his books were successful in America as well as in the United Kingdom. But he continued to write occasional journalism and undertook some lecturing in Europe and the United States.

After the outbreak of war in 1939 Lockhart rejoined the Foreign Office. In 1940 he was appointed British representative with the provisional Czechoslovak Government in exile; in 1941 he became a deputy under-secretary of state and took over the direction of the Political Warfare Executive which co-ordinated propaganda in enemy and enemy-occupied countries. He was appointed KCMG in 1943, continued in his post until the end of the war, and described his experiences in his first post-war book *Comes the Reckoning* (1947). There followed a number of other books, based mainly upon his memories of people and events.

Lockhart's books are likely to be remembered, for his easy, natural style, his knowledge of Russia and Central Europe during four stormy decades, and his many friends in high places make his writings useful subsidiary historical records as well as enjoyable reading. He had a flair for making friends wherever he went, was much loved, restless, and kind. His personality shone through his books and his enthusiasm for his friends, Scotland, and fishing is always infectious. One of his most attractive books was *My Rod, My Comfort* (1949). He was handsome in a rugged way, with an endearing smile, and, no matter how pressed for time, was always ready to exchange reminiscences, particularly if they were about Scotland and his school, Fettes, which was a big influence in his life. This had something to do with a boyish quality in his character which he never lost and which was his attraction, yet a weakness. The posthumous publication in 1973 of the first volume of his Diaries, for 1915 to 1938, provided an illuminating addition to his writings but showed him to have been self-indulgent and extravagant to an extent which somewhat undermined his reputation.

In 1913 Lockhart married Jean Haslewood, daughter of Leonard Turner, an Australian; they had one daughter who died at birth and one son. They became estranged at an early stage and the marriage was dissolved in 1938. In 1948 he married Frances Mary, daughter of Major-General Edward Archibald Beck. Lockhart's last years were spent in sickness and he died in Hove 27 February 1970.

[Lockhart's own writings; *The Times*, 28 February 1970; private information; personal knowledge.]

JAMES MACGIBBON

published 1981

LAWRENCE Thomas Edward

(1888–1935)

Known as 'Lawrence of Arabia', was born at Tremadoc, North Wales, 15 August 1888, the second in a family of five sons. His father, Thomas Robert Chapman (who had assumed the name of Lawrence), the younger son of an Anglo-Irish landowning family, had followed up a sound classical schooling with an agricultural course and some years of continental travel and mountaineering; he lived on private means permitting of comfort though not luxury; became keenly interested in church architecture and in photography; and was an enthusiastic yachtsman, shot, and (from the early days of the safety bicycle) cyclist. His mother, Sarah Maden, the daughter of a Sunderland engineer, was brought up in the Highlands and afterwards in Skye. Both parents were devout, evangelical members of the Church of England.

Having learnt his letters from hearing his elder brother taught them, Lawrence read newspapers and books at the age of four, began Latin at six, and entered the Oxford High School at eight. From the age of twelve he covered his tuition expenses by scholarships at school and a Welsh exhibition at Jesus College, Oxford. Deep love of literature, archaeology, and architecture, particularly of the Middle Ages, led him to choose as a thesis for the modern history school 'The Influence of the Crusades on European Military Architecture—to the End of the XIIth Century' (published in 1936 as *Crusader Castles*). After bicycle tours throughout England and France he journeyed alone, on foot and without baggage, through Syria, Palestine, and the southern fringe of Turkey. In 1910 he obtained a first class in history, partly on his thesis, and was awarded a four years' senior demyship for travel by Magdalen College at the instance of D. G. Hogarth, Lawrence's lifelong friend, who in 1911 sent him on the British Museum expedition that was excavating the Hittite city of Carchemish. There, after an interval in Egypt, he returned next year, assisting (Sir) C. Leonard Woolley until the outbreak of war in 1914; of this he wrote, 'it was the best life I ever lived'. He acquired some Arabic, together with the habit of eating Arab food and wearing Arab clothes. From January to March 1914 he and Woolley carried out an archaeological survey of the Negeb and country south of Beersheba for the Palestine Exploration Fund (which in 1915 published their report under the title of *Wilderness of Zin*), joining Captain Stewart Newcombe, who was already surveying that area for the War Office.

On the outbreak of war in 1914 Lawrence, being below standard height (then raised to 5 feet 5 inches) obtained but a sedentary commission in the Geographical Section, General Staff of the War Office. Dispatched to Military Intelligence in Egypt when Turkey joined the central powers, he spent two years in what was later called the Arab Bureau, which became by 1916 the Intelligence Service for the Arab campaign. In the October of that year he accompanied to Jidda (Sir) Ronald Storrs, who had initiated the negotiations which culminated in the Arab Revolt, and presented Lawrence to the Sharif Abdullah, second son of Husain, Grand Sharif of Mecca, and obtained from Husain an introduction to his third son, Faisal, who at that moment was retreating discomfited before a Turkish advance from Medina. Turkish strength in the Hejaz still amounted to nearly 15,000 rifles, 10,000 of which held Medina, 2,500 the railway between Medina and Amman, including the strongly garrisoned port of Aqaba, and 1,200 the port of Wajh. The Arabs in their anxiety pressed for the dispatch to the Hejaz of a British brigade, which Lawrence, on his return to Egypt, opposed as too cumbersome, and was himself dispatched as liaison officer and adviser to Faisal, whose confidence he soon won and whose tribal levies he helped to organize.

The secret of Lawrence's ascendancy, physical, intellectual, and moral, is best explained in his own words: 'Among the Arabs there were no distinctions, traditional or natural, except the unconscious power given a famous shaikh by virtue of his accomplishment: and they taught me that no man could be their leader except he ate the ranks' food, wore their clothes, lived level with them, and yet appeared better in himself.' Preferring to contain rather than to assault or starve the 10,000 Turks in Medina and thus compel the enemy to tie down additional troops to maintain them, Lawrence induced Faisal to threaten their communications by moving north and attacking the Hejaz railway, which thenceforth passed progressively out of effective Turkish control. It was his theory and practice that the Arabs should become 'an influence (as we might be), an idea, a thing invulnerable, intangible, without front or back, drifting about like gas, a vapour, blowing where we listed' ... 'tip and run: not pushes, but strokes ... the smallest force in the quickest time at the farthest place'. After the storming of Wajh Lawrence left Faisal there to establish his headquarters, and rode on into the interior, rousing the northern tribes and passing behind the enemy lines in Syria. Returning, he fell in with a force of the Howaitat tribe, under the celebrated Auda Abu Tayi, with it routed a Turkish battalion near Ma'an, and in August 1917 took and occupied Aqaba for Faisal. Having thus brought the whole Hejaz south of Aqaba, excepting Medina, under Arab-British control, Lawrence was promoted major and was awarded British and French decorations which he subsequently refused.

The climax of Lawrence's campaign began when, hurrying to Egypt to obtain supplies for starving Aqaba, he offered Sir Edmund (later Viscount) Allenby, the newly arrived commander-in-chief, 'to hobble the enemy by his preaching if given stores and arms and a fund of two hundred thousand sovereigns to convince and control his converts', and Allenby briefly replied: 'Well, I will do for you what I can.' Lawrence was given all he asked, and the fund was later increased to half a million pounds; thenceforward he directed Arab levies, now brigaded with the British Expeditionary Force and operating as a mobile right wing. Having defeated the Turks heavily in the model engagement of Tafila, he concentrated upon scientific train-wrecking with such success that Medina became virtually isolated, and the Turks, their rail-guards extended to Aleppo, offered a reward of £20,000 for the capture of 'al Urans, destroyer of engines', in whose protection sixty out of his bodyguard of ninety Arabs lost their lives. Towards the end of 1917, while reconnoitring alone the railway junction of Deraa, Lawrence was seized (but not recognized), forcibly enlisted in the Turkish army, and beaten senseless, but by dawn he had escaped. Next summer he persuaded Faisal to leave Aqaba in favour of Qasr Azrak for the advance upon Damascus. Finally, having broken up the Turkish Fourth Army east of the Jordan, Lawrence led the Arab troops up to Damascus on 1 October 1918, some hours ahead of the British, chivalrously allowing Sharif Nasir to precede his entry; and preserved it against serious threats of reverting to the Turks, until Allenby arrived three days later. 'In the crucial weeks while Allenby's stroke was being prepared ... nearly half of the Turkish forces [some 2,000 sabres and 12,000 rifles] south of Damascus ... were distracted by the Arab forces. With some relatively light assistance from Chaytor's Force these Turkish masses were paralysed by an Arab contingent that counted less than 3,000 men, and of which the actual expeditionary core was barely 600 strong. It would be difficult to find in the whole history of war as extraordinary a case of economy of force in distraction.' The whole payments for the Arab revolt amounted to four millions in gold, of which about half came back in purchases of food and clothing.

His task done, Lawrence retired. 'The East was sucked dry. Never outstay a climax' was his light self-dismissal, behind which, however, pressed heavily the physical toll of the sun, the snow, and the sand, battle, murder, and, never to be redeemed or forgotten, the climax of outrage in Deraa. He reached England on Armistice Day after four years' absence, and having done his utmost (though not to his own satisfaction) for Faisal and the Arab cause at the Peace Conference, settled down to the writing of his adventures. In November 1919 he was elected a research fellow of All Souls College, Oxford, and in 1921 was called by Mr. Churchill as political adviser to the newly formed Middle Eastern Department in the Colonial Office. The partnership was entirely successful. Faisal (whose ejection by the French from Damascus had been the culmination of Lawrence's disillusionment) was made king of Iraq, which was soon to become an independent state: and shortly afterwards the threat to Palestine of an unsettled Arab Transjordan was removed by the appointment of Faisal's elder brother, Abdullah, as its ruling prince on the condition that he, and his future subjects, did not interfere with French-mandated Syria. Feeling that (apart from Syria and Palestine, both already committed to the League of Nations) his 'Arab honour' was satisfied, and that he had gained his 'outlet' from public affairs, Lawrence insisted on his release from the Colonial Office in June 1922, and in August enlisted in the ranks of the Royal Air Force, changing his name to J. H. Ross in order to escape publicity, and again in 1923 to T. E. Shaw. This latter change was legalized by deed poll in 1927. Discharged from the Royal Air Force because his identity became disclosed, he sought refuge in the Tank Corps, but in August 1925 returned to the Royal Air Force. This took him in 1926 to the North-Western Frontier of India whence, in deference to Russian suspicions, he was recalled in 1928. As an aircraftman, neither attaining nor desiring officer's rank, he spent happily the last six years of his service, latterly testing, supervising, and even designing high-speed and power motor-craft at Plymouth, and later on the Solent. His service expired at Bridlington in February 1935, and he was retired at the age of forty-six, sad at leaving his work and comrades in the Royal Air Force. He bicycled to Clouds Hill, his three-roomed cottage at Bovington, Dorset, and remained there, unsettled, and evading the appointments thrust upon him in connexion with the expansion of the Royal Air Force, yet unable to enjoy his unaccustomed leisure which he planned to spend in exploring, by bicycle, the scenery and monuments of England. On 13 May, swerving on his powerful motor-cycle to avoid two boys bicycling abreast, he was violently thrown, and after lingering unconscious for five days, died in Bovington Camp Hospital 19 May 1935. He never married.

Lawrence

Lawrence was slightly but strongly built. His growth had been checked by breaking a leg in his 'teens. His forehead was high; the line of his face vertical and, in proportion to the depth of his head, long. His hair was long and fair and unruly, parted and brushed sideways. He had a straight nose, piercing blue eyes, a firm full mouth, strong square chin, and fine, careful, accomplished hands. He could be the best company in the world, holding his own with Mr. Churchill or Mr. Bernard Shaw: he could also retire within himself in any company. He preferred the society of men to that of women, with very few exceptions, and had friends in all classes. Books gave him almost as much companionship, and he was widely read in French, Latin, and Greek, as well as in English. He was a judge of painting, sculpture, architecture, and craftsmanship of every kind; and had a true appreciation of music, which he trained and gratified on a large collection of carefully tended gramophone records. He preferred neither to smoke nor to drink alcohol, and ate sparingly; but he yielded himself almost voluptuously to the 'dope' of high speed, on the swiftest motor-cycles. At eighty or ninety miles per hour he achieved 'a sense of moulding the hills and dales'.

Unique in kind as were Lawrence's exploits, their chance of historic survival would have been uncertain had he not himself recorded them in his brilliant and arresting *Seven Pillars of Wisdom* (1935) which was twice re-written during the years 1919 and 1920, after the original manuscript had been lost. Into his style, based originally upon *Travels in Arabia Deserta* (1888) by the venerated C. M. Doughty, Lawrence poured the conscious, conscientious devotion of the artist-craftsman which he had lavished upon his maps, his machinery, and his plans for battle. 'Words', he wrote, 'get richer every time they are deliberately used ... but only when deliberately used', and again, more significantly, 'Writing has been my inmost self all my life, and I can never put my full strength into anything else.' Lawrence would not have the book published in his lifetime, but issued in 1926 for subscription about a hundred copies superbly printed and illustrated by the best artists of the day. The loss of £11,000 over this thirty guineas issue was more than covered by his abridged version, *The Revolt in the Desert*, published next year (1927) at thirty shillings: but the surplus was given to charity. Lawrence also organized the re-publication in 1921 (with an admirable introduction) of Doughty's *Arabia Deserta* (the only fruit of his residence at All Souls) and made in 1924 a pseudonymous version, *The Forest Giant*, of *Le Gigantesque* by A. le Corbeaux, and under his own name a prose translation of the Odyssey, commissioned from the United States of America and published in 1932. He wrote a remarkable, if sometimes brutal, picture of his early days in the Royal Air Force, entitled *The Mint*, of which, however, he forbade publication until 1950, although a copyright edition of fifty copies (ten of which were for sale, prohibitively priced) was arranged in America in 1926.

None can begin to realize the unsuspected, the bewildering variety and versatility of Lawrence, before as well as after his Arabian exploits, until he has read *The Letters of T. E. Lawrence*, selected and edited by Mr. David Garnett in 1938. It has indeed been said that he would have survived (as would Edward Fitzgerald without *Omar Khayyam*) if only as a letter-writer. The letters emphasize the strange blend of contrasts and oppositions that made up his elusive, enigmatic, and paradoxical personality. Imperious but retiring, logical yet intuitive, profoundly impressive and provokingly puckish, on equal terms with field-marshals and Cabinet ministers, great writers, mechanics, scholars, and slaves, he bequeathed the example of one who combined physical prowess and courage under the open sky with passionate self-dedication to the testament of the great humanities, which he chose to enjoy in poverty rather than hazard the artificiality and time-wasting servitude of high position; even without his work, without his book, he was a standard and a touchstone of reality in life.

Among the portraits of Lawrence are several by Augustus John, including a painting in the National Portrait Gallery, and a pastel by Eric Kennington at All Souls College, Oxford, made for *Seven Pillars of Wisdom*. The portrait painted by James McBey soon after Lawrence's entry into Damascus hangs in the Imperial War Museum. There is a bronze bust by Eric Kennington in the crypt of St. Paul's Cathedral, and a posthumous effigy, also by Eric Kennington, in St. Martin's church, Wareham.

[*The Times*, 20 May 1935; T. E. Lawrence, *Seven Pillars of Wisdom*, 1935, *Secret Despatches from Arabia*, 1939, *Oriental Assembly*, 1939, and *Men in Print*, 1940; B. H. Liddell Hart, *T. E. Lawrence*, 1934; *The Letters of T. E. Lawrence*, edited by David Garnett, 1938; Charles Edmunds, *T. E. Lawrence*, 1935; R. H. Kiernan, *Lawrence of Arabia*, 1936; Vyvyan Richards, *T. E. Lawrence*, 1939; Clare Sydney Smith, *The Golden Reign*, 1940; Elizabeth W. Duval, *T. E. Lawrence, A Bibliography*, 1938; B. H. Liddell Hart and R. Graves, *T. E. Lawrence to his Biographers*, 1938; Sir Ronald Storrs, *Orientations*, 1937; *T. E. Lawrence, by his Friends*, edited by A. W. Lawrence, 1937; personal knowledge.]

Ronald Storrs

published 1949

COLLINS Michael

(1890–1922)

Irish revolutionary leader and chairman of the provisional government of the Irish Free State in 1922, was born 16 October 1890 at Woodfield, Clonakilty, co. Cork, the third son and youngest child in the family of eight children of Michael Collins, a farmer in humble circumstances but belonging to an old Irish family, by his wife, Mary Anne O'Brien. He was educated at the local primary school, where he was fortunate in having a teacher of unusual talents. He went to London when sixteen years of age and during ten years' residence there studied and read widely, acquiring a considerable general knowledge of business methods, economics, history, and contemporary politics, and developing a style of writing and speaking, at once easy and virile, which stood him in good stead in later times. His early years in London were uneventful; he was a boy clerk in the Post Office Savings Bank for some years, and subsequently (1910) held a minor post with a firm of London stock-brokers. He left this post during the moratorium following the outbreak of the European War in 1914, but soon afterwards found employment in the London office of the Guaranty Trust Co., of New York, where he remained until the end of 1915. He grew up a well-built man, about six feet in height, active and powerful, a good athlete, possessed of great physical endurance, with a pleasing open face, a genial and hearty manner, and a strong and self-assertive disposition. Generous in friendship, quick in temper, sparing in praise, and sharp in reproof, his strong character inspired extremes of affection and dislike, while his capacity for prompt decision and rapid action and his great physical bravery marked him as a leader in the revolutionary movement which grew rapidly in Ireland during the European War and which culminated in the establishment of an independent Irish state, of the first government of which he became head.

Collins first came into prominence on the political horizon about the year 1917. For many years prior to the outbreak of the European War, the dominant party in Irish politics was the Irish parliamentary party, which, under the leadership of John Redmond, held a practical monopoly of the parliamentary representation of the country, save in the north-eastern portion of the province of Ulster, which was a unionist stronghold. A secret revolutionary nucleus known as the Irish Republican Brotherhood had remained in existence from the Fenian times, but its membership was small and its influence of little weight. In 1913, however, the anti-Home Rule movement in Ulster led by Sir Edward (afterwards Lord) Carson, opened the way for the organization of the Irish Volunteers. This body, avowedly military in its objects, was directed from the outset by the revolutionary group. For a short period Redmond succeeded in obtaining control, but the organization split and the militant party pursued its course until the Irish Rebellion of Easter week, 1916. The eventual release of the large number of men who had been imprisoned and interned after the Rebellion resulted in the re-constitution of the Irish Volunteers, to form a body which was later known popularly, though erroneously, as the 'Irish Republican Army'.

Prior to 1916 Collins had taken an active part in the Irish Republican Brotherhood in London. He returned to Ireland some months before the Rebellion, was in close association with the leaders of the revolt, and took part in the occupation of the General Post Office in Dublin during the fighting there. After the Rebellion he was deported to Stafford gaol, and subsequently interned in Frongoch camp, near Bala, Merionethshire, with a large number of fellow prisoners from all parts of the country. He was released shortly before Christmas 1916. He was consequently well known to most of the active members of the revolutionary organizations and was rapidly accepted as the organizing genius of the Volunteer and Sinn Fein movement. In April 1918 he was arrested in Dublin, tried at Granard, and imprisoned in Sligo gaol for a seditious speech. After his release he continued to be politically extremely active; north and south the country was searched for him, but he succeeded in eluding the vigilance of the police and the military authorities.

The Irish parliamentary party had now lost prestige, and at the general election in December 1918 was practically wiped out. The Sinn Fein party dominated Irish politics and captured 73 constituencies out of a total of 105. North-East Ulster remained unionist. The Sinn Fein members met in Dublin on 21 January 1919, adopted a declaration of independence and a provisional constitution, and elected a ministry. Collins, who had been elected for two constituencies, West Cork and Tyrone, was chosen as minister for home affairs. In February 1919 he took the principal part in planning and carrying out the escape of Mr. De Valera from Lincoln gaol, and in the consequent reorganization of the Sinn Fein ministry he became minister for finance. This portfolio he retained until his death.

Collins was now in a position to command. Besides being Sinn Fein minister for finance, he was director of organization and subsequently of intelligence for the Irish Volunteers, and member of the supreme council of the Irish Republican Brotherhood. His abundant energy and his mastery of detail enabled him to keep in close touch with every aspect of the revolutionary activities, and he enjoyed the respect and confidence of his colleagues. He became an almost legendary figure to the people, and his career during the three years which followed proved remarkable.

On 12 September 1919 Dail Eireann, the revolutionary parliament, and all the other Irish revolutionary organizations were declared illegal by the British government, and their activities were thereafter conducted mainly in secret. The British military and police forces were greatly augmented and kept up a constant and growing pressure by means of raids and arrests of prominent members of the organizations. Mr. De Valera, the president of Dail Eireann, having gone to the United States of America in the spring of 1919 in order to procure moral and financial support for the movement, it was decided by Dail Eireann to float an internal loan in Ireland and an external loan in the United States. Both ventures were highly successful, each loan being heavily over-subscribed. As minister for finance, Collins was responsible for the organization of the issue; in the case of the internal loan the greater part of the work fell on his shoulders, and as the British government took every possible step to disorganize and prevent its collection, the difficulties which had to be surmounted in getting in and safeguarding the funds were enormous. Collins was completely successful in his efforts, with the result that the various activities of the Dail were amply financed during the trying period prior to 1921.

In 1920 the Irish Volunteer organization, hitherto an independent body, proclaimed its allegiance to Dail Eireann. Its numbers were considerable, but its arms and equipment were very poor. The importation of arms was rigidly controlled, and the maintenance of a sufficiency of war material was a constant problem. The efforts made by the British forces to suppress the Dail and the Volunteers aroused great public resentment, and consequently when the Volunteers retaliated by attacks upon the police and the military, they were sheltered and succoured everywhere. The attacks gradually became more numerous and feelings grew progressively embittered, with the result that from the summer of 1920 until the truce of 11 July 1921 a state of guerrilla warfare existed. Collins organized the service through which arms and ammunition were provided. In addition he created an intelligence department which had contacts in the most unlikely quarters and kept him well informed of the plans and intentions of the British military and police.

During this period the normal administration of the country had largely ceased. The Dail ministry had set up its own judicial system in opposition to the existing courts. The local district and county councils refused to obey the directions of the Local Government Board for Ireland and attorned to the rival Dail department of local government. Almost every function of government was duplicated and the whole administration of former times was daily being rendered more impotent.

Negotiations for a settlement were initiated towards the end of 1920; they took definite shape in the formal cessation of hostilities on 11 July 1921, and in an invitation from the prime minister, Mr. Lloyd George, to Mr. De Valera to meet British ministers in a conference. A prolonged exchange of correspondence followed this invitation, and a conference was ultimately arranged 'with a view to ascertaining how the association of Ireland with the community of nations known as the British Commonwealth, may best be reconciled with Irish national aspirations'. Five Irish delegates, Arthur Griffith, Michael Collins, Eamonn Duggan, George Gavan Duffy, and Robert Barton, were selected by the Dail on 14 September 1921, and endowed with plenipotentiary powers. The outstanding figures among them were Griffith and Collins. Agreement was reached on 6 December, when articles of agreement for a Treaty between Great Britain and Ireland were signed. Ireland was recognized as having 'the same constitutional status in the community of nations known as the British Empire as the Dominion of Canada, the Commonwealth of Australia, the Dominion of New Zealand, and the Union of South Africa, with a Parliament having powers to make laws for the peace, order, and good government of Ireland and an executive responsible to that Parliament'.

Mr. De Valera, however, the president of the Dail cabinet, repudiated this agreement and was supported in his attitude by two of his colleagues, Cathal Brugha and Austin Stack. A sharp division of opinion manifested itself in the Dail, and the terms of the Treaty were accepted by only a small majority of that body. A provisional government was set up on 14 January 1922, with Collins as chairman and minister for finance. The provisional government immediately set to work to arrange to take over the machinery of government from the British departments and to frame a constitution for the Irish Free State. Meanwhile the opponents of the Treaty were actively organizing their forces. The Irish Volunteers were almost equally divided, and in March the section hostile to the Treaty seceded and adopted a policy of revolt. A bitter political campaign was also begun, and the occupation of various public buildings by armed irregular forces resulted in numerous clashes in various parts of the country. Collins made desperate efforts to heal the breach, and at one time appeared to have succeeded. He was able to arrange for a general election in June 1922, at which out of 128 deputies returned 94 were supporters of the Treaty. A parliament was summoned for July. Meanwhile the situation was growing rapidly more serious, and following the seizure by the irregular forces of an officer of the head-quarters staff of the regular army, an ultimatum was issued demanding the immediate evacuation of all buildings illegally occupied. This ultimatum expired on 28 June and a civil war began.

Collins immediately took over the command of the Free State army and speedily reduced the opposition in Dublin. The main strength of the irregular forces was broken towards the end of August, although sporadic attacks continued in isolated areas up to the spring of 1923. On 22 August 1922 Collins, accompanied by General Dalton and Commandant O'Connell and other members of his headquarters staff, was returning in the evening to Cork from a tour of inspection of military positions in that county, when he and his party were attacked by a small band of irregulars in the wild and hilly country around Macroom. A severe fight, lasting nearly an hour, ensued at Bealnablath, near Brandon. The irregulars, defeated, were on the point of retiring when Collins was mortally wounded by a bullet in the head. His body was taken to Dublin on 24 August and lay in state in the City Hall until the funeral at Glasnevin cemetery. Thus ended the short career of one of the most remarkable Irishmen of modern times. His dynamic energy and powerful personality played a leading part in the struggle for independence which resulted in the establishment of the Irish Free State.

[Dail Eireann: Official Reports; *Annual Register*; Piaros Béaslaí (Pierce Beasley), *Michael Collins and the Making of a New Ireland*, 2 vols., 1926; private information; personal knowledge.]

W. T. Cosgrave

published 1937

MENZIES Stewart Graham

(1890–1968)

Sir

Head of the Secret Intelligence Service, was born in London 30 January 1890, the second son of John Graham Menzies, of independent means, and his wife, Susannah West, daughter of Arthur Wilson, of Tranby Croft. After the death of John Menzies his widow married in 1912 Lieutenant-Colonel Sir George Holford, an officer in the Life Guards and equerry-in-waiting to Queen Alexandra and extra equerry to King George V.

Stewart Menzies was educated at Eton where he won no academic distinctions but was a popular boy and a fine athlete who was master of the beagles, and president of the Eton Society ('Pop') in 1908 and 1909. Immediately on leaving school he joined the Grenadier Guards in 1909 but was transferred to the Life Guards in the following year. While in the army he acquired a love of horses and of hunting which remained with him for the rest of his life and to which he returned with special zest after his retirement. His country home was in Wiltshire and he hunted mainly with the Duke of Beaufort's hounds. He was well into his seventies when a fall in the hunting field started a decline in his health. While resident in London, Menzies enjoyed an active social life. He was a great frequenter of White's Club and also belonged to St. James's and the Turf.

Menzies first came into contact with the intelligence world during the war of 1914–18. He was sent to France in 1914 with the British Expeditionary Force and in 1915, after recovering from a gas attack, was assigned an intelligence appointment at GHQ. The work appealed to him and he showed a flair for it, which was aided by his knowledge of European languages. He ended the war with the DSO and MC and the rank of brevet major and in 1919 was again selected for an intelligence appointment: military liaison officer with the Secret Intelligence Service, also known as MI6. He thus began a career in professional intelligence which was to continue for thirty-two years. He was promoted colonel in 1932 and retired from the Life Guards in 1939.

Menzies became 'C' in full command of the Secret Intelligence Service only three months after the outbreak of war in 1939. It was a crucial moment in the history of his service. Between the wars it had been starved of funds by successive Governments and consequently entered the war ill-prepared for the tasks demanded by total warfare. Expansion and reconstruction had to take place simultaneously, and these tasks were further complicated by set-backs such as that at Venlo, when Gestapo men crossed the German-Dutch border to capture two SIS officers who had gone there to contact agents of the underground opposition in Germany. The whole character of the service gradually changed. Hitherto the staff had been recruited mainly from retired Service officers; now that it could attract men and women of talent from all walks of life the management problems were new and intricate. Added to these Menzies had to steer his service through a complicated maze of inter-Service relations, created by the existence of a new British secret service—SOE—and a new American service—OSS—operating in parallel with his own in neutral and enemy territories. In these circumstances it was to take some time before SIS could develop a momentum of its own and forge those links with Allied intelligence and resistance organizations which were to prove valuable in the later stages of the war.

Besides commanding SIS, Menzies was responsible for the over-all supervision of the Government Code and Cipher School (GC & CS), whose greatest achievement in the war of 1939–45 was the breaking of the

German 'Enigma'. This was an electro-magnet enciphering machine, which generated a wide range of separate ciphers in use by the German army, navy, and air force. German experts had rendered their machine so sophisticated that by the outbreak of the war they considered it safe even if captured. It was therefore used to communicate vital German war secrets. These began to be made available by GC & CS by the end of 1940 and by the end of 1943 they were decrypting as many as 40,000 naval and 50,000 army and air force messages a month. It is therefore not difficult to imagine the crucial importance of this source of intelligence to the Allied war effort. But it was also a highly vulnerable source for the security of which Menzies was finally responsible. This could mean refusing some forceful operational commander the right to act on one of its intelligence leads if by so doing he might endanger the source. In retrospect this responsibility was admirably discharged and the secret of the GC & CS's remarkable cryptographic successes was preserved until the end of the war. Not surprisingly, with such excellent information at his disposal, Menzies's influence with the prime minister, War Cabinet, and chiefs of staff was considerable.

The stamina and toughness Menzies displayed during the war years came as something of a surprise to those acquainted with his easy and affluent way of life between the wars. Running his service and supervising GC & CS meant exceptionally long hours of office work, besides which he became in time a member of Churchill's intimate circle of war advisers. This meant being on call to brief the prime minister at any hour of the day or night. On such occasions he had to answer for more than his own responsibilities for he was the only intelligence director to enjoy this privileged position. As an intelligence man his strength lay in a quick grasp and understanding of operational issues and in his shrewd management of a network of powerful contacts. Organization and long-term planning were not his strong points. He preferred the getting of intelligence to the mosaic work of the assessors and in this respect he resembled one of his American opposite numbers, Allen Dulles, another man to enter intelligence from a patrician background.

To many foreigners Menzies came to seem the personal embodiment of an intelligence mystique they believed characteristically and historically British. Whatever the truth of this, it contributed to his international influence and was a potent factor in establishing the Anglo-American and other Allied intelligence alliances. During the war years his service had a greater role to play than ever before. By the time he retired in 1951 the pressures of the cold war had caused the intelligence world to develop in major ways, and to acquire potent technological resources: a very different world from the one he had entered in 1919.

Menzies was appointed CB in 1942, KCMG in 1943, KCB in 1951, and received a number of foreign decorations.

In 1918 he married Lady Avice Ela Muriel Sackville, daughter of the eighth Earl De La Warr. He obtained a divorce from her in 1931 and in 1932 married Pamela Thetis (died 1951), daughter of Rupert Evelyn Beckett, nephew of the first Baron Grimthorpe, and divorced wife of James Roy Notter Garton. He married thirdly in 1952 as her fourth husband, Audrey Clara Lilian, daughter of Sir Thomas Paul Latham, first baronet. Menzies had one daughter by his second wife. He died in London 29 May 1968.

[*The Times*, 31 May and 6 June 1968; private information; personal knowledge.]

ANON

published 1981

GUBBINS Colin McVean

(1896–1976)

Sir

Major-general and leader of Special Operations Executive, was born in Tokyo 2 July 1896, the younger son and third-born in the family of two sons and three daughters of John Harington Gubbins, who was oriental secretary at the British legation, and his wife, Helen Brodie, daughter of Colin Alexander McVean, JP, of Mull. Educated at Cheltenham College and at the Royal Military Academy, Woolwich, he was commissioned in 1914 into the Royal Field Artillery.

In the war of 1914–18 he served as a battery officer on the western front, was wounded, and was awarded the MC. In 1919 he joined the staff of W. E. (later Lord) Ironside in north Russia. It was the Bolshevik revolution no less than his subsequent experience in Ireland in 1920–2 that stimulated his lifelong interest in irregular warfare. After special employment on signals intelligence at GHQ India, he graduated at the Staff College at Quetta in 1928, and was appointed GSO 3 in the Russian section of the War Office in 1931. Promoted to brevet major, in 1935 he joined MT 1, the policy-making branch of the military training directorate. In October 1938, in the aftermath of the Munich agreement, he was sent to the Sudetenland as a military member of the international commission—an experience which left him with a lasting sympathy for the Czechs. Promoted to brevet lieutenant-colonel, he joined G(R)—later known as MI(R)—in April 1939. In this obscure branch of the War Office he prepared training manuals on irregular warfare, translations of which were later to be dropped in thousands over occupied Europe; he also made a rapid visit to Warsaw to exchange views on sabotage and subversion with the Polish general staff.

On mobilization in August 1939 Gubbins was appointed chief of staff to the military mission to Poland, led by (Sir) Adrian Carton de Wiart. Among the first to report on the effectiveness of the German Panzer tactics, Gubbins had no illusions about the Polish capacity to resist. Yet the campaign left him with an enduring sense of obligation to the Poles, whose chivalrous and romantic nature was somewhat akin to his own.

In October 1939, having returned to England, he was sent to Paris as head of a military mission to the Czech and Polish forces under French command. The mission was viewed with suspicion by the French since its main purpose was to keep the War Office in touch with the burgeoning Czech and Polish Resistance movements. Gubbins was recalled from France in March 1940 to raise the 'independent companies'—forerunners of the commandos—which he later commanded in Norway. Although criticized in some quarters for having asked too much of untried troops, he showed himself to be a bold and resourceful commander, and was appointed to the DSO (1940). Back in England, he was charged by GHQ Home Forces with forming a civilian force to operate behind the German lines if Britain were invaded. Stout-hearted but utterly inexperienced, these so-called auxiliary units could not have survived for long; but their secret recruitment, training, and equipment in the summer of 1940 was a remarkable feat of improvisation and personal leadership.

In November 1940 Gubbins became acting brigadier and, at the request of E. H. J. N. (later Lord) Dalton, was seconded to the Special Operations Executive (SOE) which had recently been established 'to co-ordinate all action by way of sabotage and subversion against the enemy overseas'. Besides maintaining his connections with the Poles and Czechs, he was initially given three tasks for which he was admirably qualified: to set up training facilities, to devise operating procedures acceptable to the Admiralty and Air Ministry, and to establish close working relations with the joint planning staff. Inevitably he bore the brunt of the suspicion and disfavour which SOE provoked in Whitehall—partly because of the nature of its operations and partly because of the excessive secrecy which surrounded them. However, Gubbins had no doubt it was his duty to identify with SOE notwithstanding all the risk of misrepresentation of his motives that this entailed.

Despite frustrations and disappointments—and there were many, due mainly to the shortage of aircraft—he persevered with his task of training organizers and dispatching them to the field. The first liaison flight to Poland took place in February 1941, and during 1942 and 1943 European

Resistance movements patronized by SOE scored a number of notable successes, including the raid on the heavy water installation in Norway which aborted Hitler's efforts to produce an atom bomb.

At this stage Gubbins had no direct responsibility for SOE's subsidiary headquarters in Cairo whose activities in Yugoslavia and Greece had for some time been raising awkward issues of foreign policy. However, in September 1943 these issues came to a head; Sir Charles Hambro resigned; and Gubbins, now a major-general, became executive head of SOE. He immediately faced a concerted attack on SOE's autonomy, mounted by the Foreign Office, GHQ Middle East, and the joint intelligence committee (JIC). As always he had the steadfast support of his minister, the third Earl of Selborne, but it was not until a meeting on 30 September, presided over by the prime minister, that a *modus operandi* was agreed. Nevertheless Gubbins's position remained precarious and in January 1944 there was a further attempt to dismantle SOE. This followed the disclosure that SOE's operations in Holland had been penetrated by the Germans— for which Gubbins characteristically took the blame. Undaunted he set about co-ordinating the activities of the various Resistance movements, now supported world-wide by SOE, with the operational requirements of individual commanders-in-chief. Although control was decentralized wherever possible, harnessing the force of Resistance to the conventional war effort proved a delicate and controversial task—as often political as military—involving consultation at the highest level with the Foreign Office and the chiefs of staff; as well as with representatives of the patriot organizations, the governments-in-exile, and other allied agencies— in particular the United States Office of Strategic Services (OSS). In the event the effectiveness of organized resistance exceeded Whitehall's expectations. In north-west Europe, where SOE's activities remained under Gubbins's personal control, General Eisenhower later estimated that the contribution of the French Resistance alone had been worth six divisions.

When SOE was wound up in 1946 the War Office could offer Gubbins no suitable employment, and on retirement from the army he became managing director of a large firm of carpet and textile manufacturers. However, he kept in touch with the leading personalities in many of the countries he had helped to liberate; invited by Prince Bernhard of the Netherlands he joined the Bilderberg group; and he was an enthusiastic supporter of the Special Forces Club of which he was a co-founder. A keen shot and fisherman, he spent his last years at his home in the Hebrides. He was appointed CMG in 1944, advanced to KCMG in 1946, and appointed deputy lieutenant of the Islands Area of the Western Isles in 1976. He held fourteen foreign decorations.

Holland

Gubbins had a creative spirit that made him a natural leader of the young; and he delegated generously to those he trusted, both men and women. Above all, he was a dedicated professional soldier. With his quick brain, the imagination and energy necessary to transform ideas into action, and his force of will, he might have held high command in the field had his abilities not been confined to special operations. As it was, he left his mark on the history of almost every country which suffered enemy occupation in the war of 1939–45.

In 1919 Gubbins married Norah Creina, daughter of Surgeon-Commander Philip Somerville Warren RN, of Cork; the marriage was dissolved in 1944. In 1950 he married secondly Anna Elise, widow of Lieutenant R. T. Tradin, Royal Norwegian Air Force, and daughter of Hans Didrik Jensen, of Tromsö, Norway. He had two sons by his first marriage, the elder of whom was killed at Anzio in 1944. Gubbins died at Stornoway in the Hebrides 11 February 1976.

There is a portrait by Susan Beadle in the possession of the family.

[*The Times* 12, 17, and 19 February 1976; private information; personal knowledge.]

PETER WILKINSON

published 1986

HOLLAND John Charles Francis

(1897–1956)

Soldier and secret organizer, was born in India (probably Calcutta) 21 November 1897, the only son and elder child of (Sir) Thomas Henry Holland, geologist, and his wife Frances Maud, daughter of Charles Chapman, deputy commissioner in Oudh. Close friends called him 'Jo'.

He went from Rugby to the Royal Military Academy, Woolwich, whence he was commissioned into the Royal Engineers on 28 July 1915. He was posted to the eastern Mediterranean, arriving too late for the Gallipoli campaign, but serving on the Salonika front for most of the rest of the world war. He was mentioned in dispatches in 1917, and in the summer of 1918 was awarded the DFC for gallantry in action with the Royal Air Force. He was badly wounded in Dublin during the troubles of 1919–21, in which he admired the technical skills of his Irish guerrilla opponents.

In 1922 he reverted from temporary major to lieutenant; he was promoted captain in 1924 and major seven years later. He passed the staff college, and held a staff captain's appointment in northern command in 1934–6. In 1938, again due for promotion but medically unfit, he took an appointment as a second-grade staff officer in the War Office to research on any subject he chose. He chose irregular warfare. His branch, in which he was at first the only officer, was called GS (R).

His Irish experiences led his lively imagination well outside the normal range of military thinking at the time. Early in 1939 his branch was re-named MI R, and placed in the military intelligence directorate, though Holland concentrated rather on operations. Encouraged by A. P. (later first Earl) Wavell, he laid the foundations of several wartime secret services, and was one of the originators of the Commandos. For a few months in the summer of 1939 he worked at 2 Caxton Street, Westminster, alongside L. D. Grand, a Woolwich contemporary who ran the then inadmissible section D of the secret service. On the outbreak of war in September Holland went back to the War Office.

He gathered like-minded officers round him, and dispatched each in turn to run the service for which he seemed fit: N. R. Crockatt, whose prowess he had admired at Rugby, to secure intelligence from prisoners of war; E. R. Coombe to form the inter-services security board, which handled code-names and deception as well as security; (Sir) Gerald Templer to run the security of the expeditionary force; and M. R. Jefferis to invent and exploit secret gadgets. He sent (Sir) Colin Gubbins to the independent companies in Norway, then to command projected stay-behind parties to damage the communications of any invading German forces, and eventually to run the Special Operations Executive.

In July 1940 his staff, and Grand's, and a semi-secret propaganda branch of the Foreign Office, were all amalgamated to form the SOE. Holland thereupon went back to regimental duty, on being offered a regular lieutenant-colonel's command. By July 1943 he was back in the War Office, as deputy chief engineer and a major-general. He was appointed CB in 1945, and received also the American legion of merit and medal of freedom with silver palm. In 1947–8 he was chief of staff, Western Command; in 1949–50 he was again employed, briefly, on secret planning; and he retired in 1951.

He was a shortish, burly man who went bald early; a heavy cigarette smoker; quick-tempered, but recovering fast from anger. He married in 1924 Anne Christabel, daughter of Sir James Bennett Brunyate, KCSI, CIE, of the Indian Civil Service; they had two sons and a daughter. He died at his elder son's house in Wimbledon 17 March 1956.

[*Army Lists*; private information.]

M. R. D. FOOT

published 1993

(1897–1963)

Sir

Merchant banker, was born in London 3 October 1897, into a banking family of Danish origin, which settled in Dorset and the City in the first half of the nineteenth century. He was the elder son of (Sir) C. Eric Hambro (1872–1947), who was Conservative MP for the Wimbledon division of Surrey in 1900–7 and a partner in C. J. Hambro & Son, the family firm; his grandfather (Sir) Everard Alexander Hambro was a director of the Bank of England. His mother, Sybil Emily (died 1942), was the daughter of Martin Ridley Smith of Warren House, Hayes, Kent, and his wife, Cecilia, daughter of Henry Stuart (1808–80), of Montfort, Isle of Bute, a descendant of George III's prime minister, John Stuart, third Earl of Bute. In 1929 Hambro's parents were divorced and his father at once remarried. He had a younger brother and two sisters.

Hambro was at Eton from 1910 to 1915—in the cricket XI in 1914, and its captain in 1915, when he took seven wickets for six runs against Winchester. He went straight from school to Sandhurst, and by the end of the year was an ensign in the Coldstream Guards. He survived two years of the western front, receiving the military cross for conspicuous bravery in action. On demobilization in 1919 he went for a brief spell of training to the Guaranty Trust Company in New York, and then into the family firm, of which he soon became secretary. He played an important part in its merger with the British Bank of Northern Commerce, which led to the establishment of Hambros Bank in 1921. In 1928, when only thirty, he was elected a director of the Bank of England, and for a spell in 1932–3 he put all other work aside in order to establish, under the direction of Montagu C. (later Lord) Norman, the bank's exchange control division to deal with some of the consequences of the ending of the gold standard.

His commanding presence—he stood six feet three inches tall—and driving personality were backed by equal strength of character, loyalty, and charm. He made a notable impact in several spheres of work, particularly on the Great Western Railway, the most successful of the four great British railway companies. He became a director of it in 1928, and deputy chairman in 1934. From 1940 to 1945 he was nominally chairman, but war work took up much of his time.

On the outbreak of war with Germany in 1939, at the invitation of (Sir) Ronald Cross, the minister, Hambro joined the Ministry of Economic Warfare. In August 1940 Cross's successor Hugh (later Lord) Dalton brought Hambro into the new secret service he was forming under the Ministry's cover, the Special Operations Executive (SOE). SOE's purpose was to stimulate resistance in enemy-occupied territory, and Hambro's vigour, energy, and originality were valuable to it. He began in charge of Scandinavia, and visited Sweden in November 1940. There he arranged for some highly successful smuggling of ball-bearings, and for some sabotage in Swedish harbours, which provoked difficulties with the Swedes. He also, through the anti-Nazi journalist Ebbe Munck, initiated contacts with resistance-minded Danes, which bore useful fruit in the summer of 1944. Dalton thought highly of his Scandinavian work, and Hambro was created KBE in 1941.

From December 1940 to November 1941 he added to his responsibilities oversight of SOE's nascent French, Belgian, Dutch, and German sections, and from November 1941 for five months he was deputy head of the whole organization, in the rank of squadron leader, Royal Air Force. (Rank in SOE meant little.) He initiated an important development in January 1942, when he persuaded the Norwegians to help form an Anglo-Norwegian planning committee, from which several highly successful small operations derived, particularly the destruction on 27/8 February 1943 of the heavy-water plant at Vemork near Rjukan. When a further stock of heavy water was destroyed, in a separate operation, on its way to Germany, the Germans' search for an atomic bomb was utterly dislocated. By that time Hambro had become the executive chief of SOE (called CD) and been promoted to air commodore. Dalton's successor, the third Earl of Selborne, had appointed him in April 1942 to succeed (Sir) Frank Nelson when Nelson's health gave way—on the ground that a man who could run the Great Western Railway could run anything. An early and important task for Hambro was to arrange with Colonel William Donovan, his American opposite number, who visited London in June 1942, for co-operation between SOE and the American Office of Strategic Services. Occasional rivalries should not obscure a great deal of close and rewarding interchange.

Hambro's multifarious acquaintances in the business world were often useful to SOE. During his seventeen months of leadership, this small but lively service was transformed from a body still struggling to establish its worth into a recognized, and often highly efficient, military tool. Hambro cannot claim undue credit for this development, much of which arose from the general political and military course of the war, and some of it from the excellent work of his predecessor, Nelson, and from technicalities too abstruse even for him. A well-placed observer described him in retrospect as 'always the gentleman, among the professionals'; he was certainly not a professional in the secret-service world.

Hambro and Selborne could not agree over a protracted dispute about control over SOE by the commander-in-chief, Middle East; and early in September 1943 Hambro had to resign. Another weighty post was soon found for him. He spent the last eighteen months of the war in Washington as head of the British raw materials mission: this was cover for supervising the exchange of information between the United Kingdom and the USA which led to the first man-made nuclear explosions in July and August 1945.

He then returned to the City, and became prominent; not only in Hambros Bank, of which he was made chairman when his uncle Olaf died in 1961. He also diversified, through the Union Corporation, into mining, among other interests; supported several charitable trusts; worked himself harder than he worked his subordinates; and escaped whenever he could to Dixton Manor near Cheltenham to shoot. He married in 1919 Pamela (died 1932), daughter of John Dupuis Cobbold, DL, of Ipswich, and his wife, Lady Evelyn, daughter of Charles Adolphus Murray, seventh Earl of Dunmore; she bore him a son and three daughters. By his second wife, Dorothy (daughter of Alexander Mackay, of Oban), whom he married in 1936, he had another daughter; he had twenty-four grandchildren living when he died, in his Marylebone home, at the height of his powers and reputation, 28 August 1963.

[M. R. D. Foot, *SOE in France*, 1966, and *Resistance*, 1976; Bickham Sweet-Escott, *Baker Street Irregular*, 1965; *The Times*, 16 July 1915, 29 and 31 August, 2 and 3 September 1963; private information.]

M. R. D. FOOT

published 1981

STRACHEY (Evelyn) John (St. Loe)

(1901–1963)

Politician and writer, was born at Newlands Corner, Merrow, near Guildford, 21 October 1901, the younger son and youngest of three children of John St. Loe Strachey, for many years editor of the *Spectator*. After the death of Lord Strachie in 1936 Strachey became heir presumptive to the baronetcy created for Sir Henry Strachey, secretary to Clive of India. His mother, Henrietta Mary Amy Simpson, was a granddaughter of the Victorian economist Nassau Senior. His sister married the architect (Sir) Clough Williams-Ellis.

Strachey was educated at Eton and Magdalen College, Oxford, which he left after two years, in 1922, without a degree; his parents feared the consequences of further studies on his health following peritonitis. His elder brother had died of pneumonia in his first year at Balliol. But John Strachey had already become known as an undergraduate journalist, as editor, with Robert (later Lord) Boothby, a lifelong friend, of the Conservative journal, the *Oxford Fortnightly Review*; he was also prominent in the Canning Club; wrote poems; and both acted in, and wrote plays for, undergraduate societies. On leaving Oxford he began to work on his father's *Spectator*, writing leading articles and reviews.

In 1923 Strachey joined the Labour Party, under the influence of Sidney and Beatrice Webb, and stood for Parliament unsuccessfully in 1924, for the Aston division of Birmingham, a nomination which he owed to the influence among Birmingham socialists of (Sir) Oswald Mosley, the ex-Conservative member who was candidate for Ladywood. Although Strachey remained a contributor to, and shareholder of, the *Spectator*, he now abandoned his expectation of becoming its editor when his father died, and became an active socialist writer and pamphleteer. With Mosley, he proposed new plans for the resolution of the nation's economic problems in *Revolution by Reason* (1925), and became editor of both the *Socialist Review* and the *Miner*. In 1929 he was returned for Aston and became parliamentary private secretary to Mosley, who had become chancellor of the Duchy of Lancaster in the new Labour Government. He supported Mosley in his campaigns on unemployment in 1930, and followed him into the New Party founded in 1931. For a time he was Mosley's closest collaborator, but broke away after six months, when it seemed that the New Party was turning against Russia, which Strachey had already twice visited.

On leaving Mosley, Strachey asserted himself as an independent member of Parliament, but lost his seat in the general election of 1931. The depression in Britain was by now at its worst, and Strachey found himself drawn towards the Communist Party. He wrote for the Communist cause a succession of influential books: notably *The Coming Struggle for Power* (1932) and *The Nature of Capitalist Crisis* (1935). Strachey was never a member of the Communist Party, although his second wife was, and he would have liked to have been; but the party leaders considered him not altogether dependable and, in any case, so long as he supported the cause, more useful outside than within. Strachey's was, in fact, the most powerful intellectual voice in the Communist movement in this country throughout most of the thirties, and, as such, influenced the Left Book Club, founded by (Sir) Victor Gollancz in 1936 with Strachey's help, which became more of a movement than a book club. Strachey wrote regularly in the club's monthly *Left News*, spoke at its many rallies throughout the country, and provided the club's choice for November 1936 (*The Theory and Practice of Socialism*) and for March 1938, when, in *What Are We to Do?*, he argued for a Popular Front. In the same year his pamphlet *Why You Should Be a Socialist* sold over 300,000 copies.

Although to Strachey socialism still meant Communism, he was by now beginning to move away from Communist orthodoxy. The Nazi-Soviet pact of 1939 in the end disillusioned him about Soviet motives. Other reasons for his break with Communism were: his admiration for J. M. (later Lord) Keynes and for Roosevelt, both of whom, the one in theory, the other in practice, seemed to suggest a middle way in politics; and his interest in and personal experience of psychoanalysis. His book, *A Programme for Progress* (the Book Club choice for January 1940), seemed too Keynesian and angered orthodox Communists even before Strachey finally decided to break with the party after the German invasion of Norway and Denmark in the spring. He did so in a letter published in the *New Statesman* (27 April 1940).

Left without a political base, Strachey joined the Royal Air Force and served some time as adjutant with a fighter squadron, then as public relations officer with a bomber group. He next moved to the Air Ministry, where he eventually joined the directorate of bomber operations and became widely known to the country for his air commentaries after the BBC 9 o'clock news. This fame helped him back into Parliament as a member for Dundee in 1945 and to the post of under-secretary of state for air in Attlee's administration where he dealt skilfully with demobilization and other Service problems. Marked out for promotion, he became minister of food in May 1946.

This appointment was the most critical in Strachey's life. In many ways he was well equipped: he had made himself an able economist; he liked, and understood the meaning of, power; he knew how to use civil servants to their best advantage; he had a gift for political simplification and explanation. All these qualities were necessary, since the Ministry of Food was a politically sensitive department at a time when shortages and rationing continued and, indeed, increased (notably with the introduction of bread rationing) despite the end of the war. Strachey established a temporary mastery over the House of Commons in 1946, but he was bitterly and often unfairly attacked by the Conservative press, particularly the Beaverbrook papers. By 1949 his reputation had been severely damaged by the failure of a plan to increase supplies of natural oil by growing groundnuts on a large scale in Tanganyika. This scheme originated with the United Africa Company but was thought too large for private exploitation. The Cabinet asked the Ministry of Food to organize the scheme. After several years and over £30 millions had been invested, it was plain that ground-nuts could not be commercially or satisfactorily grown. The affair, exploited to the full by the press, hurt Strachey's political prospects, although he can be blamed only for an initial excess of zeal for the scheme, for failure to start with a 'pilot' plan, and for an excessive reliance on those whom he had named to carry out the scheme on the spot: in particular, his old friend (Sir) Leslie Plummer.

After the general election of 1950, Strachey, returned for West Dundee, became secretary of state for war, still without a seat in the Cabinet. The arrest of Dr Fuchs, the atomic spy, had led to doubts about security, and immediately upon Strachey's appointment the *Evening Standard* (2 March 1950) came out with headlines 'Fuchs and Strachey. A great new crisis. War minister has never disavowed Communism.' Strachey was advised not to sue on the grounds that the publicity would do more harm than good, although he wanted to and would certainly have been justified. Although less happy in his new post than at the Ministry of Food, and not in favour of the health service charges which brought the resignation of Aneurin Bevan, Strachey greatly admired Attlee's leadership, and remained in the Government until it was defeated in 1951. Thereafter, as shadow minister of war, he set himself to master the complexities of nuclear strategy.

In the years in opposition, Strachey attempted to steer a middle course between Gaitskellites and Bevanites in the Labour movement and accordingly incurred the obloquy of both. He voted for Hugh Gaitskell as successor to Attlee in 1955 and, in the late fifties, drew closer to the official leadership of the party. After Gaitskell died in 1963 Strachey worked for the succession of George Brown (later Lord George-Brown). Nevertheless, (Sir) Harold Wilson named him shadow Commonwealth secretary, and would have included him in his Cabinet in the following year had not Strachey died, in London, following a spinal operation, 15 July 1963.

During the fifties Strachey's main work, in his own view at least, was to attempt a new theoretical statement of his political position in a series of books: *Contemporary Capitalism* (1956), *The End of Empire* (1959), and *On the Prevention of War* (1962). In these the ex-Marxist of the thirties attempted to absorb Keynes, to analyse the real effect of empire on European economies, and to introduce the new theoretical American strategic thinking to a British audience. In 1962 he published a brilliant collection of essays, *The Strangled Cry*, mostly about the intellectual and psychological effect of Communism. In both personal and political life Strachey often seemed indecisive and perhaps evasive. He was, however, a man of great intellectual integrity, charm, and wit to his family and those who knew him well. He remained a man of culture while a politician. Physically, he was tall, somewhat ungainly, with a swarthy countenance relieved by friendly brown eyes. He remained an enthusiastic games player until late in life. As a writer, he was an extremely able expositor of complicated general ideas, whether those of Marx, Keynes, J. K. Galbraith or even Hermann Kahn. He influenced the Labour movement towards Marxism in the thirties; away from it in the forties; and towards a realistic foreign and defence policy in the sixties.

Strachey was twice married: in 1929 to Esther (died 1962), only daughter of Patrick Francis Murphy, a wealthy department store owner of New York, who obtained a divorce in 1933; in that year Strachey married Celia, daughter of an Anglican clergyman, the Revd Arthur Hume Simpson; they had a son and a daughter.

The only known portrait is one by Celia Strachey which remained in her possession.

[Hugh Thomas, *John Strachey*, 1973; private information; personal knowledge.]

Hugh Thomas

published 1981

YEO-THOMAS Forest Frederic Edward

(1902–1964)

French resistance organizer, was born in London 17 June 1902, the eldest son of John Yeo-Thomas and his wife, Daisy Ethel Burrows. The Yeo-Thomas family, which had connections with the Welsh coal-mining industry, had established itself in Dieppe in the middle of the nineteenth century. 'Tommy' was sent to the Dieppe Naval College where he early learned to defend his British nationality. Later he went to the Lycée Condorcet in Paris until war broke out in 1914. In spite of all his father's efforts to prevent it, he was determined to take part in the war and was accepted as a dispatch rider when the United States joined in. In 1920 he joined the Poles against the Bolsheviks; was captured and sentenced to death; but managed to escape by strangling his guard the night before his execution was due.

Returning to France, Yeo-Thomas eventually settled down to study accountancy. There followed a variety of employments until in 1932 he became secretary to the fashion house of Molyneux. When war broke out in 1939 he at once tried to enlist, but the two years he had added to his age in the first war now told against him. Eventually he managed to join the

Royal Air Force with the rank of sergeant. He completed radar training and was in one of the last boats to leave France when that country fell. In October 1941 he was commissioned and sent as intelligence officer to the 308 Polish Squadron at Baginton. But he was determined to return to occupied France and eventually, in February 1942, with the help of a well-known newspaper and a member of Parliament, he was taken into Special Operations Executive. Here he became responsible for planning in the RF French section which worked in close association with General de Gaulle's Bureau Central de Renseignements et d'Action. It was at this time that he was given the *nom de guerre* 'the White Rabbit'.

After the fall of France small groups of resisters had sprung up all over the country, but they were uncoordinated, ignorant of each other's identities, purposes, or often, whereabouts. It was essential that these efforts should in some way be knit together to work towards the same end. In February 1943 Yeo-Thomas and André Dewavrin, known as Colonel Passy, the head of BCRA, were parachuted into France to join Pierre Brossolette to investigate the potential of resistance groups in the occupied zone. They succeeded in uniting the various groups in allegiance to de Gaulle, pooling their resources to organize a secret army which would spring into action on D-Day. From this mission the three men safely returned in April. But in June the leader and a number of other members of the Conseil National de la Résistance were arrested and its work seriously disrupted. To help restore the situation Yeo-Thomas and Brossolette in September returned to France where movement and meeting together had become much more difficult. In November Yeo-Thomas, concealed inside a hearse, slipped through the controls, and was picked up by Lysander. Brossolette remained behind. In England Yeo-Thomas's urgent demands for supplies for his organization took him finally to the prime minister, Winston Churchill. This interview produced a considerable increase in aircraft for RF section and consequently in weapons and supplies for the resisters in France.

When in February 1944 Yeo-Thomas heard of Brossolette's capture, he arranged to be parachuted into France yet again in order to replace him and also to try to organize his escape. Another visit by one so well known to the Germans as 'Shelley' was courting disaster, which did indeed befall Yeo-Thomas. He was arrested in Paris and his long period of torture and imprisonment began: in Fresnes, Compiègnes, Buchenwald, and Rehmsdorf. Throughout his appalling tortures he said nothing of any value to the enemy. Despite several bold but unsuccessful attempts, he maintained his resolution to escape. At Buchenwald, in September 1944, when Allied agents were being liquidated, he persuaded the head of the typhus experimental station to allow three agents to exchange identity with three Frenchmen who were already dying. Yeo-Thomas, Harry Peulevé, and a Frenchman were selected, Yeo-Thomas, in his new identity, was transferred to Rehmsdorf as a hospital orderly. When the camp was evacuated in April 1945 before the advancing Allies he organized an escape from the train when men were engaged in burying those who had died on the journey. Yeo-Thomas was among the ten who succeeded in getting away. Starving, desperately weak from dysentery and other illnesses, he was captured by German troops, posed as an escaping French Air Force prisoner of war, and was sent to the Grunhainigen Stalag. He again organized an escape with ten others who refused to leave him when he collapsed and finally helped him to reach the advancing American forces.

Yeo-Thomas was among the most outstanding workers behind enemy lines whom Britain produced. He was stocky, well built, athletic (he had boxed in his youth), and his blue eyes had a direct and fearless look. His sense of humour revealed itself in a ready smile which, on occasions, broke into open laughter. His character was exactly suited to his task. He was fearless, quick-witted, and resourceful, and his endurance under hardship was supreme. He received the George Cross, the Military Cross and bar, the Polish Cross of Merit, the croix de guerre, and was a commander of the Legion of Honour.

Battered and permanently injured in health, he returned to Britain to be cared for devotedly by Barbara Yeo-Thomas, formerly Barbara Joan Dean. A marriage had ended before war broke out, two children remaining in France with their mother.

After helping to bring to trial several Nazi war criminals Yeo-Thomas returned to Molyneux in 1946 but in 1948 ill health forced him to resign. After a period of recuperation he was appointed in 1950 as representative in Paris of the Federation of British Industries. There, in its different way, he still worked for Anglo-French rapprochement. But his sufferings had taken their toll and he died in Paris 26 February 1964.

[Bruce Marshall, *The White Rabbit*, 1952; M. R. D. Foot, *S.O.E. in France*, 2nd impression, with amendments, 1968; private information; personal knowledge.]

JAMES HUTCHISON

published 1981

(1905–1973)

Sir

Head of MI5, was born at Wells, Somerset, 2 December 1905, the third of
the four sons (there were no daughters) of George Arthur Hollis, vice-
principal of Wells Theological College and later bishop suffragan of
Taunton, and his wife, Mary Margaret, the daughter of Charles Marcus
Church, canon of Wells, a grand-niece of R. W. Church, dean of St. Paul's.
His elder brother, M. Christopher Hollis, one-time Conservative MP for
Devizes, has described the early years of his family life in his autobiography, *The Seven Ages* (1974, p. 4): 'I grew up not merely as a clergyman's
son, but in a cleric-inhabited society—in a sort of Trollopean world.'

Roger Hollis was educated at Leeds Grammar School, Clifton College,
and Worcester College, Oxford. At school he was a promising scholar who
went up to Oxford with a classical exhibition. But at Oxford he read
English and in the view of his contemporaries seemed to prefer a happy
social life to an academic one. In the memoirs of Evelyn Waugh he appears
as 'a good bottle man' and in Sir Harold Acton's as an agreeable friend.
Because of this easy-going approach and for no more dramatic reason, he
went down four terms before he was due to take his finals.

After barely a year's work in the DCO branch of Barclays Bank he left
England to become a journalist on a Hong Kong newspaper. This too
proved a brief assignment and in April 1928 he transferred to the British
American Tobacco Co. in whose service he remained for the following
eight years of his residence in China. His work enabled him to travel
widely in a country torn by the almost continuous conflict of Chinese
warlords and Japanese invaders. His family possess an unusually complete
collection of his letters home—dry and witty accounts of life in China, free
of the travel romanticism then so much in vogue. A further insight into his
Chinese experiences comes from the lecture he gave to the Royal Central
Asian Society in October 1937 (see the society's *Journal*, vol. xxv, January
1938). Entitled 'The Conflict in China', it shows a considerable grasp of a
complex situation. The nine formative years in China were terminated by
an attack of tuberculosis which led to him being invalided out of the BAT
and returned to England in 1936, and a further brief spell with the Ardath
Tobacco Co., an associate of the BAT. On 10 July of the following year he
was married in Wells Cathedral to Evelyn Esmé, daughter of George
Champeny Swayne, of Burnham-on-Sea, Somerset, solicitor in Glaston-
bury. Their one child, Adrian Swayne Hollis, became a fellow and tutor in

classics at Keble College, Oxford, and a chess player of international reputation.

Hollis began his new career in the security service in 1938. It was to last twenty-seven years and to constitute his most absorbing interest. By qualities of mind and character he was in several ways well adapted to it. He was a hard and conscientious worker, level-headed, fair-minded, and always calm. He began as a student of international communism, a field in which he was to become an acknowledged authority in the service. During the war, when the bulk of the service's talents and resources were committed to German, Italian, and Japanese counter-intelligence, he managed with small resources to ensure that the dangers of Russian-directed communism were not neglected. Consequently when the war was over and the security service turned to face the problems of the cold war, he had already become one of its key figures. In 1953 he was appointed deputy director-general and three years later, when his predecessor was unexpectedly transferred to other work, he inherited the top position.

It was a post which he was to hold with quiet efficiency for the next nine turbulent years. For the whole of that time the cold war was at its height and especially manifest in the field of Soviet espionage. Spy case followed spy case at the Old Bailey: Anthony Wraight, W. J. Vassall, George Blake, Harry Houghton, Ethel Gee, Gordon Lonsdale, and the Krogers became notorious figures, while in a different context the case of John Profumo caused great political consternation. Parallel with these events new sources of information became available to the security service from Russian and satellite defectors arriving in the West. These depicted the KGB in vast and threatening terms but were difficult to assess and only rarely provided sure and certain guidance. In the light of these events and circumstances the governments of the day felt the need to allay public and parliamentary concern over national security standards, and during his nine-year tenure of office as director-general Hollis had to face on behalf of his service three major official inquiries which both he and the service survived with considerable credit. Lord Denning, in the course of his memoirs later serialized in *The Times*, commented on the confidence he felt in Hollis during the inquiry for which he was responsible.

By the time he retired in 1965 Hollis had become a respected figure in Whitehall. He was similarly respected inside his own service (and others within the intelligence community), though he did not enjoy easy personal relations with its ordinary members who tended to find him reserved and aloof. Outside these two fields he was hardly known at all, which was exactly how he would have wished things to be and how they would have remained but for the misfortune that clouded the last years of his life.

On his retirement he moved first to a house in Wells which he occupied only until 1967. In 1968 his first marriage was dissolved and he married, secondly, Edith Valentine Hammond, his former secretary, the daughter of Ernest Gower Hammond, of Stratford-upon-Avon. They moved to a new home in the village of Catcott in Somerset. Here Hollis was able to indulge his formidable skills as a golfer and to undertake some modest jobs in local government. He was then suddenly asked to visit his old service where he learned that, as a result of information tending to imply a high-level penetration of the service, he had among others become a subject of investigation. He was asked to submit himself to interrogation and agreed. Members of a service in the front line of attack by the KGB can appreciate the need for secret enquiries of this kind at whatever rank they may apply. Unfortunately some of the facts became public because of internal leaks and in 1981 *Their Trade is Treachery*, by Chapman Pincher, was published. This book's picture of the Hollis investigation implied that the former director-general of the security service had probably been a Russian spy throughout his career in the service. Not unnaturally it provoked such an outcry in press and Parliament that Margaret Thatcher, the prime minister, had to intervene. On 25 March 1981 she informed the House of Commons that the outcome of the last Hollis investigation (by Lord Trend, secretary of the Cabinet from 1963 to 1973) had been the clearance of his name and reputation. The great public interest in the matter was a severe ordeal for Hollis's family and a sad aftermath to the career of a man who had worked so hard and responsibly at his job. Hollis died at Catcott 26 October 1973.

He was appointed OBE (1946), CB (1956), was knighted (1960), and was created KBE (1966).

[Private information; personal knowledge.]

DICK WHITE

published 1986

MITCHELL Graham Russell

(1905–1984)

Deputy director-general of the Security Service, was born 4 November 1905 in Broom House, Warwick Road, Kenilworth, the only son and elder child of Alfred Sherrington Mitchell, a captain in the Royal Warwickshire Regiment, and his wife, Sibyl Gemma Heathcote. He was educated at Winchester, of which he was an exhibitioner, and at Magdalen College,

Oxford, where he read politics, philosophy, and economics. In spite of suffering from poliomyelitis whilst still at school he excelled at golf and sailed for his university. He was also a very good lawn tennis player, and won the Queen's Club men's doubles championship in 1930. He played chess for Oxford, and was later to represent Great Britain at correspondence chess, a game at which he was once ranked fifth in the world. He obtained a second class honours degree in 1927.

His first job was as a journalist on the *Illustrated London News* but his only credited article, which appeared in the 12 October 1935 edition, was entitled 'What Was Known About Abyssinia in the Seventeenth Century—A Detailed Account in a Geography of 1670'. Thereafter he joined the research department of Conservative Central Office which was then headed by Sir G. Joseph Ball.

Mitchell's bout of polio had left him with a pronounced limp and when war broke out in September 1939 he was considered unfit for military service. Instead he joined the Security Service, MI5, in November. Exactly who sponsored his recruitment is unknown although Sir Joseph Ball, who was later to be appointed deputy to Lord Swinton on the top secret Home Defence Security Executive, was sufficiently influential and well connected in security circles to have assisted his entry into the organization.

Mitchell's first post in MI5 was in the F3 sub-section of F division, the department responsible for monitoring subversion headed by (Sir) Roger Hollis. F3's role was to maintain surveillance on right-wing nationalist movements, the British Union, German and Austrian political organizations, and individuals suspected of pro-Nazi sympathies. One of Mitchell's first tasks was to assist his immediate superior, Francis Aiken-Sneath, to investigate the activities of Sir Oswald Mosley and collate the evidence used to support his subsequent detention.

At the end of the war Mitchell was offered a permanent position in the Security Service and was promoted to the post of director of F division, where he remained until 1952 when he was switched to the counter-espionage branch. While in charge of D branch Mitchell led the team of case officers pursuing the clues of Soviet penetration left by Guy Burgess and Donald Maclean, the two diplomats who defected to Moscow in May 1951. At the same time he was 'one of the chief architects of positive vetting', the screening procedure introduced in Whitehall to prevent 'moles' from penetrating the higher echelons of the Civil Service.

In 1956 Roger Hollis succeeded Sir Dick White as director-general of MI5 and selected Mitchell as his deputy. He remained in this post until September 1963 when he unexpectedly took early retirement. It was later revealed that at the time of his departure Mitchell was himself under investigation as a suspected Soviet spy. The evidence accumulated against

Mitchell was all very circumstantial, and centred on the poor performance of MI5's counter-espionage branch during the 1950s. During this period MI5 experienced a number of set-backs, failed to attract a single Soviet defector, and only caught one spy on its own initiative.

During the last five months of his career Mitchell was the subject of a highly secret and inconclusive 'molehunt' which was eventually terminated when he was brought back from retirement to face interrogation. This gave him the opportunity to answer his accusers, but did little to end the debilitating atmosphere of suspicion that at one point threatened to paralyse the entire organization, and resulted in Roger Hollis himself being accused of having spied for the Russians. Both Mitchell and Hollis strenuously denied having been traitors, leaving the whole question of the identity of the KGB's master spy, if indeed there was one, unresolved.

Tall, stooped, and habitually wearing tinted glasses, Mitchell cut a lonely figure with solitary interests, like chess puzzles and *The Times* crossword. In 1934 he married Eleonora Patricia, daughter of James Marshall Robertson, gentleman. They had a son and a daughter. Mitchell died at his home in Sherington, Buckinghamshire, 19 November 1984.

[*The Times*, 3 January 1985; *Illustrated London News*, 12 October 1935; Nigel West (Rupert Allason), *Molehunt: The Full Story of the Soviet Spy in MI5*, 1987.]

NIGEL WEST

published 1990

SPORBORG Henry Nathan

(1905–1985)

Banker and secret organizer, was born 17 September 1905 in Rugby, the elder son of Henry Nathan Sporborg, an electrical engineer, and his wife, Miriam A. Smaith, who were Americans by origin. His younger brother died accidentally in 1928. He went, like his brother, from Rugby School to Emmanuel College, Cambridge; there he took a second class (division II) in history part i (1926) and a third in law (part ii, 1927), and rowed. He was admitted as a solicitor in 1930. He joined Slaughter & May, the City solicitors, and became a partner in 1935. He married in that year Mary, the daughter of Christopher Henry Rowlands, engineer. They had a son and three daughters.

Early in the war of 1939–45 he joined the Ministry of Economic Warfare, and from it soon moved into its secret branch, the Special Operations

Executive, when SOE first needed legal advice. Most of his partners joined him; hence the unkind quip about SOE's starting troubles, 'Seems to be all may and no slaughter.' Sporborg first worked, under (Sir) Charles Hambro, in the Scandinavian section, where they encountered a mixture of failures and successes. He then took over supervision of several sections working into north-west Europe: one each for Belgium and the Netherlands, two for France, and an escape section to help all four. Some of the foundations for future clandestine work he helped to lay were sound, though troubles shortly developed in the Netherlands. When Hambro became SOE's executive head, Sporborg too was promoted.

Under the cover appointment of principal private secretary to the minister in charge, the third Earl of Selborne, Sporborg acted for eighteen months in 1942–3 as SOE's principal liaison officer both with him and with several large departments in Whitehall, none of which wished SOE well: the Foreign Office, the Ministry of Supply, and those for the three other fighting services. He also looked after SOE's relations, sometimes turbulent, with the other secret services. He continued the latter task while, from September 1943 till SOE was disbanded in January 1946, he was deputy to Major-General (Sir) Colin Gubbins, its last executive head. Gubbins handled most military business, while he left political affairs to Sporborg. One or other of them was always in London, where Sporborg was prepared to face the chiefs of staff, the foreign secretary, or the prime minister if SOE's needs required it. He saw the permanent under-secretary at the foreign office, Sir Alexander Cadogan, almost daily. He became a strong advocate of the role of subversion—SOE's main task—as a tool for unseating the governments of Axis-occupied countries, though he felt the subject too delicate and too secret for him ever to be able to give a publishable account of it. Under Gubbins's and his direction, SOE secured several significant triumphs, particularly in France, Greece, Italy, Norway, Denmark, and Burma, and ended up with a tidy monetary profit as well.

Sporborg then returned to the City, as a businessman. He joined Hambros Bank, of which he was a director for nearly thirty years, and for a time general manager. His main expertise lay in financing take-overs and mergers. His judgement was so widely respected that several large firms took him on as chairman or vice-chairman—Thorn Electrical Industries and the Sun Group of assurance companies among them; and he served on the Port of London Authority for the eight years 1967–75. He was active also in the Fishmongers Company and in various charities; he spent a decade as chairman of St Mary's Hospital, Paddington. He had an active life as a country squire as well, riding to hounds from Upwick Hall near Ware in Hertfordshire; the house where he died of heart failure 6 March 1985.

He had held the wartime rank of lieutenant-colonel on the General List, and was appointed CMG in 1945. He was also a chevalier of the Legion of Honour, and held a French croix de guerre, the order of St Olaf of Norway, the King Christian X liberty medal, and the United States medal of freedom. He was a solidly built, burly man with an affable manner, set off by a drooping eyelid. He died worth over half a million pounds.

[*The Times*, 9 March and 8 August 1985; *Rugby School Register*, 1957, 1171, 1448; private information.]

M. R. D. FOOT

published 1990

FLEMING (Robert) Peter

(1907–1971)

Writer and traveller, was born 31 May 1907 at 27 Green Street, Park Lane, London, the eldest of the four sons of Valentine Fleming, later Conservative member of Parliament for South Oxfordshire, and his wife, Evelyn Beatrice Ste. Croix, daughter of George Alfred Ste. Croix Rose, JP, of the Red House, Sonning, Berkshire. His grandfather Robert Fleming, starting penniless in Dundee, had come to London and made a fortune in the City.

Peter's childhood was clouded by a mysterious and incapacitating illness, which left him without sense of taste or smell, but he recovered in time to be an outstanding success at Eton. Although outdistanced in athletics by his younger brother Ian he became a member of Pop, editor of the school magazine, and finally captain of the Oppidans. Most of his lifelong friends were made at Eton. At Christ Church, Oxford, he was equally successful—as president of the OUDS, a member of the Bullingdon Club, and editor of *Isis*. He obtained first class honours in English in 1929.

Valentine Fleming had been killed in action in 1917 and Peter's family decided that he, the senior male heir, should carry on the flourishing family business, but a few months' apprenticeship in the New York office convinced him that his life's work lay elsewhere. After a shooting expedition on the slopes of a volcano in Guatemala he came home, and in the spring of 1931 joined, as assistant literary editor, the staff of the *Spectator*, with which he was to be associated for most of his life. Some months later he got leave to attend a conference of the Institute of Pacific Relations, and so obtained his first experience of Russia, the Trans-Siberian railway, and especially China, where he was always to feel at home.

In April 1932 he answered an advertisement in the agony column of *The Times*, which led him to take part in a crack-brained and amateurish expedition to the hinterland of Brazil, ostensibly to look for Colonel P. H. Fawcett, a missing explorer. Fleming persuaded *The Times* to appoint him their unpaid special correspondent. This mixture of farce, excitement, discomfort, and danger achieved nothing except to provide him with the subject-matter for his first book, *Brazilian Adventure*, published in August 1933. In it he blew sky-high the excessive reverence and solemnity with which travel books had hitherto been treated, mocking the dangers and himself with infectious humour. People could not believe that a story of true adventure could be so funny, and the book had immense success at home and in America.

In June 1933 he set out on his second journey to China, again as special correspondent of *The Times*, to report on the war against Communists and bandits. After reaching Mukden in Manchuria and taking part in a sortie against bandits, he travelled south, achieving an interview with Chiang Kai-Shek, the commander-in-chief of the Nationalist forces, penetrating into Communist-held territory, and finally returning home via Japan and the United States.

Again the excursion furnished him with the material for a bestseller, *One's Company*, published in August 1934. 'One reads Fleming,' wrote Vita Sackville-West, 'for literary delight and for the pleasure of meeting an Elizabethan spirit allied to a modern mind.'

At the end of August he once again set off for the Far East with a far-ranging commission from *The Times*. After a brief shooting trip with friends in the Caucasus he travelled on to Harbin in Manchuria, where he by chance met the Swiss traveller Ella (Kini) Maillart. It transpired that they both wanted to walk and ride from China to India, and though they both preferred to travel alone, they agreed to join forces. This epic journey of some 3,500 miles on foot or ponies, through the forbidden province of Sinkiang, with many dangers, hardships, and hold-ups, took them seven months, from February to September 1935. This, the most arduous of Fleming's long journeys, he chronicled in fourteen long articles in *The Times* and later in his book *News from Tartary* (1936).

In December 1935 he married the actress Celia Johnson. She was the daughter of John Robert Johnson, MRCS, LRCP. Their son Nichol was born in 1939, their daughters Kate and Lucy in 1946 and 1947.

In 1936 Fleming joined the staff of *The Times*, having declined the offer of J. L. Garvin of the editorship of the *Observer*. The editor of *The Times*, Geoffrey Dawson, was anxious that Fleming should eventually succeed him, but Fleming's interest in politics was minimal, and the idea was gradually dropped.

In March 1938, taking Celia with him, he made his fourth journey to China, to report on the Sino-Japanese war and on the completion of the Burma Road, the only remaining access to China from the west.

On the outbreak of war in September 1939 Fleming immediately joined the Grenadier Guards, on whose Special Reserve he had served for many years. In March 1940 during a week of German measles he wrote a short and very amusing fantasy of Hitler landing accidentally in England by parachute, with uproarious consequences. *The Flying Visit* was published in July, and when, less than a year later, Rudolf Hess arrived in Scotland by air, Fleming's joke began to look like prophecy.

His one desire now was to see active service with his regiment, but for almost the whole war he was seconded to various intelligence and other jobs all over the world—first in Norway with (Sir) Adrian Carton de Wiart, then training a post-invasion force of guerrillas in Kent, then in Cairo with Sir A. P. (later Earl) Wavell, then in Greece, from which he was lucky to escape alive. Next he ran a street-fighting course in London until Wavell, now commander-in-chief in the south-west Pacific, summoned him to India and appointed him head of Deception. From 1942 to 1945 he shuttled between Delhi and the Chinese capital at Chungking, besides making an unauthorized and almost disastrous glider flight into Burma with the Chindits under Orde Wingate. After the Japanese surrender in 1945 he returned to civilian life as a full colonel having been appointed OBE.

Now, with his desire to travel satisfied, he settled down to the life of a literary squire at Merrimoles, the house he had built just before the war, near his grandparents' old home at Nettlebed in Oxfordshire, and in the middle of a 2,000-acre estate which his uncle had given him. People had always imagined he was wealthy, but owing to muddled wills he never in fact had any money of his own except an allowance from his mother, until his books and journalism began to provide him with an adequate income.

He continued to write amusing fourth leaders for *The Times*, and for many years contributed a column signed 'Strix' to the *Spectator*. Then he found a new role as an extremely competent amateur historian. *Invasion 1940*, a clever analysis of Hitler's plans for the conquest of Britain and our counter-measures, published in 1957, was a great success on both sides of the Atlantic and earned him more than any of his other books. There followed *The Siege at Peking* (1959), an account of the Boxer rebellion in 1900; *Bayonets to Lhasa* (1961) on the 1903-4 expedition of (Sir) Francis Younghusband; and *The Fate of Admiral Kolchak* (1963), concerning the White Russian commander in Siberia. At the time of his death he was engaged on the official history of strategic deception in World War II, which, but for several years of official obstruction, he would have had time to complete.

Apart from these major works, his essays from the *Spectator* and elsewhere were published in five volumes: *Variety* (1933), *My Aunt's Rhinoceros* (1956), *With the Guards to Mexico!* (1957), *The Gower Street Poltergeist* (1958), and *Goodbye to the Bombay Bowler* (1961).

Fleming was slim, medium-tall, black-haired, very good-looking and attractive. He habitually smoked a pipe. Shooting, at which he excelled, was the passion of his life, and he was at his happiest on long solitary patrols of his own acres with a gun and one of his beloved dogs. On every available day he walked or rode for miles. Every autumn he went to Scotland for a shooting holiday.

His persistent shyness with strangers was sometimes mistaken for arrogance: he was at his ease with contemporaries and old friends; those who served under him in peace and war would do anything for him; and he had a special relationship with men of his father's age—Carton de Wiart, Wavell, Geoffrey Dawson—to whom perhaps this dashing young man brought memories of their own youth. He was a man of courage and imagination, a faithful and generous friend. His literary style was compounded of clarity, a large vocabulary, and his own brand of incongruous and often self-deprecatory humour.

He died at Black Mount, Argyllshire, 18 August 1971, in exactly the way he would have chosen—a glorious summer's day, a grouse shoot on his beloved Scottish moors, a right-and-left, an instantaneous heart attack. He is buried at Nettlebed. A portrait in oils by John Ward and two pencil drawings by Augustus John are owned by his family.

[Duff Hart-Davis, *Peter Fleming: a Biography*, 1974; Fleming's own writings; personal knowledge.]

RUPERT HART-DAVIS

published 1986

SWEET-ESCOTT Bickham Aldred Cowan

(1907–1981)

SOE officer, banker, and businessman, was born in Newport, Monmouthshire, 6 June 1907, the eldest of four children (two sons and two daughters) of Aldred Bickham Sweet-Escott, marine engineer of Newport and Bristol, and his wife, Mary Amy, daughter of Michael Waistall Cowan, inspector-general in the Royal Navy. Educated at the choir school of Llandaff Cathedral, and Winchester College (1921–4) he left the latter early owing to family financial difficulties. He was employed by J. S. Fry & Sons, of Bristol (1924–7), and he continued his studies privately. Through the hard work that characterized his career he took a degree at London University and in 1927 won an exhibition to Balliol College, Oxford, taking a first in *literae humaniores* in 1930.

He joined the British Overseas Bank, where he mastered the politics, personalities, and financial structures of most European countries (1930–8). After serving for a year as personal assistant to Courtaulds' chairman he joined the Special Intelligence Service, section D, concerned with organizing sabotage, where he foresaw the importance of establishing section D activities in Europe before Nazi occupation. When section D became part of the Special Operations Executive (SOE) his service with the new organization took him to many regions. In 1941 he was in London concerned with the Balkans and Middle East, becoming regional director. In July 1941 he went to Cairo, as personal assistant to the head of SOE (Sir Frank Nelson), returning to London in December to the M (operations) directorate. From July 1942 he was with the SOE mission in Washington, liaising with the Office of Strategic Services (OSS), SOE's opposite number in America. Back in London in 1943 he was briefly head of SOE's Free French section, before returning to Cairo in December, to act as adviser to SOE's Force 133 until December 1944. From January to December 1945 he was in South East Asia Command as chief of staff to Force 136, becoming acting commander during the commander's absence. He was promoted major in 1941, and colonel in 1945.

In *Baker Street Irregular* (1965) Sweet-Escott gives a reliable and entertaining account of SOE. His experience, outstanding ability, and knowledge of the secrets of the organization repeatedly frustrated his attempts to serve in the field. He was one of the few competent to deal at the top level with SOE's problems, whether in Whitehall, Cairo, Algiers, or Kandy. Whenever and wherever there was a call for staff reinforcement Bickham was the obvious choice.

In 1949 he became general manager of the Ionian Bank which, helped by his wartime involvement with SOE operations in the Balkans, he rebuilt into a banking force in Greece and those parts of the eastern Mediterranean where Greek and British influence was still important. When the Bank to his great regret was taken over in 1958 he joined British Petroleum as group treasurer. BP was at a critical stage in its development, having lost its oil monopoly in Iran, and having 'long lived in its private world of Scottish accountants and Persian oil camps'. It had to find and develop oil elsewhere, and by investing heavily in marketing to reduce its dependence on oil production alone. Sweet-Escott's task was to ensure that financial communities throughout the world 'were aware of BP, understood BP, and trusted BP'. Although at times looked at askance by the old hands, he laid the foundation of much of BP's financial success by his clear-headed guidance, his exceptionally wide banking experience, and his ability to gain the confidence of new colleagues across the world. BP's development during his period of office speaks for his achievement. He retired in 1972.

He wrote several economic and financial surveys of the Balkans and Greece, including two books for the Royal Institute of International Affairs, of which he was an active member. He was a frequent broadcaster on international affairs. He was visiting professor, international finance, at the City University, London (1970–3). He worked hard for charitable causes, especially mental health.

He was a shrewd judge of character and situations, never afraid to state his views, and unfailingly kind, especially to young people planning their careers. A keen sportsman, in his later years he took up hunting, first stag, then fox, 'pursuing both beasts as if they had been storm troopers'.

Sweet-Escott married, first, in 1933, Doris Katharine Mary, daughter of the Revd Percy George Bulstrode, of Broomfield, Taunton. The marriage was dissolved in 1950 and in the same year he married, secondly, Beryl Mary (died 1984), daughter of Trevor Phelps, businessman, of Botha's Hill, South Africa. There were no children of either marriage. Sweet-Escott died 12 November 1981 at Ipswich.

[*The Times*, 14 November 1981; *BP Shield*, no. 1, 1982; *Winchester College Register*, 1901–1946; SOE adviser; private information.]

CHARLES CRUICKSHANK

published 1990

BLUNT Anthony Frederick

(1907–1983)

Art historian and communist spy, was born in Bournemouth, Hampshire, 26 September 1907, the third and youngest son (there were no daughters) of the Revd Arthur Stanley Vaughan Blunt and his wife, Hilda Violet, daughter of Henry Master of the Madras Civil Service. His father was a kinsman of the poet, anti-imperialist, and libertine, Wilfrid Scawen Blunt, his mother a friend of the future Queen Mary; both these connections were to have a curious significance for Blunt's future career. After a childhood acquiring a lasting enthusiasm for French art and architecture while his father was chaplain of the British embassy in Paris, he went to Marlborough College; his artistic interests were further stimulated by his eldest brother, Wilfrid, a future art master. Going up to Trinity College, Cambridge, on a scholarship, Blunt graduated there with a second in part i of the mathematical tripos (1927) and a first in both parts (1928 and 1930) of the modern languages tripos (French and German). In 1932 he was elected a fellow of the college on the strength of a dissertation on artistic theory in Italy and France during the Renaissance and seventeenth century. By now he was already writing for the *Cambridge Review* and within a year was contributing articles and reviews on modern art to the *Spectator* and *Listener*. At first he championed the modern movement, which for him was a product of the School of Paris, but later, influenced by the Marxism which he had first espoused in 1934, he just as fiercely, if temporarily, attacked modernism as irrelevant to the contemporary political struggle.

While still an undergraduate he was invited to join the Apostles. The values of this exclusive Cambridge society between the wars (derived in part from the teaching of the philosopher, G. E. Moore) have been summed up as the cult of the intellect for its own sake, belief in freedom of thought and expression irrespective of the conclusions to which this freedom might lead, and the denial of all moral restraints other than loyalty to friends. An influential minority of the society's members were, moreover, like Blunt himself, homosexual, and, at a time when homosexual acts were still illegal in Britain, he seems to have relished the resulting atmosphere of secrecy and intrigue. Where he stood out from most of his contemporaries was in his phenomenal intellectual energy, powers of concentration, and capacity for self-discipline—qualities he retained into old age. Endowed with charm, vitality, and good looks, he lived an active social life and also travelled widely during the 1930s on the Continent. In 1936–7 he resigned his Cambridge fellowship, joined the staff of the Warburg Institute, lectured on baroque art at the Courtauld Institute, and allowed himself to be drawn into working for the Russian secret intelligence service by the charming, scandalous Guy Burgess. Much ink has since been spilt over the identity of the individual who recruited spies for the Russians at Cambridge in the 1930s, but in Blunt's case his fondness for Burgess, to whom he remained devoted until the latter's death in Moscow in 1963, is probably sufficient explanation. His decision seems to have been at once emotional and cold-blooded. There is no doubt of his hatred of Fascism at the time but whether he was ever a convinced communist is far from clear. Yet his sense of professional dedication would have made him as capable a spy as he was an art historian.

After a futile spell in France in the Field Security Police, he joined the British counter-intelligence service, MI5, in 1940 and remained with it in London throughout World War II. He is known to have given his Soviet controllers every detail of the service's organization and the names of all its personnel and he presumably also gave away any military secrets to which he had access. How much damage he actually did to the British war effort is hard to say; it may have been rather slight. But there was a real danger that the information he supplied might have been leaked to the Germans, so causing the deaths of Allied agents in occupied Europe, or, alternatively, used by the Russians in preparing policies hostile to the British and Americans. At the end of the war in 1945, Blunt left MI5 and thereafter had no more secrets to impart, though he remained in touch with Burgess until the latter's defection to Moscow in 1951 and he continued occasionally to see another of the Cambridge spies, H. A. R. ('Kim') Philby. In May 1951 Philby told Blunt that the security authorities were planning to arrest Donald Maclean. When Blunt passed on the warning both Maclean and Burgess were able to escape to Moscow.

All this went on concurrently with the development of Blunt's career as an art historian. Already before the war he saw that the refugee scholars at the Warburg Institute had brought with them from Hamburg both an intellectual rigour and a soundly-based historical method that were new to the study of the art of the past in Britain. In 1937–9 he published scholarly articles in the Warburg *Journal* on such diverse topics as 'The Hypnerotomachia Poliphili in 17th-century France' and 'Blake's *Ancient of Days*' and began his great work on the seventeenth-century French painter, Nicolas Poussin, characteristically with an article showing that Poussin's 'Notes on Painting' were not original but were largely copied from obscure ancient and Renaissance literary sources. Blunt also helped to establish friendly relations between the Warburg and Courtauld Institutes, becoming deputy director of the latter in 1939. In 1940 most of his fellowship dissertation was published as *Artistic Theory in Italy 1450–1600*; written with his customary lucidity and stylistic grace, it remains a useful introduction to its subject. During the war he wrote further articles in periodicals and a book on the French architect, François Mansart (1941); in 1945 he published a catalogue of the French drawings in the royal collection at Windsor Castle.

In the same year, 1945, to the puzzlement of his friends, who knew of his political sympathies though not of his activities as a spy, he accepted appointment as surveyor of the King's (after 1952 the Queen's) Pictures. One of his motives in taking the job may well have been to deflect suspicion away from himself in the event that any of his fellow conspirators was caught—for who in authority, he would have calculated, would think of doubting the loyalty of a senior royal servant? On the other hand, his activity, soon after appointment, in helping to rescue on behalf of George VI from a castle in Germany what are now said to be compromising letters from the Duke of Windsor quite possibly had no sinister implications so far as Blunt was concerned. At all events, he gave every sign of enjoying the post of surveyor, which he retained until 1972. While the day-to-day work was left to his deputy and eventual successor, (Sir) Oliver Millar, Blunt took the major decisions, including that of opening the Queen's Gallery, Buckingham Palace, in 1962. (For his services he was appointed CVO in 1947 and KCVO in 1956.) In 1947 he had become director of the Courtauld Institute of Art and professor of the history of art in the University of London. Thenceforth the Institute was to be his home (he had a flat at the top of the building, designed by Robert Adam, in Portman Square) and the centre of his life. In almost every sense he was a superb director. He had a natural authority, an infectious enthusiasm for his subject, and a winning way with students and younger colleagues. Teaching more by example than by precept, he inspired those around him to give of their best, and it was under him that the Courtauld, whose staff and student numbers more than doubled during his time, earned the position, which it had had in theory since its foundation in 1931, of being the principal centre for the training of art historians in Britain.

The first phase of his scholarly career was crowned by a masterly survey in the Pelican History of Art series, *Art and Architecture in France 1500–1700* (1953). Lucid, penetrating, and comprehensive, this is still the best study of its subject and is perhaps Blunt's single most successful book. The next dozen years were spent mainly working on Poussin, an artist for whose intellectual power, self-discipline, and personal reticence he had a natural sympathy. His erudite monograph on Poussin, based on a thorough study of the artist's ideas and including a catalogue of the paintings, appeared in 1966–7. Afterwards Blunt turned his attention as a scholar chiefly to Italian baroque architecture, on which he also wrote several books. He retired from the Courtauld and the university in 1974, covered with British and French academic honours, including honorary D.Litts. of Bristol (1961), Durham (1963), and Oxford (1971), and the Legion of Honour (1958).

Yet all this time he was at risk of exposure as a former spy. For many years he successfully resisted interrogation by the security services but in 1964, after the FBI had found a witness prepared to testify that Blunt had tried to recruit him during the 1930s, he made a secret confession in return for a promise of immunity from prosecution. In the later 1970s the pressure mounted again, as a result of investigations by independent writers on espionage relying on information leaked by former security officers. On 15 November 1979, the prime minister confirmed in the House of Commons that Blunt had been an agent of, and talent spotter for, Russian intelligence before and during World War II, although she added that there was insufficient evidence on which criminal charges could be brought. His knighthood was annulled, as was the honorary fellowship he had held at Trinity College since 1967, and immediately the press, radio, and television began a campaign of vilification. There was also much discussion by intellectuals in the serious press not only of Blunt but of the whole phenomenon of the Cambridge spies who had put belief in communism above loyalty to country in the 1930s and 1940s.

Undoubtedly some of the agitation was motivated by class hatred, and it is a striking fact that both Blunt's own actions and the treatment of him not only by the public but also by officials were pervaded at every turn by the class divisions in British society. More immediately, his career can perhaps best be explained by the fatal conjunction in him of his own outstanding gifts and his desire to be at once part of the establishment and against it; or, as an acquaintance put it, 'The trouble with Anthony was that he wanted both to run with the hare and hunt with the hounds.' He died of a heart attack, in the London flat to which he had retired near the Courtauld, 26 March 1983. He was unmarried.

[E. K. Waterhouse, introduction to *Essays in Renaissance and Baroque Art presented to Anthony Blunt*, 1967; Anthony Blunt, essay in *Studio International*, 1972; Andrew Boyle, *The Climate of Treason*, 1979; Barrie Penrose and Simon Freeman, *Conspiracy of Silence*, 1966; Peter Wright, *Spycatcher*, 1987; John Costello, *Mask of Treachery*, 1988; personal knowledge.]

MICHAEL KITSON

published 1990

CHURCHILL Peter Morland

(1909–1972)

Secret agent, was born in Amsterdam 14 January 1909, the eldest of four children (three sons and a daughter) of William Algernon Churchill, British consul there, who ten years later was consul-general in Milan, and his wife, Violet Myers. He was educated at Malvern, in Switzerland, and at Caius

College, Cambridge, where he got a pass degree and a half blue for ice hockey, a game he several times played for England. He was British pro-consul in Oran in 1933–4.

In the autumn of 1940 he was commissioned into the intelligence corps, and served with the independent French section of the Special Operations Executive (SOE); he became a captain in May 1942. He distinguished himself that spring in the tricky and dangerous task of ferrying other agents ashore on to the Mediterranean coast of France from submarines or small boats at night. He had been to France himself in January 1942, to carry messages and to find out who 'Carte' was. 'Carte' turned out to be André Girard, a painter at Antibes who claimed to control a secret army over 200,000 strong. On 27/28 August Churchill was parachuted into France to establish liaison with this army. In his new role he was almost entirely ineffective, save that he organized the reception on the Riviera of several more parties of agents. 'Carte's' army turned out to be merely notional and soon after the German occupation of France on 11 November 1942 Girard's followers dispersed. Churchill retired to St. Jorioz, a small resort near Annecy in Savoy, with his wireless operator Adolph Rabinovitch and his courier Odette Marie Celine Sansom, wife of Roy Sansom (by whom she had three daughters) and daughter of Gaston Brailly. He returned to England by light aircraft for further orders on 23/24 March 1943. There he was told that Odette Sansom was engaged in dangerous talks with a supposed German colonel, and ordered to avoid her when he returned. However, she received him when he was para-chuted back on 14/15 April, and on the following night her German acquaintance—Sergeant H. Bleicher of the Abwehr—arrested him and her, finding him fast asleep.

With more skill than truth, he passed her off as his wife and himself as a cousin of the British prime minister. He survived two years' severe im-prisonment, partly in Fresnes, partly in German concentration camps. After the war he was appointed to the DSO (1946) and awarded a French croix de guerre and Legion of Honour. He married Odette Sansom in 1947, and in her wake became something of a newspaper hero; she divorced him in 1955. He married secondly in 1956 Irene Mary ('Jane'), daughter of William E. Hoyle, sometime manager of the SPCK bookshop in Exeter: she survived him. He had no children.

He wrote three light-hearted books, cited below, on his wartime adventures; a novel, *By Moonlight* (1958), on the Glières Maquis which he had helped to arm; and a short travel guide, *All About the French Riviera* (1960), concerning the area where he spent his closing years, as an estate agent. He lived at Le Rouret, a dozen miles west of Cannes, and died of cancer in Cannes 1 May 1972.

[Peter Churchill, *Of Their Own Choice*, 1952, *Duel of Wits*, 1953, and *The Spirit in the Cage*, 1954; M. R. D. Foot, *SOE in France*, second impression, 1968; private information.]

M. R. D. Foot

published 1986

ALEXANDER (Conel) Hugh (O'Donel)

(1909–1974)

Chess master and civil servant, was born in Cork 19 April 1909, the eldest of four children and elder son of Conel William Long Alexander, professor of engineering at the University of Cork in Southern Ireland, and his wife, Hilda Barbara Bennett, of Birmingham. His younger brother became a doctor of medicine and one of his younger sisters a nun. On his father's death the family moved to Birmingham and the early years of Alexander's chess career are associated with that city. He attended King Edward's School which sent him to play in the British Boys Championship at Hastings in 1926, none of the stronger players being available. In fact he won the championship and it was not long before he was recognized as one of the future hopes of British chess.

In 1928 he went up to King's College, Cambridge, on a mathematics scholarship and signalled his arrival by winning a most brilliant game on third board in the match with Oxford University. By 1931 he was playing with great success on top board for Cambridge. He won eleven games in succession, losing only to Harry Golombek in an inter-university match that year. This meeting was the start of a firm friendship; another close friend was (Sir) P. Stuart Milner-Barry who had preceded Alexander on first board at Cambridge. These three were to be the young vanguard of British chess for the next fifteen years.

In 1932 Alexander came second in a small international tournament at Cambridge and was also second in the British Championship tournament. Leaving the university with a first class honours degree (1931) he failed to gain the star indicating special distinction and therefore also did not get a fellowship. This he rightly attributed to his spending too much time on chess. But that he was highly gifted as a mathematician was shown by the remark by Professor G. H. Hardy that he was the only genuine mathematician he knew who did not become one.

In 1932 Alexander went to teach mathematics at Winchester where he remained for the next six years. He continued to play chess, both nationally and internationally. During this period he met and married (in 1934) an Australian girl, Enid Constance Crichton, daughter of Ronald William Neate, sea captain. They had two sons, the elder of whom, Michael, joined the Diplomatic Service and was appointed British ambassador in Austria in 1982.

By now he was making a name for himself internationally. He played with success for England in the biennial international team tournaments, scoring the highest percentage for his side, albeit on bottom board, at Folkestone in 1933 and rising to first board at Buenos Aires in 1939. He also played regularly at the Hastings Christmas congresses and came equal second with Paul Keres ahead of some of the world's best players at Hastings in 1938. In that year too he won the British Championship.

He then left Winchester in 1938 to become head of personnel in the John Lewis Partnership in London, a change he enjoyed since, as he himself said, it was a relief to deal with adult minds. A new and vitally important change in his career came with the outbreak of war in 1939 when he joined the Government Code and Cipher School at Bletchley Park. He was given the task of breaking German naval codes, a problem exactly suited to his keen and vivid intelligence. Soon he was in charge of the whole operation and his two friends, Stuart Milner-Barry and Harry Golombek, who were also working at Bletchley, testified to the drive and skill with which he helped to win the battle of the Atlantic.

After the war Alexander was appointed OBE (1946), a somewhat insufficient recognition for the great services he had done, though subsequently he was appointed CBE (1955) and, when he eventually retired in 1970, CMG.

Meanwhile he scored a number of successes in the chess field. He was first at Hastings 1946–7 and joint first with the Soviet grand master, David Bronstein, in Hastings in 1953. There were many fine results too in the post-war chess olympiads. But gradually the demands of his profession (for most of the period from the end of the war until his retirement he was in charge of research and development at the Government Communications Headquarters at Cheltenham) lessened his participation in chess events.

When he retired from the Foreign Office he concentrated on writing about the game. He wrote some excellent books on chess and was chess correspondent of the *Sunday Times, Financial Times, Evening News*, and *Spectator*. He was about to set out for Iceland to report the Spassky–Fischer match in 1972 when he was smitten by what seemed a mortal illness. After a short respite he collapsed and died at Cheltenham 15 February 1974.

Hugh Alexander had a most vivid and attractive personality. A magnificent talker, he loved to argue but was ever ready to see his opponent's point of view. He had a razor-keen intelligence and the only chance of succeeding in an argument against him lay in placing the subject matter in fields of which he had not an expert knowledge. An amateur all his life, had it not been for World War II he might well have aspired to the World Championship title.

The following game was won by Alexander in the European zonal tournament at Hilversum in 1947. His opponent, the Hungarian grandmaster Laszlo Szabo, was one of the world's leading players at the time.

White Alexander Black L. Szabo Sicilian Defence

1 P–K4 P–QB4. 2 N–KB3 N–QB3. 3 P–Q4 PxP. 4 NxP N–B3. 5 N–QB3 P–Q3. 6 B–K2 P–K3. 7 B–K3 Q–B2. 8 P–B4 P–QR3. 9 O–O N–QR4. 10 K–R1 B–K2. 11 Q–K1 N–B5. 12 B–B1 O–O. 13 P–QN3 N–QR4. 14 B–Q3 N–Q2. 15 B–N2 B–B3. 16 N–B3 N–B4. 17 P–K5 NxB. 18 PxN PxP. 19 PxP B–K2. 20 N–K4 Q–Q1. 21 N–B6 ch PxN. 22 Q–N3 ch K–R1. 23 PxP BxP. 24 N–K5 BxN. 25 BxB ch P–B3. 26 RxP, resigns.

[Harry Golombek, *The Encyclopedia of Chess*, 1977; Sir Stuart Milner-Barry, 'Memoir' in *The Best Games of C.H.O'D. Alexander* by Harry Golombek and W. R. Hartson, 1976; private information; personal knowledge.]

HARRY GOLOMBEK

published 1986

BURGESS Guy Francis de Moncy

(1911–1963)

Soviet spy, was born 16 April 1911 in Devonport, Devon, the elder son (there were no daughters) of Commander Malcolm Kingsford de Moncy Burgess, lieutenant in the Royal Navy, and his wife Evelyn Mary, daughter of William Gillman, gentleman. Burgess's father died in 1924, and his mother later married John Retallack Bassett, a retired lieutenant-colonel. Burgess was educated at Eton. He went on to the Royal Naval College, Dartmouth, for two years before poor eyesight ended plans for a naval career, and he returned to Eton. In 1930 he won an open scholarship to read modern history at Trinity College, Cambridge, and he gained a first in part i of the modern history tripos (1932), and an *aegrotat* in part ii (1933).

At Cambridge he was renowned for his brilliance and charm, and his exuberance, but he also soon became notorious for his homosexuality and drunkenness, and his dirty and dishevelled appearance. Malcolm

Muggeridge later said that Burgess 'gave me a feeling of being morally afflicted in some way', and described him as the 'sick toast of a sick society'. Anthony Blunt sponsored his entry into the exclusive intellectual secret society, the Apostles. Burgess joined the Communist party, organized strikes among college servants, and joined hunger marches. It is not clear whether he was recruited as a Soviet agent at Cambridge or during his trip to Moscow in the summer of 1934. Hoping to become a history don, he embarked on research into the 'bourgeois revolution' of the seventeenth century in 1933, but the appearance of Basil Willey's *The Seventeenth Century Background* (1934) robbed him of his topic, and he left Cambridge.

At this point he announced his disillusionment with Marxism, and began to express right-wing views. As secretary to Captain 'Jack' Macnamara, a Conservative MP and member of the Anglo-German Fellowship, from 1935 to 1936, he made several visits to Germany. Burgess joined the BBC in October 1936 as a producer in the talks department, and later became producer of 'The Week in Westminster'.

In December 1938 Burgess was offered a job in Section D of SIS (Secret Intelligence Service), set up to investigate sabotage and propaganda in the event of war. It was he who managed to get H. A. R. ('Kim') Philby his first job in intelligence, in 1940. When Section D was absorbed into the newly formed SOE (Special Operations Executive) in 1940, Burgess was not given a job, and he returned to the BBC in 1941, responsible for propaganda to occupied Europe and liaison with the SIS and SOE.

In the summer of 1944 Burgess got a temporary job in the press department of the Foreign Office. In 1947 he became private secretary to Hector McNeil, minister of state at the Foreign Office, and despite his drunkenness and unreliable behaviour he not only survived but was promoted. Later in 1947 he spent three months in the Information Research Department, which was formed to launch a propaganda counter-offensive against Russia. During his time with the IRD he provided the Russians with useful details of its staff and operations. Following a period in the Far Eastern department of the Foreign Office, from November 1948, he was posted to Washington in August 1950 as a second secretary with special responsibility for Far Eastern affairs, just after the beginning of the Korean war. He clashed with his superior and was moved to a different section, and after a series of complaints about his behaviour he was sent back to England at the request of the ambassador at the beginning of May 1951.

Burgess defected to Moscow with Donald Maclean on 25 May 1951. Maclean, a Cambridge contemporary of Burgess, fellow Apostle, and fellow communist, had recently been made head of the American department at the Foreign Office. But investigations into the leaking of sensitive material from Washington had narrowed down to Maclean as chief suspect, and it seems that Burgess was detailed, probably by Philby, who was still in Washington, to warn him and organize his escape, although it does not seem to have been intended that Burgess should go too. He was not under suspicion at the time, although he was about to be dismissed for his indiscretions and outrageous behaviour. Later, Burgess was to tell friends that he had only intended to accompany Maclean as far as Prague before returning to London. Philby remained bitter towards Burgess, whose defection had thrown suspicion on him and ultimately led to his unmasking. The whereabouts of Burgess and Maclean were not revealed until February 1956, when they held a press conference in Moscow.

Once in the USSR, Burgess and Maclean spent six months in the provincial town of Kuybyshev before being allowed to settle in Moscow. Burgess was lonely and bored, missed his bohemian life in Soho, never attempted to learn Russian, and never became a Russian citizen. He did have a job in the Foreign Literature Publishing House, but he sought out any visitors from London, eager for gossip, and frequently talked about returning. Burgess was memorably portrayed by Alan Bates in Alan Bennett's television play *An Englishman Abroad* (1983).

Burgess died unmarried of a heart attack in Moscow 30 August 1963. His ashes were returned to England and buried in the churchyard in West Meon, Hampshire.

[*The Times*, 2 September 1963; B. Penrose and S. Freeman, *Conspiracy of Silence: the Secret Life of Anthony Blunt*, 1986; Robert Cecil, *A Divided Life: a Biography of Donald Maclean*, 1988; Philip Knightley, *Philby: the Life and Views of the K.G.B. Masterspy*, 1988; Anthony Glees, *The Secrets of the Service. British Intelligence and Communist Subversion 1939–51*, 1987.]

ANNE BAKER

published 1993

AMERY John

(1912–1945)

Traitor, was born 14 March 1912 at 9 Embankment Gardens, Chelsea, London, the elder son (there were no daughters) of Leopold Charles Maurice Stennett, politician, and his wife Adeliza Florence ('Bryddie'), daughter of John Hamar Greenwood of Whitby, Ontario, and sister of Hamar (first Viscount) Greenwood. At sixteen he ran away from Harrow, and set up as a film director, work which took him to central Europe and east Africa, but proved financially unrewarding. It combined ill with his taste for fast cars and high life; in 1936 he was declared bankrupt, and settled with his family that he had better live abroad. Two years earlier, experiences in Vienna on the verge of civil war had awakened in him vehement, if premature, anti-communism. Accordingly, he went to Spain when civil war broke out there in July 1936, to take an active part on the insurgent General Franco's side, smuggling arms across the Pyrenees, and receiving the Italian medal for valour in action. In 1939 bad health drove him to a sanatorium in French Savoy.

His first marriage (in Athens), which his parents disapproved, to Una Wing had rapidly broken down. He contracted a second, to Jeannine Barde, a Frenchwoman who had plenty of friends at Vichy. She died in April 1944; the following October he married another Frenchwoman, Michelle Thomas. There were no children.

During his gun-running activities he had met Jacques Doriot, a renegade French communist who had turned ardent fascist. Doriot summoned him to Paris in the autumn of 1942, convinced him that Germany was going to lose the war unless Great Britain joined against the USSR, and enlisted Amery's aid. For the next eighteen months Amery toured prisoner-of-war camps, seeking to recruit a Legion of St George—unromantically renamed by the Germans the British Free Corps—to fight alongside the Germans against the Russians and save Europe from Bolshevism. From thousands of prisoners, thirty men elected to join him; they never went into action. He also broadcast to his fellow-countrymen in England, seeking to persuade them to change sides, and gave anti-communist lectures, notably in Oslo and Belgrade.

In April 1945 he and his wife were in northern Italy, making for Switzerland, when they were captured by communist partisans. He was handed over to the British army and sent back to England. His brother (Harold) Julian's efforts to establish Spanish nationality for him did not succeed. He was arraigned on eight counts of treason before Sir Travers Humphreys at the Old Bailey on 28 November 1945. He pleaded guilty, knowing this would mean execution, and was shot in the Tower of London 18 December 1945.

[Rebecca West, *The Meaning of Treason*, 2nd edn., 1982; private information.]

M. R. D. FOOT

published 1993

TURING Alan Mathison

(1912–1954)

Mathematician, was born in London 23 June 1912, the younger son of Julius Mathison Turing, of the Indian Civil Service, and his wife, Ethel Sara, daughter of Edward Waller Stoney, chief engineer of the Madras and Southern Mahratta Railway. G. J. and G. G. Stoney were collateral relations.

He was educated at Sherborne School where he was able to fit in despite his independent unconventionality and was recognized as a boy of marked ability and character. He went as a mathematical scholar to King's College, Cambridge, where he obtained a second class in part i and a first in part ii of the mathematical tripos (1932–4). He was elected into a fellowship in 1935 with a thesis 'On the Gaussian Error Function' which in 1936 obtained for him a Smith's prize.

In the following year there appeared his best-known contribution to mathematics, a paper for the London Mathematical Society 'On Computable Numbers, with an Application to the Entscheidungsproblem': a proof that there are classes of mathematical problems which cannot be solved by any fixed and definite process, that is, by an automatic machine. His theoretical description of a 'universal' computing machine aroused much interest.

After two years (1936–8) at Princeton, Turing returned to King's where his fellowship was renewed. But his research was interrupted by the war during which he worked for the communications department of the Foreign Office; in 1946 he was appointed O.B.E. for his services.

The war over, he declined a lectureship at Cambridge, preferring to concentrate on computing machinery, and in the autumn of 1945 he became a senior principal scientific officer in the mathematics division of the National Physical Laboratory at Teddington. With a team of engineers and electronic experts he worked on his 'logical design' for the Automatic Computing Engine (ACE) of which a working pilot model was demonstrated in 1950 (it went eventually to the Science Museum). In the meantime Turing had resigned and in 1948 he accepted a readership at Manchester where he was assistant director of the Manchester Automatic Digital Machine (MADAM). He tackled the problems arising out of the use of this machine with a combination of powerful mathematical analysis and intuitive short cuts which showed him at heart more of an applied than a pure mathematician. In 'Computing Machinery and Intelligence' in *Mind* (October 1950) he made a brilliant examination of the arguments put forward against the view that machines might be said to think. He suggested that machines can learn and may eventually 'compete with men in all purely intellectual fields'. In 1951 he was elected F.R.S., one of his proposers being Bertrand (Earl) Russell.

The central problem of all Turing's investigations was the extent and limitations of mechanistic explanations of nature and in his last years he was working on a mathematical theory of the chemical basis of organic growth. But he had not fully developed this when he died at his home at Wilmslow 7 June 1954 as the result of taking poison. Although a verdict of suicide was returned it was possibly an accident, for there was always a Heath-Robinson element in the experiments to which he turned for relaxation: everything had to be done with materials available in the house. This self-sufficiency had been apparent from an early age; it was manifested in the freshness and independence of his mathematical work; and in his choice of long-distance running, not only for exercise but as a substitute for public transport.

An original to the point of eccentricity, he had a complete disregard for appearances and his extreme shyness made him awkward. But he had an enthusiasm and a humour which made him a generous and lovable personality and won him many friends, not least among children. He was unmarried.

[M. H. A. Newman in *Biographical Memoirs of Fellows of the Royal Society*, vol. i, 1955; Sara Turing, *Alan M. Turing*, 1959; *The Times*, 16 June 1954.]

HELEN M. PALMER

published 1971

PHILBY Harold Adrian Russell ('Kim')

(1912–1988)

Soviet agent, was born 1 January 1912 at Ambala in the Punjab, the only son and eldest of four children of Harry St John Bridger Philby, Indian civil servant, explorer, and orientalist, and his wife Dora, daughter of Adrian Hope Johnston, of the Indian public works department. With unconscious prescience they nicknamed him Kim.

He was educated at Westminster and Trinity College, Cambridge, where he joined the university Socialist Society and became a convinced communist. He obtained a third class in part i of the history tripos (1931)

Philby

and a second class (division I) in part ii of the economics tripos (1933). Philby was of medium height with a seductive smile. In 1933 he went on a trip to Vienna, where he met Alice ('Litzi') Friedman, an Austrian communist, whose father was Israel Kohlman, a minor government official of Hungarian Jewish origin. They witnessed the street fighting, which ended with the defeat of the socialists in February 1934, when they had a hurried marriage and left for England. By this time she had persuaded him to become a Soviet agent. While he was in Vienna, the NKVD (the Soviet secret service) had talent-spotted Philby as a potential recruit.

In June 1934, at a secret meeting in Regents Park, Philby was approached by Arnold Deutsch, a Czech undercover Soviet intelligence officer operating in London. Philby welcomed the suggestion that he should penetrate 'the bourgeois institutions'. Another of his controllers was Teodor Maly, a Hungarian who had renounced the priesthood and become an idealistic convert to Bolshevism. Beginning his career as a journalist, Philby was instructed to sever all links with his communist past and swing over to the far right. Hence his involvement with the pro-Nazi Anglo-German Fellowship. First as a freelance and later for *The Times*, he went to Spain in February 1937 to cover the Spanish civil war from the point of view of General Franco (whose planned assassination was part of his original brief), who awarded him the red cross of military merit. He left Spain in August 1939 with his overt right-wing credentials established, while his covert faith in Joseph Stalin remained untarnished by the Terror of the mid-1930s, although he had an ambivalent attitude to the Nazi–Soviet pact in August 1939. His luck never deserted him, especially permitting him to survive the ups and downs of an alternating relationship with the Moscow centre.

After the outbreak of World War II Philby went to France as a war correspondent. Returning to England after Dunkirk, he was recruited, thanks to Guy Burgess, his friend from Cambridge and a fellow NKVD agent, into the SIS (the Secret Intelligence Service or MI6) in July 1940 and soon joined Section Five (counter-intelligence) in 1941. A base in London eased his domestic problems with Aileen Furse (the daughter of Captain George Furse of the Royal Horse Artillery) with whom he had been living and producing children since 1940, but whom he did not marry until December 1946, a week after his divorce from Litzi. By then he was a rising star, having become in 1944 head of Section Nine, whose remit was 'to collect and interpret information concerning communist espionage and subversion'. When Section Nine was merged with Section Five in 1945, he alerted Moscow to the intended defection in Istanbul of Konstantin Volkov, who could have unmasked Philby. He was appointed OBE in 1946.

In 1946 the SIS posted him to Turkey and in 1949 he became their representative in Washington, where he kept Moscow informed of Anglo-American intelligence collaboration. He also saw how the net was closing in on Donald Maclean. In 1950 Guy Burgess was posted to Washington and lodged with Philby. When Maclean and Burgess fled to Moscow, Philby was summoned back to London and interrogated by MI5, who were persuaded of his guilt, but lacked the evidence of a confession to convict him. The SIS, however, in return for Philby's voluntary resignation, gave him a golden handshake. After his name had been cleared by Harold Macmillan (later the first Earl of Stockton) in 1955, the SIS fixed his cover as a correspondent for the *Observer* and the *Economist*, based on Beirut, where he arrived in August 1956.

Aileen died in 1957. There were three sons and two daughters of the marriage; Philby had no other children. In 1959 he married Eleanor, from Seattle, who was formerly married to Sam Pope Brewer, Middle East correspondent of the *New York Times*. In Beirut, Philby was successfully reincarnated as a journalist until Anatoli Golitsyn's defection to the CIA in 1962 filled in the gaps in the case against him. The SIS and MI5 then confronted Philby with a prosecutor's brief in January 1963, plus an offer of immunity if he returned to London and made a full confession. Philby admitted he had been a Soviet agent but said no more. He quietly arranged his escape and arrived in Russia at the end of January 1963. Five months later he was granted Soviet citizenship.

Eleanor soon joined him, but she so disliked life in Moscow that she left for good in 1965; she died in America in 1968. Meanwhile, Philby had been awarded in 1965 the Order of Lenin and the Order of the Red Banner. He began an affair with Melinda, the wife of Donald Maclean, who had also defected to Moscow, but this did not last. Heavy drinking and smoking dominated his life until 1970, when George Blake, another defector, introduced him to Rufina Ivanova, half Polish and half Russian, whom he married in 1971. She was the daughter of an expert on the chemical treatment of furs. In 1980 his award of the Order of Friendship of Peoples preceded his East German, Hungarian, Bulgarian, and Cuban decorations. He died in Moscow 11 May 1988, receiving his final recognition in an elaborate funeral organized by the KGB. A private buyer purchased the lion's share of Philby's papers, which were auctioned at Sotheby's in July 1994.

[Christopher Andrew, *Secret Service*, 1985; Christopher Andrew and David Dilks (ed.), *The Missing Dimension*, 1984; Nicholas Bethell, *The Great Betrayal*, 1984; John Costello, *Mask of Treachery*, 1988; John Costello and Oleg Tsarev, *Deadly Illusions*, 1993; Phillip Knightley, *Philby, the Life and Views of the KGB Masterspy*, 1988; Patrick Seale and Maureen McConville, *Philby, the Long Road*

Maclean

to *Moscow*, 1973; Hugh Trevor-Roper, *The Philby Affair*, 1968; Kim Philby, *My Silent War*, 1968; Eleanor Philby, *The Spy I Loved*, 1968; Genrikh Borovik, *The Philby Files*, 1994; Yuri Modin, *My Five Cambridge Friends*, 1994; personal knowledge.]

NIGEL CLIVE

published 1996

MACLEAN Donald Duart

(1913–1983)

British diplomat and Soviet spy, was born in London 25 May 1913, the third of four sons and five children of (Sir) Donald Maclean, Liberal politician and cabinet minister, and his wife, Gwendolen Margaret, eldest daughter of Andrew Devitt JP, of Oxted, Surrey. He, like his two elder brothers, was educated at Gresham's School, Holt, where the headmaster, J. R. Eccles, enforced the so-called 'honour system' with the aim of maintaining the highest moral standards. It may well be supposed that this system, allied to a strict upbringing at the hands of Sir Donald, a non-smoker, temperance advocate, and severe Sabbatarian, may have brought out in his son the tendency both to rebel and to deceive authority.

In October 1931 Maclean went up to Trinity Hall, Cambridge, with an exhibition in modern languages. He soon joined those on the extreme left, who aimed to reanimate, and dominate, the University Socialist Society; this group included Guy Burgess, Anthony Blunt, and H. A. R. ('Kim') Philby. Maclean, handsome, standing six feet four inches tall, was prominent both physically and intellectually among his contemporaries. He at first made no secret of his communist sympathies; but in mid-1934 he abandoned open political activity and announced his intention to enter the Diplomatic Service. This move coincided with his recruitment by the NKVD (later KGB) of the Soviet Union. In June 1934 he graduated with first class honours in part ii of the modern languages tripos, having gained a second class in part i in 1932. He entered the Diplomatic Service in 1935, serving in the League of Nations and Western department of the Foreign Office.

In 1938 he was appointed third secretary at the Paris embassy. There he met an American student, Melinda Marling, eldest daughter of Francis Marling, a Chicago businessman, whose wife divorced him in 1928 to marry a New England property owner, Hal Dunbar. Donald and Melinda were married in Paris on 10 June 1940 at the time of the evacuation of the city. Back in London he was promoted second secretary and employed in the General department until April 1944, when he was transferred to the Washington embassy, and soon after promoted first secretary. An indication that his credit with the NKVD was as high as with the Foreign Office is provided by the Soviet decision to transfer to Washington Maclean's London case officer ('control'). For some months in 1946 Maclean was acting head of Chancery; but his most important duties, from the NKVD's viewpoint, were connected with the development of the atom bomb. Early in 1947 he became joint secretary of the Anglo-American-Canadian combined policy committee, a post that gave him access to the American Atomic Energy Commission at a time when the US government was making maximum efforts to prevent leakage of information about nuclear weapons.

Two sons were born to the Macleans in the Washington years. When Maclean left in September 1948, on promotion to counsellor and head of Chancery in Cairo, he was the youngest officer in his new grade. In Cairo, however, an all-round deterioration set in, culminating in a drunken spree that caused him to be sent back to London and subjected to psychiatric examination for his homosexuality and alcoholism. The Foreign Office, believing he had recovered, appointed him in November 1950 to be head of the American department. This was a sensitive post, because of tensions resulting from the Korean war. Meanwhile the investigation of earlier leakages in Washington began to point to Maclean as prime suspect. Through Philby and Burgess he became aware of this and on 25 May 1951 defected with Burgess to the USSR. Soon afterwards his wife gave birth to a daughter in London. She later moved with her children to Switzerland and in September 1953 left secretly to join her husband. In 1967 she had an affair with Philby in Moscow.

In Moscow Maclean taught graduate courses in international relations and published *British Foreign Policy since Suez* (London, 1970). An expanded Russian edition led to his award of a doctorate of the Institute of World Economics and International Relations. By 1979 his former wife and children had left and gone to the West. He died 6 March 1983 in Moscow and was cremated there. His ashes were taken by his elder son and buried in the family plot at Penn, Buckinghamshire.

There has never been any official assessment on the British side of the damage done by Maclean as a spy; opinions differ concerning the benefit derived by the USSR from his undoubted insight into US nuclear capacity in the crucial years before the first Soviet atomic test in 1949. A report prepared in 1955 by US Military Intelligence, however, is unambiguous in attributing very grave damage to the combined activities of Maclean and Burgess. In the long term the most lasting damage was probably that suffered by Anglo-American relations, much of it arising from US criticism of the laxity of British security.

[Robert Cecil, *A Divided Life: A Biography of Donald Maclean*, 1988; official and private sources; personal knowledge.]

ROBERT CECIL

published 1990

PEULEVÉ Henri Leonard Thomas (Harry)

(1916–1963)

British agent in enemy-occupied France, the only son of Leonard Otho Peulevé and his wife, Eva Juliet Dallison, both of British nationality, was born 29 January 1916 at Worthing, where his mother and sister were temporarily in refuge from the German invasion of France. The family home was in Paris where Leonard Peulevé represented a firm of British seedsmen until the outbreak of war in 1914 when he joined the British Army. At the time of his son's birth he was a staff sergeant-major in the Army Service Corps. When the fighting in France became stabilized as trench warfare, his wife returned with the two children, moving from one place to another as her husband's unit was posted from this sector to that.

The Peulevé agency in France was not revived after the war and the family's wanderings continued while Peulevé sought to make a living, shuttling back and forth between France and England, with a period in Algiers where for a time he was British vice-consul. Thus Harry Peulevé's upbringing was as unsettled as his education was varied. His many schools included a nuns' kindergarten in Algiers, the Shakespeare School at Stratford-upon-Avon, Rye Grammar School, private schools and tutors in England and France, and finally a technical college in London where he took courses in telegraphy and wireless which led him to his first job; technical assistant in the Baird Television Company. From this he went on to the British Broadcasting Corporation in the early days of television, became a cameraman, and was so employed at the outbreak of war in 1939 when he joined the army.

Peulevé was commissioned in the Royal Army Ordnance Corps, worked on the first radar equipment, and later transferred with the rank of captain to the Royal Electrical and Mechanical Engineers, whence in 1942, as one of the earliest volunteers, he was seconded to Special Operations Executive, the paramilitary body created by the British joint chiefs of staff to organize and conduct clandestine warfare in enemy-occupied territories. Peulevé could not have been better fitted for such a task: he was bilingual and could pass as a Frenchman in France; his loyalties to that country and to Britain were equal, indivisible, and dedicated; he had an ingrained ability to make the best, even to take advantage, of the unpredictable; and he was already a specialist in wireless communication as both technician and operator. As though these qualifications were insufficient, nature had provided him with a well-built body, broad-shouldered and suggestive of considerable physical strength. Large grey-green eyes which could on occasion compel without frightening were allied with a persuasiveness remarkable in that it was always muted and made acceptable by his charm of personality. These attributes came together in developing his powers of leadership in circumstances where difference and independence in the men he commanded in the field were uncontained by the disciplines of military training. A final gift stood him in great stead in outwitting and escaping his enemies: he was able to 'withdraw' mentally, to make his mind still in the presence of those he did not want to notice him—a surer disguise than any false beard or dark glasses.

After training in a secret agent's special skills by SOE Peulevé parachuted into the Pyrenees area on the night of 30 July 1942, but, by the pilot's error, he was too low for safe landing and broke a leg. He escaped across the mountains on crutches into Spain where he was imprisoned; he got away and reached England in very poor physical condition. After recuperating he volunteered to try again. In September 1943 he was landed safely by light aircraft and established himself in the Corrèze area and extended his influence to the northern Dordogne, training and arming a large group of resistance fighters which in the course of the months reached some 3,000 men whom he led in extensive sabotage operations, on occasions joining battle in running fights with German occupation troops and inflicting considerable casualties. He acted throughout as his own radio operator in maintaining contact with SOE in London, organizing regular air-drops of supplies of arms and equipment for his increasing forces, as well as agents to assist him.

Despite the Gestapo's determined efforts to find and capture him, Peulevé evaded them until by a stroke of bad luck he was erroneously denounced as a black marketeer and arrested while operating his radio set, on 21 March 1944. Interrogated under torture he refused to talk, and the enemy never discovered who he was and the important part he had played in the clandestine war. Imprisoned in solitary confinement at Fresne for almost a year, he attempted escape, was shot and wounded in the thigh, and, since he was refused medical treatment, himself removed the bullet with the aid of a spoon. Eventually he was taken to Buchenwald where, on the eve of his execution, he was chosen by F. F. E. Yeo-Thomas as one of the two agents who with himself changed identities with Frenchmen dying of typhus. As one of the prison's forced labour group Peulevé was more easily able to escape (11 April 1945); but he was recaptured almost within sight of an advancing American unit by two Belgian SS. He persuaded the two men of the danger of being captured in uniform, suggested they undress, and while they were doing so seized one of their pistols and made them his prisoners, delivering them to the Americans. He was appointed to the DSO, made a chevalier of the Legion of Honour, and received the MC and croix de guerre.

After the war Peulevé worked for the Shell Oil Company in several European countries, Egypt, and Tunis. In 1952 he married Marie-Louise John, a Danish woman, by whom he had a son and a daughter. He died in Seville of a heart attack 18 March 1963.

[*The Times*, 25 March 1963; M. R. D. Foot (Official History), *S.O.E. in France*, 2nd impression, with amendments, 1968; M. R. D. Foot, *Six Faces of Courage*, 1978; private information; personal knowledge.]

SELWYN JEPSON

published 1981

NEAVE Airey Middleton Sheffield

(1916–1979)

Intelligence officer and politician, was born in London 23 January 1916, the elder son in the family of two sons and three daughters of Sheffield Airey Neave, well-known entomologist and honorary secretary of the Zoological Society, of Mill Green Park, Ingatestone, Essex, and his wife, Dorothy, daughter of Lt.-Col. Arthur Thomson Middleton, JP, of Ayshe Court, Horsham. He was educated at Eton and Merton College, Oxford, where he obtained a third class in jurisprudence in 1938.

He joined the Territorial Army Royal Artillery in 1939. As a lone subaltern in the chaos of the retreat of May 1940 he took part in the battle of Calais. He later described this in *The Flames of Calais* (1972). He was wounded at Calais and taken prisoner. From then on his thoughts were on escape, which he achieved from the camp at Torun, only to be recaptured in Poland. His admiration for the Poles and his later fight for a memorial for the Katyn massacre stem from that time. His interrogation then by the Gestapo, which he never forgot, made him a devotee of freedom under the laws of any country. Later this was to lead to his view that, if action had been taken outside the law by police or soldiers in Northern Ireland, the culprits should be brought to justice.

Neave was then sent to the maximum security prison at Colditz. His first attempt to escape was hindered by his colour-blindness, but ultimately in 1942 he succeeded, reached Switzerland, and then went through Vichy France to Gibraltar and back to London. His, possibly best, book, *They Have Their Exits* (1953), gives a moving account of both escapes.

He had brought back valuable intelligence information, and was soon operating at MI9 helping underground movements and training air-crews to escape. He described this period in *Saturday at MI9* (1969).

In 1942 Neave married Diana Josceline Barbara, daughter of Thomas Arthur Walter Giffard, landowner and county councillor, of Chillington Hall, Wolverhampton. After Neave's murder in 1979 she was created Baroness Airey of Abingdon. They had two sons and one daughter.

By the end of the war Neave had been honoured many times. In 1942 he was awarded the MC, and in 1945 the DSO and TD with clasp, the croix de guerre, the US bronze star, and the order of Orange Nassau. In 1947 he was appointed OBE.

Neave was called to the bar at the Middle Temple in 1943, and at the end of the war became assistant secretary to the International Military Tribunal, and thus, as a lieutenant-colonel, served the charges on the main Nazi war criminals. His last book, *Nuremberg* (1978), dealt with each one.

After the war while establishing a practice at the bar, he was from 1949 to 1951 officer commanding Intelligence School No. 9 (TA), which later became 23 SAS Regiment. But his thoughts were turning to politics. Having contested Thurrock (1950), and Ealing North (1951), he was elected Conservative MP for the Abingdon division of Berkshire in July 1953. He became parliamentary private secretary to the colonial secretary, Alan Lennox-Boyd (later Viscount Boyd of Merton), and to the minister of transport, H. A. (later Viscount) Watkinson, before becoming parliamentary under-secretary at the Air Ministry in 1959. Then came a heart attack which Edward Heath, as chief whip, thought might end Neave's parliamentary career.

But his greatest influence on events was to come. He specialized in science and technology (Harwell was in his constituency). He was a governor of Imperial College from 1963 to 1971; and a member from 1965 and subsequent chairman (1970–5) of the House of Commons select committee on science and technology. He fought a long and successful battle against the Foreign Office for compensation to former prisoners at Sachsenhausen, but in another battle he failed to get Hess released. He campaigned successfully for pensions for those over eighty. He was chairman of the British Standing Conference on Refugees (1972–4) and delegate to the United Nations High Commissioner for Refugees (1970–5).

He also played a predominant part in ousting Edward Heath as leader of the Conservative Party in 1975. Though at one time he considered among others Edward du Cann as a possible successor, he soon came to prefer Margaret Thatcher, and thereafter gave her undivided support and loyalty. When Margaret Thatcher became leader, Neave was made head of her private office, and shadow secretary of state for Northern Ireland. Although he had directorships connected largely with his energy, engineering, and scientific interests, politics and writing were his real loves.

Neave quietly, and often alone, planned, worked, and even intrigued for what he thought was right for his country. Patient, even slow, efficient, methodical, 'he thought before he fired'. Smiling often, laughing seldom, speaking in a low voice, he was almost self-sufficient. He had a cold calculating courage. Yet he had no personal ambition. He would have been amazed at the number of people at his memorial service overflowing St. Martin's-in-the-Fields, at the sums raised for his memorial trusts. He was essentially a private man. He appeared shy, almost reticent, but to friends he had a charming sense of humour, though his friendship was not given easily. He expected his friends to live up to his own high standard of integrity. He would always say when he did not know.

Neave had no ordinary recreations. He enjoyed most perfecting his own writing, and being with his wife and family. He was a good observer and listener, but would then make up his own mind. He loathed tyranny. He believed in freedom under the law. He thought that though power-sharing in Northern Ireland was not politically feasible, there should be more local government, and that if British troops were withdrawn the Catholic minority would suffer most. But to the Irish Republican Army and the Irish National Liberation Army he was a detested politician. It was by an Irish terrorist bomb hidden in his car that he was assassinated 30 March 1979 on the ramp of the House of Commons car park.

[Private information; personal knowledge.]

JOHN TILNEY

published 1986

WYNNE Greville Maynard

(1919–1990)

Businessman and intelligence agent, was born 19 March 1919 in Wrock-wardine Wood, east of Shrewsbury, Shropshire, the only son to grow up of Ethelbert Wynne, plater, and his wife, Ada Pritchard. He had three elder sisters; an elder brother had died aged one in 1915. He was brought up at Ystradymynach, a mining village a dozen miles north of Cardiff, where his father was a foreman in an engineering works. His mother died when he was fourteen. He worked in his middle teens as an electrician, and took evening courses in engineering at Nottingham University.

Called up into the army in 1939, he spent the war as a sergeant in the Field Security Police, looking after elementary security in various parts of Great Britain. He acquired the vocabulary of the Intelligence Corps, in which he served. On being demobilized in 1946 he married, on 21 September, at St Anne's, Wandsworth, Sheila Margaret, daughter of Gordon Beaton, chemist. They had a son.

He already described himself, on his marriage certificate, as a consulting engineer—a trade in which he made himself useful to exporters, with whom lay the country's best hope of staying solvent. In a decade and a half he built up a profitable small business, and came to specialize in assisting exports to eastern Europe, then under rigid communist control from Moscow. He occasionally visited the USSR to forward his clients' interests. He was a short, stocky man, with a brisk, cheerful manner, a toothbrush moustache, and smooth dark hair.

As a matter of routine, MI6 (the Secret Intelligence Service) briefed many British businessmen who travelled behind the iron curtain about points for which they might like to look out while there; Wynne was among them. Chance turned him into an important pawn in the 'great game'. Oleg Penkovsky, a colonel in Russian secret military intelligence, had been demoted from work he enjoyed in Turkey to run a Moscow committee that enquired into scientific matters—a cover for industrial espionage against the capitalist powers. Entirely disillusioned with the Soviet regime, Penkovsky sought to change sides, and through several intermediaries approached the American Central Intelligence Agency, without securing a response. He then approached Wynne, who informed MI6, which decided to take the case up, and to handle it jointly with the CIA. MI6 accepted Wynne as one of the conduits through which material could from time to time be passed to and from Penkovsky.

Wynne

Some of this material was of world strategic importance, for it enabled the Americans to outface the Russians in the Cuban missile crisis of 1962. Shortly thereafter, Wynne, who may have shown unprofessional enthusiasm at finding himself in Penkovsky's presence, unaware of the strictness with which Soviet citizens kept watch on each other, was abruptly arrested in Budapest, on 2 November 1962. He discovered after he had been flown to Moscow that Penkovsky was already in jail. After nine months' intermittent, fierce interrogation, the two were given a public show trial there on 7–11 May 1963.

Wynne stuck to his cover story that he was a simple businessman, admitting to having carried packets, but denying any knowledge of their contents. Penkovsky was sentenced to death, Wynne to eight years. After less than a year of hideous discomfort at Vladimir, some 120 miles east of Moscow, Wynne was, again abruptly, flown to Berlin and exchanged for a leading Soviet agent, Conon Molody ('Gordon Lonsdale'), early on 22 April 1964. The exchange received a torrent of publicity in the free world's news media. MI6 and the CIA paid Wynne over $200,000 compensation.

His wife had stood by him loyally; but his marriage swiftly broke up. He went off to Majorca with his secretary, Johanna Hermania, the daughter of Dirk van Buren, civil servant. They married on 31 July 1970 at Kensington register office; his first wife had divorced him in 1968. There were no children of the second marriage. Wynne wrote two books, to try to make money out of what had happened to him: *The Man from Moscow*, a life of Penkovsky and himself (1967), and the much more fanciful *The Man from Odessa* (1981), in which, for example, he claimed to have held an army commission, which he never did. He never went back to business and died of cancer in the Cromwell Hospital, Kensington, 27 February 1990.

[Greville Wynne, *The Man from Moscow*, 1967; J. L. Schechetr and P. S. Deriabin, *The Spy Who Saved the World*, 1992; private information.]

M. R. D. Foot

published 1996

SZABO Violette Reine Elizabeth

(1921–1945)

Secret agent, was born in Paris 26 June 1921, the second child and only daughter in the family of five children of Charles George Bushell, a regular soldier, and his wife Reine Blanche Leroy, a dressmaker from Pont-Rémy, Somme, France. He held various jobs in France and England before settling in 1932 in Brixton as a second-hand motor-car dealer. From her mother's family Violette picked up fluent French, spoken with an English accent. She left the LCC school in Stockwell Road, Brixton, at fourteen to work as a shop assistant. She was under five feet five inches tall, but strikingly good-looking, with dark hair and eyes and vivacious manners.

She married in Aldershot, 21 August 1940, Étienne Michel René Szabo, a thirty-year-old Frenchman of Hungarian descent from Marseilles, who had fought in Norway with the French Foreign Legion and elected to join General de Gaulle's nascent Free French forces. He was soon posted to north Africa, and never met their only child, a daughter born 8 June 1941. He died 27 October 1942 from wounds received the previous day in battle.

To revenge him, his widow joined the independent French section of the Special Operations Executive in October 1943. During the usual para-military, parachute, and security training it emerged that she was an admirable shot. She parachuted twice into occupied France, each time as courier to Philippe Liewer, an experienced agent. Her first mission began 5–6 April 1944. They found that the Gestapo had broken up Liewer's former group of saboteur friends between Rouen and Le Havre; they returned to England by light aircraft on 30 April. Between her first and second missions she was commissioned an ensign in the First Aid Nursing Yeomanry.

She and Liewer returned to France 7–8 June 1944 to set up a new group of resisters between Limoges and Périgueux. On 10 June she and two companions, in a motor car, encountered a German roadblock at Salon-la-Tour, some thirty miles south-east of Limoges. Both sides opened fire. Violette, armed only with a sten sub-machine-gun, covered her companions' retreat through standing corn for twenty minutes until she had no more ammunition, and was taken prisoner. She said nothing she should not have done under interrogation.

On 8 August, handcuffed to a neighbour on a train bound for Germany, she crawled round offering water to her fellow prisoners while the train was under attack by the RAF. She was put in Ravensbrück concentration camp, whence she went with two SOE colleagues, Lilian Rolfe and Denise

Bloch, on a working party at Torgau. They were then sent on a much fiercer one, some sixty miles eastward, at Klein Königsberg. Even her tremendously high spirits were lowered by its regime. Her companions returned from it hardly able to stand; she was not much sturdier. About 27 January 1945, shortly after their return to Ravensbrück, all three were shot dead.

She was awarded a French croix de guerre in 1944, and a posthumous George Cross in 1946.

[R. J. Minney, *Carve her Name with Pride*, 1956; M. R. D. Foot, *SOE in France*, 1968 edn.; private information.]

M. R. D. FOOT

published 1993

SZAMUELY Tibor

(1925–1972)

Historian and polemicist, was born in Moscow 14 May 1925, the eldest of three children and elder son of Gyorgy Szamuely and his wife Elsa Szanto. Both Szamuely's parents came from Hungarian Jewish mercantile stock, his grandfather on his father's side being a corn merchant. In the Hungarian revolution of 1919 his uncle Tibor, as commissar for war, was held to have been responsible for the repression under the regime, and subsequently killed himself on being apprehended by Admiral Horthy's police while trying to flee across the Austrian border.

Gyorgy Szamuely, who had worked as a journalist and had also taken part in the revolutionary government, secured passage to Moscow where he obtained employment in the Soviet trade commissariat. In this capacity he came to London in 1932 with his family though he was also secretly working for the Comintern. The young Tibor Szamuely went to Beacon Hill School, near Petersfield, which was run by Bertrand (Lord) Russell and his wife which he enjoyed and where he acquired an excellent knowledge of English. He also was sent briefly to the school at Summerhill near Leiston in Suffolk run by A. S. Neill, of which he thought less highly. In 1934 the Szamuelys returned to Moscow. Three years later Gyorgy Szamuely was arrested and condemned to ten years of jail 'without the right of correspondence'. He was never seen again.

The Szamuely family were evacuated to Tomsk in World War II, along with other Hungarians living in Moscow. Tibor Szamuely was eventually called up. In 1945 he found himself a member of the Allied Control

Commission in Hungary, perhaps working for the NKVD, the Soviet secret service. He returned to Russia after a dispute in Budapest and attended the University of Moscow to study history. Szamuely next worked as a contributor to encyclopaedias. He also had imprudent connections with the United States embassy. On 2 December 1950 at dawn, he was arrested on a charge of being an American spy, for planning a terroristic attack on Georgi Malenkov, and for uttering anti-Soviet opinions. He denied the first two of these charges but admitted the third. He was sentenced to eight years' imprisonment. He discharged eighteen months of this sentence, at a lumber camp in a marshy region, but was released on the request of Mátyás Rákosi, then the secretary-general of the Hungarian Communist Party, still a family friend.

Szamuely then returned to Budapest as a lecturer in history at the university. He formed part of the so-called 'Petöfi Circle' but, though already disillusioned about communism, played little part in the revolution of 1956 due to his family connections with the old regime. As a result of this inactivity he was named vice-rector of the University of Budapest in 1957. He was, however, dismissed from this post, and from his teaching position, for refusing to lead an attack on the philosopher George Lukács.

After this he worked in the Hungarian Academy of Sciences. At that time, he produced most of his written work such as *Modern History 1849–1945* (with György Ránki) (1959), *The Foundation of the Hungarian Communist Party* (1963), and *National Socialism* (1963). He afterwards accepted a teaching post offered to him at the Kwame Nkrumah Ideological Institute at Winneba in Ghana. He obtained this post through Kodwo Addison, whom he himself had taught in Hungary in the 1950s and who was at the time head of the Institute. He profited from a holiday in Ghana to go to England in 1964 where he remained, being in 1965 appointed lecturer in politics at the University of Reading, then expanding its activities. He became a British subject in 1969.

He swiftly established a reputation in Britain as a brilliant critic of the Soviet regime. He often wrote for the *Spectator*. His lectures at Reading were successful, though he lived in London, finally establishing himself at 17 Sutherland Place, Bayswater. He never, however, completed his long-planned history of the Soviet Union though his introduction to that work—a sparkling analysis of Soviet history—was published posthumously as *The Russian Tradition* (edited, with an introduction by Robert Conquest—Secker & Warburg, 1974).

Tibor Szamuely was a warm-hearted conversationalist, always ready to recall his tragic experiences for those who cared to interest themselves. He died 10 December 1972 of cancer in a London hospital. He was married in 1948 in Moscow to Nina Orlova, daughter of an expert in pestilence married to a doctor. Her grandfather, a merchant in old Russia, had been tortured and exiled in the first years of the Soviet regime. During the Szamuelys' London years, she taught Russian at St. Paul's Girls' School, and worked as a contributor to the *Concise Oxford English-Russian Dictionary*. She died in 1974. There were two children of the marriage, a son George, and a daughter Helen.

[Private information; personal knowledge.]

THOMAS OF SWYNNERTON

published 1986

Alphabetical Index

Alphabetical Index